Competitive Archaeology in Jordan

Narrating Identity from the Ottomans to the Hashemites

BY ELENA D. CORBETT

University of Texas Press ꙮ *Austin*

First edition, 2014
First paperback edition, 2015

Requests for permission to reproduce material from this work should be sent to:
    Permissions
    University of Texas Press
    P.O. Box 7819
    Austin, TX 78713-7819
    http://utpress.utexas.edu/index.php/rp-form

♾ The paper used in this book meets the minimum requirements of
ANSI/NISO Z39.48-1992 (R1997) (Permanence of Paper).

Library of Congress Cataloging-in-Publication Data
Corbett, Elena Dodge
    Competitive archaeology in Jordan : narrating identity from the Ottomans
to the Hashemites / by Elena D. Corbett. — First edition.
       pages cm
    Includes bibliographical references and index.
    ISBN 978-0-292-76080-6 (cloth : alk. paper)
    1. Archaeology—Political aspects—Jordan.   2. Archaeology—Political aspects—
Palestine.   3. Jordan—Antiquities.   I. Title.
    DS153.3.C68   2014
    933'.5—dc23

                                       2014017671

ISBN 978-1-4773-0990-2 (paperback)
doi:10.7560/760806

To the memory of Ustaz Farouk

Contents

List of Illustrations   **ix**

Acknowledgments   **xi**

Note on Transliterations   **xvii**

1. Archaeology Is Politics:
The Meaning of Archaeological Heritage in Jordan   **1**

2. Holy Land Core and Periphery   **20**

3. Antiquity and Modernity in Southeastern Bilad al-Sham   **49**

4. British Mandate: Core, Periphery, and Ownership of Narrative   **88**

5. Antiquities of a Hashemite State in Mandatory Space   **125**

6. Antiquity, Pan-National, and Nation-State Narratives
in the Expanded Hashemite Kingdom   **153**

7. Return to the Core   **195**

Notes   **211**

Bibliography   **253**

Index   **271**

List of Illustrations

Map 1. Ottoman administrative divisions, ca. 1914 **xiv**

Map 2. Jordan's state borders, ca. 1948–67 **xv**

Figure 1.1. Photo montage hanging in the foyer of the Department of Antiquities, Amman, Jordan **2**

Figure 6.1. The 1952 "unity stamp" **161**

Figure 6.2. 1964 papal visit stamps **162**

Figure 6.3. "Canaanite Arab from Palestine driving a pack animal" and "Canaanite Arab girl from Palestine" **174**

Figure 6.4. "Canaanite Phoenician teaching the alphabet" **174**

Figure 6.5. "Canaanite Arabic" and "Modern Arabic" **174**

Figure 7.1. The mosque and shrine of the Prophet's Companion Abu ʿUbayda ibn al-Jarrah **198**

Figure 7.2. The King Hussein Mosque, Amman, Jordan **201**

Figure 7.3. Near the beginning of the Historical Passageway **202**

Figure 7.4. Along the Historical Passageway **203**

Acknowledgments

This book began as a kernel of a conversation in what feels now like another life. Between there and here—from proposal, to grant applications, to research, to dissertation, to articles, to multiple drafts of a book manuscript—were many people and places, open doors and open hearts, that helped light the way.

A number of grants supported this journey. It would have been impossible in the first place without the chance to spend a year among amazing and patient teachers in the CASA program at the American University in Cairo. The beloved mentor and friend who made CASA possible for me, and showed me Cairo through *his* eyes, passed away shortly before I learned this book would be published. In a moment of excitement, I forgot he had gone, and I sat down to write him an e-mail to tell him the good news. The dedication of this work in his memory is a poor token for all he did for me.

Two ACOR/CAORC Fellowships (the American Center of Oriental Research and the Council for American Overseas Research Centers) and a Fulbright-Hays supported my fieldwork and data collection in Jordan, both before and after I finished my degree. I owe enormous gratitude to ACOR and its staff—Humi, Nisreen, Kathy, Sarah, Pat, Samia, Muhammad, Sa'id, 'Abed, Cesar, Norma, and Janet—led by Barbara Porter and Christopher Tuttle, for many years of continued support and friendship. Mr. Alain Mc-Namara of the Jordan Fulbright Commission has done more for me over the years than I could ever express. The faculty of archaeology and anthropology at Yarmouk University in Irbid, Jordan, and especially Ziad al-Sa'ad, offered support for my Fulbright all those years ago. A special thanks goes to Hani Hayajneh, Omar al-Ghul, and Zeidan Kafafi for their friendship and support in the years since. My research in London and Oxford was partially funded by a University of Chicago Humanities Division Dissertation Travel Grant.

Additional research in Jordan was funded by Penn State's Institute for the Arts and Humanities, and a faculty grant from Penn State University Erie, the Behrend College.

Ms. Felicity Cobbing of the Palestine Exploration Fund provided archival support in London. Ms. Debbie Usher of the Middle East Centre Archives at St. Antony's provided archival support in Oxford. Archival assistance in Jordan was provided by the vigilant staffs of the publications office of the Department of Antiquities, the Jordan National Library, USAID, the Jordan Tourism Board, the University of Jordan Library (especially the Hashemite Reading Room and the Media and Microfilms Room), the Ministry of Tourism and Antiquities, and the Department of Statistics. Mr. Michael MacDonald provided generous access to the personal papers of Gerald Lankester Harding. Archival assistance in Jerusalem was generously provided by the staff of the Truman Center Library at the Hebrew University. Mr. Awni Hadidi and the members of the Jordan Philatelic Society very generously lent their time and their stamps to provide images for this book.

My dissertation committee continues to be a source of unwavering personal and professional support. I would like to thank Mary Wilson, Orit Bashkin, Yorke Rowan, and chair Holly Shissler for all they have done. Special thanks also go to Janet Jones of Bucknell University and Thomas Parker of North Carolina State University, because of whom I found myself in Jordan in the first place.

There are many kind friends who offered untold moral and intellectual support over the years. I would especially like to thank the following people, who have shared in both the best and worst of times, grand moments or small, or just lent a helping hand when it was most needed: Dennis Campbell, Carrie Hritz, Katherine Strange Burke, Abigail Jacobson, Rusty Rook, Heather Felton, Rasheed Hosein, Carla Hosein, John Danneker, Kay Heikennen, Traci Lombre, Brian Frank, the Qaraʿeen family, the Khdeir family, the Ayyoub family, Khulood Kittaneh and Abu Alaʾ, Khalil Yusuf, Rami Daher, Ghazi Bisheh, Julie Peteet, Elise Friedland, Debby Krantz, Alison Leslie, and Lisa Findlay.

I would also like to thank the many people who have read and offered feedback on bits of this project. Morag Kersel has done so over several years and in its myriad forms. Thanks also go to Karen Britt, Kimberly Katz, Shatha Abu Khafaja, and George Potter. In the process of moving from dissertation to publication, Betty Anderson has been a hero, always giving generously of her intellect and patient mentorship. Anonymous reviewers along the way have challenged me to do better, and I am thankful for their many contributions. Any errors contained herein are, of course, my own.

The Dhiban Excavation and Development Project team has been incredibly supportive of me and this work, and the opportunity to work with them contributed greatly to the outcome. I would like to thank Ben Porter, Bruce Routledge, Danielle Fatkin, Katie Adelsberger, and Andrew Wilson for making me at home on their project.

Friends and colleagues at the U.S. Naval Academy were bulwarks of support in the home stretch of the dissertation. Special thanks go to Ernie Tucker, Ermin Sinanovic, Heidi Rey, Audrey Gaquin, and Clarissa Burt. Most of this book was written during my time at Penn State Erie, where there were many people, now scattered hither and yon, to whom I owe an enormous debt of gratitude for so many things: Catherine Bae, Elizabeth Fogle, Aileen Wang, Kathryn Wolfe, Rob Speel, Russ Hall, Michael Christofferson, Kyoko Matsunaga, Mike Gorman, John Champagne, and Jeff and Andrea Bloodworth. And for all the times my students made me crazy during this process, I want to thank them for reminding me just as often how much I love what I do, and how lucky I am to have the chance to do it. I finished this book in Amman, where my CIEE colleagues have adopted me as one of their own. A very warm thanks goes to Stephen, Jumana, Ahmad, Rana, Najeh, Zeina, Taghreed, Mohannad, Suzy, Safwat, Arafat, Ava, James, Janine, Adam, and, last but not least, Allison. Special thanks also go to Amman colleagues Zein, Hisham, Bill, and Patty.

I owe a huge debt of gratitude to editor Jim Burr and the entire team at the University of Texas Press. After hearing for many years about their incredible talent, professionalism, and humanity in getting authors—particularly first-timers—through this process, it has been a privilege to have had the chance to work with them. Copy editors are heroes, and Sue Carter is one of them.

My parents, Bob and MaryJean Dodge, have supported me in everything, no matter how crazy it was. Nothing would have been possible without them.

Finally, all love and thanks go to Joey Corbett, my best friend, the one who makes everything whole.

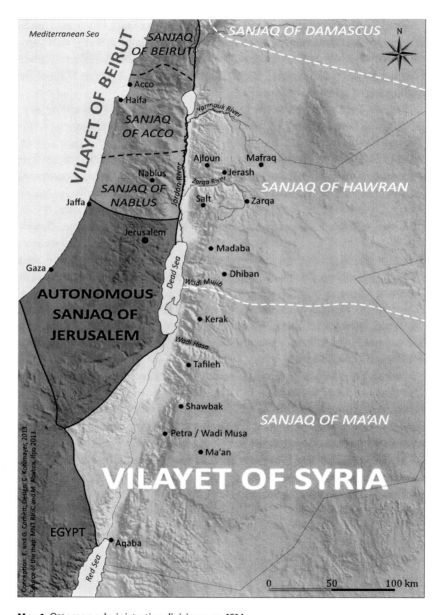

Map 1. Ottoman administrative divisions, ca. 1914.

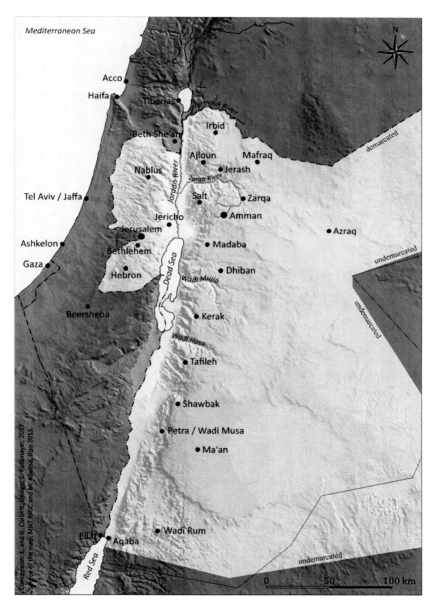

Map 2. Jordan's state borders, ca. 1948–67.

Note on Transliterations

Words transliterated from Arabic follow *IJMES* guidelines with modifications. Glottal stops *ʿayn* and *hamza* are preserved in most instances, and vowels and syllables have been added to enable ease of readability, particularly for nonspecialists.

Competitive Archaeology in Jordan

CHAPTER 1

Archaeology Is Politics: The Meaning of Archaeological Heritage in Jordan

King Abdullah II acceded Jordan's throne in 1999, the fifth of the Hashemite dynasty. Jordan's central bank shortly thereafter reintroduced the fifty-dinar bill for the first time in forty years, bearing a portrait of King Abdullah II in a suit and tie on the obverse and downtown Amman's Raghadan Palace, the primary residence built by the first King Abdullah, on the reverse. The idea that the five Hashemite monarchs in "traditional" dress could constitute the theme of five denominations of a new currency came from the Royal Court. Artist, architect, and activist Ammar Khammash designed what would be the fourth currency issue since the Central Bank's establishment in 1959.

For the first time, each Hashemite dynast is featured on his own bill, all within the same currency issue and all given equal importance. The issue thus depicts the new king as the most recent heir to a natural line of succession, the only leaders Jordan has ever known. In another departure from previous issues of Jordan's currency, Khammash featured each monarch with a landscape, monument, scene, or event with which he was contemporaneous, choosing important evocations of Jordan's modern history under Hashemite rule rather than internationally renowned archaeological sites. The bills are complex works of art, including in their design heavily stylized portions of Khammash's own watercolors and much in the way of antiquities that would be unfamiliar to many observers. "The Hijaz Railway is more us," he said, in explaining why he did not depict the sites of Jerash or Petra on any of these bills, as had all prior currency issues. "It's a pity because it has been ignored . . . the Hijaz Railway . . . and Maʿan . . . the south . . . the Hijazi stuff." Noting that Lebanon and Syria depict their Roman ruins—Baalbek and Palmyra—on their currency, Khammash said he wanted Jordan's new currency to be unique in the region. "Jerash was Roman, or Arab under the Romans," he said.[1]

The theme of five Hashemite dynasts was ubiquitous. Montages appeared

Fig. 1.1. Photo montage hanging in the foyer of the Department of Antiquities, Amman, Jordan. The monarchs are (left to right): King Abdullah II (r. 1999–present), King Hussein (Abdullah's father, r. under regency 1952–53, 1953–99), King Talal (Hussein's father, r. 1951–52), King Abdullah I (Talal's father, emir under the British Mandate 1921–46, r. as king 1946–51), Sharif Husayn of Mecca (sharif and emir of Mecca 1908–17, r. as king of the Hijaz 1917–24). Jordanian landscapes are (left to right): the Oval Forum of Jerash, Amman from the Umayyad diwan on the "citadel," the Treasury of Petra. Photo by E. Corbett, September 2002.

everywhere, superimposing images of the monarchs upon an instantly recognizable landscape that often included at least one familiar antiquities site (see fig. 1.1). Those outside the capital generally utilized a site or monument particular to that locale. The Ministry of Planning, meanwhile, hatched slogans evoking national unity and patriotic ethos in the context of a new era of development. One of the earliest included a television commercial featuring a renowned gymnast performing on a trampoline in Amman's Roman Theatre. A contemporary national sports figure was thus included in the iconography, along with one of Jordan's capital city's most recognizable ancient monuments, accompanying a specific statement of Jordan in a new age of modernization marked by aggressive privatization. The Roman Theatre is not only a tourist attraction, but also a place for Ammanis' mundane activities, even if the removal of the frenetic Raghadan bus station and other public spaces in its vicinity has worked to curtail them. Here a gymnast, a modern manifestation of classical athleticism, someone who might represent Jordan in a prestigious international venue, performed gymnastics in an archaeological place incorporated into the everyday pace of life in the capital and the daily pilgrimages of many of its citizens. It was completely natural for this young Jordanian woman to carry out one more Jordanian activity among the repertoire of daily Jordanian activities in this Jordanian place.

Since then, a variety of Jordanians, young and old, in "traditional" or "modern" garb, have smiled down from billboards. Some of the early English billboards read, "Jordan: Small Country, Big Ideas," while their Arabic counterparts read, "Jordan: You Reap What You Sow." In 2002, Amman was UNESCO's "Arab Culture Capital," and emblems commemorating this designation hung all over the city. By 2003, "*al-urdun awalan*" (Jordan First) was ubiquitous. The arms of Jordanians of various ilk—a man sporting a suit, a woman wearing a "traditional" embroidered costume, a youth in a T-shirt—together holding the Jordanian flag, appeared painted on buses, printed in newspapers, and emblazoned on trinkets hung from rearview mirrors. It came with what was reportedly at that time the world's tallest flagpole and second largest flag flying over the Raghadan Palace compound in downtown Amman, visible from almost everywhere in the city. "Jordan First" came with a series of subslogans, including "*li-ana c'ai'latak awalan*" (Because your family is first), "*li-ana huquak awalan*" (Because your rights are first), "*li-ana mustaqbalak awalan*" (Because your future is first), "*li-ana turathak awalan*" (Because your heritage is first), and "*li-ana watanak awalan*" (Because your homeland is first). Since the suicide bombings targeting three Amman hotels in November 2005, an image created by Abu Mahjoob cartoonist Emad Hajjaj—three hands (red, white, and green) grasping each other in the shape of Jordan on a black background—has been a symbol of the slogan "We are all Jordan." As uprisings sweep the region several years later, a stirring video montage mixing scenes of antiquity and modernity plays on Jordan television declaring, "*al-urdun . . . watan wa huwiyya*" (Jordan . . . homeland and identity).

In all such campaigns over the past decade and a half, Jordan has juxtaposed the language and iconography of *turath* (heritage) in its variety of forms and *watan* (nation) in its variety of meanings, all in the discourse of identity or development. Archaeological sites have been an important aspect of *turath* in this discourse. Yet while archaeology's specific role as a particular kind of *turath* in narrating the nation to audiences at home and abroad has been an issue of popular and scholarly inquiry, not least in countries of the Middle East such as Egypt, Iraq, Turkey, and Israel, little consideration in this regard has been afforded Jordan. This book seeks to address this gap by presenting a history of archaeology in Jordan and Palestine, considered through the lens of Jordanian history and the importance of Jerusalem within changing narratives of that history. It is about an ongoing and adaptive competition between foreign and indigenous powers with roots in the context of late nineteenth-century imperialism. This competition has occurred among governments, institutions, and individuals. At stake has been the ownership of archaeological artifacts and the narratives told by them, the geographies of history upon which borders were drawn, and differing conceptions of nations.

Competitive Archaeology in Empire and Nation

This historical consideration begins in the second half of the nineteenth century within the late Ottoman imperial context that laid the political and socioeconomic foundations of modern Jordan. While there was a clear territorial conception of Palestine at the time, that of Transjordan lay decades in the future, and what would become Jordan was a frontier of the Ottoman Empire. Beginning in the period of the Tanzimat (restructuring, 1839–76), and continuing until the end of the First World War, the landscapes that came to make up Jordan experienced a rapid, all-encompassing modernization. At its core were legislative reforms leading to changes in the conception of land and the centralized administration of private land ownership in southeastern Bilad al-Sham (Greater Syria), the region of the Arab parts of the Ottoman Empire of which Palestine and much of the future Jordan were a part, and inclusive of what are today Syria and Lebanon. Bilad al-Sham is used herein to capture the geographic sense of Jordan as part of Greater Syria, shaped by its proximity to and inseparability from consideration together with the peoples and places of Palestine, holistically sacred terrain for the three Abrahamic faiths—Islam, Christianity, and Judaism—and the Hijaz, the birthplace of Islam, pathway and destination of the hajj, and gateway to the rest of the Arabian Peninsula.

The components of the future Transjordan lay exactly between the holy landscapes of Jerusalem and the Hijaz, connected by proximity and people's myriad connections to those two crucial foci of late Ottoman state power projection, territorial self-conception, and image production within the context of modernization. After a disastrous war with Russia resulting in the loss of most of the remaining Ottoman lands in the Balkans, Sultan Abdülhamid II (r. 1876–1909) suspended the constitution (1878) and asserted the sultan's position, thus himself, as the Muslim caliph. Jerusalem and the Hijaz were critical to the broader rhetorical narrative that embedded concomitant religious symbolism and discourse in the ethos of modern Ottoman identity. The space between them, the future Jordan, was critical to the modernization project as a previously untapped resource to be harvested for revenues. That space was peripheral, however, to the many nuances of identity manifest in Ottoman modernity, including Ottomanism, Hellenism, Islamism, Turkishness, and Arabness.

The southeastern region of Bilad al-Sham that became Transjordan was constituted of not one territorial unit, but parts of multiple administrative units, including Jabal Ajloun, Balqa, Kerak, and Maʿan (divided into "Syrian Maʿan" and "Hijazi Maʿan"). Among and within these divisions was an incredible diversity of environments, elevations, microclimates, and access to water, including forested highlands prone to winter snows, fertile valleys that were warm year-round, the Dead Sea, desert valleys of varying size, and the borders between steppe lands and desert. Ways of subsistence varied greatly among the inhabitants of these units—which included, and not in a mutually exclusive way, larger and smaller cultivators, merchants, craftspeople, pastoralists, and seasonal and year-round nomads. Their sociopolitical organization, which originally included no major urban centers, varied accordingly, consisting of towns and villages of varying sizes, various kin and non-kin affiliations, and sociopolitical groupings such as chiefdoms and tribes that inhabited both village and hinterland space and that were fluid, and broadly understood. While the inhabitants of these four units were certainly familiar with each other and came to recognize one another as part of the same inscribed modern Ottoman administrative and cognitive reality, their ties, movements, and interactions may have been stronger and more acute with family and networks in adjoining parts of Bilad al-Sham, with Egypt, which they bordered on the southwest, with the Hijaz, or across the desert to the east with Iraq than they were with one another.

The competition over archaeology began when the Ottomans' imperial rivals, most notably England, inserted missionaries, officers, and scholars into southeastern Bilad al-Sham and surrounding regions, especially Egypt, Palestine, and the Hijaz, to draw maps for learned societies and the War Office. Important to these initiatives was knowing the natural and man-made landscapes of southeastern Bilad al-Sham, of which not only were monuments and ruins, but human inhabitants, a part. Western interests understood the identities and characteristics of the modern inhabitants by means of a past, in no small way imagined, informed by and useful for present exigencies, such as accessing and securing resources like the Suez Canal. This knowledge taxonomized colonial spaces and imperial selves against imperial and subject others, legitimizing strategic interests. New sciences such as archaeology, philology, and eugenics helped create the historicity of peoples in space, and thus a deterministic way of understanding present conditions and future potentials.

The culmination of British inroads into the study of the Holy Land was the Survey of Western Palestine (1871–77) and the less successful Survey of Eastern Palestine, a comprehensive project to give scientific articulation to the Holy Land by mapping it, using the River Jordan as the border between west and east. In mapping the Holy Land, however, the British were not engaged in an act of elucidating the extant reality in late Ottoman Bilad al-Sham, but in creating a distinct alternate reality bespeaking narratives of their ownership. The British Holy Land was one of many colonial forms of knowledge rooted in Britain's role on the global stage, embedded in its competition and cooperation with other Western powers, namely France, Germany, and the United States, and the projection of its national modernity within that framework. As designed and mapped by the British, the Holy Land had a core and a periphery that could be elucidated by the application of taxonomic science, here archaeology and related disciplines. The core was Palestine, the home of the ancient Israelites of the Hebrew Bible with whom modern British historical consciousness identified, likening the covenant with the God of Abraham and the lives of the biblical patriarchs to England's role in the Protestant Reformation and its subsequent colonial success. Finding nineteenth-century Palestine a land in need of redemption, Britain positioned itself, by virtue of history and destiny, to forge the Holy Land's path to modernity. Jews living in Palestine were potential inroads, by prospect of conversion or official protection, to a territory where, unlike rivals France, Russia, Austria-Hungary, and Germany, Britain had no indigenous co-confessional community enabling it to compete. In rendering antiquity of the Holy Land's Palestine core Jewish, the British narrative of its ownership supported the historicity narrative of the emerging Zionist movement in the same space.

Every other part of Bilad al-Sham's landscape was secondary to the most important part of the Holy Land. The landscape east of the River Jordan was particularly conceived in relation to the idea that Palestine, the home of the ancient Israelites, was a core and everything else—the home of the ancient non-Israelite peoples who also appear in the Hebrew Bible—the periphery. There was no considering any part of the periphery without relationship to the core, or any of the connotations regarding the contemporary core, periphery, and their inhabitants that went in hand with its inception.

Removing antiquities from their context for display in the museums of Western capitals was a physical dimension of archaeology's role in the competition among late nineteenth-century powers. Claiming ownership of their narratives was equally powerful, as it crafted historicity for the contemporary context and implied deterministic modern identities. While most archaeology was the work of westerners, it had an important role to play in the late nineteenth-century Ottoman Empire, which approached the competition from a position of existential danger and shrinking borders. Initiatives directed from Istanbul, particularly regarding the establishment of museums, acquisition and display of museum collections, and antiquities laws, were responses to the international competition over archaeology. As with other new sciences, news of archaeological discoveries and commentary on archaeological methods were widely available in the Ottoman Empire through periodicals such as the popular Arabic-language journal *al-Muqtataf* and similar publications in various languages. As part of the overall phenomenon of modernization, Ottomans were as engaged in discourses and initiatives contemporaneous and parallel with nineteenth-century Western efforts to apply science in the "Near East," cultivating narratives of antiquity and fostering a sense of historical consciousness for modern national identity. Late Ottoman citizens, primarily but certainly not exclusively Arabs in the case of southeastern Bilad al-Sham, embraced archaeology as they embraced other new sciences, technologies, and industries. The same archaeology, however, spoke very different narratives about both the past and the present for Ottomans than it did for Europeans. While their understanding of archaeology was heavily shaped by the Western scholars who were proactive in it, it was just as heavily imbued with their own understandings of space, place, and history as shaped by experience, the particular historical moment in which they lived, and Islamicate traditions. The contents of popular journals of science in this period, such as *al-Muqtataf*, demonstrate that crucial to late Ottoman Arab engagement with archaeology was what the new sciences elucidated about the ancient peoples with whom they identified closely in their sense of historical consciousness: the Semites and the foundational monotheistic spiritual innovation of the Beni Israel, the first of the Children of Abraham. Semitic studies demonstrated for people the most ancient historicity narrative supporting Arabism in this part of the Ottoman Empire. Evidence of the story of the Beni Israel accounted for the historicity of the confessional diversity that late Ottoman Arabs—Muslims, Christians, and Jews—lived.

Unlike westerners, late Ottoman citizens lived on and came from the spaces under scrutiny of the developing disciplines studying Near Eastern antiquity. The new upward mobility enabled by greater access to education and the proliferation of other modern institutions, meanwhile, fostered an environment in which people who lived in these spaces could engage with the new archaeological science in ways that differed not only from the paradigms established in the West, but also those preferred at the Ottoman center. Importantly, archaeology did not necessarily narrate a story of national competition, but could help account for the late Ottoman Empire's normative diversity—multiconfessional, multi-"ethnic," and multilinguistic—in a context of living under the continued pressure of existential threats from abroad.

While museums, artifacts, and antiquities laws were obvious loci for competition over archaeology, the real competition—its extraordinary dimensions and ramifications for space and geography—could not have been foreseen in the nineteenth century. In the words of a Jordanian textbook author decades later, "Is it necessary to get an international guarantee for the establishment of a national homeland and official recognition for its establishment on the basis of an ancient historical relationship?"[2] This is exactly what happened in the wake of the Great War. The author of that textbook is, of course, referring specifically to the state of Israel. But the paradigm of Jordan's ancient past as devised by Western powers also became the basis of its modern geopolitical existence after the war with the creation of the British Mandates for Palestine and Transjordan. Jordan's original conception as a space peripheral in antiquity thus had very real implications. The spaces delimited by the Survey of Western Palestine became, essentially, the Palestine Mandate. The Transjordan Mandate took shape later as a buffer zone, with neither a comprehensive historical nor contemporary narrative. This paradigm, both archaeologically and politically, has continued to affect Jordan's national existence in multiple ways throughout the decades since its independence, with an impact on contestation over its legitimacy domestically, regionally, and internationally. If there were no ancient Jordanians, what was modern Jordan?

With the establishment of the state in 1921, the competition over archaeology and narrative took on new dimensions as the British set about to rule the spaces that had been created according to both their perception of the geography of biblical antiquity and their own geopolitical exigencies in the new world order organized into nation-states. In the process, the legislation, management, and praxis of studying and interpreting the antiquity for which they were now responsible reflected not only ongoing competition among the Great Powers, but also a competition among British institutions—political and academic—and their major personalities. Those responsible for matters of archaeology and antiquity often came to clash with others who were responsible for matters of politics, despite the fact that prior to the Mandate, particularly during the Great War, the responsibilities of people in both these groups may have overlapped. In the late 1920s, American scholar Nelson Glueck canonized Transjordan's status as the land of the non-Jews of the biblical world by means of its first systematic archaeological surveys. Glueck was the first scholar to contribute real archaeological knowledge of the "others" of the Hebrew Bible and the antiquity of the ancient peoples who had inhabited what was now Jordan—the Ammonites, Moabites, Edomites, and Nabateans. While he helped raise the academic profile of these peoples, he simultaneously fashioned them in lesser apposition to their ancient neighbors, whose historicity was part of the increasingly dangerous national competition in Britain's Palestine Mandate.

A different kind of multifaceted competition was internal to the Transjordan Mandate. Emir (later King) Abdullah had been installed on the throne by the British on the basis of Whitehall's postwar strategy and a broken promise that his family would be the hereditary dynasts of an Arab kingdom that, controversially, included Palestine. The first aspect of this competition was political, as the Hashemites settled into Transjordan while machinating for something larger according to what they had been promised. The second aspect of the competition was over Abdullah's reputation and the future and character of the new state, as his interests and his way of ruling repeatedly came to clash with Britain's. The third aspect was about legitimacy, regarding what many in the international community and closer to home saw as an untenable national entity. Abdullah had in the first place won his charge by virtue of accommodation with the British, a highly problematic issue at many levels.

These three aspects of contestation in the new state of Transjordan were political in nature, and antiquities had an important function. Both before and after independence, the Hashemite state had a choice to make regarding the use of antiquities to tell its national story and speak to the identity of the new nation-state: adopt indigenous paradigms of historical consciousness resulting from engagement with archaeology, or adopt Western paradigms of core and periphery and the universal value of antiquities contained within them. As they were most legible in the international sphere, Jordan chose to promote antiquities of recognized universal value within its borders, but did so to create a Hashemite core out of its peripheral Holy Land space. In doing so, Jordan deployed antiquities such as Petra and Jerash for meanings and narratives that were *not* universally recognizable, usurping the nuances of Jordanians' personal connections to heritage and its spaces.

Geopolitical competition had a significant impact upon the narratives that could be told by antiquities. British conceptions of Jordan's territory—as devised vis-à-vis their conceptions of the territory of Palestine—had left Jordan with neither a comprehensive narrative told by its antiquities, nor, with the possible exception of Petra and the enigmatic Nabateans, a grand "indigenous" ancient civilization, and certainly none that produced written archives, upon which to draw. In this, Jordan was alone among its neighbors, with nothing to build upon like Egypt's, Iraq's, Turkey's, Syria's, or Lebanon's archaeology. While the basis of the Hashemite family's legitimacy to rule in the age of the nation-state rested physically on its leaders' approach to patronage and redistribution as patriarchs of a large national tribe, it rested rhetorically on having led the Arab Revolt, leadership of which the Hashemites owed to their political position in the late Ottoman period, which itself was based on a narrative of antiquity and genealogy: their descent from the Prophet Muhammad. Descent from the Prophet Muhammad gave the Hashemites not only impeccable Islamicate credentials, but also Abrahamic and Semitic credentials. These were the very connections so important for historical consciousness that emerged prominently in popular and scholarly interest in archaeology during the late Ottoman period. Acknowledgment of these in the postwar era, however, risked acknowledgment of what most Arabs viewed as the colonial imposition of Zionism. Jordan's Arab neighbors had archaeological evidence of their comprehensive historicity narratives from excavated ancient archives outside of and predating Abrahamic traditions; the Hashemites did not. The antiquity narrative of Hashemite legitimacy thus depended on the same Abrahamic foundations as did that of Zionism. In light of their ouster from the Hijaz and Britain's broken promises, Palestine, and particularly Jerusalem, remained objects of Hashemite desire.

When Jordan's borders expanded in 1950 to include Jerusalem, two discursive trends emerged vis-à-vis antiquity's role in the ongoing national competition: to compete with Nasserism and espouse a Hashemite vision of *qawmiyya* (pan-Arabism), historical narratives of the ancient past supporting the Semitic/Abrahamic/Islamic pedigree of the Hashemites; and development narratives of archaeology and other kinds of heritage as related to receipts from tourism, espousing a Hashemite vision of *wataniyya*, or nation-state nationalism, for the expanded kingdom. Jordan's territorial expansion had fulfilled the Hashemite dream of obtaining a larger hereditary possession, one that included Jerusalem. It highlighted, however, the Hashemites' gains at the expense of the Palestinians, and in further collaboration with the British and the new state of Israel. Egypt's revolution of 1952 reinvented the competition again in short order. The rise of Gamal Abd al-Nasser, the assertion of non-alignment in the Cold War, Arab Socialism, Baʿathism, and the denouement of British rule in the region made the Hashemites' position vis-à-vis Palestine, Israel, and the struggle against colonialism, imperial hegemony, and their legacies even more tenuous. During the turbulent period in regional politics that coincided with Jordan's control of what it christened the "West Bank" (1950–67) and ruled distinctively from Amman, King Hussein and the Hashemite throne faced a number of existential threats from both within and without, the most serious of which was a successful popular leftist movement that the monarchy suppressed while simultaneously usurping its platform.[3]

Hashemite rule over Palestine from its core east of the river, specifically Jerusalem and the cache of highly visceral meanings that its antiquity carried, was the key to Jordan's competitiveness. It was not only part of the competition over the discourses of pan-Arabism and nation-state nationalism, but also part of the competition with the state of Israel, which shared a long border and the basic framework of an antiquity narrative with Jordan. While the winners and losers of this competition were ultimately determined on the battlefield, Israel prevailed in the discursive competition whereby antiquity was a necessity for legitimacy, largely due to the paradigm established and cultivated by Western interests for nearly a century, which taxonomized heritage into "archaeological" and "living," and saw universal value in "Judeo-Christian," as opposed to Abrahamic, antiquities. Without Jerusalem in the post-1967 era, Jordan has had to recalibrate its antiquity narrative without that which it coveted, gained, made a centerpiece of its identity during a formative era, and catastrophically lost. That strategy has enabled the continuance of the discursive division between antiquity for tourists and antiquity for the domestic audience, who have been actors and agents in the Islamization of the truncated Hashemite kingdom based, in the official discourse of Islamization as directed from above, on the familiar genealogical narrative of the Hashemites. The antiquity narrative and strategies for deploying it have been deeply affected, as always, by regional events and socioeconomic issues.

A View from Jordan: Problems and Problematization

This consideration of a long and complex competition for archaeology and its narratives in Jordan and Palestine through the lens of Jordan's history seeks to add broadly to conversations across multiple disciplines while beginning a conversation that has been missing from scholarship of the history and archaeology of both Jordan and Palestine. At the general level, historians, anthropologists, archaeologists, and specialists in cultural heritage, cultural studies, religious studies, literature, and area studies will see methodologies familiar to their own disciplines herein, and much that relates to broad interdisciplinary considerations of colonial and postcolonial studies. It is ultimately a political study, but rooted in the analysis of what many would fail to recognize as political. Archaeology *is* politics.

This study is, more specifically, an intervention into the discourse of both Near Eastern archaeologists and historians of the modern Middle East. Until quite recently, most historical considerations of archaeology in the Middle East have been written by archaeologists themselves, who write histories of their discipline devoid of expertise in the historical context that provides the critical lens onto their discipline as a unit of study. More anthropologically oriented archaeologists have better come to terms with awareness of being engaged in a postcolonial act rooted, as is so often the case, in its colonial predecessor. These archaeologists are fewer and farther between in the Middle East, where they do not predominate in the archaeology of historical periods (this is left to the more Bible- and classics-oriented scholars), and where interest in historical periods—particularly those related to the Hebrew Bible, the time of Jesus, and early Christianity—tends to outstrip interest in prehistory or other historical periods. Indeed, much of the archaeological soul-searching and sensitivity that is observable where the issue of "first nations" and the concomitant recognition of colonial legacy has a high profile—in the Americas, for instance—is largely lacking in the foreign archaeological community that works in the Middle East. Acknowledging the colonial legacy of their discipline—which still privileges the mastery of dead languages over the mastery of languages of the countries in which they spend their lives working and routinely advocates, or at least fails to question, "national" archaeology—would force them to take uncomfortable political positions in a place where so many archaeologists claim that they are "not political," while maintaining a position that practicing archaeology is not a political act. And with the exception of archaeologists who focus in heritage of the "Islamic period," archaeologists working in the region where Islam is the non-monolithic religion of the majority have no training to properly work in it, as their profession does not require such training. While most will affirm, and quite sincerely, their sensitivity to "Islamic period" heritage, they come equipped with no capacity to see the world in Islamicate terms, let alone use Islamicate sources to shed light on traditions involving place or antiquity; the Abrahamic story doesn't end with the coming of Islam, and endures precisely because Islam is rooted in its predecessors, tied to their notions of antiquity, landscape, and identity. The "Judeo-Christian" misnomer casts a long shadow, and many of today's archaeologists are committing the same sins as their colonial predecessors, unable or unwilling to recognize their engagement in political acts and the perpetuation of foreign paradigms of knowledge. Much of the discourse and initiatives regarding "looting" over the past decade, particularly in the context of the Iraq war and the Arab uprisings, are complex evidence of that.

For historians of the modern Middle East specifically—who tend to be unfamiliar with archaeology, its methodologies, and its disciplinary discourse—this is an intervention into the disciplinary discourse of the history of Arab nationalism, uniquely here through the lens of the history of archaeology in Jordan's imperial, colonial, and postcolonial spaces. Like other historical considerations of Arab nationalism in recent years, nationalism herein is not considered a failed monolithic or binary product of developmental political processes tied to the discourse of states and elements subversive to them. It is, rather, a wide range of enduring modes of identification embedded in the engagement of modernity in both conception and performance, the whole of cultural experience expressed on an active canvas of participation that invents, borrows, and calibrates without concern for cognitive dissonance or linearity, as there is neither. While the bulk of this study is dedicated to exploring hegemonic uses of archaeological heritage to compete in the nation-state context and manipulate people's sense of identification with Jordan, it offers prospects for future considerations of subaltern and hermeneutic approaches to identity and heritage in Jordan, Palestine, and beyond. As notions of *watan, turath,* and identity are uniquely loaded and problematic in the Jordanian context, this study contributes to recent literature that has complicated the consideration of Jordanian history and historiography, locating these interventions in the context of modern Arab history and historiography more broadly.

There have been no extensive considerations of the uses and meanings of archaeological heritage in Jordan. Historical, anthropological, and literary studies such as those of Donald Reid and Elliott Colla (Egypt, Egyptian archaeology, and Egyptology), Magnus Bernhardsson (Iraq), James Goode (the Arab world broadly), and Nachman Ben-Yehuda and Nadia abu el-Haj (Israel) have been entirely lacking.[4] The reasons why lie in both real issues and scholarly paradigms.

The Hashemite monarchy and the various narratives of it are one complication. The Hashemites' goal was to secure a hereditary dynasty in the post-Ottoman order. Throughout the twentieth century, the Jordanian part of the family demonstrated its willingness to take unpopular positions, accommodating, for instance, the British, the Yishuv and Israel, the United States, and other international, regional, and domestic powers to achieve that end. What was a history rooted in self-interest and self-preservation was intertwined in real and rhetorical trajectories that were much larger, including the unfolding course of events for Palestinians, the Cold War, and an era during which Egypt and Gamal Abd al-Nasser loomed so large. Hashemite motivations in the context of these events have produced no shortage of academic and popular interest, much of it focusing on the monarchy and taking pro- or anti-Hashemite positions that ultimately reinforced the monarchy's own legitimacy discourse in scholarly and other circles, from historical and other perspectives. Mary Wilson, Avi Shlaim, and Laurie Brand were among the first to examine the role of the Hashemites and perceptions of that role in this history in critical ways.[5] Linda Layne, Eugene Rogan, Michael Fischbach, Joseph Massad, Andrew Shryock, Betty Anderson, Kimberly Katz, and Yoav Alon have made invaluable contributions to this discussion, shining light on the role of Jordanians—largely absent from earlier historical or other considerations—and the socioeconomic, intellectual, and cultural dynamics of land and citizenship law, the military, state-building, locales of spiritual significance, nationalist discourses, history writing, and political movements.[6]

The physical and rhetorical dimensions of Jordan's borders are a further complication. Of all the Middle Eastern states carved from the Ottoman Empire, Jordan is often considered the "least real" of all the imagined communities. This is simultaneously ludicrous and true; people identified no more or less with locality or region in Jordan than anywhere else, nor were its borders any more or less contrived. The notions, still spoken aloud, that modern Jordan is "southern Syria" or "Palestine" or "northern Arabia" are easily countered, even though various regions of the modern state may have had stronger connections with Syria, Palestine, Egypt, or Arabia in a pre- or early-state past than with one another. The state was, however, conceived as an afterthought, its borders articulated by the British after and in relation to the territories that had already been included in Britain's Mandates, Palestine and Iraq, and those of France, Syria, and Lebanon. Jordan's borders vis-à-vis Saudi Arabia's were, moreover, decades in the settling. More importantly, its border with Palestine has been, in Joseph Massad's words, "elastic." The western border institutionalized by Winston Churchill in 1921 expanded to include the "West Bank" and East Jerusalem with the 1948 war, and contracted again with their loss in the 1967 war. Until its disengagement twenty-one years later, Jordan maintained the institutions of its statehood in Occupied Palestine, retaining its stewardship of Jerusalem's Muslim holy sites through its special role in *waqf* (religious endowments), enshrined in its peace treaty with Israel in 1994.

The physical, institutional, and rhetorical elasticity of Jordan's borders in the context of Hashemite leadership and its real and discursive nuances gave added dimension to the complexity of identity and identity politics. Identification or lack thereof with *turath* in its many forms has had important dimensions that are both within and without the *watan*, the dimensions of the *watan* have been both conceptually and physically elastic, and the *watan* in those many forms comprises a diverse population within and beyond it. Those within it have been affected by waves of migration, often under duress, and their identity in Jordan institutionalized in larger frameworks of Hashemite national discourse.

The terms "Transjordanian" and "Palestinian" are at the heart of this complexity, and are tricky and sensitive. In this book, I use the term "Jordanian" broadly and inclusively to mean all those who hold, or should hold, Jordanian citizenship. Outside that meaning, and even in many ways embedded within it, are extremely sensitive distinctions recognized by Jordanians. Herein I use the term "Transjordanian" to mean Jordanians descended of families who were late Ottoman Transjordanian citizen-subjects. It is thus an imperfect term, and a term based primarily on recognition of political and socioeconomic existence and participation in the late Ottoman Transjordanian world (where no such geographical configuration or term as "Transjordan" existed) rather than on kinship or origin stories such as those described by the subjects of Andrew Shryock's research. Many kin groups of settled, nomadic, or semi-nomadic background would not recognize "Transjordanian" to mean such, and might adhere to either a more exclusive or inclusive definition. "Transjordanian" and "Jordanian Jordanian" exist as terms to distinguish those expressing their identity as such from another category, "Palestinian Jordanian," which can carry a range of value judgments. The term is used herein to mean those Jordanian citizens whose family origins are in Palestine, and who found themselves in myriad ways, often as refugees, workers, civil servants, and/or entrepreneurs, within (roughly) Jordan's present borders at various moments since 1921. While such distinctions are generally not made in the following pages, there are socioeconomically, politically, and culturally relevant shades of being "Palestinian Jordanian" having to do with how, when, and from where one has arrived in Jordan.

Organization of the Book

In chapter 2, I examine British and American study of the "Holy Land" in the late nineteenth and early twentieth century, understanding the emergence of the discipline of archaeology in the context of international competition. Modern science had a crucial role to play in that competition, and archaeology was particularly useful in this regard, tied to important competitive activities such as mapping and collecting for national museums. The science of archaeology, particularly in the Near East, rather than working in opposition to religion, shared a comfortable hybridity with religious studies in tandem with a broad ethos of competitive modernity. This modernity was projected with specific national peculiarities in the archaeological endeavors of westerners in the Holy Land, helping affirm their identity and postures in the global competition that helped define them. The Protestant, capitalist expansionism that characterized British and American modernity (and self-identified with the Chosen People of the Hebrew Bible) rendered the future Transjordan, its people, and their study imaginable for what they were not. In other words, the spaces of Transjordan were delineated negatively vis-à-vis Palestine, identifiable for being the land not of the biblical Israelites, but of their adversaries. British realizations of biblical Transjordanian space have, like their maps of biblical Palestinian space, had a lasting effect on the course of regional events.

While the British and Americans mapped previously imagined spaces into reality, the Ottoman Empire was modernizing its reality in the same spaces to survive an international competition in which they were increasingly weaker, indebted, and existentially threatened. The spaces of the future Transjordan were a focus of frontier settlement to increase productivity and taxation, but were also the spaces set between two important foci of religio-national identity building: the Arabian Hijaz and Palestinian Jerusalem. Chapter 3 explores the environment of bureaucratic, economic, and sociocultural change and expectation experienced in southeastern Bilad al-Sham during this period, focusing on the growing reading and increasingly upwardly mobile late Ottoman Arab society and its engagement with the narratives of antiquity that Western scholarship was creating out of the contemporary spaces in which it lived. I focus specifically on the popular journal *al-Muqtataf* and its presentation of biblical archaeology and advances in Semitic studies. Knowledge of Near Eastern archaeology was widely disseminated by means of *al-Muqtataf* and other journals to an Arabic reading and listening public that embraced it as other sciences and understood biblical and Semitic studies as affirming their own history and identity. While the competition over artifacts and museum collections raged, the same archaeology spoke narratives in different ways for late Ottoman citizen-subjects and westerners, differing paradigms of knowledge and identity that would help set the stage for competition not just over archaeology, but over national borders and the identification of those who would be organized into them. In Jordan's case, that ethos would be heavily imbued with ideas about bedouin and tribalism.

Chapter 4 begins at the end of World War I, focusing on how the British, having mapped, excavated, and imagined Palestine's and Transjordan's spaces into reality, devised interventions and policies in that territory regarding antiquities when they were the Mandatory authority, creating in the process an enduring separation between "living" and "archaeological" heritage that was as unnatural as the new borders they had helped determine. An enterprise that was previously one of imperial competition was now one of forging law, a fusing together of archaeology and politics in a new and stark manner, the competition over archaeology affecting not only international dimensions but also the relationships among British institutions and individuals. Transjordan, meanwhile, was problematic; having been defined in terms of what it was not and created as a colonial afterthought, Western archaeology could offer no real, consistent narrative of antiquity that bound this oddly shaped territory together. It yet contained archaeological heritage requiring the same kind of institutions and care as did that of the Palestine Mandate, but with even more limited coffers. A comprehensive narrative told by Transjordan's antiquities did not begin to emerge until the end of the 1920s. That narrative was devised by American archaeologist Rabbi Nelson Glueck, and relied heavily on the notion, established in the decades prior to World War I, that Transjordan was the landscape inhabited by ancient non-Israelite peoples, and was therefore unequal by comparison. The modern bedouin in this narrative were reminiscent of the biblical patriarchs, further linking contemporary Arabs to various notions regarding the identifying characteristics of ancient Arabs. To compete with colonial and nation-state narratives constructed by British officials and Glueck, meanwhile, Arab intellectuals, drawing on Western archaeological and philological research, wrote about history and archaeology in a distinctively pan-Arab idiom shaped by their experience under the Mandate and the increasing national tension with the growing Jewish community in Palestine.

In chapter 5, I examine the role of archaeology and antiquities in Emir (later King) Abdullah's efforts at state-building, in which his challenge was to turn the peripheral space he was given into a Hashemite core. Transjordan had no comprehensive narrative for its antiquities recognized as having universal value, its borders remained unfixed, and the Hashemite family coveted a much larger hereditary possession that included Jerusalem. Yet Transjordan's landscape and the antiquities it included became an important means of building a recognizable core. Stamps and currency designed and issued during Abdullah's tenure, for instance, used archaeology to send nuanced messages about what lay specifically within Transjordan's borders. Playing on Western notions of universal value recognizable outside those borders, these discourses simultaneously subsumed the personal narratives that people had to the *turath* of antiquity and its landscape that would not have been recognizable to foreign audiences. Intellectuals such as Transjordan's poet 'Arar (Mustafa Wahbi al-Tal, 1899–1949), meanwhile, straddled both thematic worlds and all aspects of the competition over place and identity, but by means of his words gave rhetorical content and form to the physical Transjordanian state beyond that enabled by official discourses.

In chapter 6, I consider the role of antiquity in the ongoing competition once the Hashemites realized their long-standing goal of obtaining Jerusalem. Having spent the Mandate period building a Hashemite core without Palestine, Jordan set about to rule, from Amman, what it would name the "West Bank," an audacious rhetorical and spatial reconfiguration of the paradigmatic construction of the Holy Land. Jordan would subsume Palestine's Holy Land iconography accordingly, particularly for foreign audiences. Jordan's primary and secondary history and social studies textbooks of this period, however, tell a complicated story of antiquity's role in owning both pan-national and national narratives in the context of King Hussein's competition with primarily Gamal Abd al-Nasser to control the discourse(s) of Arab nationalism, and with Israel and Palestinians to own the narrative of Palestine as Jordan. Hashemite narratives of antiquity in this period depended on pan-Arab precedents for history writing and implicit understandings of the Hashemites' relationship to the Prophet Muhammad and earlier Abrahamic patriarchs. As that required recognition of Israel's antiquity narrative and renders Hashemite Jordan's uncomfortably similar to it, and as archaeology had a primary role in creating the state of Israel's historicity in Palestine, the writing of history and archaeology are almost entirely discursively separated in the schoolbooks of the expanded kingdom. While both could carry aspects of pan-national and national narratives, history was less problematic than archaeology for owning Hashemite historicity in the Holy Land's contested spaces. History writing thus made emotive narratives of Jerusalem and the West Bank Holy Land, while discussion of antiquity unrelated to spiritual matters was about the modern state and citizen, development, and benefits related to the tourism sector, enabled by and reinforcing the cognitive and physical separation between religious and antique heritage. Both kinds of writing emphasized, first and foremost, the unity of Jordan across the river.

I conclude this book by considering how Jordan, in light of the discursive history of its antiquities, recalibrated those narratives after losing Jerusalem and the West Bank in 1967. One aspect of this recalibration manifested in an "Islamizing" project to renovate the shrines and tombs of the Prophets and Companions, something the Ottomans had done in the late nineteenth century. This project sought to provide renewed pilgrimage spaces in Jordan, enabled the Hashemites to control Islamic discourse in the kingdom, and provided new spaces with which to promote the aspect of their legitimacy based on family connections to the Prophet Muhammad and their historical role as protectors of holy places. I also explore initiatives to promote specifically Christian tourism and the development of new museums. More recently, remote and sensitive antiquity—from the Neolithic through the Iron Age—has become part of the more familiar antiquity narratives developed over the decades. I approach these issues in the context of Jordan's neoliberal development program and the backlash to such projects that have characterized the region since late 2010.

Archaeology's power to realize the nation lay in the historical context of its disciplinary emergence. A taxonomic science like so many others to which it was related, it created knowledge of a world in which industrialized powers' ability to compete with one another depended on securing colonies. In that competition, archaeology narrated scientific affirmation of a past that explained the present and envisioned a positivist future. Based on ideas of value rooted in such affirmations and explanations, it drew borders, assigned people to them, and gave antiquities a monetary value like any other resource. Archaeology was among the forms of knowledge used to create the modern

Middle East. As those categories, nearly a century later, fracture amidst unspeakable human suffering while heritage is smashed, stolen, and sold, a historical consideration of archaeology's role in narrating nations can help elucidate the interstices of such tragedies, and open an interdisciplinary dialogue regarding what lay beyond them.

CHAPTER 2

Holy Land Core and Periphery

In the waning days of hostilities between the Central and Allied Powers, British Orientalist David Hogarth, director of Oxford's Ashmolean Museum, mythic figurehead of the Cairo-based Arab Bureau, and soon-to-be Middle East commissioner at the Paris Peace Conference, wrote to his mother:

> I offered myself four years ago for my special knowledge of one theatre of this War, and . . . was put in charge of our policy in the Near East . . . I don't collect intelligence but interpret it, ie. I advise on the policy to be pursued under given circumstances in the Arabian and Palestinian theatres . . . In particular I have had to take a leading part in running the Arab Revolt, as a movement allied with us, since it started in 1916 . . . I am supposed to be essential to our political and military success in the Near East and I know that in certain respects, my knowledge is greater than anyone else's now. But I also know that, in reality, "il n'qa pas d'homme necessique," and if anything happened to me, the show would go on all the same![1]

As the epic trial-and-error management of the Great War by an informal network of well-connected adventurers gave way to the bureaucratization and violent banality of colonial rule in the Middle East, Hogarth's letters revealed growing frustration with his service. Patriotism had motivated Hogarth to volunteer for England's war effort, offering the "special knowledge" he had acquired while extensively traversing the Arab regions of the Ottoman Empire over the course of his academic career. Like many of his contemporaries—Gertrude Bell, T. E. Lawrence, Leonard Woolley, Ronald Storrs, Ernest Richmond, and Harry St. John Bridger Philby, among many others—Hogarth would bear witness as the knowledge gained in his scholarly life and deployed to support the war effort was enshrined in treaty and policy.

Hogarth's "special knowledge" of the Middle East was the result of deliberate production, not acquisition. It resulted from a process by which the British grafted tangible results of surveillance and intelligence onto an ethereal geography, a spiritual terrain seen in the mind's eye and felt in the soul, an Edwardian knowledge beyond that gained in the Victorian era by what had since become conventional, scientific means.[2] In the spaces that Hogarth and the other scholar-soldier-policy-makers—among them archaeologists, historians, philologists, ethnographers, linguists, classicists, Orientalists, eugenicists, Social Darwinists—sought to know, the officialdom to which they had volunteered their services drew the borders of new nation-states after the Great War, shattering the temporal and spatial boundaries between the old order and the new. It thus fell to those who straddled the prewar and postwar era, struggling uncomfortably under the weight of socioeconomic and spiritual dislocations of imperial modernity and re-evaluative challenges to its framework, to serve as the bridge between those radically different orders.

Victorians had set this process in motion, having in the Near East turned the tabula rasa of their Western imaginations into something very real, conceiving what would become the historicity, modernity, and national parameters of new states sanctioned after the war by the world's major powers. They surveyed, mapped, studied, and excavated to create and consume narratives intertwining empire, science, and God. Among the *realia* that emerged from this process were the spaces that became the Holy Land and those who populated them. The Holy Land was, in the process, further realized as core and peripheral space, more important and less. In such a taxonomy, the attributes of its inhabitants were logically determinative of both historicity and modernity. In such a context, what would become contested national spaces of Palestine and Jordan came to be.

The Holy Land *realia* were born of competition. Nineteenth-century Western powers both imagined and filled the spaces that would become the post-Ottoman Near East, offering physical, preliminary answers to the Eastern Question in a broad context of imperial competition and cooperation appropriate for their particular national contexts. Just after the mid-nineteenth century, a rapidly modernizing Ottoman Empire found itself shackled to European powers under increasing debt, flanked on land and sea by England, France, and Russia and forging a strengthening friendship with the German-speaking world—Austria-Hungary and an ascendant, ultimately united Germany. The world had looked quite different just decades before. Whereas Russia and the European powers along its borders had long capitalized on the Ottoman Empire's territorial losses in the Balkans, Napoleon's march across Europe and his 1798 invasion of Egypt signaled acute danger—to Ottomans and Europeans alike—for the Mediterranean and Arab lands. While France was quickly repelled from Egypt, the projection of Western power in such manner had come to the region, never to be dislodged. Among its manifestations was study of the landscape in a way that reflected the broad cultural context at home and refracted an image of that context and its deployment abroad on the competitive imperial world stage.

England entered the competition by setting out to map what it already imagined as the Holy Land, assigning narratives to these imagined spaces, first measured and then further explored, according to intellectual and cultural values shared with the nineteenth-century United States and heavily influenced by German method and methodology. While their national contexts, trajectories of expansionism, and involvements in the Near East were quite different, these three Western powers, led by England, looked to apply science to foster a more intimate, personal knowledge of the biblical Holy Land specifically for English, American, and German Protestants. This ethos characterized the formative years of archaeological exploration in the "biblical land" or "Holy Land," from about 1840 until the onset of the First World War.

At the beginning of this period, classicist historicism was well entrenched in Europe, incorporating a long-held Greek dichotomy between itself and the eastern barbarian in combination with Rome's universal civilizing mission into a modern imperial cultural milieu for which antiquity—its study, its appropriation, its history lessons—was the unquestioned consciousness of imperial modernity.[3] During the period, Charles Darwin's work emerged to offer new conclusions for taxonomic enterprises that, infused in emergent racial and social theory, cast the relationship between European empire and colonial periphery in a deterministic characterization of progress and its opposite, while the United States engaged this historicism in a way concomitant with its own young colonial and postcolonial expansion.[4] At period's end, the consequences of the Great War, which settled this phase of global competition, would require antiquity's narratives of imperial national historicism to be recast in a framework of bureaucracy and nation-state historicism with new colonial logistics and vocabulary. England's particular role in the competition over ancient and modern spaces and narratives laid the groundwork for the physical and rhetorical dimensions of the British Mandate, the conflict in Palestine, and the creation of the modern state of Israel.[5]

In this chapter I argue that we must consider Jordan in the same light, and propose an intellectual framework in which the physical definition of this space came to exist for the British who would control it after World War I. Protestantism was an important component of British imperial modern identity, having complex interstices with capitalism and ideas of progress.

In what those in the "West" called the Near East, Protestantism, capitalism, and progress manifested a particular affinity for Old Testament spaces, spaces critical to what Protestants understood as the unadulterated covenant of the days of the biblical patriarchs, spaces that no one else had claimed because they were not linked to long-held Orthodox or Catholic traditions and were now discoverable only by means of science. In this paradigm, the land upon which lived the ancient Israelites, whose story is the root of the Hebrew Bible, was of primary importance. When the British set forth to discover the Holy Land with science, it was the homeland of the ancient Israelites and evidence of their presence as related in their own scriptural text that they intended to find. As such, their understanding of the landscape of the "Holy Land" had a core and a periphery. The core was what they understood as the land of the ancient Israelites of the Hebrew Bible, and the periphery was everything else—what, according to the Bible, constituted the "homelands" of the non-Israelites, who are often portrayed in a fraught light vis-à-vis those who are naturally the protagonists of the Hebrew scriptural tradition. It is in this way that the British mapped Palestine and an "east of Jordan," with the River Jordan serving as the boundary between the two. The core and its contents had a ready-made comprehensive narrative; the periphery did not. The core and its contents thus constituted a definable and desirable priority; the periphery was an afterthought. The core became the modern borders of Palestine; a large chunk of the periphery became Jordan. The core had a Jewish identity applicable to "Judeo-Christian" and "Western" civilization; the periphery did not. What it was *not* thus defined the periphery. This idea, based on a spatial and narrative imaginary of modern identity and historicity understandable by the application of science in a context of international competition, would become the basis of the geopolitical configuration of the post-Ottoman Middle East, destined to affect narratives of both ancient history and the contemporary milieu of Palestine and Jordan until the present day.

Catholic and Protestant Imperial Modernity in the Near East

When Napoleon invaded Egypt in 1798, he brought with him teams of savants—specialists in everything from botany to philology—and with them began the modern scientific study of the Holy Land. The French milieu in the Holy Land was rather exceptional when compared with that of other powers, above and beyond the religious and consular representations that now materialized beyond Istanbul in Jerusalem. Because of Charlemagne's diplomacy and the circumstances of the Crusades, France's king had historically assumed the role of protector over Latin Christian interests in Jerusalem. France's historic role was recalibrated for modern times when it assumed protection over Catholic interests by means of the Capitulations in the sixteenth century, while Russia's czars would make similar claims on behalf of Greek Orthodox Christians.[6]

The French had a broad understanding of biblical geography, and early in the nineteenth century began excavating and reading ancient texts at sites from the Mediterranean coast to Persia. By the mid-nineteenth century, the French were ahead of their Western peers in developing archaeological methods and excavating in Egypt, Greece, and Mesopotamia, seeking both the "Classical" and the "Oriental."[7] Major French excavations in the Holy Land were tied to areas of France's own strategic imperial interests, primarily in Lebanon, and were therefore concentrated at Byblos, Tyre, and Sidon, especially after Mount Lebanon became an autonomous district under international guarantee, particularly French protection, in 1861, France having exploited a wave of sectarian violence in which it intervened.[8] Because of their Catholic history, however, French interests in the Holy Land were focused on the places where Jesus was thought to have lived, the spaces of Palestine and the future Transjordan, with the River Jordan at their core.[9] These New Testament spaces were long sanctioned by Rome and traveled by Christian pilgrims for nearly two millennia. French intellectuals, among them members of various Catholic brotherhoods, eagerly applied scientific method in these spaces as they did elsewhere in the Near East. Recognized for more than 1,500 years, however, the spaces in which Christ lived could not be easily erased, and ultimately required no scientific sanction to render them legitimate. French exploration in the Holy Land would not seek holy sites to venerate in lieu of those already venerated, even if Protestant attacks on the authenticity of sites important to Catholics, sites upon which France claimed official, national protection, did bring the French to their vigorous defense and encouraged them to expand the scope of their research.[10]

The other Western powers that entered the competitive sphere of Near Eastern scholarship were Germany, England, and the United States. As France's intellectual endeavors were characterized by its Catholicism, those undertaken by these three powers were characterized by their Protestantism.[11] German scholarship would provide the catalyst, and British and North American scholars would reinvent the epicenter of the Holy Land in accordance with the legacy of the Reformations and Enlightenments and the holistic cultural context of their national expressions of modernity.

Just as Enlightenment thought had constructed the interdependency of modernity and historical consciousness, so were science, religion, and philosophy similarly inseparable. Paradigms that frame analyses of intellectual history in terms of "science versus religion" or "reason versus faith" are thus misleading.[12] Every advance in the various fields of science informed the development of the study and practice of philosophy and religion. Among the modern sciences was philology, which was the primary means of studying the ancient world in the nineteenth century. Forms of material culture other than texts provided secondary support for understanding the ancient written word. German scholars had a well-earned reputation for dominance and innovation in philology, not only in classical languages but also in the ancient languages of the Near and Far East.[13] By applying philological science, German scholars had, by the mid-nineteenth century, made startling cases against the historicity of the Bible.[14] German scholar Julius Wellhausen's synthesis of biblical criticism, *Prolegomena zur Geschichte Israels* (1882), deconstructed the time frame during which the Hebrew Bible was composed and the doctrine that it was a product of divine inspiration.[15] Given the doubt cast upon the Bible's literality, German endeavors in the field of Semitic languages and Holy Land archaeology were characterized by a scientific Protestant ethos seeking to purify the faith by understanding its roots.[16] For many German intellectuals, the roots of faith had more to do with the origins of man and civilization than the origins of the Israelites. Assyrian and Babylonian texts that long predated the Hebrew Bible attested to experiences of God similar to those recorded in the Jewish scriptures. This demonstrated for many that the ancient Israelites were not, in fact, unique, and intellectuals within and outside Germany began understanding the roots of faith and civilization in terms of pan-Babylonianism. In this respect, German interest in the Near East and the Bible had, like French interest, a broad scope. The particularities of the German approach, however, would distinguish its archaeological and philological work—and that of those who worked in the German tradition and methodology—in the Holy Land from that of other national projects. German methodology, in seeking to peel away what intellectuals believed had profaned the true faith, led German scholars and many of those who trained in their midst away from the Hebrew Bible and the imagined space of the ancient Israelites. As would happen throughout the Western academy, German scholars' quest to apply science for understanding the Bible had the effect of taking intellectuals further from faith, even if the German public did not necessarily follow.[17] German-speaking evangelical Protestants, meanwhile, set forth to proselytize to the contemporary peoples of the Holy Land.[18]

The expression of German intellectualism in such a progressive framework of faith reliant on science was appealing to British and North American Protestants. While "secularization" is widely used to describe European and

American culture in the nineteenth century—accounting for changes in cultural norms and paradigms of knowledge—multidenominational Protestantism on both sides of the Atlantic accounted for values associated with competition, progress, industrialism, expansion, prestige, and anti-Catholicism. Progress was simply unattainable without the advancement of science. In the words of Bruce Kuklick, "A full-blooded Protestant Christianity dominated educated life in nineteenth-century America."[19] This progressive ideal, with the limitless promise of its new institutions and opportunities for immigration and advancement, helped Germans and German methods assume a special place in American universities.[20] German scholars bound for North America thus joined the back-and-forth transatlantic pilgrimages of British and American intellectuals, men for whom science, philosophy, and religion were often one and the same. These were men of letters who took a wide variety of positions in contemporary controversies, such as when Darwin forever altered the course of intellectual history with *Origin of Species* in 1859 and in 1871 with *Descent of Man*, and when Julius Wellhausen's Documentary Hypothesis soon thereafter did the same for biblical studies.[21] They enjoyed fame and notoriety on both sides of the Atlantic, crisscrossed the ocean to speak, published widely in both places, and corresponded and debated regularly with one another.[22] Learned and voluntary religious and scientific societies, which had grown numerous since the late eighteenth century, had counterparts in both countries, and shared British and American members.[23]

When British and Americans, largely on missionary and religiously inspired initiatives, arrived in the Holy Land in the opening decades of the nineteenth century, they brought the national peculiarities of their lived Protestantism and its imagined pilgrimages. The life world of Christ having been so long defiled by Rome, Protestants expressed a particular affinity with the Old Testament and thus with the ancient Israelites whose narrative is so colorfully contained within its pages. As modern bearers of the true faith, British and American Protestants saw themselves, like the Israelites of old, as a chosen people.[24] In England, this affinity was, in part, the legacy of having led the people from darkness to light through the Reformation, and a hallmark of their competitive superiority in a contemporary global competition.[25] Similarly, from the earliest days of their settler-colonial project in the New World, Americans' connections to the Old Testament were linked by their religious and community leaders to patriotic ideals.[26] As they hacked their way through the wilderness, building shining cities on hills and violently proselytizing to the indigenous heathens, they bestowed their towns and cities with the names of their imagined Old Testament landscape.

If Catholics considered Palestine generally and Jerusalem particularly the epicenter of the Holy Land because it was the sanctified terrain of Jesus, for Protestants the importance of this same geography was that it was the terrain of the ancient Israelites. Protestants had long since turned their backs on the biblical geography of the papacy in favor of an idealized vision of the holy terrain that occupied the internalized space of the spirit rather than a physical space in a faraway land. They were thus unconcerned with the historicity of the papacy's New Testament landscape. Two things were quite apparent, however, when British and American missionaries, officers, explorers, adventurers, treasure hunters, and millenarians encountered the real Holy Land.[27] The Old Testament landscape upon which had trod the footsteps of the patriarchs did not exist, either. Worse, the land of milk and honey as envisioned in Protestants' imaginary pilgrimage was decidedly un-magnificent—its cities simple, its people a backward rabble, its water a breeding ground of malaria and other pandemics.[28] It was a land in need of redemption, discovery, and modernity, and a battlefield for global competition among strong colonial powers.

Redeeming the Spaces of Patriarchs

At the inaugural public meeting of the Palestine Exploration Fund (PEF) in London in 1865, William Thompson, the archbishop of York, infamously linked English Protestantism, patriotism, destiny, science, and England's role in a global colonial competition with this oft-quoted bit of his closing remarks to the gathering:

> This country of Palestine belongs to you and me. It is essentially ours. It was given to the Father of Israel in the words "Walk the land in the length of it and in the breadth of it, for I will give it unto thee.". . . We mean to walk through Palestine in the length and in the breadth of it because that land has been given unto us. It is the land from which comes the news of our redemption. It is the land towards which we turn as the fountain of all our hopes . . . it is the land to which we may look with as true a patriotism as we do to this dear old England, which we love so much.[29]

From encounters with a land and people in need of redemption to such an imperial conflation was a path of only a few decades. The centrality of the Old Testament Holy Land and the understanding of scientific method that characterized nineteenth-century Protestantism provided the ethos and rigor with which Americans and British undertook their systematic study of the biblical Near East just before mid-century. Western projects set forth across thousands of miles of vastly different territories, all with some bearing on what had been imagined as the Holy Land. While German methods were critical to these endeavors, British and American methodology, particularly at what it would create as the epicenter of the Holy Land—the River Jordan and what lay just west of it—was quite distinct. Many British and American intellectuals set their sights on the heart of the Holy Land, setting forth to use science to make a space previously only imaginable into something real. Their first step was to survey and map the land, making the terrain known only through biblical literature into a real space conceivable for modern times.

American Congregationalist Edward Robinson published *Biblical Researches in Palestine, Mount Sinai and Arabia Petraea* simultaneously in English and German in 1841, inciting a pre-Darwinian intellectual and popular revolution on both sides of the Atlantic.[30] One of America's greatest intellectuals of the time, the conservative New England scholar turned his cutting-edge philological training, obtained in Germany, in the opposite direction from German intellectual trends, using it to cast light on the veracity and historicity of the Bible, upon which science had been used to launch attacks and cast doubt. Like most Protestant scholars, artists, and other travelers to the Holy Land, Robinson held the Catholic- or Orthodox-sanctioned New Testament and other religious landmarks in contempt, steeped in superstition—an issue that had been of increasing international diplomatic concern in recent years.[31] While walking in the footsteps of Christ meant an unpalatable connection with irrationality, the paths trod by Palestine's Old Testament heroes, off the beaten path and found out-of-doors, offered a real pilgrimage space for the Protestant enlightened.[32]

Robinson and his colleague Eli Smith, an American missionary based in Beirut, traveled the region for three years. Using their broad knowledge of Semitic languages and history, they sought to link the Arabic toponyms (place names) of contemporary Palestine with those of Old Testament locales, thus creating the first scientific geography of the Hebrew Bible. Robinson used scientific method and cutting-edge methodologies in an innovative way, making it work *for* believers—and ultimately for God—rather than against them. In doing so, he established the paradigm by which all future study of the Holy Land would be undertaken. His research, created by and for Protestants, enabled them to step forward in light of their imagined, indelible connection to the ancient Israelites and claim the spaces he had identified, knowing them firsthand in the modern world. Robinson's was the first major step in making an imagined geography real, and this work earned him a gold medal from England's Royal Geographical Society. His books became guides for a Holy

Land tourist industry that soon emerged with Thomas Cook and Sons at the helm.[33]

Seven years after Robinson and Smith published *Biblical Researches in Palestine*, American naval commander William Francis Lynch became the first westerner to complete a voyage of the Dead Sea, hoping to use it one day to broaden international trade horizons for Virginia cotton and tobacco.[34] To build on the work of Robinson and Smith, Lynch, and the expedition of English cleric and scholar H. B. Tristram (1863–64), the most famous of the scientific societies dedicated to Holy Land research, the British Palestine Exploration Fund (PEF), was founded in 1865.[35] Its first incarnation was the Jerusalem Water Relief Fund, an organization established to address missionaries' harrowing experiences of water-borne pandemics in Jerusalem, as well as conditions for agricultural and commercial development and exploitation. With donations and the influence of the society's elite members, the Royal Engineers—that is, the military—were recruited to map Jerusalem. The results of the survey would be used to overhaul the city's water system.[36]

While surveying Jerusalem, the Royal Engineers, led by Captain Charles Wilson, couldn't help but find enigmatic archaeological remains. Because the survey was meant to modernize the city's water systems, Wilson had reason to explore extant cisterns, aqueducts, channels, and sewers. These took his team underground, where they found architecture and artifacts attesting to multiple periods of the city's settlement.[37] Press coverage of the mission and its finds ignited popular interest back home. Prominent members of the Jerusalem Water Relief Fund, most notably the evangelical Sir George Grove, harnessed public interest and secured the benefaction of a wealthy imperialist, Walter Morrison, to establish a permanent society to support Palestine exploration.[38] At the inaugural public meeting of the PEF, its intended functions, taxonomic and ethnographic, were described as "exploring Jerusalem, and other Holy Land sites, for archaeological purposes; surveying the land; and investigating flora, fauna, and the natural resources of Palestine."[39] It was likewise hoped that "biblical scholars may yet receive assistance in illustrating the sacred texts from the careful observations of the manners and people of the Holy Land."[40]

Author John James Moscrop understands the PEF as a microcosm of Victorian society and as an environment in which all the factors contributing to Britain's larger intellectual, social, and political climate are observable. Its very existence emerged from the broad-based application of science and critical scholarship to an understood, primordial religious and national truth, and a conviction that England was most competitive and best suited to elucidate knowledge that was there for the taking. The PEF succeeded in building an organization with a membership reflecting the organization of the British Empire. While certainly its membership, and particularly its administration, counted the political, financial, intellectual, and clerical elite—all English and Anglican—its general membership was varied. Subscribers came from all religious backgrounds—including Catholics and Jews—from other countries, and from the expansive middle class.[41]

The PEF's stated goals were likewise broad enough to appeal to a wide range of intellectual and political tastes, although some members were more comfortably affiliated than others.[42] Its religious foundations were appealing to a wide audience of believers, whether wed to the traditionalism of biblical revelation or advocating a modern, rational approach. A basis in hard science and critical scholarship appealed to scientifically and theoretically minded believers and nonbelievers. The patriotism with which the PEF's mission was imbued was innocuous enough to draw both political liberals, who tended to question the many-faceted notion of empire, and political conservatives, who held a range of views regarding England's imperial enterprise.

Archbishop Thompson's injunction at the PEF's inaugural meeting must have appealed greatly, however, to the competitive wiles of imperialists and military strategists, for whom walking in the length and breadth of Palestine would bring the power of boots on the ground to make maps, secure resources, fortify access to them, and deter and challenge competitors. Besides the importance of practical experience and careful observation of landscape to science, knowledge of the land of Palestine was of utmost strategic importance in the international competition. Wars in the Crimea and India were recent memories, England and Russia were locked in a life-and-death struggle for supremacy in Asia, and the Eastern Question remained unresolved.[43] Given the impending opening of the French-built Suez Canal and the power implicit in the Suez Canal Company and its shareholders, Whitehall acutely felt the need to protect West Asian and Mediterranean assets, part of a larger strategy to protect England's Indian and African interests, access to which was radically enabled by the canal's opening. Captain Wilson's expedition to map Jerusalem had included a secret reconnaissance survey mission in the Sinai, the first of what would be many excursions there.[44] A military role in the PEF was thus established long before its inaugural meeting. Given the broad-based membership of the PEF and the "patriotism" to which the Archbishop of York refers, it may not have mattered to its subscribers if the fund's relationship to military strategy had been more overt.

Competition for Mesha, Harbinger of National Spaces

By 1874, the PEF had made a generous gift to the Louvre of the Moabite Stone, the most important Holy Land archaeological discovery made to that date, and among the very few extra-biblical inscriptions that has ever been recovered. Known also as the Mesha Stela, the stone bears a monumental inscription relating to a biblical episode from the third chapter of the Book of Second Kings and other biblical passages. This find came not from the epicenter of Holy Land exploration—Jerusalem particularly and Palestine generally—but from east of the river in what would become Jordan. The ninth-century BCE text is Moabite, and was found by bedouin some fifty kilometers from Jerusalem in what was then an area inhabited by pastoral nomads between the towns of Madaba and Kerak known as Dhiban, the name of which is nearly identical to the ancient toponym Dibon. Dibon was the seat of biblical Moab, an Iron Age (ca. 1200–550 BCE) communal entity contemporaneous with the kingdoms of Israel and Judah. According to the inscription, Mesha, King of Moab, had erected the stela upon the high place dedicated to the Moabite god Kemosh in the city of Dibon. The inscription is a record of Mesha's deeds, chief among which was the defeat of Israel, which had, by the hands of the house of its king Omri, and the will of the Israelite god Yahweh, occupied and oppressed Moab for generations.[45]

The Mesha Stela was a unique and incredible find. Since its discovery, there have been few inscriptional finds related to the history of the Israelites during the biblical period. Within a few years of the discovery of the Moabite Stone, for example, a Paleo-Hebrew inscription of the eighth century BCE commemorating the building of a tunnel was found in Jerusalem outside the Old City walls at Silwan. The inscription may bear witness to King Hezekiah of Judah's efforts to protect Jerusalem's water supply from the Assyrians (2 Kings 18; 2 Chronicles 24). In 1896, Flinders Petrie found an Egyptian stela commemorating Pharaoh Merneptah's defeat of an entity called Israel near the close of the thirteenth-century BCE, the period when many scholars believe the Israelites first appeared in Palestine. An Aramean inscription, possibly from the ninth century BCE, was found in northern Israel at Tel Dan in the early 1990s and commemorates the defeat of an entity possibly known as the House of David, that is, the Kingdom of Judah. These later finds, along with the Mesha Stela, compose the bulk of uncovered philological evidence specifically concerning the biblical Israelites.

If the British raison d'être in Holy Land exploration was to illuminate the world of the Hebrew Bible with new sciences, why turn over one of the most spectacular finds in the history of biblical archaeology to competitor France for display in its national museum? This was not a show of beneficence, but the last act of a lengthy imperial drama that made local, regional, and international politics of Mesha's stela. The episode would ultimately focus England's Near Eastern regional course, strategically and scientifically, for decades to come. There may be something to John James Moscrop's subtle speculation that the English gave the Moabite Stone to the French in exchange for the abandonment of an impending French Holy Land survey, a vast mapping project upon which the PEF, assisted in no small way by the military, would itself soon embark, and which would ultimately lay the foundations for the nation-state order of the post–World War I Middle East.[46] From the British point of view, the Moabite Stone was a small price to pay to prevent the French from reaping the fruit of what they themselves expected—and believed was rightly theirs to narrate, find, and possess—of Palestine's past and future. Letting go of the record of Mesha's deeds might have been a calculated and competitive means to an end.

In the years immediately following its founding, the PEF struggled for finances and members. Charles Wilson and the Royal Engineers were again dispatched to Jerusalem by arrangement with the fund and the Ordnance Survey, but the cost of survey and excavation work was prohibitive and an extended mission was ultimately aborted. Only a few months would pass, however, before Royal Engineers were sent to Jerusalem under Lieutenant Charles Warren for survey and excavation work with the cooperation of the PEF and the Ordnance Survey. Much to Warren's dismay, their project was perpetually impoverished, its potential thus greatly diminished. In a plea for donations, the PEF describes its lack of funding for Warren in early 1869 in terms of Archbishop Thompson's "patriotism" and competition:

> To abandon these works at such a moment would be most lamentable;
> it would be to proclaim to America, to Germany, and to France, that
> England—the country where the Bible has been most loved and most
> studied—will not from her great wealth spare a few thousands yearly to
> carry on the work of elucidating and explaining the Bible history.[47]

If Warren's foray into Jerusalem was not, in fact, a deliberate diversion for the sake of competitors, he was certainly forced to play Peter to Wilson's Paul.[48] While Warren struggled to make ends meet in Jerusalem, Wilson was dispatched with another team of Royal Engineers and a directive from the Ordnance Survey, accompanied by members of the PEF's executive committee, for an extensive study of the strategic Sinai. A sudden infusion of cash into the PEF's coffers and private donations from a church-based group seeking to find the route of the Exodus helped put the PEF, the Ordnance Survey, and the War Office on the ground in this most crucial arena.

The Moabite Stone

Warren's presence and tenuous financial situation, meanwhile, would make him a central figure in the sensational drama of the Moabite Stone. In summer 1868, bedouin of the Bani Hamida tribe showed their guest, Reverend Frederick Augustus Klein of the Anglican mission in Jerusalem, the large, mysterious stone with the substantial inscription. He made a tracing of a few letters. A German born in France, Klein took the tracing not, as might be expected of one ordained in the Church of England, to British representatives, but to the Prussian consul, who was an accomplished linguist. The consul recognized the importance of Klein's tracing and obtained permission for him to make an offer to purchase the stone from those who had shown it to him. The Bani Hamida were allies of the more powerful Beni Sakhr; making the calculation that they might draw the ire of the Ottoman center at Istanbul and others should they take German money for themselves, they declined to sell it.[49] Negotiations continued to no avail, owing to various rivalries among and concerns of local kin groups and the dynamics of the relationship between Istanbul and the Ottoman periphery.[50] On the occasion of Crown Prince Frederick William's visit to the Holy Land in 1869, the Prussian consul convinced the governor, Istanbul's representative in Nablus, to intervene.[51]

Warren, meanwhile, heard rumors of the stone.[52] He sent word to the PEF for advice and to Klein offering assistance, receiving, in return, silence from the first and hostility from the second.[53] Yet another player, an upstart Orientalist in diplomatic service at the French consulate named Charles Clermont-Ganneau, was less scrupulous. Clermont-Ganneau readily took advantage of bedouin rivalries, sending emissaries on a secret mission to make a plaster squeeze of the stone. All the crew were caught in the act save one, who made off with what he could of the squeeze and delivered it to the Frenchman.[54] Shortly thereafter a *firman* (decree) arrived from the Ottoman governor of Nablus demanding that the bedouin turn over the stone to the Ottoman authorities, who had already reached a deal to sell it to the Prussians. Believing that the Europeans must have wanted something valuable inside the strange black stone and recognizing the trouble it had brought them, the bedouin on whose land it stood broke it apart. Finding nothing inside it, they divvied up the parts and hid them.[55]

A bedouin soon approached Warren with fragments of the stone and the tale of its destruction. Horrified at the destruction of what was rumored to be a Phoenician discovery, he teamed with Clermont-Ganneau to gather as much information about the relic and to buy as many pieces of it as they could.[56] With no help from the PEF, Warren was forced to pay out of his own pocket. Clermont-Ganneau, meanwhile, had made a rough translation of the squeeze. The Frenchman went over Warren's head and published his translation. It quickly hit the press and caused an instant popular and intellectual sensation on both sides of the Atlantic.[57]

The Germans reacted bitterly. The PEF, which had impoverished Warren's own project and ignored his news of the Moabite Stone, shamed him publicly for not trying to obtain it sooner. England castigated France for publishing the find. In France, Clermont-Ganneau became a national hero, actively discrediting Warren in the European press. The PEF then ordered Warren to obtain rubbings of the stone and photographs of the rubbings. Since Klein had made the discovery in the first place, Warren recommended that the fragments of the stela go to Berlin. In the buildup to the Franco-Prussian war, however, the French consul in Jerusalem was adamantly opposed to the idea. Once back in London, Warren turned over the fragments of the stone he had purchased to the PEF.[58]

Charles Wilson, meanwhile, learned that the French had begun what promised to be an extensive survey of the Holy Land. Given the physical importance of Palestine to England's regional strategy, and its conflation with the cultivated English ethos for Palestine, news that the French were mapping the Holy Land certainly met with great consternation in many English circles. Using Wilson as a mediator, the PEF contacted the French team. The organization had, meanwhile, made casts of the stela fragments in its possession. Clermont-Ganneau tried to sell his own pieces of the stone to the PEF, which was desperately short of funds and could not afford them. The PEF tried to sell its pieces to the Louvre, which refused to buy them.

Within a month of the eruption of hostilities between France and Prussia (1870–71), the French Holy Land survey came to an end, never to be finished.[59] In 1871, England's Royal Engineers, led by Claude R. Conder and Horatio H. Kitchener, embarked on the Survey of Western Palestine, a comprehensive mapping project that would last for six years. A year later, Clermont-Ganneau entered the PEF's service as its resident Jerusalem archaeologist, a job he would keep as long as he held his diplomatic station at the French consulate.[60] By 1874, thanks to a generous gift of the PEF of its fragments to the Louvre, the surviving parts of the Moabite Stone had been reassembled and gone on permanent display in Paris, where they remain.[61] The Royal Engineers were hard at work making the first comprehensive maps—

English maps—west of the River Jordan, without competition from anyone. This foothold was a crucial step along England's unfettered, unthreatened access to India and beyond, and the stage was set for unimaginable repercussions in the future.

It is difficult to discern the extent to which England's lag in archaeological advancement vis-à-vis its European rivals played a role in the affair of the Mesha Stela and decisions made to advance both the discipline and imperial strategic interests in its aftermath. Biblical archaeology was still in its infancy in 1870, and the British, unlike the Germans and French, had yet to put their own nationals on the ground as professional archaeologists in any part of the Near East. Two explorers, E. H. Palmer and Charles Tyrwhitt Drake, were dispatched by the PEF on survey to the Desert of the Tíh and the Country of Moab. The first part of their journey took them to the Sinai, the supposed location of the Israelites' forty-year exile, and the second part to biblical Moab east of the River Jordan. To that point, exploration east of the river had been very limited. During the second portion of their journey, Palmer and Tyrwhitt Drake went specifically to Dhiban, where the Moabite Stone was reportedly found. Despite the similarities between the ancient toponym (Dibon) and the modern name (Dhiban), the obvious presence of not one but two side-by-side archaeological tells, and the fact that the Mesha Stela had been found nearby, it was determined that the area was not worth further investigation.[62] Palmer and Tyrwhitt Drake searched Dhiban and its environs for more inscribed stelae, but failed to find any, at least on the surface. Palmer reported that excavations in Moab's ruins would no doubt yield many things, but owing to the expense, lack of Ottoman security, and Arab "mania for stones" brought on by the Mesha debacle, "a mere visit even of scientific men to the country will be attended with nothing but disappointment and annoyance."[63] This was in marked contrast to George Grove's comments on the Moabite Stone and his announcement of Palmer and Tyrwhitt Drake's expedition:

> The indications of Isaiah xv. and xvi. imply that the nation of Moab was more civilised and important than we are apt to suppose, and the general interest attaching to the discovery of such a portion of its literature is therefore naturally great . . . To find a passage of Moabite chronicle so parallel in date to a portion of the Bible, is an event of no mean importance; and it should stimulate us to further researches in the same direction.[64]

Given the interest and sensationalism generated by the Mesha Stela and the investment in an exploratory mission to Dhiban, it seems that the PEF was intimidated enough by Palmer's report that it decided to forego an investment of greater resources east of the river. The extent to which the PEF's military associates might have been involved in this decision is unknown. Given the competitive regional situation, the Ordnance Survey likely had more pressing mapping priorities than this part of Moab.

At the same time, the British did forsake the opportunity to explore an archaeological tell in close proximity to a major find with extraordinary historical and biblical significance. While it was known that, across this part of the world, tells were an indication of where antiquities could be found, initial surveys and reports on tells east of the River Jordan were still a decade away, and another two decades would pass before more extensive studies emerged, at about the time Flinders Petrie made the archaeological tell a unit of serialized, specialized investigation.[65] In his report, Palmer mentions ruins, architecture, and walls at Dhiban and says that "the village is built upon two hills."[66] It seems that he and Tyrwhitt Drake did not recognize that these were, in fact, tells with associated monumental architecture and probably countless surface finds.

It is also likely that the British looked forward to putting surveyors and professional archaeologists to work west of the River Jordan, certain to find countless inscriptions more important to them than Mesha's for both competitive and other purposes. Westerners had already begun to find evidence of the vast quantities of written documents produced elsewhere in the Near East under the auspices of ancient Egyptian, Syrian, Anatolian, and Mesopotamian kings. Reports of PEF meetings and lectures, found not only in *Palestine Exploration Quarterly* but in the Arabic journal *al-Muqtataf* in the 1880s and 1890s (see discussion in chapter 3), certainly demonstrate the organization's tantalizing thoughts about the prospects for future research. If the Moabite king was indeed "civilised," as George Grove wrote, and had produced such a thing as this documentary stela, what would be found of the Israelite kings—Mesha's enemies and England's forebears? Israelite inscriptions would bear further witness to the presence of the Israelites on the land, offering greater illumination of the landscapes of the Hebrew Bible and the historicity of those spaces. Only a few years earlier, Wilson and Warren had scratched the surface of Jerusalem's ancient shafts, tunnels, and pools. Knowledge of the existence of such ancient and mysterious places must have offered endless and exciting possibilities for discovery and claims of English patrimony. In light of those possibilities, limited resources had to be deployed where the chances of more important discoveries were most promising. While its discovery and translation was a sensation at the time, no one, not even the French, to whom the British gifted their pieces, could have known at that moment what a unique and fortunate find Mesha's inscription really was.

It would not be fair to say that the British valued the Mesha Stela less than the French did, but it might be said that they valued it differently. France took a broader view in terms of its national interests in biblical archaeology, where England took a more focused view. It would likewise be inaccurate to look askance at France's decision to forego its Palestine survey. Due to their increasing political entrenchment in Mt. Lebanon, the French, while not abandoning archaeological work elsewhere, were increasingly concentrated in northern Bilad al-Sham in the second half of the nineteenth century. That is where they excavated the grand tell sites of biblical eras—the Canaanite cities of Ebla and Ugarit, for instance—many of which, unlike sites in Palestine, yielded extensive archives.

The French no more abandoned Western Palestine to the British than the British abandoned Mesha to the French. England and France made their choices of landscapes to map and explore, sites to excavate, and narratives to create of them based on a perspective forged in intellectual discourse particular to their national contexts and their economic and strategic interests in consideration of the competition in which they were engaged, particularly with each other.[67] The narratives and *realia* created out of this phase of the competition fashioned the landscapes of post-Ottoman Bilad al-Sham in perpetuity. England's project to map Palestine established narratives of core and peripheral landscapes that sit at the nexus of the modern relationship among Israel, Palestine, and Jordan.

Creating a Core and Periphery of Holy and Holier Spaces

With the French surveyors otherwise disposed and the Moab debacle settling, the PEF, armed with its evangelical and scientific charter, set out to bring biblical and classical geography into the modern world.[68] Armed with the PEF, the War Office set out to make maps of strategic territory. The most ambitious of the PEF's projects was the Survey of Western Palestine (1871–77), conducted by the Royal Engineers under the leadership of Claude R. Conder and Horatio H. Kitchener.[69] Dividing its conception of Palestine into a western and eastern portion separated by the River Jordan—a core and periphery of the Holy Land—the PEF gave the eastern half as a survey project to its newer American counterpart, the American Palestine Exploration Society (APES, founded 1870), in what was a collaboration designed to maintain England's interests and prestige.

The geographical parameters of these surveys were designed around the primary landscapes of the lives of the ancient Israelites. In defining both ancient and modern space, by extension they did the same for both ancient and modern people. The surveys sought to define the lands of the Bronze Age Canaanites (ca. 3300–1200 BCE) and the Iron Age kingdoms and peoples described in the Bible—Israel, Judah, Gilead, Ammon, Moab, Edom, and the Philistines. This conception of ancient space would endure; the map of Palestine created by the PEF with the work of surveyors from the War Office essentially became the map of Britain's Palestine Mandate after World War I and defined its border with France's Mandate in Lebanon. Its legacy formed the basis of proposals to divide the land between Palestine's Arab and Jewish populations, and ultimately defined the borders of the State of Israel, and thus at least one border for several modern Middle Eastern states.[70]

The surveys likewise had serious implications for the long-term understanding of the archaeology and cultural remains of those states, perhaps more pointedly in Jordan than anywhere else. By means of the surveys, the PEF realized a biblical geography based on the texts of the ancient Israelites, with whom its audience felt profound identification as being "chosen." As such, all other biblical peoples were consigned to the category of "others," defined primarily in terms of their interactions with the Israelites as recorded for posterity in the Hebrew Bible. According to the biblical writers, these relationships were more often antagonistic or hostile than neighborly. The lands in which the other biblical peoples lived likewise played supporting roles in the story of the Israelites, and were considered similarly as their peoples. Just as the Western Survey ultimately defined the borders of the State of Israel, so the lands of most of the Israelites' neighbors are located today within the borders of modern Arab states.

While there is no reason to doubt that the non-Israelite peoples of the Hebrew Bible also left texts behind, nothing thus far is known to exist on the scale of the Old Testament; there are only a handful of inscriptions and ostraca and, of course, Mesha's inscription. Despite what is known of the biblical writers, knowledge of the narrative traditions of their neighbors is almost entirely lacking. The literary understanding of them is thus dependent on the archaeological record, the framework of which was established in light of what the writers of the Hebrew Bible had to say about them.

This situation is especially tricky for understanding the Iron Age in the Holy Land, particularly where Jordan, Occupied Palestine, and the State of Israel are concerned. The cultural heritage of the Iron Age, defined roughly as 1200–550 BCE, is that which has been most used and misused to make claims and counterclaims of the ancient past as a basis of national legitimacy. Because the largest and most comprehensive textual synthesis of this era is found in books comprising the Hebrew Bible, the Iron Age is most famously the era of David, the development of monotheism, Solomon's Temple (the First Temple), the unity of Israel and Judah, and the subsequent splitting of that united Israelite monarchy on bad terms. By the end of the Iron Age, Jerusalem was lost and the people of Judah forced into exile in Babylon.

There were at least three Iron Age kingdoms in what is now Jordan—Ammon, King Mesha's Moab, and Edom—their borders and populations with one another and with their neighbors in Israel and Judah in flux. Whether such toponyms existed before or after the Iron Age was irrelevant; the idea of the linear rise and fall of kingdoms with definable geographic boundaries on the landscape, linkable to an idea of ethnos and race, was something that modern science and its emphasis on classification enabled nineteenth-century Europeans and Americans to understand.[71] Mapping these kingdoms rendered them facts on the ground, providing historicity and narratives that Europeans and Americans sought and the knowledge that the application of scientific method to Bible study could illuminate for them.

In this way, the Holy Land was divided into two distinct parts—*cisjordan* and *transjordan*; one was identified as Israelite/Jewish and the other was not. Christians worship the Israelite god Yahweh, and not the Ammonite Milkom, the Moabite Kemosh, or the Edomite Qaws. *Cisjordan*, "this side" of the river, was thus important for understanding the roots of Christian civilization and *transjordan* was not. Transjordan, the name eventually given to Britain's Mandate east of the river, is a translation of *Oultrejourdain*, a term used at the time of the Crusades to refer to what lay "beyond the Jordan" from the perspective of one standing west of the river, to which the east was tied by its inclusion in the Kingdom of Jerusalem.[72] Transjordan was defined by what it was not. To this day, the Iron Age on the western side of the river remains far better elucidated than that on the eastern side.

In carrying out its survey west of the River Jordan, the PEF's interest in scientific exploration of the Holy Land melded on a grand scale with that of the War Office in mapping an area of strategic importance. The PEF was perpetually cash-strapped, lacking its own surveyors and equipment, and dependent on non-British scholars like Charles Clermont-Ganneau for archaeological experience, and its partnership with the War Office had become crucial to fulfilling its own charter. For its part, the War Office utilized the PEF when it could fulfill a strategic need. Ancient Canaan, Philistia, and other places sought by the PEF happened to be vital to British imperial interests stretching from the Mediterranean to India. While the PEF's relationship with the War Office was obviously no secret, the extent to which the War Office likely funded the Western Survey and the strategic nature of its impetus for doing so was not widely advertised.[73]

Correspondence between the PEF and its new American cousin, the APES, resulted in the proposal for a Survey of Eastern Palestine. The APES was founded in New York in conjunction with PEF activities in North America, counting among its numbers men of letters and finances, including membership with connections to America's missionary stronghold in Beirut and the Syrian Protestant College.[74] In addition to asserting an American national presence in what had been a European realm, the APES's purpose was largely to refocus attention on the centrality of Palestine to biblical studies, which had increasingly become the purview of Assyriology and German national archaeological efforts.[75]

While not a border in a similar sense for the region's inhabitants, the border between the survey areas, and thus between western and eastern Palestine, was the Jordan River.[76] The Americans both volunteered for this part of the survey and were volunteered for it by the British.[77] While appearing in the biblical narrative, the lands east of the River Jordan did not encompass the kingdoms of the Israelites and were not crucial facts on the ground, either to the world that Protestants sought to make real or, at that particular moment and with a couple of exceptions, to the intelligence needs of the War Office. Adding to the importance and mystique accorded the western side of the river, with the exception of the north Jordan River Valley and its adjacent landscapes, territories east of the river were not so well explored by comparison, and at that time lacked the abundance of recognized ancient tells reported on the western side. What had shaped notions of antiquity on the eastern side of the river were what had been identified and defined by Western explorers for Western audiences, much of which was monumental and, with notable exceptions, fairly late in date compared with antiquities sought on the western side of the river. These included what were deemed the very important sites of Roman Jerash (Ulrich Seetzen, 1806) and Nabatean Petra (Johann Burckhardt, 1812), both of which, although Jerash more than Petra due to the comparative ease of the journey, were visited by several subsequent nineteenth-century European and American travelers whose accounts were widely published.[78] These two sites, along with several others, such as those called the "Desert Castles" (believed to be Sassanian or Islamic) and castles related to the extensive Crusader era, formed the bulk of knowledge of antiquity east of the River Jordan. In addition to Seetzen and Burckhardt, other explorers to have ventured over the river included Austen Henry Layard (in the late 1830s to early 1840s, before excavating Nimrud near Mosul in the

1840s); Edward Robinson and Eli Smith (in the late 1830s); H. B. Tristram (in the early 1840s); and Charles Warren (in 1867).

The PEF had devised and claimed the Western Survey and was ready to act. If the Americans wanted a piece of the action, the Eastern Survey would have to do. They had been largely absent from the scene since the Lynch expedition to the Dead Sea in 1848 and were unable to dispatch a team to the field immediately.[79] This likely suited the PEF and the War Office quite well. The Eastern Survey established a means of intellectual and military cooperation with the Americans but enabled the British to retain the most prestigious part of the project, and that most vital to British geopolitical interests. It also spared the British the problems and expense anticipated by E. H. Palmer in light of his frustrating 1869 expedition to Moab, described above.

Due to their long absence from Holy Land exploration, the Americans had lost their competitive edge in Holy Land exploration and were almost completely dependent on British contacts, now well established, for conducting their work.[80] The British sphere of influence could thus reach far beyond the eastern banks of the Jordan River without their direct input. An American presence east of the river offered the added advantage of avoiding a direct British entanglement with France and Germany.[81] With the Americans conducting a survey, the French and Germans would be less likely to do so. Nearby French and German interests might also feel less threatened by an American presence than a British one. In addition to European survey and archaeological projects, Istanbul increasingly dispatched Germans to Arab regions of the empire, particularly east of the River Jordan, to implement Ottoman infrastructure development projects such as the railroad and telegraph systems.[82]

First assigned to West Point graduate Lieutenant Edgar Z. Steever, the Eastern Survey failed to meet either PEF or War Office standards.[83] American Holy Land experience was severely curtailed by the Civil War, and its military was, by the 1870s, far less experienced than the Royal Engineers in up-to-date survey techniques. The APES's funding situation was even less certain than the PEF's, and though the U.S. Army paid for its own engineer, Steever, and later Colonel James C. Lane, it did not have triangulation equipment. The eastern side of the Jordan River also posed the logistical difficulty of remaining largely off the beaten path of explorers and archaeologists. Only lately and due to Ottoman efforts at modernization and centralization had it witnessed interest in infrastructure and security that had come to Palestine west of the Jordan in somewhat earlier years.[84] By 1880, agreements between the APES and the PEF regarding the surveys and publishing the results had crumbled and both the APES and its Eastern Survey were defunct.[85] Conder took up the Eastern Survey for the PEF and the War Office in 1881–82. Working without an updated *firman*, he surveyed five hundred square miles of what was considered biblical Gilead (the northeastern Jordan Valley) and Moab before Istanbul, understandably suspicious of British intentions, requested that he be withdrawn, and thus ended the second attempt to survey the PEF's eastern Palestine.[86] In the 1880s, nine published volumes resulted from the Western Survey, whereas the Eastern Survey produced only one.[87]

The realization of landscape created from the surveys and explorations of the core and peripheral "Holy Land" was intimately tied to roles its contemporary peoples were assigned that were temporally ambiguous and incongruous.[88] If the Holy Land that Europeans and Americans encountered was a landscape in need of redemption, it follows that its inhabitants were, if not beyond such redemption, in a similar state of need, the agents of desolation in this sacred land.[89] At the same time, however, they were romantic caricatures of the imagined ancient community of biblical protagonists that was believed to have inhabited that landscape. Neil Asher Silberman writes that the shepherd boy became David and the peasant girl drawing from the well became Rachel.[90] The bedouin were "the enemies of agriculture," but they were also living incarnations of the world of the biblical patriarchs.[91] These Janus-like characteristics of the Holy Land's inhabitants were rooted in modern travel and scholarship; explorers like Burckhardt and Charles Doughty described bedouin lifestyle in a way that was reminiscent of biblical figures such as Abraham, Isaac, and Jacob. Such descriptions were woven into the fabric of philology and linguistics, particularly biblical criticism and Semitic studies. Julius Wellhausen himself was just one ardent proponent of studying modern Arab bedouin to understand the ancient Israelites.[92] The inhabitants of the Holy Land were thus frozen in time for the Western observer.[93] In the context of the Darwinian revolution and what followed, it was easy for observers to contrast the Holy Land's inhabitants with Western perceptions of progress and modernity, understand those appositional trajectories in relation to the inherent characteristics of Western and Eastern peoples, and appropriate the landscape accordingly and in light of competitive ambitions.[94]

Emergent historicist disciplines and ethnography would be easily incorporated into the development of archaeology, with important consequences in the Holy Land. On the one hand, archaeology turned a fledgling discipline of treasure hunting into a science with careful methods emphasizing chronology, and therefore dependent on stratigraphy, pottery seriation, and context. On the other hand, it wrought particularist methodologies that would lead to a range of archaeological artifacts and architecture knowing neither borders nor specific peoples—such as the collared-rim jar or the four-room house—being called after, and therefore attributed to, the ancient Israelites. These were then used to carve legitimizing spaces for settler-colonialist national aspirations and those who, for a complicated host of reasons linked to millenarianism and both anti-Semitism and philo-Semitism, supported them.[95] That those engaged in such scientific developments, such as Petrie and Leonard Woolley, were also actively engaged in or eminent proponents of developments in eugenics is beyond the scope of this discussion, but is a crucial component of the context in which this trajectory unfolds.[96]

Early Western encounters with Petra illustrate the impact of this paradigmatic conflation of core and peripheral space with the taxonomic classification of people. Petra emerged in the confluence of philological and archaeological study as particularly Nabatean, and was therefore assigned to the category of the ancient Arab. It was not immune to biblical associations, as numerous local and literary traditions tied it to the Abrahamic patriarchs. Such associations in the nineteenth-century Western cultural milieu were, however, ultimately negative. The late nineteenth-century American landscape painter Frederic Church was inspired by Edward Robinson's illumination of biblical geography to travel to the Holy Land, experience it firsthand, and paint it. His paintings and writings about Petra were particularly meaningful for him.[97] Petra was located in what was understood to be biblical Edom. Numerous Old Testament prophets say that God smote the Edomites, the descendants of Esau, because of their infractions against the kingdom of Judah; the Edomites had supposedly prevented the Israelites from crossing through Edom during the Exodus.[98] A trip through Edom, scene of such ancient divine wrath against the enemies of Israel, was for westerners a poignant testament to biblical truth, especially when one gazed upon the ruined splendor that was Petra. Church's Petra paintings and their few Arab subjects were interpreted in the West as timely reminders of ancient glory reduced to contemporary depravity and desolation.[99] It was the message from God so clear to the Western traveler, so completely lost on the ignorant Arabs who inhabited this ruined place. As John Davis writes, "Such racial and religious denigration served an important ideological and competitive end."[100] It was a hallmark of Anglo-American Orientalist art and literature throughout the nineteenth century.[101] Petra's ruins, meanwhile, held quite different meanings, real and positive meanings bridging a distant past to a lived present, for the people who inhabited its environs and for broader Arab audiences. Such meanings are a crucial and often overlooked component of the dynamic competition for archaeology and narrative, and are discussed extensively in the coming chapters.

Bedouin of the East

The consequences of schizophrenic paradigms rooted in Western interactions with landscape and bedouin for the future Jordan and its people were as acute as those of the taxonomies that would provide a framework for the colonial and settler-colonial projects west of the river. For European explorers, particularly the British, the bedouin of the nineteenth-century Near East were a peculiar combination of uncivilized and sagacious, enterprising and lazy.[102] Unlike their effete, urbanite contemporaries—of which there were infinitely more west of the River Jordan—they were the "real" Arabs, a noble people of deep faith, abiding tradition, and excellent manners and hospitality. They were thought to be especially close to God, their desert circumstances resulting in the practice of an uncorrupted monotheism and great gentlemanliness. The gentlemen authorities of the British (Protestant) Empire fancied themselves similarly, and thus believed they had a special knowledge of and affinity for the "real" Arab bedouin.[103]

The lands that came to make up Jordan were conceived peripherally to the extent that their village organization and the complexity of interactions between village and hinterland were completely marginalized in narratives and symbologies that followed, not just in terms of core spaces from which they were excluded, but within the conception of spaces to which they were assigned. Western scrutiny cast pre-state Transjordanian space as that of many deserts and a few sown; it was a simple binary without differentiation and in which the sown were practically invisible. Bedouin thus inhabited the landscape and behaved according to the characteristics of their classification. These conceptions and misconceptions of both landscape and people established the framework of British rule in Transjordan after the Great War, the organization of the nation-state thereafter, and both academic and popular conceptions of it to the present day.[104]

In this framework, the bedouin inhabitants of the periphery east of the river were set up to be tribal citizen-subjects of a state, the function of which was to fill a spatial vacuum in proximity to the core. Supposedly inured to paternalism, they were subject to the extraordinary might and use of imperial power and the co-optation of the leadership of the nation-state supported by that power. They would be charitably cleaned and dressed to be saved from starvation while serving as the faceless, mobilized representatives of the nation, publicly lauded, yet publicly chided for their backwardness, personal embodiments of the canard of rustic authenticity and national modernity.[105] The bedouin were destined to be a category apart from the rest, both socially and symbolically, what Joseph Massad has called "metonyms" of the nation.

As the physical and rhetorical spaces of the core and periphery expanded and contracted over the course of the coming decades, they would also provide a foil for the other Jordanians—those with origins in the Palestine core—to be assigned categories apart from the rest. Like a tribal shaykh or family patriarch, the emir/king's legitimating role would be to reconcile their interests in the context of shifting core and peripheral spaces.[106]

Competition Becomes War

The Western and Eastern Surveys of Palestine were enormous steps in the maturation of the study of the ancient past in what was now, thanks to these mapping projects, popularly recognizable in the West as the Holy Land. An esoteric, ancient landscape had been made a contemporary reality for the British and Americans with the help of modern scientific method and methodology as understood at the time. Scripture's place as a tool in that methodological kit was well established and accepted, although scholars inclined to secular humanism increasingly—and often painfully and uncomfortably—shied away from it.[107]

Trouble in Egypt and the Sudan in the 1880s had taken the PEF and the War Office into surveys farther afield—to the Sinai, east of the River Jordan to Kerak, and south of the Dead Sea to the Wadi Araba.[108] By the late 1880s and early 1890s, however, the English and American focus on landscape surveys gave way to excavation initiatives. Earlier forays, particularly in Mesopotamia, built collections for British museums, but were professionally incomparable to advances in archaeological methods and methodology made by other Europeans. Britain and the U.S., however, quickly came to equal their French and German counterparts in terms of professional development, scale of excavation, and field methodology. Large-scale excavation projects of such interest groups as the Egypt Exploration Fund (EEF) and the Babylonian Exploration Fund (BEF), in conjunction with British and American institutions of higher learning, began in Palestine, Egypt, and Mesopotamia.[109] American Frederick Jones Bliss, from the most elite circles of Syrian Protestant College, apprenticed with Sir Flinders Petrie at Tell el-Hesi (1890) and, on behalf of the PEF, conducted the first modern archaeological excavations in Palestine.[110] More scholarly inquiries were made east of the River Jordan, by H. B. Tristram, Frederick Klein, Conrad Schick, Gray Hill, Bliss, and others. At the turn of the century, seeds of the defunct American Palestine Exploration Society had been gathered again to establish the multi-institutional American Schools of Oriental Research (ASOR) with its first permanent base in Jerusalem.[111] In

1910, Duncan MacKenzie mapped the two tells at Dhiban. While pessimistic about overcoming the difficulties of excavation there—due mainly to security issues and problems with the local inhabitants—he writes that "scholars who are interested in Semitic origins as they bear upon the early history of the Hebrew race will hardly be satisfied to remain indefinitely content with the extraordinary fact that no single site east of the Jordan has been investigated through excavation."[112] MacKenzie had not only recognized the tells but also identified their ancient inhabitants in relation to their neighbors on the other side of the river and their context in the larger realm of Semitic studies.

Investigation through excavation east of Jordan would have to wait, however, until after the Great War. In 1913, the War Office engaged the PEF for the first time since the surveys of the 1880s. In its only recorded instance as deliberate cover for the War Office, the PEF dispatched Leonard Woolley and T. E. Lawrence on the Wilderness of Zin Survey, mapping large parts of the Wadi Araba and the Negev Desert that had gone unrecorded in previous efforts.[113] By the time conflict in the Balkans erupted into the First World War in 1914, numerous tell sites on the western side of the River Jordan had been the subject of excavations with an eye toward stratigraphy and pottery seriation, including Bliss's projects along Jerusalem's walls, by which he sought a better understanding of the city's chronology.[114]

Given the growth of Middle Eastern archaeology and philology in general and expansive excavations outside of the Palestinian Holy Land, Palestine archaeology was increasingly linked to developments in the archaeology of Egypt, Mesopotamia, and the rest of North Africa and Asia Minor. Americans and British played a significant role in incorporating a biblical archaeology based in Palestine into advances in the contemporary fields of regional archaeology, philology, linguistics, comparative religion, anthropology, and so many others, adding an Anglo-American perspective.[115] That perspective was based on a particular concept of landscape—a holy, idealized, Old Testament landscape—that they had mapped into reality and filled with narrative *realia* by means of archaeology. That none of it directly or specifically corroborated the Bible, but merely provided some historicity for its broad context, demonstrating that it contained some allusion to the reality of life as it was and the way the biblical writers saw their world, was not at issue. For believers, there was nothing to disprove the holy book and plenty to tantalize and suggest its veracity, while for skeptics these developments represented the advancement of science, knowledge, and national achievement in a global competition. Holy Land tourism, a trickle at mid-nineteenth century only for the intrepid wealthy, was a booming middle-class enterprise by 1900. London-based Thomas Cook and Sons, rooted in evangelical Protestantism and the temperance movement, shuttled the growing transatlantic petite bourgeoisie, contracting with the War Office and the PEF.[116] For Americans who couldn't make the trip, the Holy Land came to them courtesy of organizations like Chautauqua, heavily infused with Methodism and the participation of individuals such as William Foxwell Albright, the future "father" of American biblical archaeology whose name would eventually be given to ASOR's Jerusalem institute.[117] In the Chautauqua Institution's Palestine Park in western New York State, visitors could wear costumes, participating in dramatizations of biblical and contemporary life as illuminated by the Bible and the scientific study of the Holy Land.[118]

It is important to remember that the rapid advancement of field archaeology in Palestine and the Middle East as a whole had an international context in which the global competition among strong powers was increasingly understood as leading to an inevitable conflagration.[119] All parties to the impending conflict were, by the dawn of the twentieth century, players on the Middle Eastern stage. The pace of change at home for each of these players—the Ottomans, British, French, Germans, Americans, and so many others—ran unabated, linked to and inseparable from the competitive, international world in which they now found themselves. How these players assumed their roles on the Middle Eastern stage was inextricably part of how they dealt with their changing world at home. Here culture, intellectualism, religion, patriotism, social good and ill, economic issues, and geopolitics merged in a mix of national and personal interests that cannot be disentangled. Thus emerged a Holy Land for the West.

As did David Hogarth, when global war finally erupted in 1914, many of those who had played extensive roles in establishing British scholarship on the ground in the Mediterranean, Near Eastern, and Arabian landscapes joined the war effort outright, and were particularly important to the intelligence sector.[120] In the same letter to his mother that opened this chapter, Hogarth explained his motivations:

> The last four years have been a time in which there has been no question of a Government as apart from the individuals of the Nation, or of an army as opposed to Civilians. Everyone, who could do anything, has had to become part of the Government or the Army. It is a People's, not a Government's, War![121]

Patriotism and a sense of duty clearly motivated the scholar-officer-diplomats, and as historian Magnus Bernhardsson observes, their firsthand experience of Near Eastern languages, peoples, and geography made their service truly valuable to the Great War effort.[122] Whether that familiarity translated into sound frameworks for policy during or after the war is beyond the scope of this discussion. The crucial point to recognize is that scholars created knowledge on the landscapes of the Near East based upon what they imagined for the past and understood as the competitive exigencies of the present and future. By means of their academic profession, many of them had a hand in strategy and policy making. Their knowledge thus helped create certain facts on the ground, and those facts were and are colonial in their inception. The story of the Middle East in the years since and the study of what came before it are legacies of those facts, with the nation as the unit of organization for archaeology and its narratives. In Jordan and Palestine, the study of the past occurs within a conception of a holier, Western core comprehensively narrated in what is widely understood as "Judeo-Christian" tradition, and an Eastern periphery that is not. This dichotomy resulted in the shape of the present—national borders and peoples—and the implementation of the multivariate colonial and settler-colonial projects that would characterize both. The historicizing and institutionalizing of this paradigm would be contested in perpetuity, owing to the continued hegemonic nature of its implementation and the fact that its design was either unwilling or unable, in the first place, to account for the inhabitants' range of identifications with space, history, modernity, God, science, antiquities, and one another. The following chapter considers the interstices of these identifications within the context of late Ottoman "Transjordan" and Palestine.

CHAPTER 3

Antiquity and Modernity in Southeastern Bilad al-Sham

While Europeans spent the several competitive decades leading to the Great War imagining ancient landscapes in southern Syria, the generations of contemporary peoples who lived and understood those spaces as home experienced a protracted era of dynamic modernization. The Tanzimat (ca. 1839–76) reforms were, in the first place, intended to restructure the Ottoman Empire to save it, to strengthen its position in a global competition that had very quickly developed to threaten its very existence. These reforms sought to build centralized institutions, exploit the productivity of land in the context of global capitalism, collect revenues from private ownership of land, and inculcated notions of the rights and responsibilities of citizenship. By the end of the Tanzimat, such notions were embedded in the ethos of patriotism tied to the Ottoman territorial homeland articulated by the Young Ottomans, the statesmen and intellectuals among the first generation to emerge from the era of modernization.

The decades that followed witnessed many things. Sultan Abdülhamid II oversaw the promulgation of the Ottoman constitution in 1876 and suspended it in 1878. The mass popular mobilization that characterized the Young Turk Revolution and restoration of the constitution (1908) helped oust Abdülhamid in 1909. That revolution met frustration with the onset of constant, total war (the Italian invasion of Libya and war in the Balkans, 1911–13; World War I, 1914–18; the Turkish War of Independence, 1919–23). Meanwhile, modernization as tied to notions of land, belonging, and institutions was manifest in emerging discourses—official, academic, popular, and personal—of what we would articulate today as "cultural heritage."[1] The process of Ottoman imperial identity building by defining and utilizing cultural heritage was thus no different from other imperial identity-building projects of the same era. Both the Ottoman and European empires sought, in the study and manipulation of cultural heritage, a narrative that lent authenticity, and thus justification, to their imperial frameworks across vast, multi-ethnic landscapes. Across the domains of the Ottoman Empire, multiple imperial powers simultaneously sought to construct narratives of their identity—and that of others—based on the same landscape. This was the first phase of a competition binding together antiquity, narrative, and land that would assume an entirely different character with the implementation of the nation-state system after the Great War.

While the Ottoman Empire and European powers may have all competed using cultural heritage, the context and the objectives of the competition were quite different in two basic ways. First, Ottoman initiatives involving cultural heritage were rooted in the antiquity of home, while such European initiatives were by necessity entangled abroad. Ottoman objectives in the deployment of cultural heritage were, moreover, rooted in Ottoman territory in the context of an ethos that was intended to be unifying, and, unlike European imperial objectives (practically if not always rhetorically), were neither colonial in the way that European powers were, nor any longer expansionist. Second, a crucial difference between Ottoman and European perspectives in the competition for cultural heritage was that the Ottoman Empire was on the defensive, trying to maintain its territorial integrity, whereas the European powers, unburdened by the Capitulations regime to which Ottoman modernization was tethered, sought to extend the influence and reaches of theirs.

This chapter stands in comparison and contrast to the last, proposing a hermeneutic framework for considering how narratives of antiquity might have fostered modern identity in the Arab Ottoman spaces that became contemporary Palestine and Jordan. As in European capitals, an official discourse directed from the Ottoman center in Istanbul was rooted in such efforts, contemporaneous and parallel with nineteenth-century Western projects to apply science for various purposes in the "Near East." Also as in the West, unprecedented opportunities for upward mobility enabled by greater access to education and the proliferation of other modernized institutions fostered an environment in which people could engage with the new archaeological science in ways that may have differed from official paradigms. Unlike westerners, late Ottoman citizen-subjects lived upon and came from the spaces under scrutiny of the study of antiquity. This created the potential for a kind of engagement with the new archaeological science that wasn't possible for Western audiences, one heavily influenced by the Western scholars who were proactive in it, but imbued with people's own understandings of space, place, and history as shaped by experience, the particular historical moment in which they lived, and Islamicate traditions. It was upon such extant understandings of identification and narrative in the late Ottoman Arab world—holistic and lived—that Western imaginaries of holy and holier land, of core and periphery, of Palestine and Jordan, would be grafted after the Great War, turning an international competition among great powers into a new phase of resistance against colonialism and acute national struggle.

Throughout this chapter, I understand the Ottomans' role in the competition, and thus the connection between antiquity and identity in Jordan and Palestine in this period, through a consideration of modernization in these regions of the late Ottoman Empire. The chapter begins with a discussion of the development of museums and antiquities laws as a component of official Ottoman engagement in the global competition of this period. I suggest that there is a connection between the institutionalization of antiquity as directed from Istanbul and implications for multiple official and subaltern identity discourses vis-à-vis the relationship between the imperial center and its Arab provinces. The discussion proceeds to consider both tangible and intangible aspects of modernization that bound together antiquity and identity and helped the Ottoman Empire compete. Manipulation of space was a highly tangible element in the competitive Ottoman modernization project. As two intimately holy Abrahamic spaces, Istanbul focused special attention in this regard on the Hijaz and Jerusalem, and what became Jordan was not only an underutilized frontier space, but also a physical corridor between two politicized sacral spaces and, thus, an Ottoman periphery. Manipulation of intellectual and discursive space was equally important in late Ottoman attempts to compete, and thus bind together, antiquity and identity.

It is, however, a less tangible element of modernization, as official narratives are fairly easy to identify, but the range of personal and collective narratives and the personal and collective agencies that give substance and voice to them are less easily discerned. I thus connect the tangible and intangible by considering the growth of literacy, the growth of opportunities to be educated in new knowledge, and upward mobility in the context of the range of possible antiquity narratives tied to modern spaces—particularly Palestine, Jordan, and the Hijaz—that Istanbul manipulated in various ways in an effort to strengthen its competitive hand, and that people understood as a component of their identity in the modern world. In proposing a way to understand why and how Arabs in the late Ottoman milieu engaged with one type of the new knowledge capital—the science of archaeology—I analyze its presentation in a widely circulated popular science journal of the time, *al-Muqtataf*.

Popular journals like *al-Muqtataf* are important because, in the absence of other kinds of evidence, they offer insight as to how people understood the nature and function of archaeology, what kinds of archaeological stories interested the audience most, and what kinds of artifacts were important to their readership. What they cannot do in so many words is explain why people understood the nature and function of archaeology in a particular way, or why they were interested in particular kinds of archaeological stories and artifacts. Archaeology as found in the pages of *al-Muqtataf* thus offers the potential to consider a range of narratives tying together space, antiquity, and identity in the formative, competitive, and modernized fin de siècle. I argue that the Arab readership of *al-Muqtataf* and similar journals embraced archaeology as it embraced other new sciences, technologies, and industries. The same archaeology, however, spoke different narrative outcomes to Arabs and Europeans about the Arabs' past and present. Importantly for Arabs, archaeology and its related disciplines helped account for the late Ottoman Empire's diversity—and their crucial role in its past and future—at a time when the empire faced existential threats assuming its dissolution into emergent discrete territorial units based on homogenization of this diversity, the "unmixing of peoples," as Lord Curzon infamously called it in the aftermath of the Great War and instantiation of the nation-state order. Critical to specifically Arab engagement with archaeology was how the new science contributed to historical consciousness, harmonizing modern taxonomic identities with traditional modes of identification, and thereby elucidating two themes that connected all Arabs at their very noble origins: the antiquity of the Semites and the foundational monotheistic spiritual innovation of the Beni Israel, the first of the Children of Ibrahim (Abraham), from whom all Muslims, Christians, and Jews are believed to be descended. By the end of the era under consideration here, Arabs and Muslims found themselves the largest subgroups of identification in the modern Ottoman whole, soon to be separated from it into a series of nation-states according to European strategic interests and European narratives of antiquity that were embedded in their articulation. Arabs' senses of historical consciousness and range of identities spoke very different narratives about the possible shapes of the post-Ottoman order, thus setting the stage for a new phase of competition once the terms of peace were clear, and serving further to bind together the national fates of Palestine and Jordan. The range of identities available in the late Ottoman Arab context were all manifest in the spaces that became Jordan. Those spaces, however, were peripheral to all of them. The new state thus entered the postwar competition with a rare flexibility in determining its identity.

Law, Museum, Space, Consciousness

The international framework for considering modernization, competition, survival, and the prelude to total war as presented in the previous chapter was legible in Ottoman as much as in European museums. As in European museums, official deployments of cultural heritage conveyed messages calibrated for domestic and foreign audiences alike. Antiquities could be widely cited as evidence of manifold layers of Ottoman legitimacy on Ottoman soil. In museums established in the capital—particularly the Imperial Museum—and the provinces, Ottoman officials adopted display strategies that, Wendy K. Shaw writes, imitated European museums precisely to subvert them.[2] Museums in Western capitals told a positivist narrative of imperial development, with stark implications given modern Western European strength and power. European museums presented antiquities such that the course of human history appeared, like biological evolution, to develop along an inevitable trajectory from less evolved to more evolved. History thus led to the present moment—and the future as imagined in it—in which the inherent characteristics of peoples and societies, elucidated by the developing taxonomic methods and methodologies of modern science, had naturally determined their current milieu.

Ottoman museums displayed objects such that they visually declared the roots of Ottoman supremacy over, and eventually descent from and inclusion among, the bygone civilizations that had thrived and fallen on the empire's soil, tying them to the modern imperial center by virtue of their primacy in collections, particularly in the Imperial Museum.[3] These were the same ancient civilizations that European museums glorified as the forebears of the greatness of modern "Western civilization," and the objects that conveyed the Ottomans' epistemological message were tied, as in European museums, through their Greek-ness to a Helleno-Byzantine narrative that served European interests in both classical and, perhaps ironically, Christian traditions. Statesmen-intellectuals of Sultan Abdülhamid II's time invoked land, religion, ancient architectural remains, relics of ancient peoples, and the modern peoples who inhabited the diverse Ottoman domains to envision a strong, powerful, idealized modern Ottoman state and citizenry. In this framework, Helleno-Byzantine antiquity was meant to be a national meme projecting historical-cultural supremacy, natural inclusion in a great epic of world civilization, and modern Ottoman political and moral legitimacy.[4] Such heritage was not only used to contest a European concept of "Western civilization" and its epistemological greatness, but it also had acute competitive relevance at home. Greece, newly independent from the Ottoman Empire, used the same antiquities to legitimize its narrative of past and future, all the while threatening the increasingly tenuous Ottoman hold on its remaining vital assets in the Balkans.

Antiquities in the Arab lands of the Ottoman Empire were governed and tied to museum development by a succession of Ottoman legislation, the antiquities laws of 1874, 1884, and 1906.[5] The author of the 1874 law, Anton Philip Déthier, was German, appointed by reformers in the Ministry of Education to head the Imperial Museum. The law contained a deliberately broad definition of antiquities, had several loopholes, and was not always well enforced. Subsequent laws were authored primarily by Osman Hamdi (1842–1910), an elite, French-educated Ottoman career bureaucrat who was an artist, intellectual, and excavator. He was the architect of display strategies in the Imperial Museum, and, while serving as the head of the Jerusalem Department of Public Instruction, recruited Frederick Jones Bliss to help establish there by decree the first archaeological museum and its collections in 1901.[6] With each incarnation of the Antiquities Law he penned, Osman Hamdi deliberately sought to define antiquities more substantively and comprehensively. He and other like-minded individuals also engaged in public awareness campaigns using the press to educate people about the importance of antiquities and the detriments of looting.[7] The 1906 law established the primacy of the Imperial Museum in the administration of antiquities and enforcement of antiquities legislation. All three laws were met with great consternation by European excavators, as much due to the seemingly haphazard issue and enforcement of them as to their imperial and personal biases.

While at the beginning of the nineteenth century Sultan Selim III permitted—with trepidation—Lord Elgin to pry the Parthenon Marbles from the Athens acropolis and carry them away for display in philhellenic England, by mid-century Ottoman intellectuals asserted the invaluable symbolic importance of cultural heritage in keeping with the empire's efforts to assert itself as a modern imperial player, and grew increasingly frustrated as antiquities left the confines of the empire, pawns in the imperial competition among the Great Powers and the very personal ambitions of individuals such as Heinrich Schliemann, famous and infamous for his excavations of Troy.[8] Shaw contends that, by the late nineteenth century, the random enforcement of Ottoman antiquities legislation was a great point of contention between the professionals who had emerged within the Imperial Museum and the Ministry of Education and the sultan. Whereas the cadre of highly educated cultural heritage professionals sought to enforce the antiquities code, Sultan Abdülhamid II still allowed exceptions and deliberate violations of it as he saw fit, most notably when dealing with Germans. This was, of course, in direct violation of the ideal envisioned by late Ottoman statesmen—the uniform rule of law as opposed to its random application at the decree of a sultan.[9] After making a gift of the façade of the early Islamic "desert castle" of Mshatta (along the Hijaz Railway in what became Transjordan), then assumed to be a Sassanian Persian structure, to Kaiser Wilhelm II of Germany, Sultan Abdülhamid is reported to have scoffed, "Look at these stupid foreigners. I pacify them with broken stones."[10] Osman Hamdi was outraged.[11] He had dedicated his life and career to the care of such heritage and to educating an empire about its value.

This was perhaps, however, indicative of the high cost of subversive mimesis. If Helleno-Byzantine antiquities had to serve the hegemonic narrative, other antiquities could not. Even as Sultan Abdülhamid undertook to promote Islam and pan-Islamism as crucial to his modernization program, Islamic heritage was thus not, and could not be, incorporated into the Ottoman Empire's antiquities narrative as was Helleno-Byzantine heritage. Islamic cultural products, in fact, were considered, as they were in Europe, a thing apart from the Helleno-Byzantine narrative—arts to be discursively separated from antiquities. Islamic arts were increasingly and controversially removed from their religious contexts and from everyday use for display, unconnected to the dominant historical/cultural narrative told by antiquities.[12]

If Helleno-Byzantine antiquities were so crucial to the official Ottoman antiquities narrative, the ancient Eastern or Anatolian heritage, like Islamic heritage, could not serve such a function, either. Many such antiquities of less value to the paradigm would leave the Ottoman domains for Europe during this period.[13] Those that remained could potentially be displayed in a hall of the Imperial Museum reserved for them, largely separate from the Greek, Roman, and Byzantine hall.[14] Biblical archaeology was in its infancy during the first half of the Sultan's reign, but would soon come to dominate much of the archaeological paradigm for Europeans in the Ottoman Empire, while offering Ottomans, like the Arab reading public discussed later in this chapter, scientific affirmation of their origins as they already understood them, or at least new ways to think about old narratives of their relationships among one another.

While the debate regarding the extent to which the late Ottoman modernization project shared characteristics of European colonialism is ultimately beyond the scope of this discussion, it bears mentioning here.[15] Osman Hamdi is himself a problematic figure representative of the complexity of this issue. He is a hero of analyses focusing on cultural heritage discourse of the Ottoman imperial center in this period and a "good Ottoman" of European and American archaeological lore. By means of excavations and the Imperial Museum, however, he was as much engaged in removing antiquities from their local contexts—from Saida (ancient Sidon on the Lebanese coast), for example—for display in the imperial capital as were his European counterparts.[16] Through his writings, moreover, Osman Hamdi reveals himself to be representative of the ethos of the "civilizing mission" in which the imperial center was engaged with its periphery, predominately Muslim and Arab as this period wore on—what Selim Deringil has called "borrowed colonialism" and Ussama Makdisi "Ottoman Orientalism."[17] Much as Shaw contends that mimesis in museums was an act of competitive subversion, Makdisi argues that Ottoman modernization was characterized by Istanbul's appropriation of important tenets of European Orientalism as a means of resistance and nation building; the Ottomanist imperial project thus created its own Orientalized "other" in an attempt to de-Orientalize its whole.[18] The de-Orientalized whole was represented by its enlightened imperial center, responsible for pulling its recalcitrant Oriental frontier kicking and screaming into a strong, national modernity. As war drew ever closer, the racial and ethnic Turkish-ness of the center was a greater point of emphasis, as concomitantly was the Arab-ness and bedouin-ness of the frontier.[19] As Makdisi notes, this was not entirely a top-down process. "Ottoman modernization in an age of Western empire," he says, "produced and anticipated multiple Orientalist discourses."[20] It is this multiplicity of discourses and their complexities, relating to cultural heritage, Orientalist and otherwise, that the inquiry embedded in this chapter assumes.

Makdisi's "multiple discourses," whether in line with official or subaltern discourses, are possible because people's direct contact with antiquities is deeply personal, reflecting the power embedded within antiquities and individuals themselves, and the entirety of experience with which individuals engage antiquities. These can work in tandem with or in opposition to the hegemonic and sometimes contradictory discourses that construct narratives around them, which in this case were many, including Ottomanism, Hellenism, Islamism, Turkishness, and Arabness. If British maps of Palestine created real spaces for the West because they laid a grid upon a collectively imagined but personally extant landscape, for those who actually lived on the landscapes of the late Ottoman Empire under discussion here, the space itself, rather than being imagined, was already real, an enduring landscape of ties and movements, of history and sacredness, of action and interaction. The modern recalibration of that space in a context of scientific colonial competition took many forms; people internalized their consciousness of history and space in new ways, recognized the monetary value of "invaluable" antiquities, and both accepted and rejected official discourses regarding antiquities in whole or in part. It is a mistake to assume that if people disregarded the scientific value ascribed to antiquities, using them instead, for instance, as building materials and means of subsistence, such uses precluded the personal narrative value of either those antiquities or the places from which they came. In similar fashion, Europeans tended to disregard narrative values of antiquities other than those that modern science ascribed to them. This study, in and beyond this chapter, operates with such agency of both antiquities and individuals in mind.

Wendy K. Shaw writes that Europeans, and not Ottomans, had ultimate control over the "antique space" within the Ottoman domains. In other words, the most important part of constructing identity based on antiquity—conceiving the space and its contents, naming it, mapping it, digging it, convincing others of it—was a power that the Ottomans almost entirely lacked vis-à-vis the West, despite extensive national excavation efforts conducted largely at the behest of Osman Hamdi.[21] Such lack of Ottoman power and its consequences, however, would not be evident until after the Great War and the implementation of new nations along the lines of maps created in the context of studying antiquity. Even then, the Ottomans' lack of control over "antique space" was not universal across the former imperial domains, as demonstrated by cultural heritage discourse in an independent Turkey, which hinged on that very ancient "Eastern" history that had been previously deprioritized in favor of the Helleno-Byzantine narrative.[22]

If the Ottomans had lost the hegemonic power over "antique space" to the West, then one has to assume that there was neither agency nor power in Makdisi's "multiple discourses," or in antiquities or individuals. Without such agency, however, hegemonic projects of appropriation have nothing upon which to draw in the first place. The growing corpus of literature regarding the appropriation of cultural heritage in the context of twentieth-century national and other political projects in the former Ottoman domains suggests otherwise.[23] What was for westerners terra incognita onto which they grafted their knowledge, ideologies, and ambitions—in so doing defining the "antique space" for themselves—was *home* for its inhabitants, delineated by a diversity of socioeconomic and political interactions, shared cultural and historical experiences, and the lived terrain of the present informed by everything that was part of it both now and in the past—from shrines, monuments, ruins, artifacts, and natural phenomena to poetry, legend, scripture, and genealogy enshrined in both oral tradition and various genres of text.[24] As an unquestioned space, home had needed neither imagination nor justification—it simply *was*.[25] Modernization and taxonomic science, however, served to turn that unquestioned space into conscious space; justifying claims to ownership of that space would eventually depend on historical consciousness and ownership of its narrative. As Osman Hamdi and the diverse cadre of elite Ottoman intellectuals throughout the empire readily engaged with European narratives ascribed to their cultural heritage—disseminating them, nuancing them, molding them, challenging them, adapting them, considering them in the context of their lived terrain—so did their fellow citizen-subjects in the framework of a holistic modernity. This may not have translated into the power, after the Great War, to completely influence the delineation of new political spaces crafted from narratives of antiquity, but it certainly helped solder the tangible and intangible elements of the late Ottoman milieu into conceivable cultural landscapes drawn on the canvas of the mind's eye, understood and felt among the various collective, hybrid, and fluid modes of belonging, participation, expectation, and resistance in the modern world.

Ottoman Holy Lands, Cores and Periphery

If modern Ottoman identity discourses—Ottomanism, Hellenism, Islamism, Turkishness, and Arabness—had nodes of overlap in their contradictory impulses, the landscapes that became Jordan were peripheral to all of them. The future Transjordan lay between—and was connected by proximity and its people's connections to—two crucial foci of late Ottoman state power projection, territorial self-conception, and image production—Jerusalem and the Hijaz. That projection of power was rooted in a sultan who, after a disastrous war with Russia resulting in Ottoman loss of much of its remaining Balkan territory, suspended the Ottoman constitution (in effect 1876–78), asserting the sultan's position, and thus himself, as the Muslim caliph. While Europeans and Americans imagined, albeit vaguely and peripherally, an East of Jordan, a very different inhabited space emerged there through a process articulated by and directed from the Ottoman imperial center at Istanbul, aiming to incorporate this frontier space and the citizen-subjects within it into its broader modernization program.

Ottoman efforts to better link its center with its periphery in the last decades of the empire aimed primarily to increase revenues. Achieving this goal was a complex and multifaceted process that created new legal and institutional realities on the ground, applied with some flexibility according to local conditions and traditional patterns of usufruct and social organization. Among developments in this frontier during the last half century of Ottoman rule were the registration of private landholdings and potential conscripts, settlement programs for Circassian and Chechen refugees and local bedouin, a more extensive deployment of administration and a security apparatus to enforce land and settlement programs, improved management of agricultural surplus, co-optation and punishment of local populations and their leaders, population growth, greater productivity, greater urbanization and monetarization of the economy, the improvement of infrastructure for transport and travel, and the extension of railroad and telegraph lines.[26]

In addition to its potential to generate revenue, the future Transjordan was of interest for other reasons. Ottoman education reform sought to defend against the proliferation of European missionary schools targeting local Christian populations, growing in number with the increasing European presence in the region generally and, in the case of Transjordan and its Christian populations, in Jerusalem specifically.[27] Given the extent of its bedouin populations and its numerous locales commemorated for their importance to Islamic history, Islamic Ottoman missionary work in the future Transjordan went hand-in-hand with education reform and the appropriation of Islamic symbolism in concert with deployment of the kinds of iconographic displays deployed by any other contemporary world power, such as seals, banners, ceremonies, parades, anthems, museums, almanacs, and building projects.[28]

In the process of such developments, the Transjordan districts had become, in new ways, conduits and adjacent cultural landscapes for two symbolic pivots of modern, late Ottoman identity realized in lived antique space: Jerusalem and the Hijaz. In the former, the projection of Ottoman power was refracted between center and periphery against the increasing projection of Western power; in the latter, it was meant as a reflection of political legitimation in an Islamic idiom, and where Ottoman space was surrounded by Britain. The narratives of Ottomanism, Hellenism, Islamism, Turkishness, and Arabness functioned variously in one or both contexts.

Crucially, however, their wide-ranging symbolic importance rendered Jerusalem and the Hijaz inseparable from Sultan Abdülhamid's infusion of Ottomanism and Islamism. At the heart of this infusion was the empire's territorial integrity, the population of which was predominately Muslim after the 1870s, and the geography of which incorporated all territory under the sultan's rule, for which a sense of a sacralized Ottoman patriotism crossing religious and linguistic lines had been articulated by Young Ottoman intellectuals and those who were influenced by them.[29] Within this framework, Sultan Abdülhamid reasserted the Ottoman sultan's role as caliph, investing himself with a reinvigorated sacral role alongside his dynastic, political role, giving complex nuance to what had traditionally been considered an earthly authority (sultan) and a pious authority understood to come with the acknowledgment and acceptance of the religious community (caliph).[30] Both roles were paternalistic. The integrity of imperial space and the well-being of Ottoman citizen-subjects were, under Abdülhamid's long reign, invested in the sultan, who was likewise the caliph responsible for the leadership of the Muslim community and the protection of its institutions. At the same time, the edicts of 1839 and 1856 and the Nationality Law of 1869, hallmarks of the Tanzimat reform process ensuring the equality of all Ottomans, were the law of the land, and Abdülhamid saw himself as the sultan of all Ottomans, even having suspended the constitution for most of his reign. In Istanbul's late reach into Jerusalem and the Hijaz, we can better understand how this approach was meant to be a pragmatic, deliberate means of maintaining the integrity of a centralizing, modernizing, multiconfessional, multi-"ethnic," multilinguistic empire stretching from North Africa, to Europe, to Asia Minor.

Jerusalem as a late Ottoman core was, in the final decades of the empire, a vibrant and diverse city. While not of the same size or metropolitan hue as Istanbul, Beirut, Damascus, or Cairo, it was a locus of religious, intellectual, and broad cultural life and a site of complex interaction among intra- and intercommunal identities, with a long history of organization, as throughout the empire, into *millets* (confessional communities).[31] At the center of this rich cultural life and interface of diverse peoples was the fact that Jerusalem was a sacred terrain for the three Abrahamic faiths, all represented in significant numbers in the Ottoman Empire, with highly nuanced understandings, especially for those who lived there, of their personal and collective connections to that symbolically rich landscape. Istanbul's extended reach into the city, then, can be understood both in terms of imperial policy throughout the Arab provinces that aimed to increase arable land and raise revenues, but also in terms of its projected Islamic character and role as caretaker of a multiconfessional, multilinguistic, multi-"ethnic" imperial body. Jerusalem thus offered the sultan a space in which all facets of his authority could be displayed and all acts of those who lived within the imperial framework under his rule could be performed. The Islamization of Ottomanism and the Ottoman Empire constituted a certain appropriation and Ottoman expression of the Arab experience, as Islam was revealed to the Arabs and, until the fall of Baghdad to the Mongols in 1258, the caliph was Arab and the caliphate originally an Arab institution. The sultan, meanwhile, had a duty according to law to safeguard all Ottomans, and Abdülhamid, as caliph and by default an exemplar among Muslims, had to uphold the well-being of the *ahl al-kitab*, or People of the Book, Jews and Christians. The traditional responsibilities assumed by the deputy or successor of God's Prophet Muhammad were thus understood to exist comfortably with the responsibilities of a modern, enlightened ruler. Jerusalem, with its sacred richness, mixed population, and Arab provincial location, was a perfect locus for the expression of this multifaceted late Ottoman ethos. It was also, however, a prominent site of Ottoman interaction with the global community, given the influx of tourists, scholars, and permanent religious and diplomatic communities. A growing population of Jews included early members of the Zionist movement, North Africans fleeing European colonialism, and others with messianic proclivities.[32]

Istanbul designated Jerusalem the capital of an independent *sancak* in 1874.[33] Becoming a *sancak* meant that it was not considered or administered as part of a larger administrative unit, the *vilayet* (province). It was, rather, due to its "sensitivity or importance," administered directly by the Ottoman Ministry of Interior in Istanbul.[34] Istanbul thus thrust itself into Jerusalem and Palestine—and the foreign communities there—in a tangible and unprecedented way according to its emphasis on the territorial integrity of the empire, law, bureaucracy, efficiency, ideas of ownership, public security, and the application of new technologies. The power of appointment to both religious and secular posts and the administration of *awqaf* (religious endowments) also lay in Istanbul. Through this control, the sultan and his statesmen had power over an enormous cache of religious symbols for many audiences at home and abroad. Highlighting the sultan's direct control of Jerusalem emphasized the Islamic identity of the Ottoman Empire, which simultaneously promoted the idea that the sultan and his government acted as caretakers of the holy places for a diverse polity. While other imperial powers made increasing diplomatic, commercial, and religious inroads into Jerusalem, the city's affairs, those of Palestine as a whole, and those of the empire's Arabic-speaking population more broadly were increasingly linked to the imperial center as the center itself became increasingly tied to Palestine. Jerusalem's residents were among the first in the empire, after Istanbul, to organize leadership efforts among the local population by means of a municipal council; it also elected its own deputies to the Ottoman parliaments of the 1870s and the postrevolutionary (post-1908) period.[35] This experience laid the groundwork for Jerusalem's place in people's identities beyond the 1908 revolution and Sultan Abdülhamid. At both the intellectual and popular levels, Jerusalem's inhabitants imbued its space with recalibrated meanings. No longer a landscape for demonstrating the confluence of the sultan's religious/political responsibilities, the various Abrahamic communities sacralized the constitution and the *hurriyya* (freedom) it bestowed upon Ottoman citizens in scriptural language tied directly to the geographical contours of the homeland, of which Jerusalem and its people considered themselves a representative part.[36]

Both the physical and the symbolic aspects of the late Ottoman reform program also shaped the development of the empire's relationship with another core, the *vilayet* of the Hijaz, in the late nineteenth and early twentieth century. This region, home of the *haramayn* (the two protected holy sanctuaries, Mecca and Medina), destination of the Muslim hajj, traditionally held a practical importance for the empire that Jerusalem, an important destination but neither a requirement of pilgrimage nor alternative to hajj, had not previously shared. The Hijaz was an obvious and physical locus of Ottoman Islamic identity, as it was the duty of the sultan to ensure the safe passage of the world's Muslims making the hajj through his empire. It was under Abdülhamid that the Hijaz Railway was built, which could be used for purposes of both the pilgrimage and defense.[37] In terms of the sultan's appropriation of Arab experience to his political infusion of Ottomanism and Islamism, the land of the Revelation—and its language, its people, and their customs—there was no better space for Abdülhamid's projection of Islamic legitimacy for audiences both at home and abroad. He undertook, with state money and his own, repairs and upkeep of the holy sites of Mecca and Medina, including the embroidered cloth mantle, or *kiswa*, that covered the Ka'aba. The exchange of the old and new covering, which bore the sultan's name, was made with a dramatic pilgrimage on foot of tens of thousands of the world's Muslims from Damascus to Mecca during the hajj, tying together all the locations on this journey in celebration and providing the needs of its participants at state expense.[38] Jamal Badran (1909–99), Palestinian artist and specialist in traditional Islamic crafts, credited this journey with his interest in Islamic arts, and his formative experience as a child in Haifa indicates how impressive the scene of the pilgrimage must have been. Bearing the *kiswa* and the *mahmal*, a ceremonial carriage covered with similarly brocaded verses from the Qur'an, the pilgrims made their way from Damascus to Haifa and Gaza, a yearly festival held in each place, before setting sail for Jeddah.[39]

While the sultan certainly inserted himself and the state into the Hijaz in an unprecedented way, assertion of Ottoman control there differed in important respects from the centralization project in Bilad al-Sham and the *vilayet* of Syria. Arable land and population were sparse in the Hijaz. The state heavily subsidized settled residents of the Hijazi towns and holy cities, who were also exempted from taxes and conscription. Nomadic tribes of the Hijaz, meanwhile, were heavily subsidized by both the state and hajj pilgrims in exchange for their peaceful interactions with the pilgrimage.[40] As William Ochsenwald notes, the Hijaz was a drain on Ottoman resources, a great symbolic, but hardly a financial, asset.[41] Its existence encapsulated in religious significance, its demographics, its ultimate lack of financial contribution to the empire, and its distance from the imperial center meant that the Hijaz functioned fairly autonomously, power and notability was localized, and the exponential change that characterized the other Arab provinces of the empire was quite a different, and more limited, experience there.

Although Istanbul had established the position of governor of the Hijaz as the reform program took shape in the mid-nineteenth century, that appointee had to share his power, notably with the sharif and emir of Mecca.[42] Given that religion was the defining characteristic of the Hijaz and the region's general autonomy, the sharif and emir of Mecca, a descendant of the Prophet of Islam charged with protecting and administering the holy places and ensuring the safety of the hajj, was a coveted Ottoman appointment. An appointee of the sultan, the sharif and emir of Mecca executed his duties by using financial coercion and strong-arm tactics to control local tribes, who often demonstrated their opposition to Ottoman policies by sabotaging the security of the pilgrimage. Ottoman administration of the Hijaz throughout most of the era of centralization had thus largely meant its exemption from the *vilayet* law and the assertion of both the sultan's and the emir's authority in a mutually beneficial relationship. The sultan appointed the emir, and the emir showed his clout with the tribes of the Arabian Peninsula by ensuring an uneventful hajj. The emir thus demonstrated his loyalty to the sultan, and the position of both was elevated.[43] The last person to hold this position was Sharif Husayn bin 'Ali, who would ultimately launch the Arab Revolt and whose descendants are the Hashemite kings of Jordan.

Following the revolution of 1908 and the return to constitutionalism in the Ottoman Empire, the appointment of Sharif Husayn as emir of Mecca was one of Abdülhamid's last acts as sultan, the circumstances of which are some matter of debate.[44] The Hijaz would no longer enjoy the relative autonomy it had previously known. After the revolution, Ottoman leadership (in various hands of the CUP, the Committee of Union and Progress, which had played the major role in the organization and execution of the revolution) sought in the Hijaz as everywhere in the empire to further centralize its authority within a context of greater political awareness and participation. In the last years of the empire, Sharif Husayn and the CUP engaged in a mutually beneficial relationship of push, tug, and redirect, each to achieve his own ends. Husayn understood the extension of invasive infrastructure and technology, troop deployments, legal reforms, the separation of Medina from the rest of the Hijaz by designation as an independent *sancak* (like Jerusalem), and attempts to apply the *vilayet* law in the Hijaz as projections of the power of the imperial center at the expense of his power as a local notable.[45] Istanbul realized that its success was limited in this, and Husayn was not necessarily pliant, but he was a greater asset than he was a liability in terms of steering affairs in its favor. And Husayn, who greatly valued his own power and position, likewise understood his relationship with Istanbul as more apt to elevate his position and achieve his ambitions than to undermine it. On the cusp of the Ottomans' entry into the Great War, however, the CUP embarked on an aggressive Islamization campaign and appointed a reform-minded, centralizing governor to the Hijaz who served the additional function of commander of the armed forces.[46] This move was steeped in the context of the broader international conflict, the rivalry between the Ottomans and the British for control of the Arabian Peninsula, and fear of potential British-Arab machinations to reestablish an Arab caliphate, and Husayn, recognizing the threat this posed to his family's position, began making contingency plans involving the Ottomans' rivals.

The Past as Intersection of National Modernity, Space, and Citizen

The foregoing pages have offered an overview of the legal and bureaucratic classification of the peripheral Arab spaces that would become Transjordan, framing that discussion in the context of their proximity to two centers of religious-national focus, the Hijaz and Jerusalem, and the vast change they underwent in the rubric of late Ottoman statecraft. This is crucial context for considering the role of antiquities in realizing the modern space of the late Ottoman Empire, in its entirety and in its parts, and encouraging the performance of complex and flexible identities in them.

Attempts by the likes of Osman Hamdi to promote what was everywhere in the world a modern idea with extensive implications—that antiquities had value in and beyond their monetary worth—have been extensively chronicled.[47] Understanding how people who were not directly linked to the arena of archaeology and antiquities internalized—or not—this emergent sense of tangible and intangible cultural heritage and notions of value attached to them is problematic. Many people who were engaged in related activities would not have understood themselves to be so. Because engagement with antiquity through religious observance or reverent or ritualized interface with nature, despite the importance of nature and landscape to early exploration of antiquity, has largely been institutionally separated from the realm of archaeology and antiquities, the answer is even more elusive, in the Ottoman context as well as today. Value operates at numerous levels vis-à-vis cultural heritage, but the power to determine value in the modern context is derived from both market forces and scholarly interpretation, which often require the separation of what is valued, either physically or intellectually, from its primary context. The same antiquities can be valuable to different people for different reasons, while some antiquities can be more valuable to some than to others; a foreign archaeologist does not approach a site in the same way as does a local population that might bury the dead within its ruins.[48] While that may seem obvious and benign, who gets to make those determinations and the complex reasons why they make them are not. It is in this way that cultural heritage is inseparable from the power embedded in imperialism, colonialism, nationalism, hegemonic iterations of postcolonialism or resistance, and most recently neoliberalism.

Most westerners who first physically encountered the archaeology of the vast Ottoman world did so in the heavily discursive context of museums and exhibitions. Many Ottomans, on the other hand, first encountered them through their ordinary daily pilgrimages, pastimes, or ritualized activities upon the landscapes of home before possibly encountering them in a provincial museum or the Imperial Museum. The disciplinary development of archaeology, from treasure hunt to cartographic exercise to excavation, offered new twists to such ordinary encounters, and a grand reframing of them in the modern context of pious capitalism, science, and nationalism. The race for antiquities, whether driven by Western antiquarians or empires or responses to them, meant that an increasing number of people encountered archaeology in the rubric of competing notions of value not only in school and public discourse but also through the process of looting and smuggling; antiquities had become a lucrative trade, perceptions of government behavior had made it a means of compliance or resistance, and notions of intangible value did not and do not necessarily preclude it.[49] Yet others, particularly in the context of the early large excavations in Egypt, Mesopotamia, and Anatolia, began to encounter archaeology as laborers, fulfilling a range of duties for projects run by Europeans.

What did archaeology mean, however, for those who had no direct, or who had limited, involvement in its production? Whether living in the shadow of antiquities or not, what did they speak for people? What was their role in modern identity discourses such as Ottomanism, Hellenism, Islamism, Turkishness, and Arabness? What did they speak for Arab Ottomans, given Shaw's demonstration that the mimetic Ottoman museums of the late imperial capital consciously subverted their European counterparts by emphasizing Helleno-Byzantine antiquity over vestiges of "Eastern" heritage? As treasure hunts became archaeological excavations and an emergent European and North American discipline across the Arab world, did this challenge the hegemonic Helleno-Byzantine paradigm, either of the Ottoman center or Europe? And what "multiple discourses" thus emerged? What relation, if any, did archaeology have to religious heritage, particularly Islamic heritage, given the seeming incompatibility between Islam's sacrosanct place in late Ottoman identity, its simultaneous consignment to the ambiguous "other" of (not quite) antiquities discourse, and the removal of its cultural products from their primary role as ritual objects to become items of national and international display?

While there are no quantitative answers to this line of questioning, it is possible to approach it with reference to the broader context of modernization. Archaeology was available to a public that was increasingly able and desirous to consume it. *Al-Muqtataf*, one popular journal of science and culture and one of the most heavily circulated Arabic-language periodicals throughout its run, offers a lens through which to view the availability, context, and content of archaeological knowledge.

Popularizing the New Science in the Modern World

Charles Darwin's impact on every aspect of intellectual life that followed him was not just a Western phenomenon, and the life of *al-Muqtataf* is ultimately rooted in the late nineteenth-century Darwinian context and subsequent phenomena such as Social Darwinism.[50] The journal was founded in 1876 by former students of the Syrian Protestant College, later the American University in Beirut. Yaʿqub Sarruf, Faris Nimr, and Shahin Makarius were Syrian Christians who, with their journal, hoped to extol for the Arabic-speaking and -reading audience the virtues of modern science and accompanying Social Darwinist peculiarities of mid to late nineteenth-century Anglo-American capitalism.[51] As such, they were part of the diversity of Arab intellectuals— the religious-minded modernists, secularists, and those in between—who helped mobilize the *nahda* ("renaissance" or "awakening"), the sweeping cultural modernization of the nineteenth and early twentieth century in which Arabic language played a central role in the translation, creation, and transmission of knowledge and discourses of identity rooted in ideas of the nation, called at the time variously the *watan*, homeland, or the *umma*, a term that, throughout Islamicate history, referred to the community of believers, but, in modern usage, carried various broad, pan-national connotations.[52] Sarruf and Nimr stayed on as lecturers at the college, from which they were removed after a nasty falling-out with more conservative forces over teaching Darwin.[53] Given new opportunities available for Christians in nominally Ottoman Egypt, and their support of the British occupation there at that moment, Sarruf and Nimr went to Cairo in 1885 and took the journal with them, where it would be published until shortly after Nimr's death in 1951.[54]

Much has been written about *al-Muqtataf* and similar journals, the intellectuals who contributed to them, what influenced them, the vast influence they had, and their place in the broader context of intellectual and nationalist thought.[55] This project is more interested in who was reading *al-Muqtataf* and how, both in terms of physical access and the personal associations with which its audience may have approached its content as pertains to the sciences—namely archaeology and philology—that helped mold what Yoav DiCapua has described as "historicism." Historicism was a "new language" that "sought to understand the past from the point of view of the final outcome of progress: that is, the future," and through which modern historical consciousness emerged.[56] Much like displays in European and Ottoman museums, historicism was thus an innovation viewing time as a progressive developmental trajectory in a defined territorial space. Like Ottoman display strategies, it drew on European paradigms, but was crafted in both Ottoman and localized idioms characterized by all the trends discussed in this chapter, fear about competitiveness and the future clearly among them. In the Arabic pages of *al-Muqtataf*, historicism was subject to the "multiple discourses" of a diverse audience with various experiences of and reactions to their modern subalterity, and the fact that much of the emerging archaeological record, so important to modern historical consciousness, was part of their lived landscape. *Al-Muqtataf* serves here as a lens for better understanding this interface of personal connection and revolutionary knowledge.

It is necessary first to consider the issues of literacy and access to journals. The extent of literacy in the late Ottoman Arab world, as elsewhere in the empire during its final decades, is difficult to quantify. Rates of illiteracy were high. At the same time, an exponential rise in literacy was a global phenomenon in this period as, in the words of Benjamin Fortna, "throughout the world universal education and literacy were the vehicles through which the state was to pursue its aim of both creating and then shaping national identity and loyalty."[57] There are many data regarding numbers, types, and locations of schools and numbers of pupils in the final decades of the Ottoman Empire.[58] These demonstrate a steady increase in the number of public and private religious and secular schools at all levels in both urban and rural contexts, in the number of teachers, and in the number of both male and female students. Ami Ayalon estimates that by the start of World War I, 20 to 28 percent of the Arab school-age population of Palestine, for instance, was receiving some kind of school-based education, whether in state, private (often Christian missionary), or *kuttab* (Qur'anic recitation) schools. It was likely a far greater percentage than at the turn of the century.[59] In Transjordan, the first state primary school for boys opened in Salt in 1880, and by the end of the century, primary education was available to boys in Kerak, Tafila, Shawbak, and Ma'an, while a large secondary school opened in Kerak. By 1915, boys could obtain a primary education in numerous villages and rural tribal lands, while girls could obtain a state primary education in Salt and Kerak. There were also advanced primary state schools for both boys and girls.[60]

As for access to journals, Ayalon's study of texts and reading in Palestine, particularly his focus on *al-Muqtataf* and similar publications, demonstrates that *al-Muqtataf* in particular had subscribers all over the Ottoman world, "from Aden to Adana" and beyond, prior to the turn of the twentieth century.[61] Its individual subscribers were those who could both afford the cost of subscription and were motivated to read it. Among Palestinian subscribers Ayalon notes for Butrus al-Bustani's universal encyclopedia (*Da'irat al-Ma'arif*), advertised in one of *al-Muqtataf*'s contemporaries (Bustani's own Beirut-based biweekly *al-Jinan*), were individuals of the new and upwardly mobile professional classes—teachers, doctors, lawyers, engineers, translators, government officials, merchants, and clergy of different religious affiliations—"the elite layer of the country's literate public."[62] That layer was growing throughout this period and was widespread, with subscribers in both urban and rural contexts.[63] Ihsan Turjman, the young resident of Jerusalem whose diary offers a vivid account of wartime life as an Ottoman soldier and resident of the city at period's end, is a prime example of one such urban subscriber to both *al-Muqtataf* and Jurji Zaydan's *al-Hilal*.[64] There were also institutional subscribers such as schools, indigenous and foreign religious institutions, book-lending shops, public reading rooms, and libraries endowed at the initiative of individuals or cultural, literary, and scientific clubs and societies, particularly in urban contexts.[65] Readers described having shared or discussed what they'd read in their own family, work, and social circles, and teachers discussed what they read with students in their classrooms.[66] Those who were unable to read could listen to news, books, and journals read aloud in cafes or, where no cafes existed, in communal gathering places, both public and private, in rural villages.[67]

Archaeology and the Scientific Affirmation of Understood Origins

Al-Muqtataf was a product of its time, demonstrating the confluence of scientific, socioeconomic, and political thought in the context of modernity, competitive late nineteenth-century imperial and colonial projects, and the language of nation that accompanied them. Archaeology in Arab spaces was just one among thousands of topics gracing its pages. As a journal of popular science, it provides a window into how people conceived of archaeology. Along with advances in the study of languages, the editors, contributors, and readers of *al-Muqtataf* understood archaeology as a modern science that expanded the methods of history, itself a newly reified science the development of which enabled people to better understand both their origins and their modernity. From the range of identities available to late Ottoman citizen-subjects, archaeology spoke Arabness. Arabness had its origins in Arabs' racial and ethnic identification as Semites whose historicity could be read in the archaeological record. It was an adaptable modern identity because it was easily conflated with notions of origins linked to the intersection of religious and genealogical traditions.

Approaches akin to those developing in Europe were at home in the context of the Arab *nahda*, where European knowledge was disseminated in Arabic and intellectuals such as Egypt's Rifaʿa Rafʿi al-Tahtawi had introduced the classical works of Arab and Islamicate intellectuals such as Ibn Khaldun to new generations of Arabs who would debate his legacy.[68] The ideas of the fourteenth-century North African historian, especially his *al-Muqaddima* (Prolegomena), were important in the intellectual life of the Ottoman Empire.[69] By the mid-nineteenth century, they had also been integrated into European knowledge.[70] As *al-Muqaddima* scientifically describes the rise and fall of civilizations, it could fit comfortably in the context of modern global competition and the ability of science to explain it. Ibn Khaldun describes civilization as cyclical; nomads conquer civilized societies, become like the sedentary peoples they conquered, and are in turn conquered by a wave of nomads. Both nomads and sedentary civilization have varying strengths of social cohesion. Sedentary civilization is the ideal, yet what makes it ideal renders it weak, vulnerable, and ultimately unable to survive. Nomads bring about the destruction of the ideal, but by means of admirable social characteristics they ultimately forsake in achieving the ideal. For an Ottoman Empire losing ground in a global competition, for Arabs who had nomads living among them, and for Europeans contemplating the success of their colonial endeavors, Ibn Khaldun's paradigm was at work in their world. It enabled all parties to extrapolate narratives to support their role in the competition.

In like fashion, pre- and early-modern considerations of ancient architecture and artifacts as lessons of history—cautionary tales of haughty men such as Pharaoh laid low, or objects of contemplation as to man's place in the world—gave way as Arabs of the late Ottoman period embraced archaeology as they did new scientific developments and intellectual paradigms more generally.[71] Archaeology was embedded in a range of narratives recalibrating knowledge of ruins and artifacts to reflect new notions of identity that were varied and flexible in time and place and could be incorporated into broader intellectual and political discourses. Archaeology and philology offered a modern way for a modernizing society to explore its origins in the framework of shared history and historicism, even if, as developed in Europe, it was meant to separate and categorize. Archaeology and philology offered Muslims, Christians, and Jews who could identify communally as Arabs and Ottomans a tangible ancient communal identification as Semites and children of Abraham outside the oral, textual, and experiential traditions with which they were familiar. Near Eastern archaeology's development at the confluence of science and religion was thus as natural a fit in the Arab Ottoman world as it was in the West, able to work in tandem with the long tradition of Islamic sciences and an extensive corpus of oral tradition and literature that included scriptures and extrascriptural literature, genealogy, poetry, history, geography, and other genres drawn from the great thinkers of the ancient world to those of the present moment, from numerous religious communities, and in countless languages, spanning the western Mediterranean throughout the entirety of the Asian world.

Archaeology as presented, and no doubt as read or heard, in the pages of *al-Muqtataf* reflects this intersection of identity, science, modernity, and religion — the confluence of old and new knowledge. There is no reason it wouldn't; its purpose was the dissemination of knowledge in Arabic to an Arab audience. It was thus not just a vehicle for translating European knowledge; it deliberately drew upon the vast and diverse corpus of knowledge that was a longstanding component of Arab and Islamicate civilization. And new European knowledge regarding the study of the past depended upon that shared history. The conscious justification of relationships and claims to space that had previously been understood without articulation was a process that emerged in this period. In the Arab Ottoman case, that shared history reflected the character of the contemporary world around them. At that moment in the life of the *nahda*, there seems to have been no sense, nor should there have been, that inflexible modern political justifications to match the inflexible imposition of nation-states would be made of it, especially when consideration of the idea of nation and identity was vast and porous.

An article entitled "Usul al-Tarikh" (The Sources of History), by Emir Amin Mujid Arslan, published in *al-Muqtataf* in 1888–89, stresses the importance of the past as both a positive and negative example for the present, and, one can infer, for the future.[72] Arslan says that there are cornerstone sources for history — the relation of news and events, archaeology, and poetry — which all have strengths and limitations, and can corroborate or contradict each other in complex ways based on the reliability of one source versus another, which may be up to the observer to discern. Relation of news and events, which depends on oral and written transmission, is subject to the same principles that guide the tradition of *isnad*.[73] Archaeology is most like poetry, which, due to its fixity, is difficult to alter over time. Whether rooted in the ground or transportable to a European museum, Arslan explains, archaeology offers indisputable evidence that can confirm or deny historical events or explain why commonly held views of history must be changed, especially in the absence of other kinds of evidence.[74] He uses the example of what European archaeologists working at Sidon (Lebanon) thought might be the sarcophagus of Alexander the Great to potentially challenge Alexandria's (Egypt's) claim to being the location of his burial.[75] Alexander is a figure who looms as large in pre-Islamic, Islamic, and Islamicate oral and textual traditions as he does in the West. He is imbued, in fact, with spiritual importance largely missing from sources outside the Islamicate. Given the ongoing debate in the pages of *al-Muqtataf* and elsewhere as to the extent to which Egyptians had Arab origins, and the broader context of the *nahda*, in which Arabs from Lebanon took great pride in their involvement, the possible burial of Dhu al-Qarnayn (Alexander) in Bilad al-Sham would have been cause for excitement. Arslan also uses the example of Baalbek's (Lebanon) ruins to shed light on the city's unknown history and challenge aspects of recorded history.[76] Unstated in this analysis, in so many words, is that the artifacts and ruins in the ground, like the enduring structure of poetry, may be indisputable, but their interpretation in context is what establishes and carries a narrative.

This is not an omission on Arslan's part, as he clearly understood the interpretive power of the new science. What his analysis may highlight is a fundamental difference between European and Arab understandings of archaeology's power to inform modern historical consciousness, particularly given its logical extension in national origin narratives. The role of archaeology in Arab spaces for Europeans was applied science in an imperialist/colonialist framework. This served to categorize those spaces, thus defining the subject-colonial periphery vis-à-vis the imperial power's center in a way that carried a message of positivist development of civilization and culture and an immediately recognizable national "self" against the "other." This was couched in a discourse of legitimizing superiority with embedded racial, religious, and ethnolinguistic hierarchies and an implied binary of modernity against its opposite.

For Arabs, the consideration of and search for historical origins was fundamentally quite different. By this time they were the largest subset of a multi-"ethnic," multilingual, multiconfessional empire, the geography of which was a complex and dynamic terrain of homeland whose fellow citizen-subjects came from a diversity of backgrounds and had a wide range of communal identifications, and who neither had a colonial project nor saw their own imperial center, currently engaged in a project for its very survival, as a colonial power in the way Europe was, nor as something from which to gain independence. The lands that Europeans were exploring, mapping, and ultimately digging were Arabs' *own* lived reality; thus there was no inherent need for them to appropriate it, and the categorization of peoples was, to varying degrees of consciousness, a flexible exercise in what was natural, providing validation of their relationships among one another as they understood them, offering the broadest possible basis for communal and intercommunal identification, rather than the narrowest contrivance of "self" and "other."

Two central themes that emerge in *al-Muqtataf* in discussions of archaeology and its relation to language and history in the years before the Great War demonstrate this clearly. The first is the potential of archaeology to shed light on the Exodus, a seminal event in the history of the community of Abraham's children through which Pharaoh's failure to submit to the will of God in his epic confrontation with Moses and the Beni Israel (Israelites) has an extensive legacy in Qur'anic and extrascriptural Islamicate literatures.[77] The second, a logical extension of the first, revolves around the power of the new science to elucidate the history and origins of the Semites, from whom Abraham's children came and among whom, in their submission to God through Abraham's covenant, they distinguished themselves.

The two themes are conflated because scholars of the new sciences categorized the Beni Israel (among numerous other ancient peoples) and modern Arabs as "Semites," those whose language is based on a system of roots and patterns, and for whom these shared linguistic roots provide one aspect of an extensive framework of shared cultural experience. While the term "Semite" emerges from the context of late eighteenth-century German scholarship, it draws on biblical roots, specifically the way the writers of the Book of Genesis describe their origins and their relationships with those around them.[78] "Semite" derives from Shem, one of the sons of Noah (Genesis 10). Among Shem's descendants, as described in biblical and extrabiblical genealogies, are Joktan, who is identified in Arabic traditions as Qahtan, the progenitor of the southern Arabs and thus all of Yaman, and later Abram, who is chosen by God and becomes the patriarch Abraham/Ibrahim, the first "submitter," or *muslim*.[79] A woman of Qahtani descent is believed to have been the wife of Ishmael/Isma'il, from whom is descended 'Adnan, progenitor of the northern Arabs, who is understood to be a direct forebear of the Prophet Muhammad. In this way, the Prophet Muhammad is connected genealogically in Qur'anic and extra-Qur'anic literatures and traditions to Abraham, the founding patriarch for Jews, Christians, and Muslims, and in his person ties together the lineages of all the Arabs specifically in the peoples whose origins are in the Arabian Peninsula.[80]

In the origin narrative taking shape in the late nineteenth century based on new methods and methodologies of history such as archaeology, philology, linguistics, and taxonomy, it is from the Arabian Peninsula that intermittent waves of Semites emerged throughout history, moved by inherent social and martial characteristics, along with particular physical characteristics and language that constituted a "race" apart from the rest, to populate the reaches of the contemporary Arab world.[81] While European scholars, particularly in the German tradition, may have been at the forefront of such paradigms, mixing new philological inquiry with ideas attributable to Ibn Khaldun, those paradigms worked quite well in tandem with relationships as Arab Ottomans already understood them through long-standing textual and oral traditions. This is hardly surprising, as European scholarship to this end was ultimately based in the same literary traditions and the same scriptural framework.[82] Popular modes of genealogical identification in Bilad al-Sham in this period, for instance, included descent from either the Qays or the Yaman, in reference to ancient, pre-Islamic Arabian ancestors, Qahtan being among the most important.[83] These weren't fixed, determinative ways of understanding the origins of one's ancestral kinship, but permeable and flexible categories of identity that could shift accordingly to accommodate a range of socioeconomically or politically beneficial alliances among people over time. Identification with Qays or Yaman transcended both village and religious identity, as villages in Palestine and the future Jordan had residents from both groups, and Qays and Yaman each had many Christians and Muslims among their descendents.[84]

The Exodus and the Semites

Coverage of archaeology in the pages of *al-Muqtataf* demonstrates great interest in two specific themes: first, what could the new science reveal about the Exodus; and second, what could it reveal about which ancient peoples were Semites, and who were the earliest among them? People understood that the whole of Islamic history began at Creation and included every aspect of pre-Islamic history and scriptural traditions.[85] Archaeology offered people hope of better understanding those ancient epochs about which they read in scriptures and related literatures or in the accounts of ancient historians, such as Herodotus and Islamic historians such as al-Tabari, and poets with a historical style such as Homer or Arab poets such as 'Amr bin 'Adi al-Lakhmi, all cited in the journals.[86] As the developing discipline of archaeology in the Near East revolved around the Bible, furthermore, it revolved around the Beni Israel. The audience of *al-Muqtataf* was interested in evidence of the Beni Israel because it was evidence of their own origins, and in events like the Exodus because it was a seminal moment in the historical consciousness of the community of submitters to the God of Abraham. This sentiment is alive and well today. As a Jordanian archaeologist told me, "I hope my ancestors were Jewish. That means they believed in one God thousands of years ago. I don't want to think they were pagans."[87]

While the modern historical narratives told from studying the landscapes of Palestine and Transjordan are ideally of most interest to this discussion, it is important to remember that in the final decades of the Ottoman Empire, most advances in Near Eastern archaeology were actually made in Egypt (nominally Ottoman but under British occupation as of 1882) and Iraq. Egypt, in addition to having a landscape etched with the monumental remains of pharaonic civilization, was the scene of much of the story of the Beni Israel, particularly the Exodus. While Egyptian antiquity might have been attractive for Europeans, it was loaded in very different ways for Arabs.[88] Iraq, meanwhile, set the stage for the monumental Sumerian and the Semitic Assyrian and Babylonian civilizations, was the home of Abraham, and was part of the land of exile of the Beni Israel. Syria sat midway among the great ancient civilizations, influenced and coveted by each. As for the Hijaz with its holy places, it required no elucidation by archaeology.

Interest in the themes of Semitic origins and the Beni Israel is reflected in specific axes around which the contents of *al-Muqtataf* revolve and in the organization of their presentation. There is both a local and regional focus on archaeology, with a clear sense that it was important to consider the details of local archaeology as part of the broader regional picture and offer syntheses of finds and the historical narratives they served. There is also a clear intent to keep the reading public up to date on archaeological discoveries, as readers got word of new discoveries almost in real time. In this way, *al-Muqtataf* serves as a time capsule; it shows how artifacts and their contexts were understood upon their discovery, and can be compared with more recent conclusions drawn from studying them and considering them in conjunction with other finds over the course of more than a century.

Letters and comments from readers are perhaps the most compelling aspect of *al-Muqtataf*'s contents for purposes of this discussion, as they demonstrate the nature of interaction not just between the worldwide audience of readers and editors of the journal, but between the diverse reading public, who clearly sought to harness new kinds of knowledge to better understand their origins and their modernity and the natural/divine and man-made worlds. The science of archaeology and its relationship to history and linguistics gave readers, who were obviously well read or well versed in a variety of religious and intellectual traditions (or actively seeking to become so), new ways to think about matters of historical-religious interest. *Al-Muqtataf* was supposed to be the readers' as much as the editors' journal. It was one resource among many that readers and listeners actively used to inform their historical consciousness. By writing to the editors they had the ability to shape the journal's contents. An 1886–87 article, "Musa wa al-Faraʿun wa Banu Isra'il" (Moses, the Pharaohs, and Beni Israel), alludes to this phenomenon.[89] It serves as a response to the most frequently asked question submitted to the journal by readers, who, notes the author, know well their religious books, know of the Egyptian archaeology in the museum at Bulaq (Cairo) and in foreign museums in Paris, London, Berlin, and others, and know history from the likes of Herodotus. Readers, says the author, want to know whether researchers in Egyptian archaeology have found any evidence corroborating the Torah as regards Moses, the Pharaoh, and the Beni Israel. The editors compiled a comprehensive corpus of work of the most famous researchers to offer answers to this question.

What else were *al-Muqtataf*'s readers asking in their letters?

In 1902, Ahmad Effendi Fahmy from Jamjoum (likely Lebanon) writes asking for recommendations for ancient and modern tourism books that describe the ancient nations (for which he uses the term *al-umam*) and their cities.[90] The editors tell him that he must start with Herodotus, the "father of History," followed by the likes of Diodorus Siculus and Tacitus, among others, who all followed in the footsteps of Herodotus and traveled the many nations. Among famous Arab geographers, the editors suggest that he read Yaqut al-Hamawi, Ibn Battuta, and Ibn Jubayr. From among the *afranj* (foreigners) they recommend, among others, Marco Polo and more recent explorers such as Captain James Cook, missionary David Livingstone, and Henry Morton Stanley (sent to Africa to find the missing Livingstone).

Salim Effendi al-Taneer of Beirut writes to the editors in 1886, worried that in a recently printed edition of one of the books of al-Kindi, Arab polymath of ninth-century Baghdad, he read that Abraham was about ninety years old when God came to him, whereas the Torah says that Abraham was, in fact, seventy-five years of age. Which, Salim Effendi wants to know, is more trustworthy, al-Kindi or the Torah? The editors of *al-Muqtataf* reassure him that the Torah is more trustworthy.[91]

Niqula Khuri Suleyman, a self-described *khawaga* (foreigner), writes in 1919 from Brooklyn, New York, concerned about the languages Abraham may or may not have spoken.[92] He has read in the Torah that after the death of Sarah, Abraham negotiated a burial place with the Beni Hith (Hittites; see Genesis 20). Suleyman wants to know what languages Abraham spoke with the Hittites if he didn't know anything except Chaldean, which the Hittites didn't speak. The editors answer, "We can't say because we don't know where you learned that Abraham didn't speak anything but Chaldean and that the Hittites didn't speak it." They explain that Egyptian and Assyrian archaeological evidence includes political and financial correspondence among Babylon, Syria, and Egypt penned in one another's languages. The Assyrian language was, furthermore, close to the Hebrew in which the Torah was written, and the agreements concluded between the Hittite and Egyptian kings were written in Assyrian and Egyptian. It is therefore not strange, they assert, for it to be written in Genesis that Abraham spoke with the Hittites and was understood.

In 1911, 'Abd al-Malik Effendi Kiriakus from Mlayh writes asking about the capital of Egypt in the age of the Beni Israel.[93] "What was the name of the seat of the Egyptian kingdom when Abraham, Joseph, Jacob, and his children came to Egypt?" he wants to know. Where is it located now? Was it under Egyptian rule in the time of Moses and the Exodus and did it remain under their rule until the time of Christ? What were the names of the kings who were contemporary with those mentioned, and have writings and inscriptions been found to corroborate these stories as presented in the Torah, he wonders? The editors answer that the Torah doesn't mention the name of the Egyptian capital in the time of Abraham, Joseph, Jacob, Moses, and Christ. Nor is there among the archaeological evidence any mention of these figures, except Christ. Mention of Israel as an *umma* resident in Palestine is found, they note, from the time of the Egyptian King Merneptah of the Nineteenth Dynasty. Experts in Egyptian archaeology have ideas, however, about when the various patriarchs entered Egypt, but the editors decide to leave such a discussion for another time. They end by noting that Christ, as written in the Bible, was born in the time of Augustus Caesar, when Egypt was subservient to Rome and its seat was Alexandria.

Possibly from the same reader, or perhaps from the editors themselves, a question follows about the location of the land of Jasan (Goshen).[94] "Where is the land of Jasan in which the Israelites settled, and to what country does it extend?" After some background about sources for this information, including the Torah, they place it in modern-day Egypt between Zagazig in the north, Belbeis in the south, and Tell al-Kabir in the east. Another follow-up question that may have come from either the reader or the editors themselves asks, "In which part [of Egypt] did the Christ reside and is this determined by ancient archaeology and history?" There is no evidence, the editors answer, from the Bible or from archaeological or historical evidence, of the place where Christ stayed in Egypt, and the legend may have either come from the time of Christ himself or been perpetuated by a later historian. They write that traditions hold that he and his mother resided in al-Matariyya, on the northern outskirts of modern Cairo.

Letters such as these offer little indication about the extent to which the landscapes upon which *al-Muqtataf*'s audience lived, particularly the rich Arab landscapes of the late Ottoman world, were a resource for understanding as were books, journals, and a range of traditions. They were, however, the landscapes of home, fluid and flexible, understood both locally and as a whole, and in new ways based on a perspective of historical consciousness. From official maps of the time to personal maps understood in the mind's eye or created through daily pilgrimage or extraordinary travel, we can begin to imagine what readers and listeners visualized about artifacts and monuments in the landscape. These letters do offer a more explicit window onto the ideas with which *al-Muqtataf*'s audience, strongly shaped by literary, scriptural, and various other traditions, approached the journal's coverage of archaeological discoveries, which were generally presented by means of short reports and incorporated into longer and broader syntheses.

Artifacts of Semitic Language

If the audience for journals like *al-Muqtataf* was deeply invested in the archaeology of the Exodus and the Semites, and the journal's editors responded specifically to interest in these themes, it stands to reason that coverage of particular archaeological discoveries follows a similar pattern. Archaeological discoveries covered in *al-Muqtataf* tend to fall into two main categories, architecture and objects, or those involving philology and linguistics. All of these were generally or specifically connected to some scriptural tradition. Given the importance of Abrahamic traditions, the modern emphasis on origin narratives, the ability of science to assist in creating or verifying them, and Arab intellectuals' general interest in language as a unit of modern identification, archaeological discoveries with bearing on advances in philology and linguistics were more pointedly and easily synthesized than those relating to architecture or artifacts of cultural expression or everyday use. By means of finds related to language, it could be determined which ancient peoples were Semites, and who among the Semites was the most ancient. If ancient Semites were the forebears of modern Arabs, discoveries related to language were an important connection for identities that were spread across not just vast spaces, but epochs.

By way of example, reports of R. A. S. Macalister's work at Gezer (a site about halfway between modern Jerusalem and Tel Aviv) were of interest because Gezer was originally a Canaanite city-state, and as the discourse of origins ran deeper, the Canaanites were identified as the earliest native Semitic civilization in Bilad al-Sham. Discussions of Gezer are full of references to finds related to worship of Canaanite deities such as Astarte, but also in a disambiguated way to the quite disconnected activities and periods of Solomon, the Beni Israel, Samson, Egypt's Middle Kingdom, Simon Maccabee, and Christ.[95] It is important to bear in mind that while archaeological initiatives in Bilad al-Sham lagged behind those elsewhere in the region, by the late 1890s scholars were considering the archaeological landscape of Bilad al-Sham in the context of major discoveries elsewhere, particularly those involving writing, such as the Amarna Letters and the Merneptah Stela, a monumental inscription of the thirteenth century BCE elegizing the victory of Pharaoh Ramses II's son over Gezer that mentions the defeat of a nebulous people called "Israel."[96] The archives of letters discovered at Tell al-Amarna demonstrated that the kings of Egypt, Hatti, Babylon, and Assyria were engaged in rich, regular correspondence and broad regional diplomatic and economic contact during the fourteenth century BCE (Late Bronze Age).[97] When the editors of *al-Muqtataf* responded to Nicola Khuri Suleyman's letter regarding the languages spoken by Abraham, it was discoveries such as the Amarna Letters that they had in mind. The Amarna Letters were of particular interest to Arabs because they were the main textual resource for studying Canaan (ancient Bilad al-Sham) and its inhabitants outside of and predating the Torah.

Discoveries related to language were important to a sense of historical consciousness for the taxonomic reasons of classification and chronology. Language helped determine which ancient peoples could truly be classified as Semites. Such classifications could then be tied to things like martial and physical characteristics and ultimately race. Hittite writings found in places like Hama (in modern Syria) and Carchemish (in modern Turkey) thus demonstrated that the Hittites were *al-maghul*, a term that conveys the meaning of barbarian tribes that infiltrated West Asia.[98] The Amorites and their many descendants throughout the region, including the biblical Canaanites, meanwhile, were Semites, despite the fact that the Bible describes them as descendants of Noah's son Ham.[99] These categories, therefore, could be fluid and contradictory, and there was not necessarily universal consensus about who belonged in which one.

The issue of the Amorites is important because it was the root of the idea that Semitic populations had nomadic origins. European scholars studying texts unearthed at sites like Ebla (in modern Syria) and Alalakh (in modern Turkey) discovered numerous Sumero-Akkadian (2500 BCE) references to the Amorites, whom the Mesopotamian elite clearly considered foreigners, and worse, an inferior, nomadic, barbaric civilization living somewhere to the west. The term probably best described a rural, pastoral lifestyle that was widespread throughout the region west of the urban centers of Mesopotamian civilization at this time (much like the later term *'arab* described a nomadic lifestyle). European scholars, however, understood the term as a taxonomic ethnic moniker that worked well in conjunction with the popularization of Ibn Khaldun's ideas about cycles of civilization and the relationship between nomads and settled peoples. Beyond Semitic Wave Theory (discussed further in chapters 4 and 6), these ideas would form the basis of the Amorite Hypothesis, which distinctly rooted the story of Abraham as related in Genesis, along with the accompanying cultural, religious, and legal framework of the region, into the contrived ethnic context of the Amorites.[100]

Particular peoples who ruled over ancient Egypt, so crucial to historical consciousness because of their relation to the origins of the Beni Israel and the Exodus story, presented one important area of disagreement over the taxonomy of ancient peoples.[101] The Hyksos, described as "foreign" kings or chieftains from West Asia who arrived and took power in Egypt, are remembered as kin to the biblical Yusuf/Joseph and Y'aqub/Jacob, and their ultimate origins are presented as an issue upon which scientists cannot agree. Possibilities are that they were wandering tribes of eastern Egypt, Arabs, Amorites, Philistines, Jebusites, Hittites, or Phoenicians.[102] The most famous hypothesis, according to *al-Muqtataf*, is that they were ancient Chaldeans expelled by the Elamites, and that they were in part, like the Hittites, *al-maghul* and Tatar.[103]

There was perhaps no greater interest, however, than in the origins of Ramses II, whose mummy was discovered in 1881 and went on display in the Egyptian Museum of Antiquities in Bulaq. Iconic figure of the Nineteenth Dynasty, he easily took on all of the connotations of the Qur'anic stories about Pharaoh, especially he who enslaved the Beni Israel, repudiated God's messenger Musa/Moses, and refused submission to God. The editors of *al-Muqtataf* state that Ramses, based on the Assyrian origins of his great-grandmother, portraits, and the physical features of his corpse on display in the Bulaq museum—his nose, forehead, and chin—is obviously not Egyptian.[104] For the journal's editors, these lines of evidence help affirm that Ramses was of Assyrian origin, and therefore a Semite.[105] Ample evidence of Semitic words, both Hebrew and Arabic, particularly in the land of Goshen, could be evidence of the Beni Israel and potential evidence of historicity to the Exodus story. Reliefs discovered from the time of Ramses and his son Merneptah show people with physical features indicating they are not Egyptians but Semites, people who are called in Egyptian texts the *hapiru*, another nebulous social group of the Late Bronze Age.[106]

Al-Muqtataf's editors clearly thought it important to make the case that Ramses was a Semite. In the absence of affirmative, although perhaps suggestive, evidence of an Exodus event, the body of the man who could have been the larger-than-life nemesis of Musa/Moses was especially well preserved and could be visited in the museum in Cairo. This was just as God had revealed in *Surat Yunus* (Jonah) in the Qur'an; as punishment for his treatment of the Beni Israel, Pharaoh's corpse would be preserved as a sign to those who would disobey Him (Qur'an 10:90–92). In the modern scientific addendum to the story of Pharaoh, *al-Muqtataf* makes him a son of those who were among the earliest Semitic peoples. He is therefore related to the contemporary Semitic peoples, the Arabs. That he enslaved the Beni Israel—another earlier Semitic people, also related to the Arabs, and submitters to the one God—presents no conundrum, as he is an Arab Semite on all counts, and *this* was the important point.

Once Semites had been distinguished from others on the basis of language, finds could be used for their second important purpose, chronology, helping determine which Semitic people was the most ancient and had the most influence on those who followed. At this point, what one of those ancient Semitic people might have perpetrated against another is irrelevant, an issue that changes in the nation-state era of later decades, particularly during the Cold War. When discoveries of ancient archives across the region demonstrated that Syria had very ancient walled cities and temples, this was important evidence for the dating and endurance of toponyms.[107] If Egyptians in the time of Tuthmoses III (fifteenth century BCE) knew the names of Syria's cities, this helped demonstrate that the cities mentioned in the Torah were originally Canaanite and not Hebrew (the Hebrews came along later) and allowed *al-Muqtataf*'s editors and contributors to make important connections between the Canaanite language and the Assyrian language. The Moabite Stone likewise demonstrates for *al-Muqtataf*'s editors that the Moabite language was like the language used in northern Syria, which rendered it older than Hebrew and more akin to Canaanite. Phoenician writings discovered in Yaffa, Akka, Sur, Sidon, Jubayl, and Cyprus, they say, do not appear later than the sixth century before Christ, and Hebrew supplanted Phoenician via the Moabite language. The oldest Hebrew writing yet discovered, they write, was that written in the days of Hezekiah (eighth century BCE) upon the spring of Siloam (Silwan).[108] The emphasis upon the relative youth of the Hebrew language in comparison with other Semitic languages is not necessarily about competition at this point, but rather an exercise in trying to create a chronology for a sense of historical consciousness. If, likewise, the majority of Syrian cities mentioned in the Israelites' book retained their names, the editors of *al-Muqtataf* take it as evidence that those who wrote it lived in Palestine. As the search for the origins of Semitic languages was not yet the national competition it would become, this observation was not a political issue. Its acknowledgment represented people's understanding of their own history, their interest in science as a tool to help reveal their earliest origins, and their relationships to their ancestors and each other in the idiom of modern science.

Different Semites and the Limits on Owning Them

This consideration of coverage of archaeology in *al-Muqtataf*'s contents demonstrates its audience's scientific acceptance of, or at least an interest in, the notion of a Semitic race and its conflation with ancient and modern Arab identity. As a modern identity, Arabness is the more important designation, occupying a space elevated beyond the amalgamation of a way of life (nomadism and animal husbandry), speaking one of a variety of root-and-pattern-based languages together having been designated the "Semitic" languages, and martial and physical characteristics that went with that way of life and language. *Al-Muqtataf*, moreover, represents the view that modern Arabs are to recognize a common relationship and differences between them and other contemporary peoples, such as modern Turks, based on their descent from ancient peoples.

Which ancient peoples were Arabs and Semites is not necessarily an issue upon which everyone agrees; thus the Egyptians sometimes appear as some other race entirely.[109] Like all other regional peoples in ancient times and the present, however, they were subject to mixing due to intermarriage and several movements of "Asiatics" and "Arabs" into and out of the region over time. The tendency to conflate Arabism and Semitism, meanwhile, made it possible for one author to claim that the Beni Israel hailed from the Arab tribes that moved westward into Egypt, and for Jurji Zaydan to talk about Hammurabi as both an Arab and a Semite. He wrote this in the context of an article that begins by lamenting that no Arab was involved in the new science by which the ancient Arabs could be studied.[110]

It was a theme frequently mentioned throughout this period, as *al-Muqtataf* made a point to cite experts in the field. The journal's audience knew the names of famous archaeologists such as Flinders Petrie, Frederick Jones

Bliss, R. A. S. Macalister, Ernst Sellin, and Charles Warren, and read the minutes of Palestine Exploration Fund meetings. One reading both *PEQ* and *al-Muqtataf* can see that the first was often a source for the second during this period. As *al-Muqtataf* was based in Cairo, *PEQ* would have been available to its editors. Given their connections to the archaeological community through Bliss and others, they also likely had access to public lectures and scholars. *Al-Muqtataf* often thanks foreign scholars, particularly civilian and military officials of the British occupation who supported archaeology, for their service to the science of the Arabs, while simultaneously leveling stinging self-criticism at their own society. "It might please the reader," writes one author in the 1890–91 issue, "that the learned people of the West take upon themselves the most difficult of burdens and carry the greatest expense, spending their days and nights between the ruins of Egypt and Sham and other countries of the East exploring sections of rock and sherds of pottery between the ancient ruins, delighting in carved rock sections more than they delight in simple gold ingots."[111] The author says that it is this attitude toward the value of knowledge, science, and history by which the West has distinguished itself from the East in sectors such as agriculture, industry, and trade and so "raised its banner above the greater part of humanity . . . We are kidding ourselves," he adds, "if we think we can impel our learned people to study the archaeology of our ancestors, because until now we are not united in necessities such that we can be interested in these luxuries."[112]

This was not, however, a comfortable position. Among the Western scholars lauded in the passage above would have been French Orientalist Ernest Renan, who claimed in his 1855 book, *General History of Semitic Languages*, that the Semitic peoples were lacking in many characteristics of civilized peoples, including wit and humor. Like so many scholars of his time, Renan engaged in other intellectual debates, such as ideas of nationalism and the role of religion in modern life. His work, highly reflective of his ideas of racial determinism, led to his most direct encounter with the Arab and Muslim world, in which many intellectuals, most famously the Islamic modernist thinker Jamal al-Din al-Afghani (1838–97), very publicly engaged him in European platforms refuting his assertion that Islam was incompatible with science. A decade later, an anonymous author took Renan's conclusions about Semitic humor to task in *al-Muqtataf*, publishing an article entitled "Mazah al-Samiyyeen wa Badahatuhum" (The Humor and Wit of the Semites). It offers several old literary examples of Arabic-language humor, saying, "This is from the Arabs and those assimilated to their way of life, and there remained among the Semites another *umma* [nation] of great importance in past ages and until now, and that is the Jewish *umma*."[113] The article proceeds to offer numerous examples of Jewish humor with reference to scripture, extra-scriptural literature, and history. After this consideration, the author says, "Perhaps the Syrians and Phoenicians were like the Arabs and Jews in humor and wit."[114] In this example, we see a deployment of the word *umma*, a sense that the Semitic umbrella has numerous *umam* (nations), the idea that the Syrians and Phoenicians were not Arabs or Jews, but were somehow kin by language, by extension kindred in characteristic wit, and, one might extrapolate, character and race.[115] This example also illustrates that, at the end of the nineteenth century, one mode of historicized taxonomic thought held that the Jewish *umma* had, at some point in history, become separate from the Arab *umma*. The Semitic umbrella could thus foster at least two modes of Arabness: one that recognized the modern descendants of all the ancient Semites in the Arab spaces of the late Ottoman Empire—Muslims, Christians, and Jews—as able to constitute one nation, and another that enabled their recognition as different nations. The strengthening Zionist movement in Palestine complicated these formulae.

Competition

Ideas about ethnic and racial origins found in the pages of *al-Muqtataf* and the scientific basis they offered for understanding the relationships among modern peoples and their legitimacy in space laid the groundwork for syntheses that emerged after the war. Given the range of identities available to people in the context of the modernizing late Ottoman Empire, a range of nationalisms and their vocabularies were manifest as the Ottoman Empire gave way, self-determination met frustration, colonialism took root anew, and the ongoing international competition took on a new character. Historicity as interpreted through archaeology played a significant role in these processes. Throughout most of the period under discussion here, there was no reason for Arab Ottomans to have thought that the science they embraced would provide a blueprint for something unthinkable. The power to define the space of antiquity was not something they realized had been lost, or had been necessary to win. Jerusalem, the most contested spatial component of holy and holier land between the Ottoman Empire and the West, would, perhaps inevitably, be the flashpoint where that realization would crystallize.

By the time an illicit dig within the Jerusalem *haram* (1911–13) created an uproar in the press and spurred popular mobilization, with both Arab parliamentarians and Jerusalem's citizens making accusations against Ottoman officials and publicly pleading with them to adhere to the rule of law, Italian intentions in Libya were obvious, the Balkan Wars were under way, re-volts against the Ottomans in the Hawran and Kerak were recent memories, intercommunal relations in Palestine were under increasing strain, and the world stood on the brink of all-out war.[116] While the dig—a hunt for the in-famous "temple treasure" based on ciphers "discovered" by a Finn in various books of the Hebrew Bible—was the work of non-experts unaffiliated with any legitimate scientific organization, the fact remained that the Ottoman government appeared complicit and the breach occurred on the most sacred bit of holistically sacred terrain. Ottoman authorities stood accused of taking bribes, behaving without transparency, and enabling foreign theft of objects of great historical and monetary value. Jerusalem's citizens sought official ac-knowledgment of accountability and for the Ottoman government to remon-strate with British authorities to get back what had been stolen. All of this was widely reported in the press.[117] At that time in the hands of the CUP, the language of criticism chides the "unionist" Ottoman government for its ignorance of the value of archaeology, for being disdainful of the concerns of its *umma*, and insists that only a caliph—of which there was none since Ab-dülhamid II, having asserted his role as such so vehemently, had been over-thrown—could authorize such undertakings on the *haram*.[118] The promises of the 1908 revolution had not materialized, the relationship between the holy core of Jerusalem and the CUP had deteriorated, and the connections of sacred space and archaeology to Arab identity in an Islamicate framework had rendered archaeology in Jerusalem a political grievance. Embedded in this grievance with Istanbul, there was competition with the Zionist movement.

Licit digs continued apace just beyond the *haram* in Silwan, located out-side the Old City walls. Not only did illicit excavation tar legally sanctioned archaeology with its brush, but given the entirety of the context at that mo-ment, what Nadia Abu El-Haj suggested in the early twenty-first century was a phenomenon not entirely without recognition early in the twentieth: What is the difference between archaeology motivated by science and archaeology motivated by other desires when both affirm the dominant taxonomic para-digm?[119] Critiques citing the lack of benefit to locals from foreign archaeo-logical work grew sharper, in terms not only of self-effacement but also of criticism of those foreign initiatives.[120] That Palestine archaeology became a subject of interest at the Zionist Congresses, and that Baron Edmund de Rothschild, the most important benefactor of Zionist settlement in Palestine, was allowed to conduct archaeological research in Jerusalem and offered to found a museum there for archaeology that was of importance to the Jewish people, was not lost on the Arab press.[121] Osman Hamdi and Frederick Jones Bliss had long since, and by Ottoman decree, established an archaeological museum for Palestine in Jerusalem. The reaction to the illicit dig on the *haram* occurred because people had embraced the archaeological science that made such museums possible, understood what science had displayed there as meaningful to their identity in the modern world, and understood it in a broader political context.

The days of largely apolitical or at least less blatantly competitive archaeological discourse were over. It would take on decidedly sharper nuances as the "unmixing of peoples" separated longtime cousins into new, highly contested national and pan-national groups, filling contestable spaces assigned them that had been cut from the Ottoman whole based on how European science and exigency had understood them.[122] Moving forward after the war, intellectuals of the new Arab states would eloquently and opportunistically assert their syntheses of modern historical methods to compete in the rubric of the new political reality.

On Being Peripheral

The spaces that would constitute Jordan were peripheral to all the intellectual trends and identities manifest in the late Ottoman Arab world. This would likewise render them peripheral to the determination of spatial delineations after the war and considerations of who belonged within them. In being peripheral to identity discourses, however, they were still subject to the Ottoman Empire's modernization initiatives. It was, in fact, the incorporation of southeastern Bilad al-Sham's spaces into the centralized late Ottoman bureaucracy that laid the institutional framework for the postwar state. The Hashemites and the British would graft the new state onto a village society that was characterized by its experience of being incorporated as such. They could do so with adaptability because Jordan's spaces, unlike the Hijaz and Palestine, for instance, experienced the modernization process without the identity baggage that had been so crucial to their late Ottoman recalibration or the international competition that characterized it.

The military certainly incorporated the future Jordan's spaces into new maps it produced for the reformed school system, but they had no special designation among the Ottoman spaces oriented toward an Anatolian center.[123] When a revolt rooted in opposition to centralization initiatives erupted in Kerak in 1910 and spread south, that same military restored order, and Istanbul instituted swift and punitive justice.[124] Istanbul likewise intervened in Jordan's holy spaces, but, of course, not in the way it did in the important holy spaces of the Hijaz and Jerusalem. Ottoman largesse built or rebuilt mosques in Transjordan, some of them new, prompted by population growth, others with history, dating as far back as the time of the Prophet and the early caliphs. As Ottoman officials did for similar sites throughout the empire's Arab provinces, in Mu'ta, a southern village of Kerak, they saw to the repair of the shrines and tombs, visited by numerous pilgrims, of the Prophet's Companions who were martyred in one of the most famous existential battles of early Islamic history.[125]

As everywhere in the empire, Jordan experienced the expansion of state schooling, which, among its many goals, intended to check the growth of foreign missionary schools. By the time these efforts bore fruit, the Greek Orthodox Church (under Russian protection), the Latin Church (under French protection), and the Protestant Church (Anglican, under British protection), which all had bases in nearby Jerusalem from which to operate, had schools in Salt, and would continue to extend their influence southward into Kerak throughout the remaining years of the empire.[126] One special school, the Tribal School (Aşiret Mektebi), targeted Jordan's sons. It accepted students from prestigious Arab tribes and recruited from a system of provincial quotas for a five-year, state-sponsored course in Istanbul that served as preparation for advanced education at the civil or military service academy.[127] There they underwent a rigorous amalgamation of advanced primary and secondary schooling, drilling, surveillance, cloistering in austere living conditions, and ritualization of religious observance, all in the cosmopolitan imperial capital. While the Tribal School did incorporate hundreds of tribal sons into the civil and military apparatus of the state, it was never quite able to fill its provincial quotas and closed in 1907.[128]

The Tribal School served a less tangible function connected to the schizophrenic identity Arab tribes conjured in the parlance of Ottoman officialdom, which enabled the imperial center to paint an enlightened picture of itself and had interesting parallels to the dualistic British view of "tribes." On the one hand, "tribes" were "wild," "uncivilized," and a threat to Istanbul's centralizing reforms and the empire's modern character. Arab tribes, however, the particular target of the Tribal School, simultaneously held a special, elevated allure. Abdülhamid II's interest in his Arab subjects was directly related to the role Islam played in his sultanate. In the official view, those ancestrally closest to true Islam were the Arabs, and among the Arabs the roving desert tribesmen, particularly those of the Hijaz, were, much like their role as biblical caricatures in Western imagination, reminiscent of the days of Revelation and the great legacy of early Islamic history.[129] Their day-to-day lives in the present, however, were marked by animism, superstition, ignorance, and practices that were un-Islamic.[130] For this reason, as well as to counteract foreign

Christian missionaries and their institutions while promoting late Ottoman reform of shariʿa, Istanbul deployed Muslim missionaries to Transjordan to set the frontiersmen right in both knowledge and practice, "correcting" their observance of Ramadan and better ritualizing their religious lives.[131]

If there were multiple official identity discourses available in the Arab spaces of the late Ottoman Empire, they all had some manifestation in the future Jordan, but its spaces were not embodied in them. Ottomanism, Hellenism, Islamism, Arabness, and Turkishness, along with a range of subaltern identities that we might consider, could all be read in Jordan's antiquity and modernity, but Jordan was not an amalgamation of space that could be used to own any one of those narratives or the nodes at which they overlapped or competed. Of official discourses of identity, those with the broadest potential appeal were Islamism and Arabness. And while Arabness in the Transjordanian spaces no doubt had the same foundation in Semitic origins and science as everywhere else, their Arab character in this period was as much, if not more, rooted in the dualistic notion of Arab "tribes" shared by both the Ottoman center and the West. As the relationship between Istanbul and its Arab provinces grew more strained in the years before the war, urban-based activists seeking greater decentralization from the imperial center seized upon events such as the Kerak Revolt of 1910 as part of a larger discourse of Arab political identity in the Ottoman framework.[132] After the war and their acquisition of Transjordan, the Hashemites would narrate the Kerak Revolt as an Arab nationalist prelude to their own. They would ultimately cultivate many and varied aspects of Jordan's holistic landscape, weaving together antiquity and modernity, to recalibrate narratives of the nation as circumstances dictated. The ability to do so lay in the adaptable identity narratives of modernization in peripheral space.

CHAPTER 4

British Mandate: Core, Periphery, and Ownership of Narrative

Archaeologists are notoriously touchy and quarrelsome, even for men of science, and there will probably be great difficulties in reaching any agreed form of organisation and, still more, of policy, but it might be well to consult Sir Arthur Evans, Mr. Hogarth and one or two other leading British authorities (a) on the provisions to be inserted in the various mandates and (b) on what international organisation, if any, should be recognised under the League of Nations. The matter is of some importance both because archaeology proper is a fruitful cause of jealousy and friction and because archaeology is an extremely useful camouflage for politics.[1]

Archaeology not only was a camouflage *for* politics, but proved after the war to be the very essence *of* politics. The archaeological literature of the British Mandate reflects this, the narrative of the Holy Land core (Palestine) and its periphery (Transjordan) contextualized in the framework of the nation-state. It promoted not just the realization of a Holy Land narrative developed in the decades leading to the Great War, but England's supremacy in a recalibrated postwar global competition: bringing the peoples of its spheres of interest into modernity, securing its interests in the new world order, and leading the new nations of the region to their future, positivist reward of self-determination in line with Woodrow Wilson's Fourteen Points.

The three editions of *The Handbook of Palestine and Transjordan* (published 1922, 1930, and 1934) opened with these words to the traveler from Herbert Samuel, first high commissioner of Palestine (1920–25):

He may find among the Bedouin of Beersheba precisely the conditions that prevailed in the time of Abraham; at Bethlehem he may see the women's costumes and, in some respects, the mode of living of the period of the Crusaders; the Arab villages are, for the most part, still under mediaeval conditions; the towns present many of the problems of the early nineteenth century; while the new arrivals from Eastern and Central Europe, and from America, bring with them the activities of the twentieth century, and sometimes, perhaps, the ideas of the twenty-first. Indeed, it is true to say that in Palestine you can choose the climate, or the century, that you prefer . . .

Palestine has witnessed many and great changes in the four thousand years of her recorded history. But it is necessary to go back to the time of the Crusades for a change as fundamental as that which is involved in the ending of the Turkish Administration and the substitution of a British Mandate.[2]

Samuel penned these words—an updated taxonomy of both romantic and unenlightened backwardness and promise for British rule and Jewish immigration—for the first edition of the book, published while the existence of Transjordan under Hashemite rule remained provisional. They were never updated for subsequent volumes, despite the addition of a special, albeit short, section about Transjordan to the second and third editions of the book. The *Handbook*'s authors were Harry Charles Luke (Palestine Mandate colonial administrator, assistant governor of Jerusalem 1921, high commissioner for Palestine 1928) and Edward Keith-Roach (Palestine Mandate colonial administrator, governor of Jerusalem 1926–45).[3] Dr. John Garstang (University of Liverpool, first director of both the British School of Archaeology in Jerusalem and the Palestine Department of Antiquities, author of the antiquities laws for Palestine and ultimately Transjordan, 1920–27) and George Horsfield (chief inspector of antiquities for Palestine, and ultimately Transjordan, under Garstang) contributed archaeological notes. The third edition is 549 pages long, with 430 of those dedicated to Palestine. The geography, history, and archaeology of Palestine, along with information for tourists, are taken up in three separate sections, constituting approximately 185 pages total. Transjordan's geography, history, and archaeology, by contrast, constitute only one section of approximately twenty-six pages. "Palestine is Mediterranean, Trans-Jordan is Arabian," write the authors, "and the rim of the Arabian plain, tilted askew to the east, here finds its highest western levels. The Hijaz Railway, lying on the watershed running north and south, marks the limit between the desert and the sown, whence start valleys flowing west, dividing the country into sections. These deep valleys become in historic periods the political frontiers."[4] For the authors, geography was taxonomy, a taxonomy serving as the basis of nation-state narratives and, by extension, at least some conceptualization of the peoples who composed them. The limits and frontiers to which they allude were arbitrary at best and actually had little relationship to "political" or other divisions in previous historical periods. There wasn't, moreover, much for them to write about Transjordan.

Cook's Traveller's Handbook to Palestine, Syria and Iraq, also of 1934, is likewise interesting for what it says—or does not say—about Transjordan, as it suggests itineraries for travelers.[5] Part 2 of the guidebook is called "Palestine (with Trans-Jordan)," and Garstang is again a source of archaeological information for this volume. The suggested Transjordan travel itinerary constitutes only 22 pages of a volume of 496 pages.[6] This itinerary guides the tourist from Jericho to Amman by way of the city of Salt by going north some distance before crossing the Jordan River Valley to cut southward toward Amman. It then provides details on possible excursions from Amman, which included crossing various biblical-era rivers on the way to the famous monumental city of Jerash, understood to be classical, and Ajloun Castle, fortress of the enemies of the Crusaders. From there, tourists could go by way of Irbid back to the River Jordan or to the monumental city of Umm al-Jimal en route to Syria. Other excursions to monumental sites outside Amman are suggested, including Iraq al-Amir (a Hellenistic palace), Hesban (believed to be the biblical Heshbon), the Christian ruins at Madaba and Mount Nebo, Mukawwir (where John the Baptist reportedly lost his head), and well-documented desert castles at al-Qastal, Jiza, and Mshatta. The next logical attraction is thus the Crusader-era fortress of Kerak, followed by Petra. From Petra it is an easy trip to the town of Ma'an, from whence one could go to Aqaba. On the road tourists would see signs for "Rum," which, the book notes, was made famous by T. E. Lawrence. From Aqaba, which, according to the book, may have been King Solomon's port city of Ezion-Geber, tourists could proceed to Egypt. Cook's guidebook thus devised excursions that crossed biblical rivers and passed an Old Testament site now and then, but in contrast with the western side of the River Jordan, Transjordan was thought to have few antiquities sites, and fewer of interest. With the obvious exception of Petra of the Nabateans, "identified with the Nebaioth of Genesis xxv., the first-born of Ishmael," antiquities sites east of the river had been labeled, since the explorations of the nineteenth century, as classical, Christian, Islamic, and Crusader—and easily viewed en route to somewhere else.[7]

The shared fate of the two sides of the river in the wake of the war thus mirrored the paradigm of history that had been contrived in the decades just prior to it. That paradigm had its origins in Britain's strategic interests in a global competition in which protection of its most vital colonial resources was paramount. Exploration, study, and collecting related to antiquities were among Britain's vital competitive tactics. The River Jordan became a border in a new way, and the fate of antiquities on its eastern side had, in the global academic and popular ethos, become linked by their relative relationship to that of the antiquities that lay on the western side, which were England's priority. That link was based primarily on the importance of biblical heritage to British and American Protestantism, fixing a privileged historical narrative to sites and artifacts thought to bring the Old Testament and its Israelite protagonists alive.

By means of the peace treaties following the Great War, the nation-state system legalized this paradigm, and with the Mandates recognized Britain's responsibility to modernize what had been created from its historicity. In this framework, Transjordan was as tangential in its modern existence as it had been in regional history understood in the West, a new colonial afterthought meant to serve Britain's strategic needs and challenges in the era of the nation-state. General Allenby's triumphal entry into Jerusalem on 11 December 1917 grafted a British administrative and political reality onto a late Ottoman one, providing a new context for the shared fate of everyone and everything on the western and eastern sides of the River Jordan.[8] A military governor ruled over Cisjordan (Palestine) by means of the Occupied Enemy Territory Administration (OETA) before the implementation of the stewardship of a high commissioner and the Mandate. Transjordan's incorporation into that framework and a direct British presence there came more than two years later.[9] By then, the consequences of McMahon's promises to Sharif Husayn, the Arab Revolt, and the secret deal between Sykes and Picot were apparent, and Faysal's Damascus-based kingdom would fall before a frustrated Abdullah would, with his father's blessing, set forth from the Hijaz on a mission to realize that kingdom again. Britain's attempt to rule Transjordan, after the collapse of Faysal's kingdom, as separate local governorates—Ajloun, the Balqa, and Kerak—headed by young British officers quickly proved futile.[10] As Abdullah made his way north through Transjordan forging alliances and daring the British to act, Britain, in an attempt to mitigate French, Arab, and Zionist aspirations that San Remo and the Treaty of Sèvres did not lay to rest, saw in him someone who might be able to fill the power vacuum left in Transjordan, consolidate a state to act as a buffer between its possessions in Bilad al-Sham and those of the French, provide Britain with an uninterrupted path by which Iraqi oil could reach the Mediterranean, and ultimately add to Britain's sphere of influence linking India and the Mediterranean.[11] Newly appointed colonial secretary Winston Churchill met with Abdullah in Jerusalem shortly after the Cairo Conference of March 1921 to delineate a Transjordanian Mandate for Abdullah to rule on a provisional basis, originally of six months.[12] By the end of that summer, Faysal was on the throne as king of Iraq. Sharif Husayn and his sons would, however, continue to covet a larger hereditary possession inclusive of what they had been promised by McMahon. The British were happy to make deals using that carrot, meanwhile claiming to maintain the status quo in Palestine.[13] This meant maintaining the rights of each religious community, an impossible task given that only one had been promised help to realize a nation there, while the others were promised merely that their civil and religious rights would not be prejudiced. The ongoing global competition was thus in a new phase marked by multifaceted state- and nation-building exercises. In the case of the Palestine and Transjordan Mandates, these aimed to secure the core the British created there in the context of securing an array of interrelated British interests.

As prior to the war, antiquities had an important and contentious role to play in this competition. Britain, as the occupying and Mandatory power with the responsibility, sanctioned by the world's major powers, to prepare the occupied peoples to one day be properly self-determined, had to translate its prewar aspirations and the whole of the ethos that came into being with the colonial foundations of interest in, study of, and care for antiquities into policy that could not appear colonial in the same way as before the war. It claimed, meanwhile, to maintain the status quo in coveted Palestine, a task that was paradigmatically impossible given both the historical narratives and contemporary exigencies that underpinned its creation as a core landscape. It was not enough to occupy with military strength and self-serving economic policy; the right to rule was a responsibility requiring demonstrations of ownership not just of spaces and their contents, but their narratives.

This chapter is about contested demonstrations of ownership of heritage in the British Mandates of Palestine and Transjordan. The British undertook both physical interventions into cultural heritage and legislative initiatives to govern every aspect of its being. They did so in the language of restoration and redemption of decayed space, institutionalizing cultural heritage, and further taxonomizing it into that which was archaeological in nature and that which was "living" and generally religious. This reinforced the idea that heritage was interesting to particular people for particular reasons, and left certain kinds of heritage undefined, thus rendering it devoid of status as heritage at all. This process, which revolved around the question of who owned antiquities or had the right to keep them in trust, was not only a deliberate means of punishing the losers of the Great War and imposing the Mandate, but also, as a consequence, a means to feed a contest within and between British institutions and among British individuals themselves, particularly in ways that pitted scholars, many of whom had contributed to the war effort, against Mandate bureaucracy. It happened in Palestine first, leaving an American rabbi, Nelson Glueck, to institutionalize an archaeological paradigm for the eastern side of the River Jordan in peripheral relation to what had been established for the western side, creating a historicity narrative of space and people mirroring the creation of Arab and Jewish national space from the Holy Land. The chapter concludes by exploring Arab syntheses of narratives of ownership over the same heritage and antiquities. These narratives drew on western archaeological and philological research, subsuming the personal narratives that people had to the *turath* of antiquity and its landscape, devising a pan-Arab idiom to contest the colonial impositions of Zionism and nation-state borders.

Jerusalem and the Restorative Powers of Western Civilization

Colonel Ronald Storrs, military governor of Jerusalem (1917–20), immediately intervened to carve the modernity, order, and systematization of British rule into the spaces of the city's heritage. In so doing, British rule in the centerpiece of the Holy Land core added new threads for the narrative it had woven before the war: legal frameworks for managing heritage and people's interactions with it, for defining heritage, and for the development of industries related to heritage. In this respect, Storrs serves as a prototype of the production of knowledge for the exercise of colonial power.

He issued Public Notice No. 34 in April 1918, forbidding any alterations to anything within a 2,500-meter radius of Jerusalem's Damascus Gate without the written consent of the military governor, under pain of heavy fine.[14] As Storrs, in a language of occupation and development familiar to our own time, writes in his autobiography, "The inhabitants of a place are not exhibits to be held back in picturesque discomfort in order that the sentimental tourist may enjoy her anticipated thrill . . . It is not enough to stop men doing ill: you must help them to do well."[15] To this end, he also established the Pro-Jerusalem Society, describing it as "in effect the Military Governor civically and aesthetically in Council," which brought together leaders and representatives of the diverse communities of Jerusalem for consultations regarding the care and development of the city. While Storrs took this initiative very seriously, it certainly wasn't a new idea; as noted in the previous chapter, the residents of late Ottoman Jerusalem had extensive experience organizing and governing local and municipal affairs.[16]

Storrs quotes the society's official charge as

"the preservation and advancement of the interests of Jerusalem, its district and inhabitants . . . The protection of and addition to the amenities of Jerusalem, the provision and maintenance of parks, gardens and open spaces, the protection and preservation with the consent of the Government, of the Antiquities, the encouragement of arts, handicrafts, and industries in consonance with the general objects of the Society" and certain other cultural activities.[17]

Based on this charge, colonial officials encouraged the establishment of similar societies in other cities and towns.[18] The Antiquities Ordnance of 1920 (see below) would specifically charge the Pro-Jerusalem Society to see to the upkeep of all confessions' holy sites in Palestine, which were mostly architectural in nature.[19] In a terrain that had been imagined and articulated in the first place as holistically sacred, the discursive separation between "holy" sites and "antiquities" sites, between "living" and "historical" heritage, between sites of tourist pilgrimage and those of religious pilgrimage, began to be instantiated in colonial institutions and law.

The Pro-Jerusalem Society was entirely self-funded by subscriptions in denominations large and small drawn from wide audiences both locally and abroad. The society was originally chaired by Charles Robert Ashbee, a prominent designer, architect, and Socialist who had been instrumental in the cooperative handicraft movement among London's urban poor and who was teaching in Cairo at the time of his appointment to the Pro-Jerusalem Society. In an initiative suited to the narrative of development in Britain's Mandates, Ashbee came to Jerusalem to enact the same kinds of development projects that had characterized the Arts and Crafts movement he had supported at home, in light of his view that "Islamic art was an extension of personal, public and secular space" and his experience linking such concepts to the importance of traditional handicrafts and "a bond between manual labor and communal living."[20]

Storrs's governorship and initiatives such as the Pro-Jerusalem Society mark only one chapter in an extensive record of promoting and manipulating what he defined as the authentic cultural identity of every post to which he was assigned—Egypt, Palestine, Cyprus—while governing these places as multi-ethnic components of the British Empire.[21] Based on his successful career incorporating heritage into colonial governance, Whitehall eventually dispatched him to serve as governor of Cyprus (1926–32), where his specific charge was combatting Greek nationalism by fostering an ethnic Cypriot identity, which he did with the help of a Swedish archaeological team that claimed to have found evidence of an indigenous Iron Age people called the Eteocypriots.[22]

Storrs sought to implement British rule not only by articulating and organizing the varieties of Jerusalem's modern and ancient pilgrimage spaces with legislation and socioeconomic and civic engineering, but also by making direct physical interventions into those spaces. One of his first such projects, to restore the tile façade of the Dome of the Rock, is a case in point. While couched in the language of the Mandate authority's responsibility to care for and control living heritage spaces and respect the spaces and traditions of those over whom Britain now ruled, the narrative of such projects bespoke British hegemony in a global competition in which Jerusalem was a strategic and symbolic prize. In this narrative, restoration is necessitated of a state of decrepitude caused by inferiors and enemies. A return to a more glorious past could materialize, however, only through the enterprise of the new foreign, Western power ruling over the space.

A report by Major Ernest Richmond of the Egypt Expeditionary Force (EEF) details the condition of the tiles composing the façade of the Dome of the Rock at the end of 1918.[23] Richmond had served as architect to public works in Egypt from 1900 to 1914 and to the War Office from 1914 to 1916.[24] Storrs brought him to Jerusalem to serve as consulting architect to *al-Haram al-Sharif* (the Noble Sanctuary, consisting of the Dome of the Rock, al-Aqsa Mosque, and their environs) because of his architectural training and familiarity with Islamic institutions and antiquities.[25] His report upon undertaking this project demonstrates how the various threads of ideology and scientific inquiry that came together to create the Anglo-American conceptualization of Palestine's landscape before the Great War carried over into Britain's physical administration of that landscape once the war was over. Survey and classification remained the path to knowledge, of which the British, now in charge, were capable of—and had the responsibility for—gaining and using for a greater and universal good.

British authorities' imperative vis-à-vis the Dome of the Rock was to prevent further decay of the façade. Preventing decay meant acquiring intimate knowledge of its details. Procuring this knowledge depended on establishing a good working relationship with those most familiar with the building. Richmond writes:

> The question of dealing with the tile facing of the Dome of the Rock requires the devotion of a considerable amount of time upon the spot and under the guidance of an exact knowledge of all the data at our disposal. Fortunately we stand at a time, which may never be repeated, when an interim government, with the cordial cooperation of the traditionary guardians of the shrine, has given an opportunity for gaining this knowledge by allowing me the privilege of living for several months in the presence of the Dome of the Rock.[26]

Richmond's project was certainly painstaking; he mapped the tiles of the building's façade and compiled a register detailing each one. He combed the entire site for pieces of old tile that had fallen, were in disuse, or had obviously been discarded. These he cataloged in a building on the *haram* given for his use by the grand mufti of Jerusalem, Kamil Effendi al-Husseini.

Richmond was convinced that British restoration work was absolutely necessary and, in fact, Britain's responsibility. "The Dome of the Rock is not merely a building of archaeological and artistic interest," he writes, "but also a building of every-day use and a symbol, at least in the eyes of Muslims, of something still very much alive." Discarded tiles he recovered would never be enough for "filling the ugly gaps in the tile facing," so new tiles would have to be produced. British restoration did not threaten to produce "a corrupt document for future generations" because the chaotic façade, as it stood, was "already a patchwork of effort extending over many generations."[27] Tiles provided by the British were thus a logical step forward.

But who would the British commission to make new tiles? Richmond clearly understood Commander David Hogarth to believe that tiles good enough for the Dome of the Rock could be produced only in *Europe*. Richmond, however, suggests founding "a small experimental workshop in Jerusalem."[28] He says:

> It may well be . . . that the East is quite incapable of doing again what it has done before. But a consciousness of this possibility does not imply that it would be altogether unreasonable to give the East a chance; moreover, it certainly is possible that research and enquiry may bring to light the continued existence of knowledge and traditions upon which may be based at least a hope for reviving this art.[29]

With all due respect to European advancements in the knowledge and art of tile-craft, Richmond notes that many of the Dome of the Rock's tiles looked European and that locals believed them to be European. The building's caretakers informed Richmond that the tiles were, in fact, the product of defeated enemy Germany. "These melancholy specimens," he says, "afford Muslims no very encouraging advertisement of European skill." The Germans had not only affixed their inferior tiles to the façade of the Dome of the Rock, but they had also, at some point in the decades leading to the Great War, carried old tiles back to Germany.

Work on the façade perpetrated by the Ottomans, that other vanquished enemy, fares no better in Richmond's report. While many, including Hogarth, seem to be under the impression that the majority of the extant tiles date from the reign of Suleyman the Magnificent, Richmond assures otherwise:

The whole of the great "Ya Seen" inscription dates from 1872 and is composed of tiles of inferior quality. A considerable work of repair or rather "restoration" was carried out in 1818 and the degree of respect accorded by restorers in the past to the older tiles can easily be appreciated by anyone who takes the trouble to walk round the building and to note the relative importance of the positions occupied by the older and the newer tiles as well as the lamentable manner in which most of the older tiles have been reset without reference either to the positions they were originally intended to occupy or to the relationship, implied by the design, of one tile to another. Moreover large numbers of the finest tiles have been ruthlessly cut up to fill spaces which the restorers found awkward to deal with.[30]

Neither Richmond's budget nor the parameters of his assignment were adequate to undertake the kind of survey and restoration he believed was necessary for the Dome of the Rock. Hogarth agreed.[31] He had misjudged the amount of money available from the Ministry of Awqaf (Religious Endowments) and there was not sufficient funding for such an enormous project.

The matter of whom to find to make the tiles was, furthermore, not an issue easily solved:

> I think it is absolutely necessary to re-tile in the interests of the aesthetic effect of the building; but I do not want it done till the best possible tiles, in imitation of the originals, have been procured. Lt. Col. T. E. Lawrence recently told me that Damascus still produced tiles almost equal to its 16th century fabric, but, after some research there last week, I failed to find any but very inferior specimens.[32]

In a Foreign Office memo, Major William Ormsby-Gore, political officer of the EEF attached to the Zionist Commission, likewise mentions an Armenian artisan who designed a room for Sir Mark Sykes's home in Yorkshire and might replicate "old Damascus tiles" very well. "If he has not been massacred in the interval he might provide the necessary tiles. The Dome of the Rock is probably for the most part the work of Christian workmen."[33] That the man who secretly helped divide British and French geography in the Levant orientalized his English home notwithstanding, and the crass humor with which Ormsby-Gore writes of the Armenian aside, such a statement in such a context could not have been more loaded. The implication, of course, hardly subtle, is that the iconic Dome of the Rock, categorized as a Muslim site, was spectacular only because Islam had had to call on what came before it, Christianity, to produce it. It was thus natural that a similarly advanced "Christian" civilization, England, should intervene to restore it to its original condition.

This idea fit comfortably into the broader restoration narrative that began with nineteenth-century British interests in the Holy Land and its development, seen in Herbert Samuel's comments from *The Handbook of Palestine and Trans-Jordan* linking the modernization of Palestine, British rule, and Jewish immigration from the West. With Jewish immigration under the British Mandate serving to realize Zionist aspirations and the promise of the Balfour Declaration, the competitive narrative by which modernization and concomitant nationalization in a desolate land could be attributed to the "return" of Western Jews logically followed. That colonial officials, here a liaison to the Zionist Commission, spoke and acted in accordance with such narratives, demonstrates clearly the complicated linkage of heritage and antiquities to politics.

Complicating these links further was the place of such spaces as the Dome of the Rock in coalescing narratives of tourism, which, in the Holy Land, is a loaded kind of pilgrimage.[34] The experience of visiting an "antiquities" site like Megiddo, for instance, was, at some level, to have the same significance for the tourist audience as visiting a "religious" site like the Church of the Holy Sepulchre, at least for Christians. No similar phenomenon was intended for non-Muslim audiences regarding places such as the Dome of the Rock. The importance of the Dome of the Rock in books for British tourists and military personnel lay in its architectural and historic significance and its religious significance to Muslims. Missing was any spiritual and emotional significance that might interest non-Muslims who nevertheless identified with Abrahamic traditions. Tourism literature may have directed non-Muslims to bask in the grandeur of the Dome of the Rock, but it did not make the connections for them to the biblical world that preceded it. Missing from the literature is that *al-Haram al-Sharif* sits atop what remains of the platform that supported the Second Temple, itself believed to have been constructed on the site where Solomon's Temple once stood and where Abraham nearly sacrificed his son, Isaac/Ishaq or Ishmael/Isma'il, depending on Jewish or Islamic tradition. In other words, those who produced and consumed the pilgrimage narrative largely failed to recognize that *al-Haram al-Sharif* was viscerally and intentionally part of that same world they rendered "biblical." While the handbooks and travel itineraries do articulate the Abrahamic traditions embedded in *al-Haram al-Sharif*, they largely fail to connect them to one another. The Dome of the Rock and the Western Wall are noted as important to Muslims because of the Prophet Muhammad's Night Journey, presented as something separate from the site's extensive Abrahamic past, as opposed to a continuation of it.[35] The pilgrimage narrative of Palestine under the Mandate was thus a continuation of the scientific delineation of "our tradition" and "other tradition" masked in enlightened stewardship. One was a priority to be actively studied, known, and experienced. The other was to be maintained out of a sense of imperial pride of duty, political status quo, and local sensitivities. These are distinctly unequal imperatives.

Storrs and Richmond's restoration of the tiles of the Dome of the Rock was delayed, finally beginning a few years later with money raised by the Supreme Muslim Council.[36] By that time, Charles Robert Ashbee had found exactly the Armenian workmen for whom Ormsby-Gore had been looking, the Karakshian and Balian families. While "technical and budgetary problems" delayed the project and the participation of the Karakshian and Balian families, they both made Jerusalem their home, establishing their famous workshop, Palestine Pottery, on Nablus Road.[37]

To put in perspective the importance of British rule over the Holy Land core it helped create and the role of Jerusalem and its heritage, such as the Dome of the Rock, in the narrative of British possession of this strategic landscape, it helps to consider an iconic example in another "liberated" city. By contrast with Britain's involvement in restoring the Dome of the Rock, British officials decided not to intercede when asked to do so at the Aya Sofya (St. Sophia) in Istanbul, a Helleno-Byzantine monument appropriated for the narrative of Western civilization. Mr. Thackeray Turner, chairman of the Committee of the Society for the Protection of Ancient Buildings, cites the dismal report of a Mr. Thomas Jackson in an urgent letter to foreign secretary Lord Curzon.[38] Jackson's report apparently suggested that "St. Sophia" was in danger of collapsing. Turner writes:

> My Committee does not specially urge that the building should be returned to Christendom, but in that event it would ask the British Government to see that the structure be secured from the danger of collapse . . . ; and secondly it would ask the British Government to prevent any damage by "restoration," renewal or removal of any of the objects of art which the building contains, objects which are also of great historic value.
>
> In the event of the building remaining in the hands of the present owners my committee would ask your Lordship if it would be possible or even desirable to suggest to the Turkish Government that a building which is so much the centre of the history of the arts of Western civilisation might not be better repaired under the auspices of the best brains of that civilisation than by the representatives of one school of Thought only.

Turner's plea met with little sympathy, likely due to Istanbul's status, as opposed to that of Jerusalem. The minutes accompanying the letter allude to the undetermined status of the Ottoman capital at that time. British officials assumed that "Constantinople and the Straits" would be internationalized in the form of a Mandate. That was still very much undecided, and any desire to work on St. Sophia would have to be undertaken with whatever administration came to be.[39] Another reason for the negative response is that British renovation of St. Sophia was being sought for inclusion in the peace treaty, and the minutes stipulate that "there is no intention of taking Santa Sophia from the Moslems."[40] That would have been contrary to British policy and antithetical to the image the British wanted to portray of themselves and their governance throughout their empire and to the outside world. Whereas British control over the spaces of Jerusalem and the broader Holy Land core served to protect its strategic interests, similar interference in Istanbul could have served to undermine its position over that regional core.

Historian Arnold J. Toynbee, however, then serving at the Foreign Office, thought that the status of what he called Hagia Sophia would certainly come under treaty provisions for antiquities. He asks if it wouldn't be possible for Hagia Sophia to have a dual designation, as a living religious site under the jurisdiction of the proper Turkish religious authorities and as an international monument under the jurisdiction of the antiquities authority of the future Mandatory government of the Straits zone. He cites recent British architectural inspection of the Mosque of 'Umar in Bethlehem as a precedent.[41]

Toynbee's example, however, is apt demonstration of the very issue at hand. The British fully understood the delicacy of the context of their rule in the Holy Land, and went to great lengths to care for the holy sites of all the confessions now under their authority. The Mandatory status of Istanbul was not finalized. And unlike the situation in Jerusalem, there was not in Istanbul a *millet* of the defunct Ottoman system emerging as a national movement, threatening the status quo that the British claimed they were intent on upholding.[42] Other officials privy to the minutes advise that leaving the matter to the future Mandatory was the safest option.[43] Peace negotiations were ongoing, and the fate of not only the landscapes of the former Ottoman Empire but also the antiquities and heritage found within them would be enshrined in the ensuing treaties and legislative actions of nascent nations.

Legal Matters

Discourses regarding England's intervention at the Dome of the Rock and its refusal to intervene at Aya Sofya must be seen in the context of broader initiatives to legalize ownership of antiquities after the war in a way that reflected the new order. Richmond's report that Germany had taken tiles from the Dome of the Rock piqued interest at the Foreign Office. He wondered if measures couldn't be taken in the peace agreement to get them back, while other officials enumerated more "good stuff" taken from former Ottoman territories, including the façade of Qasr Mshatta in "TransJordania."[44] The issue fell before secretary of state for foreign affairs Lord Curzon, who forwarded it to foreign secretary Lord Balfour.[45] A significant effort was under way by terms of the peace negotiations to make the vanquished Germans, Austrians, and Turks surrender antiquities to the Allies. As the British military representative at Smyrna wrote to the Foreign Office, "All those interested in antiquities bear England a grudge for having had many objects of the greatest interest and beauty removed from Asia Minor."[46] The irony of this statement, of course, is that he does not acknowledge Britain's (or other allies') role in denuding the former Ottoman territories of movable antiquities, but chides Britain for allowing Germans or Turks to have them at British expense.

Without the Ottoman Empire, to what antiquities legislation would its former territories be subject? Embedded in this question was that of ownership in the postwar order and how to punish the losers. Having spent three-quarters of a century self-styling a landscape, the powers that emerged victorious—here the British—clearly saw the unprecedented opportunity to institutionalize and regulate the physical reality of the ancient space they had conceptualized for the modern world in a new geopolitical order they had been key to designing. This would be done, of course, in a manner that demonstrated British prestige and legitimacy to govern.[47]

The major point of contention in this facet of postwar competition was the issue of who owned antiquities, which raised many questions.[48] Should antiquities be the property of the nation in which they were discovered? What if that nation was new, and had been part of an empire that no longer existed when the antiquities in question were found? Should antiquities belong to the nation of the excavator who discovered them? What if the excavator had been a citizen of an empire that didn't exist anymore, and the excavator's new citizenship were in question? What if the excavator was French but worked in British service at the time of the discovery? Should antiquities belong to the nation that financed their discovery? What if that nation no longer existed? What if that nation were among the Central Powers? Should antiquities belong to the nation that was currently in power where the discovery was made, even if the boundaries of that territory had yet to be determined, or if it remained undecided which power would ultimately have control over that territory? Or should antiquities belong to the nation that "could most easily appreciate their value"?[49] And what kind of value was implied—cultural, historical, religious, scientific, monetary? Did this allow for different nations to value the same antiquities differently, or did it assume a hegemonic discourse by which antiquities were to be "appreciated" by which nations? Did "appreciation" also imply rights to cultural and political appropriation? And was there a certain chauvinism implied regarding the abilities of some nations over others to appreciate some antiquities, or a binary understanding that some antiquities had meaning only for some groups and other antiquities had meaning only for others?

Britain's interest in the role of antiquities in the peace process was not for those antiquities to be repatriated to whatever new state might be their nation of origin, but for the sake of the colonial powers now in charge and their allies. Guaranteeing access to antiquities for itself was a vital component of Britain's legal framework for its Mandates.[50] It was simultaneously an awesome responsibility; care of antiquities required a significant investment of money and manpower.[51] There were thus attempts to legislate a peace whereby the war's losers would have to bear the financial weight of the new order for antiquities. A proposal that the Turkish government pay for an international commission responsible for antiquities oversight in former and future Turkish lands rationalized this in frameworks of both retribution and development. Sir Frederick Kenyon, director of the British Museum, reasoned that the Turkish government should pay,

> first, because its neglect of its obvious duty in the care of an inheritance from the past to which conquest is its only claim, is the sole cause of the need for the Commission; second, because the country would benefit greatly by the proper administration of its antiquities—not because they can be sold and generally exploited by the illicit dealers, as at present, but partly because the museum of the country would receive an ample share of them, and partly because they attract civilised travelers. Under proper administration, Asia Minor should become as much a resort for tourists as Egypt.[52]

Complicating discourses of antiquity in terms of ownership, punishment, and economic advancement, numerous factions were interested in the legislation of antiquities after the war. The fate of archaeology was a battleground upon which the Allies could compete with one another, and upon which British offices, institutions, and individuals at home and in and beyond the Mandates could compete among themselves. Historian Magnus Bernhardsson writes, "What may seem to be a petty intergovernmental rivalry actually had critical repercussions for the status of antiquities and archaeology in Middle Eastern nations under British influence."[53] Many of the same characters whom Bernhardsson identifies as vying for control and influence over Iraq's cultural heritage did the same in Britain's Levantine Mandates. Sir Frederick Kenyon used his position as president of the prestigious British Academy to create the Joint Archaeological Committee (JAC).[54] In the same memo, Kenyon describes the JAC as "appointed at the invitation of the British Academy to deliberate on matters relating to the Archaeology of the Near East." Essentially Kenyon had, as president of the British Academy, invited himself, as director of the British Museum, to form a body to bend the ear of government as regards antiquities policies. The committee's purpose was to offer counsel to the British authorities as they organized institutions and devised antiquities legislation throughout the newly ordered empire.[55] He writes:

> The defeat of Turkey, and the meeting of representatives of the Entente and the U.S.A. at the Peace Congress, afford an opportunity such as can never recur to remedy this deplorable state of affairs [i.e., the status of antiquities under the Ottoman antiquities law]. The success of the varied Inter-Allied organizations during the War suggests the possibility of an international solution of the problem.[56]

Kenyon laments the corrupt administration of the Ottoman antiquities law. He says that under the law, officials could delay applications for a *firman* to work. The treatment, furthermore, of one's *firman* and one's project had been subject to one's country's diplomatic relations with Istanbul and the relationship between one's head of state and the sultan. Kenyon's references are specifically to Germany and Austria, which Britain, France, and the United States believed had received preferential treatment from the Ottomans, and were thus as guilty of violating the antiquities law as the Ottomans were of failing to enforce it.[57]

While British officials frequently sought advice from Kenyon and the JAC, they didn't necessarily follow it or view it favorably.[58] As in their refusal to intervene in the matter of Aya Sofya, described above, they sometimes found scholars' interests in archaeology difficult to countenance in terms of their own overall objectives and necessities of diplomacy and governance.[59] By way of example, the JAC's—that is, Kenyon's—proposed League of Nations commission for the administration of antiquities, and thus Turkey's divestiture from control over them even in its own postwar possessions, was not legally and financially in accord with the progress of diplomatic negotiations with Turkey as carried on by Allied statesmen. Such proposals and their larger ramifications were not, however, unique to Kenyon or England. A Professor Westermann, archaeological consultant to the U.S. delegation to Versailles, proposed a very similar system in March 1919 whereby "four persons, all of whom shall be trained archaeologists, [shall] be appointed by the Higher Council of Ten, representing the four powers, France, Italy, Great Britain and the United States."[60]

Archaeology as a complicated nexus between politics and scholarship, and a point of contention between diplomats and scholars, lay in the fact that ideologically, interests such as Kenyon's and the JAC's in organizing and legislating antiquities were directly in keeping with the purpose of the Mandates: a kinder, gentler "civilizing mission" in which the British maintained a kind of patrimonial trust for the nascent entities they were to bring along as nations in the modern world. The language with which Kenyon describes the JAC's efforts to advise the Foreign Office and Colonial Office about antiquities is similarly a declaration of the raison d'être of Mandate in the euphemistic language of appropriation, rehabilitation, development, and eminent domain:

> The antiquities of these lands are the inheritance of the whole civilized world. The Governments of the Associated Powers will assuredly not be going beyond the objects for which they have waged war, if they take measures to protect from further destruction not only the native populations of the lands that have suffered from Turkish oppression, but also the records of their past history. It is to be expected that, even in that portion of their former Empire which will remain in the hands of the Turks, there will be, as a consequence of the new conditions, an extensive economic revival. The development of the country, in itself so desirable, will involve increased danger to antiquities. Hitherto they have been allowed to fall into decay to be plundered by villagers or by military authorities for building purposes, to be destroyed in the course of building roads or railways, or, in the case of movable objects, to be exploited by dealers. Unless a properly administered law of antiquities can be brought into being, not only will these evils continue, the last two in increased measure; but in addition new settlements will spring up over sites which ought to be excavated first, and the cost of expropriation will render future excavations difficult or impossible.[61]

If Ronald Storrs's intervention at the Dome of the Rock was one means of grafting British ownership—and the narratives of history, competition, restoration, and economic development that went with it—onto Jerusalem and the Holy Land core, the interventions of Kenyon, the JAC, and the British Mandatory governments to overhaul the Ottoman antiquities law functioned in a similar way in and beyond that core. In terms of the fundamental issue of ownership, however, the British showed themselves willing to refer to the

Ottoman antiquities law when it suited them. Regarding the Lisbon Collection, which involved antiquities that Germany removed from Assur (Iraq, Mesopotamia) and that Portugal seized in port at the outbreak of the war, the British argued for their return to the "administration of Mesopotamia"—in other words, themselves under their own Mandate—based on the fact that exporting antiquities was illegal under the Ottoman statute.[62] As for antiquities that had been removed from the Ottoman Empire by enemy powers before the war, such as tiles from the Dome of the Rock and the façade of Qasr al-Mshatta, it was eventually determined that they were not subject to terms of the Versailles Treaty and would remain where they were.[63]

The JAC contended that Ottoman legislation actually encouraged the destruction of antiquities.[64] It alleged that the requirement subjecting landowners to prosecution if they did not report the finding of any antiquities on their property, and the unstated part of the law requiring that reporting be made at the expense of the owner, led people to destroy antiquities they found. Historian Jens Hanssen's account of the 1887 discovery of the Saida necropolis in Lebanon, however, in the context of which the landowner, the community, and the authorities worked well in tandem and within the law, challenges the universality of these claims.[65] The strict prohibition against exporting antiquities, the JAC argued further, increased their value for smugglers and also led to the destruction of artifacts' contexts. This could be remedied, suggested the JAC, by legislating a division of finds among the government, archaeologists, and anyone who might find antiquities. Such an arrangement would ensure that those who found antiquities were financially compensated while archaeologists were compensated with subjects for research.

This approach was characteristic of how the British Mandate governments legislated antiquities.[66] It had the appearance of "preserving . . . the records of their subjects' past history" while simultaneously guaranteeing the rights of Western archaeologists to "the inheritance of the whole civilised world," as Kenyon describes it in the quote above. Since the early twentieth century, European countries had drafted antiquities legislation guaranteeing that "all undiscovered antiquities of a movable character are the absolute property of the government."[67] The laws enacted by the British in their Middle Eastern governments, however, adhered to this paradigm in a particular way. Meeting nationalist resistance throughout the Middle East, most famously in Egypt, Palestine, and Iraq, and having reaped the benefits of the lack of enforcement of antiquities laws throughout the nineteenth century until World War I, the British were as interested in maintaining their own access to Middle Eastern cultural heritage as they were in administering it as a trust for their Mandatory subjects. Bernhardsson notes that a prohibition on the export of antiquities from India and Cyprus was met with absolute derision by Kenyon, who claimed that as the museum of the imperial capital, all the empire should be showcased at the British Museum, of which he was the director.[68] Antiquities legislation in Middle Eastern British possessions was thus ultimately not much different from that which governed concessions for industry and natural resources.[69]

Specific to antiquities and their institutionalization in the context of the Holy Land core, Kenyon and the JAC established, in 1919, the British School of Archaeology in Jerusalem (BSAJ), appointing Dr. John Garstang of the University of Liverpool as its director.[70] As a result of the peace negotiations, the care of antiquities was left to the governing powers and established the framework by which the Ottoman antiquities law was to be replaced.[71] Garstang, also serving as honorary adviser to the military authority, was thus largely responsible, at the behest of Herbert Samuel, British high commissioner for Palestine, for the formulation of the Palestine Antiquities Ordnance. This provided the framework for the Department of Antiquities of Palestine for the study and maintenance of Palestine's archaeological heritage, and for some kind of official sharing of responsibilities between the BSAJ and the department.[72] Some of the important points contained in the new legislation were as follows: an antiquity was deemed to be anything made before AD 1700 (automatically discounting more than two hundred years of Ottoman heritage); the director of antiquities was to be counseled by an international advisory board composed of a representative of the British, French, and American Schools, and an Italian, two Jews, and two Muslims appointed by the high commissioner (embedding the Mandate's taxonomy with international control over antiquity); all antiquities were the property of the government, but the excavator of any project had the right to a fair division and export of finds after the completeness of the museum's collection was assured; any object owned and still used by an ecclesiastical body was not an antiquity (enshrining discursive separation of taxonomies of heritage); anyone who found or reported the discovery of antiquities was entitled to compensation; as the governing body of historical sites, the care of antiquities sites could be entrusted by the Department of Antiquities to other entities; the sale and export of antiquities was legalized (inscribing the link between heritage and monetary value).[73] A few years later, this legislation would also serve as the basis for the establishment of the Department of Antiquities of Transjordan and control of that Mandate's antiquities.

While John Garstang may have successfully produced antiquities legislation with enduring elements, there was one issue over which he and Mandate officials would never agree. Throughout the mid-1920s, he repeatedly tried to convince High Commissioners Samuel and Plumer and Colonial Secretary Amery that the antiquities departments of Palestine and Transjordan should be separate entities with adequate numbers of personnel, and have bigger budgets and reserve funds from HMG's treasury partially paid by a tax levied on tourists to both countries.[74] While he ultimately lost the argument, the reserve fund was an important concept. Garstang proposed that at least a fraction of the revenue from tourism receipts be used to establish a fund to go directly into the budgets of the antiquities departments. If there were to be no revenues obtained from charging tourists admission to sites, he proposed a tax be levied at the point of tourists' entry to the countries. The high commissioner was against this idea, given the pilgrimage nature of much of this tourism.[75] Appeals to the responsibilities of Mandate, those of international tourists, and the potential embarrassment to Britain should tourist sites under their governance be found in a state of disrepair did not move colonial officials.[76] In their denials of his requests, they cited expense and lack of urgency for the agendas Garstang proposed. As it was, the antiquities departments didn't have a specific allotment from HMG's treasury, but were given small slices out of the general budget for Palestine and Transjordan that were in no way related to the amount of revenue drawn by antiquities.[77] If this exacerbated financial difficulties for the antiquity of the core, the situation was even worse for that of the periphery.

The Department of Antiquities on the Other Side of the River

The same perceptions of heritage, antiquities, and their role in British ownership of its Mandates governed their legal status in Transjordan. In the peripheral space, however, British interventions into heritage lagged behind those in Palestine or were missing altogether. The various treaties and policies resulting from the war legalized and institutionalized Transjordan's dependent but peripheral relationship with Palestine in a way that reflected the scientific realization of the Holy Land prior to the war. From 1921 until 1946, Transjordan was intimately tied to Palestine's Mandate government. The arrangement initially assigned a chief British resident to Amman who reported to the high commissioner in Jerusalem. At that time, the Palestine and Transjordan budgets were calculated separately, Transjordan receiving a grant-in-aid from HMG's treasury, and each government was responsible for its own expenses. As of spring 1924 and in the midst of a tense showdown between Emir Abdullah and the British over Transjordan's governance, however, the treasury canceled the grant-in-aid, to the extreme financial detriment of the emirate and at the expense of what little independence it had, either from the Palestine Mandate government or Whitehall.[78] To the detriment of Transjordan, of course, both budgets henceforth came out of the same treasury allotment for Palestine, and Transjordan's finances were vetted by the officials in Jerusalem.[79] This was to have serious ramifications for antiquities, given Britain's secondary interest in Transjordan vis-à-vis Palestine and Jerusalem, which was, in the first place, derived of the secondary interest in its heritage.

In May 1923, two years after his Jerusalem meeting with Churchill and in the midst of a tumultuous period of early state formation, Emir Abdullah signed an accord with His Majesty's Government that essentially recognized Transjordan's statehood and promised its eventual independence. After a trip to Jerusalem that year during which he was privy to the work of the Department of Antiquities of Palestine, the emir wanted to establish the Department of Antiquities for Transjordan.[80] The law constituting the Department of Antiquities was issued in 1923 and the first antiquities law was passed in 1924, the same year the British began to consolidate authority in the emirate through the development and control of institutions.[81] One of the emir's first acts was to have Amman's Roman Theatre cleared for use and guards posted to protect Jerash.[82] The emir also ordered the leveling of a wall of a Byzantine basilica to make way for Amman's first congregational mosque, the al-Husseini Mosque, which still stands in *Wust al-Balad*. The British resident in Amman, Harry St. John Bridger Philby, was dead-set against what he saw as destruction of antiquities.[83] The emir called on the religious status of the building in progress and its importance to Muslims in protest against Philby's interference.[84] This final row in 1924 between Philby and Emir Abdullah—over an antiquities site—is legendary. It was the end of a bad relationship based on differing visions of governance between the emir and the chief resident, and Philby gladly left for more lucrative pastures with Ibn Saʿud in Arabia.

The falling-out, over the destruction of a Byzantine church, drove the high commissioner in Jerusalem to seek the advice of John Garstang, still director of the British School of Archaeology in Jerusalem and part-time director of the Palestine Department of Antiquities. Despite a tiny, inadequate budget and all the responsibilities for Transjordan falling on the shoulders of Garstang's own staff in Palestine, they provided some security and consolidation for sites that had represented Jordan's heritage for nineteenth-century explorers—Jerash, Amman's Roman Theatre, and Kerak Castle. Jerash was actually the first location for the department's offices. George Horsfield acted as Transjordan's chief inspector. Garstang and Horsfield initially worked in Jordan with Rida Tawfiq Bey, a distinguished, Ottoman-era philosopher whom the emir appointed as the administrative head of his antiquities department. That department passed antiquities ordinances in 1924 and 1925 that recalled certain aspects of the old Ottoman laws and incorporated parts of the new laws adopted in Mandatory Palestine. All local headmen throughout Transjordan were to look after the antiquities in their regions and report any damage or abuse, including the removal of architectural elements, to the government in Amman. Anyone who found antiquities was to report to the government within one week; the government was ultimately responsible for finding and protecting antiquities and enforcing the new laws.[85] Under the laws, an antiquity was defined as "any structure or any art object made by human effort before the year 1700."[86] This replicated the definition of antiquity as established in the Antiquities Ordinance that Garstang had written for Palestine, leaving more than two hundred years of Arab Ottoman heritage devoid of legal protection or consideration.

When Ma'an and its environs became a district of Transjordan in 1925, coveted Petra, one of the few spaces of Jordan's heritage that nineteenth-century explorers had promoted, finally fell under the jurisdiction of the emir's fledgling antiquities department.[87] Developing a tourist industry for Petra, originally Philby's collaboration with the American Express Company, became another of the department's projects.[88] Garstang and Horsfield were able to work there, while Jerusalem physician Tawfiq Canaan, an ethnographer and member of both the Palestine Oriental Society and the Pro-Jerusalem Society, undertook the kind of study he normally completed on the other side of the river, publishing *Notes on Studies in the Topography and Folklore of Petra* in 1930 (see further discussion in chapter 5).[89] Between the late 1920s and the Second World War, archaeological work also began at places that were known well or hardly at all: Ajloun Castle, the tomb of the Prophet's Companion at Mazar near Mu'ta, Mount Nebo, and Teleilat al-Ghassul. Multinational projects at Jerash and Kerak Castle continued.[90]

While the organization of the Mandates tethered Transjordan to Palestine until its independence in 1946, Transjordan's Department of Antiquities gained independence from Palestine's in 1928.[91] Garstang had resigned in 1927, likely over his frustrated attempts to convince colonial administrators that he needed a budget commensurate with the revenues that antiquities brought to the treasury.[92] The unknown author of a colonial office memo detailing the situation writes, "Generally it seems to have been a case of the scholar and archaeologist finding himself unable to cope with the ordinary ways of bureaucracy, and apparently without the ability to get either Lord Plumer or Colonel Symes to appreciate his difficulties and ease his position." Ernest Richmond, restorer of the tiles of the Dome of the Rock, assumed the post. The likely catalyst for the individualization of the two departments and their finances was the reorganization of the Palestine Department of Antiquities in preparation for the establishment of the Palestine Archaeological Museum with an endowment from John D. Rockefeller.[93]

George Horsfield became chief inspector of antiquities for the newly independent department in Transjordan, and Rida Tawfiq moved the departmental offices from Jerash to Amman's Roman Theatre, centralizing government control over antiquities in the capital.[94] An Italian excavation at the Amman Citadel (1927–30) may have been the first foreign, nondepartmental team granted a permit to excavate in Transjordan. In recognition of the event, Chief British Resident Henry Cox (Philby's replacement), Prime Minister Hasan Khalid Abu al-Huda, an unnamed head of the Department of Antiquities, the Catholic parish priest, and the director of Amman's Italian Hospital received the team. Emir Abdullah himself visited the dig and invited the team to dinner.[95] A team from Yale working at Jerash in conjunction with the British School of Archaeology in Jerusalem followed the Italians a year later. Foreign teams have been excavating in Jordan ever since.

The Italian team's work, however, indicates much about the dominant paradigm that would carry into the 1930s for understanding Jordan's very ancient archaeology. "We were therefore in presence of the sacred rock of the Ammonites," wrote excavator Renato Bartoccini, "the oldest place of worship of that warlike people, against whom the army of David, inured to war, had to struggle for three years."[96] Regarding the same site and the Italians' work there, "it seemed to be without doubt that the fortified city—under whose walls, by the will of King David, was slain the General Uriah, husband of Bathsheba—would be found in this, the highest part of the third terrace of the Acropolis of Amman."[97] This formulation is quite different from the stories of landscape and locals' personal connections to it described in the pages of author Abd al-Rahman Munif's autobiography of his boyhood, spent in Jordan's capital city in these early decades, or as related by those trying to involve marginalized local communities in sustaining cultural heritage today. It is not, however, locals' connections that form the basis of the antiquity narrative of the site, nor of downtown Amman more generally.[98]

Nelson Glueck and the Other Side of the Jordan

An ambitious young American rabbi named Nelson Glueck revolutionized archaeology in Transjordan in the 1930s.[99] Yigael Yadin, Israeli archaeologist, war hero, and antiquities collector, eulogized Glueck thus:

He was a Jewish Victorian type—strange and unique. He was romantic, even a little childish. He was entranced by the magic of his people's past. The moving force in his life was his faith in the God of his fathers and the history of his people. He wandered to and fro in the desert, not like Lawrence, who was blinded by the oriental charm of the Bedouin, but rather like one who viewed the Bedouins as Abraham, Isaac and Jacob, still wandering about the face of the land.[100]

Yadin's memorial swipes at T. E. Lawrence, remembered as a figure sympathetic to Arab causes, and British colonialism more generally, by arguing that Glueck's Jewish faith authenticated his encounter with the Holy Land in ways that British Protestant experiences of it could not. It was exactly this kind of temporal disambiguation and conjunction of progress and faith, however, by which British and other explorers understood the landscape and people they encountered, and gave form to a Holy Land with a core in Palestine rooted in the origins of Judaism. Both Yadin and Glueck had worked to Judaize that core by means of its archaeology. Before Glueck helped shape the character of the core from within, however, he spent his early career contributing to its narrative by devising one for its periphery. Glueck's early scholarship enhanced the narrative of the core by creating knowledge to reinforce Transjordan's status as a non-Jewish periphery. His archaeological approach to the eastern side of the river thus mirrored the political framework of the nation-state paradigm.

Nelson Glueck was intimately shaped by the influence of Reform Judaism—for which he would become one of the leading twentieth-century figureheads—and his belief in the scientific pursuit of biblical studies.[101] To this end, he left his hometown of Cincinnati to pursue a prestigious German PhD and then went to study with William Foxwell Albright in Jerusalem. Albright, then head of the American School in Jerusalem, is remembered as the father of American biblical archaeology and as a scholar who, like his American counterparts, took seriously both scientific excavation and the historicity of the Bible. The professional path that had led him to Palestine was not all that different from Glueck's. Having grown up in a proselytizing Methodist environment in the American Midwest, Albright undertook biblical studies in the German tradition at Johns Hopkins University. Sources disagree as to whether it was going to Palestine that made him believe in the accuracy of the Old Testament, or whether at a young age he decided, as the American Congregationalist scholar Edward Robinson had several decades before, to infiltrate the world of German biblical criticism to use it in the service of a belief he had never forsaken.[102] Albright and Glueck thus shared the intellectual tradition of their profession and American midwestern roots, but what may have drawn Glueck to his archaeological mentor and his mentor's faith in biblical historicity was a shared sense of personal connection to the land of Palestine.[103]

It isn't clear why Albright and Glueck decided to focus on Transjordan, although Glueck's biographers suggest that they may have thought Jerusalem too crowded with excavations or the environment too tense given the political strife of the late 1920s.[104] After some early explorations, in 1929 Glueck addressed the annual meeting of the Central Conference of American Rabbis (CCAR), which adopted a resolution to support Hebrew Union College's (HUC) participation in excavating a Jewish historical site in Palestine. HUC was the intellectual bastion of the Reform Judaism movement, and enthusiasm for archaeology as the scientific study of the past must be understood in this context. The same emphasis on science and intellectualism that was a hallmark of nineteenth-century Protestantism was likewise a characteristic of Reform Judaism, and Glueck invoked the PEF, its broad program of exploration and study, and its Survey of Western Palestine in seeking the community's support.[105]

Glueck's survey of Transjordan was the first full-fledged archaeological survey of such magnitude east of the Jordan River. While survey was the method of the earliest explorations of the Holy Land in the nineteenth century, Albright and Glueck had brought it into the twentieth. Nearly thirty years had passed since Flinders Petrie's excavation revolution at Tell el-Hesi (originally believed to have been biblical Lachish), when he linked pottery types to particular phases of the site's stratigraphy. Based on his excavations at Tell Beit Mirsim (which he identified as biblical Debir, an identification now rejected), at which Glueck participated, Albright was able to construct a comprehensive pottery chronology for Palestine. By means of this chronology, however, Albright linked pottery types with ethnicity, itself a modern contrivance. While his chronology, especially its divisions of periodization and the insistence upon linking particular pottery types with specific ethnicities, has undergone a substantial amount of tweaking in the past eighty years, in many respects it remains intact and is still the first point of reference for reading pottery at Palestinian archaeological sites. Using a combination of his pottery chronology and observation of landscape features, Albright identified sites in the landscape and categorized them into chronological periods.

This is the method with which Nelson Glueck, who had replaced Albright as head of the American School in Jerusalem, undertook his work in Transjordan in late 1932. He applied a broad definition of biblical archaeology that, on its surface, seemed revolutionary, encompassing the prehistoric through the historical epochs of all the biblical lands.[106] He set out "intending to locate as many biblical sites as possible east of the Jordan River, to define the boundaries of the ancient kingdoms of Edom and Moab, and to gather information on other strata of settlement."[107] Glueck covered an extensive amount of ground in three seasons and was the first archaeologist to visit a great many sites, publishing prolifically on landscape features, pottery, and his analyses of what these suggested about the history of Transjordan's ancient peoples in light of biblical texts. He covered the landscape of Transjordan in a way that could never have been imagined by the proponents of the Eastern Survey in the late nineteenth century. Glueck's primary conclusions concerned Transjordan's ancient, enigmatic peoples—the Moabites, the Edomites, and the later Nabateans.

Glueck and Gerald Lankester Harding, the British first director of the Department of Antiquities of Transjordan, revolutionized the scholarly understanding of the Nabateans when they excavated the Nabatean temple below Khirbet al-Tannur, a black volcanic mountain that rises above Wadi al-Hasa just south of the border between Moab and Edom, in what today lies between the central and southern parts of Jordan.[108] While a synthetic understanding of Nabatean civilization remains largely absent to this day, in the 1930s it was hardly a blip on the archaeological radar. Harding's and Glueck's work was the first major excavation of a site with Nabatean levels, or at least the first recognized as such. What Glueck really introduced to Nabatean studies was an appreciation of the complexity of the Nabatean spiritual world, and the framing of their religion and religious practice within the broader framework of Semitic religions. Glueck biographers Jonathan M. Brown and Laurence Kutler write, "In its austere isolation, it [Khirbet al-Tannur] is comparable to Mt. Sinai, where the freed Hebrew slaves in the Exodus narrative encountered their God. Glueck noted that both sacred sites shared the qualities of remoteness and desert locale, thus investing them with a spiritual dimension, given that the Semitic concept of holiness involves a spatial separation from everyday life."[109] Glueck saw the similarities between Khirbet al-Tannur, which had a central sanctuary containing a carved altar, and other Nabatean shrines throughout Transjordan and eventually the Negev. He drew further parallels between these kinds of shrines, the Dome of the Rock in Jerusalem, and the Ka'aba in Mecca.[110] Glueck published his synthesis of Nabatean archaeology and culture in a popular book, *Deities and Dolphins*.[111]

Long before Nabatean civilization left its imprint on the landscape, the central and southern highlands of Transjordan—the biblical lands of Ammon, Moab, and Edom—teemed with life. Nelson Glueck was the first archaeologist to offer any elucidation of the material culture of these people, which he always related to the biblical narrative. His conclusions dealt mainly with cycles of settlement and desertion, civilization and lack thereof, and the first pillar of his synthesis went so far as to intimately relate the material culture and history of the Bronze Age with the personal lives of the biblical patriarchs. According to Glueck, sedentary civilization heavily settled Ammon, Moab, and Edom in the Early Bronze Age (3300–2300 BCE), and deserted them in what he called the Middle Bronze Age (2000–1550 BCE), during which time primarily nomadic civilizations thus inhabited them. Glueck attributed the desertion to the destruction of Sodom and Gomorrah as related in the Book of Genesis. These lands were similarly settled again early in the Iron Age (1200–550 BCE), which buttressed his argument for what is considered a "late date" for the Exodus and the Israelite conquest of Canaan as described in the Book of Exodus.[112] According to Glueck, the land was deserted again until about the fourth century BCE, when the Nabateans appear on the scene.

The second part of his paradigm for understanding the biblical lands east of the River Jordan was that the cycles of settlement and nomadism he observed in the landscape were due to political and socioeconomic, not climatic, factors. In such a formulation, nomadic populations naturally had a negative impact on sedentary civilization. The final part of his formulation dealt specifically with the Moabite and Edomite peoples of the Iron Age. He maintained that they existed simultaneously with each other, had a shared culture, and, to a degree, shared destinies. Despite the clear problems in his methodology, Glueck was the first to give agency to these peoples, demonstrating through his survey work that theirs were high civilizations, on equal footing with their Israelite and Judahite contemporaries, at least in most respects.

In the latest edition of his popular book *The Other Side of the Jordan*, published a year before his death in 1971, Glueck observes:

> Despite all the growth and change in manner and custom and culture among the Arabs in Transjordan and particularly in Palestine today, there is one group which shows less change than any other in this part of the world. That group is composed of the Bedouins, particularly those who tent and wander in the desert . . . the nomads of greater Arabia are but little different today from their predecessors hundreds and thousands of years ago. Always they are hungry, and unceasingly they cast longing eyes upon lands which to them are lands flowing with milk and honey.[113]

Such a sentiment, much like Yadin's description of Glueck's worldview, offers a contradictory and troubling window onto Glueck's essentialist paradigm of Jordan's history and archaeology. On the one hand, he equates the biblical patriarchs to contemporary nomads, but on the other highlights nomads as the degrading force upon settled civilizations throughout Jordan's history. It bears striking resemblance to that of early Western experience in the Holy Land and narratives of Arab spaces, particularly frontiers such as Transjordan, constructed at the Ottoman imperial center, with the added scientifically based nuance that the local inhabitants have *always* been responsible for cycles of destruction and habitation. This is not a role reserved for contemporary peoples in need of redemption, but, much like genetics, is in their very nature.

Glueck's paradigm is more troubling in consideration of the general state of affairs and tensions in the Mandates when he was conducting his work in the 1930s. Particular to Transjordan, a number of its relatively small population were to some extent nomadic, and these people, the ubiquitous "bedouin," were co-opted and cultivated, often under conditions of life-threatening economic and physical insecurity, by the British and the Hashemites to produce a particular character and reality for the Transjordanian state in terms of its borders, its governance, its security apparatus, and its symbolic recognizability.[114] As Glueck surveyed the landscape, Transjordan's nomadic and seminomadic populations struggled for their subsistence under the imposition of borders and definitions of citizenship, their situation made worse by an extended period of drought. Such great suffering compelled the British and Hashemites to act; much as the Ottomans had by means of the Tribal School, Transjordan's leadership would incorporate this social welfare into a broader discourse of development, modernity, and patrimony. Through their inclusion in martial and other institutions of state, the "bedouin" and their heritage would eventually come to represent Jordan in narratives for those at home and abroad.

In a final troubling twist to Glueck's narrative, while he had indeed given agency to the ancient civilizations that had graced Jordanian soil—the Ammonites, Moabites, and Edomites—he rendered them distinctively unequal in comparison with the peoples on the western side of the river. In the introduction to his 1971 *festschrift*, Glueck is quoted describing the Ammonites, Moabites, and Edomites thus: "They spoke the same language as the Judeans, perhaps with a slightly different accent; they used the same kind of script; they built the same kind of buildings; they wore the same kind of clothes; and they fashioned the same kind of pottery. Yet," he emphasizes, "they disappeared, while the Jewish people, physical and spiritual descendants of their Judean contemporaries, lived on to transmit the perennial tradition of Jewish religion."[115] In *The Other Side of the Jordan*, Glueck ponders the "disappearance" of the transjordanian Iron Age peoples and the "genius" in the enduring

Abrahamic monotheism of a small minority of their cisjordanian contemporaries.[116] While he leaves the reader to wonder if this was by the will of God or an accident of history, there can be little doubt as to how Glueck might have answered that question. Western observers had easily answered that question for themselves decades earlier through their scientific realization of the Holy Land. Glueck had taken it a step further, devising a comprehensive archaeological narrative that Transjordan had previously lacked and that supported the creation of an Arab state in the Holy Land periphery, which, throughout history, resembled what it was supposed to be in modern times. It was the foil for the Jewish state that was under restoration in the Holy Land core.

Before leaving his explorations of Transjordan's archaeology behind in the late 1930s, Glueck had already turned his scholarly attention to narratives of the core itself. He excavated for multiple seasons at Tell el-Khelifeh, now in Aqaba, Jordan, and against the border with Eilat, Israel. The findings convinced him that he had found King Solomon's port of Ezion-Geber.[117] He equated the nearby copper mines of Timnah, today in Israel, with the legendary mines of King Solomon, and the American press widely published stories about the project.[118] While the relationships of Tell el-Khelifeh and Timnah to King Solomon have since been successfully challenged, and there remains to this day no physical evidence of either a king of Israel and Judah or a man named Solomon, the idea that somewhere in or between Aqaba and Eilat lies Solomon's port city remains, as in the old tourist books quoted at the beginning of this chapter, a popular story.[119]

Glueck never again worked in Jordan, turning his scholarly interests in new ways to affect narratives of current events. He even graced the cover of *Time* magazine on 13 December 1963, under the banner, "The Search for Man's Past." Not only had he created narratives, he clearly had the ability to disseminate them in ways that mattered. Glueck volunteered for service during World War II in the North African, Middle Eastern, and Arabian theaters, during which he was an undercover intelligence officer with the Office of Strategic Services (OSS, forerunner of the CIA) posing as an archaeologist—much like Lawrence and Woolley had on the Wilderness of Zin Survey—and during a period in which all archaeological exploration had ceased.[120] Later he gave the benediction at President Kennedy's inauguration. He would guide Hebrew Union College's new archaeological institute in Jerusalem through the 1967 war. He had long since been a publicly active Zionist, taking part in organizations, lectures, popular and academic publishing, and fieldwork that helped enhance the connections between the modern State of Israel and the world of the Jews of the Hebrew Bible.[121]

Many narratives that Glueck enabled with his scholarship have endured in whole or in part—the complicated symbolism of "bedouin" and archaeological precedents for the states of Jordan and Israel, for instance—even if his methodology and paradigms have been successfully challenged. Many decades have passed since his Transjordan surveys, and until today archaeological projects in Jordan still begin with reference to Glueck's surveys, as he was the first to identify many Jordanian sites. Many of his conclusions have been revised, however, owing to more recent and extensive archaeological fieldwork and general advances in the field.

Most significantly in Jordan, scholars have challenged two primary aspects of Glueck's synthesis: that archaeological evidence can be linked to divisions understood by reading the Bible, and that the archaeological record was substantively different on the eastern side of the river than on the western side. Writing in 1986, James Sauer was the first to undertake, in writing, a comprehensive, critical evaluation of Glueck's analyses of the archaeological record of ancient Jordan.[122] Sauer was, in the first place, critical of the role of the Bible as applied to archaeological analysis.[123] For Sauer, the Bible can be understood only hermeneutically, and represents just one small part of the biblical world from the perspective of one small group of its peoples. No archaeological evidence can link the "Patriarchal Period" to the Bronze Age, as the patriarchal stories were compiled and edited many hundreds of years after the fact. Sauer argues that Glueck's linkage of archaeological evidence to events in the Bible, even in later periods when biblical texts might be considered more contemporary, must be carefully assessed. Subsequent fieldwork showed that Jordan was not, in fact, completely devoid of settlement in the Middle and Late Bronze Ages. Sauer writes that Jordan's archaeological record, in fact, fits squarely within the lively context of the rest of the Levantine biblical world during those periods, no more or less part of a much larger *corpus* of people and events that has no relationship to modern political borders.[124]

Nor was there, argues Sauer, a gap in Jordan's habitation in the Late Iron Age. Glueck presumed that when the Neo-Babylonians destroyed Judah and took the elite among its population into exile in 586 BCE, the Transjordanian kingdoms of Ammon, Moab, and Edom had suffered a similar fate. In fact, says Sauer, the archaeological evidence suggests that they seem to have prospered. Biblical and extra-biblical sources written during this period would thus naturally portray these peoples in a negative light; they thrived while their neighbors suffered through destruction and exile.[125] Glueck's analyses might leave us to wonder if the "disappearance" of Ammonite, Moabite, and Edomite culture, as he believed himself to have observed it and as related in the Bible, was the divine price these peoples east of the River Jordan paid for prospering from the Israelites' pain.[126] There is little room for alternative

popular narratives, however, when scholarly narratives of the past are enshrined in law and nation-state.

Archaeology in the Service of Self-Determination

In this chapter, I have considered the ways in which British ownership of antiquities, heritage, and their narratives served larger narratives of both the
legitimacy of the postwar geopolitical order and Britain's role in it. The end of
the Ottoman order was supposed to usher in an order of self-determination,
and Arabs, now subjects of a euphemistic colonialism on a detour with a positivist end somewhere in the future, also claimed ownership of their heritage
and its narratives. Such narratives depended on people's personal sense of
connection to antiquity and landscape articulated as historical consciousness,
as described in the previous chapter. During the interwar period, however,
Arab intellectuals drew on the Western scholarship they had embraced prior
to the war to articulate those narratives anew, challenging the impositions of
the Mandates and justifying their right to self-determined nationhood.

At the outbreak of World War I, an anonymous call from Cairo for Arab
secession from the Ottoman Empire was addressed to the "Sons of Qahtan,"
meaning the Arabs. This was not a mainstream position, but its language is
important for its merging of historical consciousness and political goals, and
a secret society of the prewar era composed of intellectuals and officers had
named itself similarly.[127] Recall that Qahtan, progenitor of all the southern
Arabs, is the descendant of Shem, progenitor of all the Semites, whose descendant married Isma'il/Ishmael, son of Abraham, from whom was born
Adnan, the link between the northern and southern Arabs. Hashim, progenitor of the Hashemites, is descended of the northern Arabs (those of Isma'il's
line) by patriline, and is shown in canonized genealogy to have married a
woman outside of that patriline—and from that of the southern Arabs (those
of the ancestor Qahtan's line, known in the Bible as Joktan, son of Shem
and grandson of Noah). As Daniel Varisco notes, this "internationalizes" the
Prophet Muhammad's (and the Quraysh tribe's) lineages, linking the two
branches of Arabs as delineated according to mythic ancestors.[128]

After the war, Arabs went to work realizing the institutions of the new
states in which they found themselves living. Many intellectuals were, however, thinking and writing another nation, an ancient Arab nation that surpassed those newly imposed borders and Arab-ized the landscape and its
peoples from remotest antiquity. In chapter 3, I argue that before the war, the
intellectual and literary *nahda* and self-reflective Arab and Islamic modern-

ism considered the past and present social condition and used new paradigms of knowledge to articulate what had previously been an unquestioned sacrality of heritage. After the war, intellectuals added an ethnolinguistic positivism rooted in the kinds of archaeological and philological research seen in the pages of such popular journals as *al-Muqtataf*. C. Ernest Dawn's general observations about the writing of history in this period are helpful here:

> The Arab nation, the culmination and heir of the Semites, established its rights to the national territories. This achievement was not accomplished without meeting the aggressions of determined enemies. Throughout history, other peoples, Aryans and Turco-Mongols, had intruded into the Semito-Arab homeland. The common view of Semito-Arab history implicitly divided it into two periods of greatness, the ancient Semitic and the Islamic, each followed by two periods of decline in which the alien dominated.[129]

This narrative drew upon the confluence of the archaeological sciences that were the purview of the West, but enabling the Arab articulators of emergent *wataniyya* to produce meta-narratives that "Arab-ized" virtually all of the ancient peoples who had roamed the pre-modern Arab world—Hebrews included—finding their origins in various waves of Arab Semites who emerged from the Arabian Peninsula.[130] In this framework, *wataniyya* was a nationalism linked to a broad physical territory beyond nation-state borders that offered an identity narrative to all ancient and modern Arabs who had lived within it.

As the shape of the post–First World War order emerged, Arab intellectuals consolidated and promoted earlier strands of intellectual inquiry into the Arabs' ancient past, writing in both Arabic and English to help articulate *wataniyya* and combat colonialism, with an emphasis on combating Zionism. Deploying the ancient past for this purpose required a formulation of the ancient landscape of the modern Arab world, its history, and its monuments that was primordially Arab. Such a formulation had to fulfill three further goals: first, demonstrate a shared ethnicity for all Arabs; second, demonstrate that an ancient Arab nation or nations existed before that of an ancient Jewish nation; and third, account for the shared ethnolinguistic, religious, and historical connections between Arabs and Jews and the diversity of Arabs. Denial of Muslim and Jewish history was difficult, for denial of Jewish history equaled denial of Muslim and Christian history.[131] Devising an appropriate narrative of ancient history thus required an Arab framework that fit the contemporary geopolitical context, a solution that would be found in an Arab-centric, pan-Semitic narrative with the etiological and teleological possibilities described by Dawn.[132] In the years immediately after the Great War, in school textbooks that were produced in major urban centers and used all over the Arab world, in history and travel books, in poetry and allegory, in the press and popular journals such as *al-Muqtataf*, Arab writers promoted the synthesis of ideas that emerged in the late nineteenth century, a paradigm by which all Semitic peoples came in waves out of the Arabian Peninsula to populate the space of the contemporary Arab *watan*, giving rise to the panoply of ancient Middle Eastern civilizations.[133] The Hebrews are among these Semitic Arab peoples, who were preceded by their Semitic Arab cousins in Palestine, the Canaanites.

This formulation of pan-Semitic historical consciousness was internationalized in no small way by *Ancient Times*, the textbook written by American Orientalist James Henry Breasted of the University of Chicago's Oriental Institute, first published in English in 1916.[134] Breasted contended that Arabia was the ancestral home of all the Semites, who, throughout history, have given up their original bedouin ways of life and developed successive urban-based civilizations throughout the Middle East. The rough-hewn Hebrew nomads, he claimed, wandered over time out of Arabia into the urban Palestinian society built by the Semitic Canaanites, who had earlier wandered out of Arabia to settle Palestine. Upon seeing the comfortable and prosperous urban life that the Canaanites had created, the Hebrews, Breasted says, adopted Canaanite civilization as their own.[135]

Speaking about ancient peoples as Arab Semites was nothing new. German scholars in particular were doing so at least as early as the 1860s, based on philological evidence from which, when considered together with alleged sociocultural and physical characteristics of the peoples who used them, was contrived the Semitic race. Crucial to these "racial characteristics," writes George Barton, describing the work of A. H. Sayce, is the fact that a large chunk of the Arabian Peninsula is a desert: "Intensity of faith, ferocity, exclusiveness, imagination—can best be explained, [Sayce] thinks, by a desert origin."[136] This adds a second, important component to the origin narrative of the Arab Semites derived in the West. The word *'arab* appears to have originally described a lifestyle—nomadic pastoralism—to which the desert is crucial, although unlike notions of the earlier "Amorites" in the texts of Mesopotamian urbanites described in the previous chapter, there is speculation that this may have been what the *'arab* called themselves.[137] The bedouin lifestyle that travelers such as Johann Burkhardt and Charles Doughty described bore a striking resemblance to the lifestyle of the patriarchs and peoples of the Hebrew Bible, an idea seen clearly in the thought of scholars such as Nelson Glueck.[138] In the late Ottoman context, it resembled that of the community to which God made his revelation through Muhammad. That the origin of the stories of the biblical patriarchs should therefore be sought in the Semites of the Arabian Peninsula was an idea whose proponents included Julius Wellhausen, the recognized father of biblical criticism.[139]

The inherent characteristics of desert dwellers of the Arabian Peninsula provide a third aspect of the narrative. Much as Ibn Khaldun describes and Glueck and others saw in the landscape, society exists in cycles by which nomads become settled, settlements grow, the remaining nomads are squeezed out, and in this way, nomads move farther and farther from the center of the land of their origins to settle places far afield.[140] This is how it became vogue to imagine Semitic Wave Theory—Arabs emerging from the Arabian Peninsula throughout history to settle the lands of the contemporary Arab world, among them Canaanites, and later Hebrews and so many others. In publishing his comprehensive synthesis intentionally as a school textbook at the same time that post-Ottoman borders began to materialize, and in Arab-izing both the Canaanites and the Hebrews within a broader, widely accepted ethnic origin narrative, Breasted offered postwar Arab intellectuals a pan-national narrative with roots in Palestine that predated, and thus countered, the narrative of ancient history deployed by the Zionist movement.[141]

These ideas took on revolutionary nuances given the new colonial and nation-state realities after the war. In 1919 Muhibb al-Din al-Khatib, a prolific essayist and textbook writer, published a synthesis of the Semitic Wave Theory in a Damascus newspaper.[142] In 1920, an editorial in the Palestinian newspaper *al-Quds al-Sharif* espouses the Canaanites-Hebrews narrative in the context of developing relations between the Zionist movement and Palestinians in Jerusalem, differentiating between Palestinian Jews, who were considered part of the community, and European Jews, who were considered outsiders.[143] By 1923, ʿUmar Salih al-Barghouthi and Khalil Tutah had published the first of what would be many editions of their textbook, *Tarikh Filastin* (The History of Palestine), which was used for many decades in classrooms throughout the Arab world.[144] Al-Barghouthi and Tutah provide a detailed account of Jewish history based on Muslim, Jewish, and Christian sources, all within the framework of a detailed pan-Semitic narrative of shared origins.[145] They were also part of what Salim Tamari has called a "circle" of ethnographers, in which the major figure was the Jerusalem medical doctor Tawfiq Canaan, who wrote in English for the *Journal of the Palestine Oriental Society* (*JPOS*) from its inception in 1920 until the mid-1930s. Canaan and the other Arab members of this "circle" recorded native Palestinian culture and peasantry out of a belief that they were under threat and that they represented "—through their folk norms and material artifacts—the living heritage of all the accumulated ancient cultures that appeared in Palestine (principally the Canaanite, Philistine, Hebraic, Nabatean, Syrio-Aramaic, and Arab)."[146]

122 Competitive Archaeology in Jordan

Canaan's work specifically linked folk and religious traditions to landscape and all of its components, such as water, fauna, home, and monument.[147] Much like his contemporary, Palestinian intellectual, activist, and civil servant 'Arif al-'Arif (who would spend much of his career in service to Jordan, including as mayor of Jerusalem), Canaan's ethnographic research included localized studies of both fellahin and bedouin.[148] Another member of the *JPOS* circle, Stephan Hanna Stephan—Mandate civil servant, archaeologist, and curator of the first Palestine Museum—worked extensively with literary and oral tradition, comparing, for instance, contemporary Palestinian folk songs about love and sex to the Song of Songs in the Hebrew Bible.[149]

As for Breasted's textbook, its earliest Arabic edition, al-'Usur al-Qadima (Ancient Times), was published in Beirut in 1926, from which it was disseminated for decades in the Arab world, Arab writers frequently referencing it or quoting it directly.[150] Among those to write about history and antiquity in this idiom, Palestinian writers Muhammad Darwaza (1887-1984) and Darwish al-Miqdadi (1898-1961) were among the leading authors of textbooks, publishing between the late 1920s and the late 1930s seminal volumes that would be used widely in schools throughout the Arab world and in multiple editions.[151] Their books drew upon all available antiquity narratives, and in ways that enabled various and fluid national and pan-national discourses.

It should not appear paradoxical that the literatures of nationalism, anti-imperialist and anti-Zionist at their core, would present narratives to their own audience within the framework produced by Western scholarship. Such scholarship, its emphasis on classification and existing in its codependency with Western strategic interests, ultimately aided and abetted the delineation of unnatural postwar national boundaries. The maps, surveys, and knowledge Europeans devised in this context were those with which they entered the war, and those that would determine strategy. While seeing the result—a nation-state system grafted upon the discourse of "nation" that had very different territorial understandings of itself and its constituent parts—as a process may be inescapable in hindsight, there would have been little reason, either for Arabs or Europeans, to have fully anticipated the outcome prior to the cataclysm of the Great War.

As their encounters with the West developed over the course of the nineteenth century, educated Arabs enthusiastically engaged in the discourses of new knowledge that those encounters presented them. Much of that knowledge was produced within the rubric of scientific method and the classification and definition of things and people. At the very least, educated Arabs were active in learning about their past and were open to Western approaches to it, and easily enveloped Western approaches into the broader *nahda*. For those within the context of the literary and cultural continuum of Islamicate civilization, it was not too great a leap for such Western approaches to work in tandem with Arab and Muslim paradigms for understanding the continuum of ancient history. From the Exodus to cycles of nomadism and settled agriculturalism, the archaeological, philological, and linguistic sciences were compatible with Abrahamic scriptures, associated literatures, and oral traditions in their many languages. Flinders Petrie's synthesis of the life of the Beni Israel in Egypt, cited in the pages of *al-Muqtataf*, ultimately challenged no belief, and Orientalists' Semitic Wave Theory had much in common with Ibn Khaldun's *al-Muqaddima*.[152] If Western scholars such as Nelson Glueck wanted to see biblical patriarchs in the bedouin, and Zionists of Jerusalem's Bezalel School of Arts and Crafts wanted to paint, sculpt, and draw the biblical figures they claimed as their own forebears as Arabs and bedouin in an idiom of nationalist production, Arab intellectuals and nationalists could make such paradigms work for their interests, too.[153] In this way, scholars such as Tawfiq Canaan could render Palestine's fellahin a locus of the record of Arab civilization on its landscape.

The point is that archaeology may have been mired in the essentialism of mainstream Western intellectualism, but given its compatibility with non-essentialist "native" history and non-essentializable understandings of identities, they didn't necessarily carry such a message for an Arab audience until it was clear that they would be used as justification for modern geopolitical ends. If acceptance and gratitude for European research as seen in the pages of *al-Muqtataf* discussed in the previous chapter seems naïve, the simultaneous acknowledgment that no Arabs were engaged in these endeavors does hint at reservations, as did the Ottomans' selective curtailment of European archaeological activities in their territories in the empire's final decades. The British occupation of Palestine, the entire Mandate system, and the dependence on native figureheads to maintain that system had certainly shown those earlier reservations to have merit, and as the dust settled, clearly there was recognition that archaeology was a serious piece of a much larger colonial project. Antiquity as evidence of new geographic realities was a vital component of the nation-state. Demonstrating the perennial nature of the imagined national community within the geographical boundaries of state was a prerequisite for self-determination. Intellectuals engaged in the articulation of official and subaltern nationalisms were not simply borrowing and creating new knowledge; they were framing their discourse within a hybrid and fluid paradigm of knowledge that best fit the political and socioeconomic organizational context in which they found themselves. While striving to supersede the essentialist nature of colonial paradigms of historical consciousness, Arab nationalism as thus articulated would serve to reinforce it, all the while existing in a complex relationship with simultaneously emergent pan-national and nation-state nationalist ideas and institutions. With the geopolitical nuances of the archaeological and historical record came other aspects of anticolonial discourse that would further essentialize the relationship between East and West, Semite and Ayran, Muslim and non-Muslim, and imperialism and capitalism versus socioeconomic justice.[154]

Historians Tarif Khalidi and William Cleveland have argued that George Antonius, Lebanese-Egyptian civil servant of the British Mandate, wrote his seminal book on Arab nationalism, *The Arab Awakening*, to show his readers, primarily in the West, that the efforts and circumstances of contemporary Arabs rendered them worthy of self-determination. Historian Salim Tamari has compared the efforts of Tawfiq Canaan and his "circle" of Palestinians writing in English about heritage to those of Antonius. The authors whose work is mentioned herein wrote with a similar purpose, showing their readers in the classroom, coffeehouse, reading rooms, village gathering places, and in the British Colonial Office that Arabs met the criteria by which ancient historical relationships were an important component for staking the legitimacy of modern nations, whether those be territorial states or the entirety of a particular people across a vast landscape of habitation.

Britain set forth to rule its nation-state Mandates in Bilad al-Sham as it had imagined their spaces prior to the war: a Palestine core and a periphery that became a solution called Transjordan. This was in accord with Britain's strategic interests in the postwar world order. By means of physical and legal interventions, Britain sought to own not only antiquities and antiquity's spaces, but also their narratives, and therefore asserted its legitimacy to rule based on notions of restoration, order, and positivism. As Palestine was more important to Britain's narrative, such initiatives and interventions were lacking in Transjordan. There, an American supporter of Zionism synthesized a comprehensive narrative of Transjordan's antiquity that mirrored the creation of an Arab national periphery from the Holy Land to complement the Jewish national core. In this context, Arabs wrote about archaeology and ancient history to deploy their own narrative in the fight against colonialism, a narrative that conflated Arabs and Semites, Arab-ized all ancient peoples within the borders of the broad Arab *watan*, and demonstrated that the Arab presence on the landscape was older than any other. East of the river, meanwhile, Abdullah of Transjordan sought to own the narratives of his own space, and used antiquity to turn the periphery into a Hashemite core.

CHAPTER 5

Antiquities of a Hashemite State
in Mandatory Space

*The Amirate of Transjordan which emerged from those struggles to have him as
its prince is now a kingdom, and he its king. This undulating tableland beyond
the Jordan, the land of Gilead, Moab and Edom, where the splendid "oaks of
Bashan" still abound, and where David crowned his conquests with the capture
of Rabbath-Ammon (Amman), goes forward in ordered progress under his wise
governance, and with the help of Britain. Its nomads, trained and disciplined
for the first time in history, and its sturdy peasantry, comprise the ranks of the
famous Arab Legion, and in the campaigns of Syria and Iraq, brothers in arms
with British soldiers, they supported the loyalty and friendship of their prince
to Britain. In his capital at Amman, well may he say as did Joab before him in
his song of victory, "I have fought against Rabbah, and have taken the city of
waters."*[1]

If antiquities and their narratives were important components of an ongoing
colonial and nation-state competition, Abdullah bin al-Husayn, emir of
Transjordan, engaged in it with the deck stacked against him. With leadership over the Holy Land periphery came the challenge to render it into its
own core. In the first place, Emir Abdullah's family had colluded with the
British against the Ottomans, yet the Arabs were not ultimately united in
a kingdom under Hashemite suzerainty, as had been the goal. Britain and
France had divided the Arabs into states under their own rule, and Palestine had been promised as a Jewish national home. France ousted brother
Faysal from kingship in Damascus, and Ibn Sa'ud summarily expelled the
family from the kingdom of the Hijaz, forcing them from the sacred spaces
of Mecca and Medina, over which they had served as protectors, their descent from the Prophet Muhammad having enabled them great prominence
among late Ottoman statesmen. In terms of antique space, brother Faysal's

consolation prize, the Kingdom of Iraq, had what Britain's other regional possessions—Palestine and Egypt—did: tidy categories of high-interest monumental antiquities attributable by science to particular ancient peoples and meta-narratives that could explain historical consciousness and the borders and institutions of modern states. The antique space of Abdullah's Transjordan consolation prize was, however, as problematic as its contemporary milieu. Years would pass before its borders were fixed (and even then they were to expand and contract), the British governed its territory in a trial-and-error fashion, Abdullah had complex dreams of a larger hereditary possession and a loftier title, and its small population interacted within the shifting parameters of the new state, walking the fluid boundaries of pre-state alliances and national and pan-national interests.

Amidst talk of various confederations that might absorb Palestine, the Transjordanian Hashemites and representatives of the Yishuv, the Jewish community in Palestine, approached their interactions and negotiations in terms of the historicity of the Jewish presence in Palestine as related by scripture and shared history. In early 1924, a prominent delegation of leaders from the Yishuv composed of Col F. H. Kisch, David Yellin (a member of the Palestine Oriental Society and regular contributor to its journal), and Rabbi Jacob Meir met in Amman with Emir Abdullah on the occasion of the visit of his father, Sharif Husayn.[2] The delegates of the Yishuv appealed to the Hashemites openly on the basis of the common Semitic heritage of Arabs and Jews and their shared role in the advancement of learning during the medieval period. Sharif Husayn proceeded to reassure the delegation that he was ready to share his territory with Jews. Emir Abdullah insisted that the Zionists recognize the political rights of Palestine's Arab population, but spoke in terms of the paradigm of shared history: "I feel and I understand the feelings of the Jewish people which longs for its homeland and its country, and I would have been very glad had it not been expelled from its country 2000 years ago."[3]

It was critical for the Hashemites to speak of history in such terms, and it was a narrative that would carry across the decades with important nuances as determined by the course of events. While certainly they owed their position of prominence in the Hijaz to their relationship with Istanbul, the Hashemites' eligibility to be protectors of the holy cities was based on their descent from the Prophet Muhammad through his great-grandfather, Hashim. This is the only real aspect of antiquity as a basis of their modern legitimacy to which the Hashemites could refer, especially given that they were literal outsiders in both places the British installed them, and in proximity to others with whom they sought to collaborate in an effort to secure a larger hereditary state. The Hashemites, in a sense, posed themselves as the basis of the telos of a *watan*, their religiously significant genealogy emphasizing Muhammad and Ibrahim on one hand, which had a paradigmatic scientific counterpart linkable to Shem and Qaḥtan on the other. Hashim, the ancestor from whom they took their name, brought the two together.

Fortunately for the Hashemites, the ancient basis of their legitimacy was viscerally linked to the contemporary realm of the spiritual and therefore widely applicable beyond nation-state geography and outside the place in which they were not outsiders—Arabia—the very same place in which they had installed themselves on a throne that they quickly lost to Ibn Saʿud. Adherence to faith tradition as the primordial leg of their legitimacy required at least some recognition, however, of the ancient historical narrative deployed by the Zionist movement on what had become contested land. That recognition figured widely in discourses of emergent pan-nationalism—*wataniyya*— Arab-izing the panoply of ancient Semites in an effort to subvert the narrative seeking to separate Arabs along strange territorial divides, dispossess them of land and resources, and colonize them with foreign settlers.

It was certainly Abdullah's misfortune, however, that within the territorial borders of the emirate he had been given to rule was nothing like ziggurats or pyramids that other new Arab states had to evidence the ancient greatness of which the nationalists wrote. A look at Transjordan's landscape, far less explored than most, most importantly its counterpart Palestine core, suggested that the ancient ages of great civilizations had largely passed it by, mostly leaving some prehistoric, classical, and Islamic antiquities, hardly the best of those, and nothing that offered a comprehensive narrative of historical consciousness for a proto-Transjordan. With the important exception of Petra, large monuments on the landscape that foreigners wanted to visit were linked in the first place to the presence of Western occupiers—Rome and the Crusaders. While ancient Egypt, Anatolia, Iraq, and Persia and their peoples are certainly important components of the Semitic scriptural narrative, the extant written record of their civilizations discovered through archaeology lay mostly outside the Bible and the corpus of Semitic scriptural texts. Unlike the narrative of great civilizations of which Western archaeologists and the Arab nationalist writers were so enamored, the story of ancient and modern civilization in Transjordan emerged as one ultimately dependent on a story as told by Abrahamic scriptures, rendering the story of Transjordan under Hashemite rule as told by archaeology much like the story of Palestine as told by archaeology for the West and the Zionist movement. This hegemonic story had "othered" the ancient people on what was now Transjordan's side of the river, a relationship reflected in the contemporary nation-state condition that was contested among Jewish and Arab national groups.

In promoting an antiquity narrative, Transjordan's leadership thus faced a considerable challenge to turn the periphery it was given into a core unto its own. The landscape was irreparably carved and categorized, and not in a way that recognized local and regional modes of historical consciousness. Utilizing familiar antiquity within its original borders evoked no immediate notions of a proto-Transjordan or Hashemite legitimacy, and ultimately relied on Western narratives that had established exactly what of antiquity was familiar and important in the first place. Brashly deploying its ancient Arabs was potentially riskier, whether seeking to make proto-Transjordanians out of the ancient Semites who predated the Beni Israel or those who lived contemporaneously with them. The ancient Arab Semites identified as living before the Israelites were idolators and, given the real and contentious prospect of a Jewish national entity in contested space, risked demonstrating the uniqueness and legitimacy of the ancient Hebrews and surrender of not only Hashemite interests in and claims to that idea and the space that had been delineated for it, but also those of all who were not included in the narrative designated as "Judeo-Christian." For Transjordan to promote itself as the ancient home of the Ammonites, Moabites, and Edomites was just as tricky. They could likewise be identified as Arab Semites, but they were also idolators. Worse, they were biblical "others" vis-à-vis the Beni Israel, and usually antagonistic "others" at that. To incorporate them into an antiquity narrative thus risked serving the new geospatial dichotomy, carved in the first place by foreign efforts to map the land of the Israelites. Conjuring ancient Transjordanians, meanwhile, would have undermined the *wataniyya* narrative served by the unity of the broad category of Arab Semites. Even if the Hashemites were willing to trade pan-Arabism to secure their own interests in a *watan*, they could not appear to so do.

To walk these fraught lines, Transjordan represented itself with antiquities of universal value that could carry highly nuanced meanings. This chapter considers how the early Hashemite state of Transjordan used antiquity to create a core within its problematic ancient and modern spaces, all the while subservient to Britain and coveting the recognized core of Palestine, particularly Jerusalem. It begins by briefly discussing the late Ottoman intellectual and political life of Abdullah I as insight for considering the nuances of the Hashemites' legitimacy narratives in Transjordan and Palestine after the Great War, especially given the role antiquity would play in helping articulate both nation-state and pan-national Arab identities in the postwar order. While working toward the goal of a larger and heavily symbolic hereditary possession, however, Abdullah nonetheless began deploying the antiquities within Transjordan's borders as symbols of the state. These, particularly Petra and Jerash, had obvious "universal value" as granted in the West, and represented Transjordan on its early stamps and currency. While the Hashemite state adopted "Western" modes of representing the nation for creating a recognizable core from both within and without, I argue that a hermeneutic consideration of antiquities as logos of the nation offers possibilities for understanding the complexities of the messages intended for domestic and regional audiences, who had personal identifications through proximity, tradition, or education to these new national symbols that were (and remain) largely unknown or unappreciated in the West. Having explored how early Transjordanians might have ideally been meant to understand their identity in the rubric of antique cultural heritage, I conclude the chapter by suggesting possible subaltern identifications with landscape and antiquity, using examples of the verse of the poet 'Arar and the recollections of a man who lived a lifetime where Mesha's stela was found on the tells of Dhiban.

A Future King in a Late Ottoman World

How Abdullah bin al-Husayn came to rule Transjordan is a well-known story, both in history and historiography. It did not mark the beginning of a political career for his generation of the Hashemite family, something for which it had been aptly groomed for a very long time. After spending his early childhood in Mecca and Taif obtaining a traditional education learning the Qur'an, Abdullah and his brothers left in 1891 for a gilded cosmopolitan exile in Istanbul.

Like other children throughout the empire, Abdullah and his brothers engaged in its modern educational program, which strictly emphasized Turkish language, math, geography, and history, particularly that of "Muslim Turks."[4] In and out of their lessons, they experienced the diversity of the Ottoman Empire as represented in Istanbul and shared the company of many Hijazi and Turkish notables.[5] The family returned home in the wake of the 1908 revolution after Husayn was named emir of Mecca.

In the context of challenges both to the family's and Ottoman authority, particularly from tribal alliances and rivals such as Ibn Sa'ud, Abdullah took his first political charge in 1909, successfully accompanying the leader of the hajj caravan, the *emirülhac*, the Ottoman official charged with leading the pilgrims, assuring their safety, and maintaining contact with the interior ministry. For Istanbul's part, the central government maintained its official duties and in so doing elevated its partisan in Mecca, while the emir of Mecca had given a powerful demonstration of his family's clout to his more local constituents. That all of this happened in the context and space of the hajj, conflating the political and the sacred with far-ranging pomp and circumstance, so much the better.[6] Abdullah then served as his father's deputy in Mecca while the rest of the family was on campaign against Ibn Saʿud before returning to Istanbul. Husayn had used his clout with notables to get Abdullah elected as the Meccan deputy to the Ottoman Parliament, where he would serve two terms.[7] Brother Faysal, meanwhile, served as the parliamentary representative from Jidda.[8]

On his return to Istanbul, Abdullah stopped in Egypt, where he visited the Khedive and had an audience with none other than Sir Ronald Storrs (eventual military governor of Jerusalem) and Lord Kitchener, who had come a long way from his PEF survey days and was at that time high commissioner in Egypt. While this meeting has been remembered differently in various sources, it paved the way for Britain's overtures for an alliance with Sharif Husayn against the Ottomans.[9] Before engaging Husayn in those fateful talks, the British contacted Abdullah, and Abdullah served as Britain's conduit for financing preparations for the revolt.[10] Based upon his early and ongoing contacts with the British, Abdullah may have been the first convert to the idea of an alliance against the Ottomans, even if it was Faysal who would take center stage by way of his connections with intellectuals and nationalist movements, made while on Damascus reconnaissance for his father in 1915.[11]

When Ottoman military defeats in the region began mounting, and with the CUP executing a reign of terror against perceived opposition in Syria and Lebanon, a regional famine, and a British blockade of foodstuffs directed against the Ottomans that affected the entire region, it was no longer tenable for Husayn to keep his lot with Istanbul. Abdullah prosecuted the Hashemites' end of the revolt in the south while Faysal went north, and the results of the Great Arab Revolt were perhaps less great in the execution than in the repercussions. The British had, meanwhile, promised a national homeland for the Jews in what Husayn had reason to believe was promised to him, and the Bolsheviks withdrew Russia from the war. France and Britain's promise to carve up the Arab parts of the Ottoman Empire between themselves was now common knowledge. Husayn and Abdullah carved a kingdom from the Hijaz and claimed its titles, only to incur the immediate, continuous, and ultimately disastrous incursions of Ibn Saʿud, both father and son demonstrating a vulnerability and lack of legitimacy at the local level that numbered the days of their Hijazi kingdom from its beginning.[12] Faysal had much greater success, although this proved fleeting in the establishment of rule on the ground in Damascus.[13] Elegaic remembrances of the revolt's unified nationalist moment have shown themselves infinitely more complex, as idealistic post-Ottoman/pro-Turk sentiments, Syrian territorial nationalism, and pan-Arab nationalism with secular and religious flavors and both pro- and anti-Hashemite underpinnings mixed with elite mobilizations from above and often contrary popular mobilizations from below.[14] By the time Faysal lost Syria to the French, many Syrians themselves were not party to his inner circle's vision of rule and accommodation with the Mandatory power.[15]

That vision was a hereditary Arab kingdom ruled by his family. While Faysal went to Cairo to receive his consolation prize—the throne of Britain's Mandate for Iraq—Abdullah forged alliances with tribes and strongmen in an effort to retake Damascus, making his way north through Ma'an, Kerak, the Balqa, and Ajloun, where the British had left hapless young officers in charge.[16] A large Hashemite Arab kingdom including Bilad al-Sham and, importantly, Jerusalem was the goal, and the emirate of Transjordan as part of the British Mandate was a step on the path to its implementation.

Narratives of Antiquity and the Conundrum of Periphery and Core in the Postwar *Watan*

Abdullah set about ruling a periphery that had no antiquity narrative in either his or its own favor, all the while coveting a core where antiquity narratives could, theoretically, be more favorable to both. As he settled into Transjordan, rocky as the transition often was in the early years, the prospect of retaking Damascus or returning to the Hijaz slipped away. On the brighter side, brother Faysal and his heirs held the throne of Iraq immediately to the east, and Palestine, that British Mandate to which Transjordan was so closely tied, remained the locus of potential territorial accommodation. That Jerusalem was intended for inclusion in any such accommodation was clear, and interring Sharif Husayn's body next to al-Aqsa Mosque when he passed away in 1931 was the first physical step along the path to making Jerusalem, and by extension Palestine, the logo of a modern Hashemite political identity.[17]

Without access to the holy cities of the Hijaz, Jerusalem, and the site of Husayn's burial on *al-Haram al-Sharif*, offered a physical locus for expression of one of the pillars of Hashemite political legitimacy, one that was intimately tied to the spiritual: the Hashemites were eligible to guard the holy places of the Hijaz in the first place because of their descent from the Prophet Muhammad. No longer able to perform this function in the Hijaz, Jerusalem was a logical choice and, in its religious diversity, a place where the very real duty of pious Muslims—previously held by the caliph—to see to the protection of all "peoples of the Book" could be enacted.

The Dome of the Rock is the most recognizable of holy sites on the *haram*, and perhaps all of Jerusalem. The Umayyad caliph 'Abd al-Malik built it at the end of the seventh century, and scholars and pundits have spent the last century pondering why: was it an expression of personal largesse and piety, an alternative place of pilgrimage at a time when revolt made travel to Mecca dangerous, or was it something with which to spite Christendom?[18] What is important is that it commemorates, in the first place, the lives and deeds of prophets such as Ibrahim/Abraham, Suleyman/Solomon, and Muhammad. The location is identified in Abrahamic scriptures, related literatures, and traditions as the place where the patriarch nearly scarified his son Ishaq/Isaac or Ismaʿil/Ishmael, depending on the narrative and one's beliefs, and the location upon which Suleyman built his temple.

The revelation of the Qur'an and the prophethood of Muhammad are linked to these traditions by means of the Night Journey (*al-Israʿ*). In this, the Prophet Muhammad sojourned from his home in Mecca on a winged steed to "the farthest mosque" (*al-masjid al-aqsa*, Qur'an 17:1) before ascending to heaven from the locale of Ibrahim's sacrifice and Suleyman's Temple. According to tradition, he left his footprint in the bedrock upon which ʿAbd al-Malik would have the Dome of the Rock built.

Muhammad's genealogy as later canonized reflected his direct descent from Ibrahim.[19] The Hashemites take their name from Hashim, the great-grandfather of the Prophet Muhammad, who is a key link in the genealogical canon. Descent from Muhammad thus means descent from Ibrahim. Sharif Husayn's burial on the *haram* was a visceral gesture embodying multiple layers of ancient and contemporary strands of complex religio-national identity.[20] And while it depended on the wide range of Palestinians' and Arabs' personal connections to the site, those were subsumed in this emerging narrative by the connections of the Hashemites to it as once and future figureheads.

Abdullah operated comfortably within the borders of both the nation-state and the pan-national *watan*. As artificial, imposed, and imperfect as these new borders may have been, people had imagined their communities at many levels—the family, the locality, the region, the *millet*, the *umma*—with one person's understanding of each of those terms and associations being perhaps different from someone else's. In a certain respect, the multiple levels at which the nation-state system was to function, complete with regional associations and alliances, had the potential to work with those entrenched understandings of identity. What rendered the physically unnatural borders intellectually and viscerally unnatural, however, were two interrelated aspects of the new paradigm: (1) the idea that identities had to be conscious and articulated, and thus defined, understood, and justified; and (2) the fact that there would be strict limits on the fluidity and hybridity of identities, both now and in historical consciousness, related to imposed cartographic projections and accommodation of a range of hegemonic interests, many of which had their roots in the taxonomizing of antiquity.

In this context, Transjordan, like its neighbors, began to symbologize itself by means of what was found within its borders, frequently vestiges of antiquity and the messages comprehensive landscapes that included them could convey. Antiquities and their associated landscapes, much like maps as described by Benedict Anderson, thus became logos of the nation.[21] While Transjordan deployed those symbols and messages of the new state through its institutions and objects such as postage stamps and currency, intellectuals, crucial to the work of those institutions, were simultaneously writing another nation, an ancient Arab nation that surpassed those newly imposed borders.

Antiquity as Visual Cues of the *Watan*

If Abdullah accepted Transjordan as a transitory stage of a larger, fluid, and sacred pan-national spatial vision, it was nonetheless a space that had to bespeak meaning and performance of national statehood under his leadership. Vestiges of antiquity, representing historical facts on the ground within such novel borders were, in Jordan as everywhere else, vital components of such state- and nation-building exercises.

Institutions emerged writ large in Transjordan ahead of and after the Organic Law (1928), the basis of the institutionalized emirate, its leadership, and its citizens. These included ministerial administration, the recasting of duties of tribal leaders in official capacities, a legislative council, the emergence of a military and clearer delineation of borders, and means of providing services, including a postal service to issue stamps and an organization to issue currency.

While state institution-building was ongoing, British officials launched a massive and invasive program through Transjordan's Land Department, much like the Ottomans had previously, to expand agricultural output and increase tax revenues by determining individual land ownership, updating the land regime that the Ottomans had put in place in its final decades. Michael Fischbach writes, "A key ingredient in the formulation of a modern nation state is the creation of an identity tied to a specific terrain."[22] The land program, carried out between 1927 and 1952, proved instrumental in ensuring the title of small property holders, securing the interests of larger landholders—many of whom were enmeshed in the institutions of state—and in the process expanded the bureaucracy and increased citizen interaction with the emirate. It helped secure Transjordanians' interests to the state and impart the reality of a Jordanian nation upon them.[23] Throughout the many years that the land program was in effect, the very landscape and its features into which Jordan's citizens were being organized was often the subject chosen for its stamps and currency. Together with images of the emir, what was ancient and modern upon Jordan's landscape graced these small, circulating national portraits, thereby demonstrating continuity, development, and legitimacy, all for the good of the nation in which Transjordanians were now living.

Petra and Jerash as Logos of the Nation

Images of Petra and Jerash have appeared on Jordan's stamps and currency frequently across the decades.[24] They were among the scenes to grace Transjordan's first stamps (1933) and newly independent Jordan's first currency (1949). The two most widely recognizable antiquities sites on Transjordan's side of the river naturally became the earliest logos of the nation. And while they told no comprehensive narrative of antiquity that bespoke a proto-Transjordan, one had a visceral religious meaning and together with the other offered a comprehensive narrative of modernity. While the international audience's recognition of these sites as Transjordanian was important, the deployment of these images to the domestic and regional audience depended on people's personal associations with them or unquestioned traditions related to them.

Shortly before Nelson Glueck began his surveys of Transjordan, Tawfiq Canaan was dispatched to Petra in 1929 with Transjordanian DOA inspector George Horsfield on an expedition funded by British financier Henry Mond. Using the same methods and methodology by which he had studied Palestine's fellahin and bedouin and devised a nativist paradigm of antiquity from such work, Canaan spent three weeks conducting an ethnographic study of Petra's people and their folklore, and in 1930 published *Notes on Studies in the Topography and Folklore of Petra*.[25]

Given the centrality of locale and landscape to his examinations of ethnographic questions, Canaan is particularly interested in the Bdul and their stories, reporting that of all the people who call the Petra region home, they know more place names than other locals. Every bit of land has a name, Canaan says, possibly a recent name based on some aspect of tribal history.[26] Place-names, he says, may also come from their relationship to color, to a particular tree, rock, *wadi*, or landmark. A place or a feature may likewise be known by multiple names, and those names may be applied to more than one locale.[27] Canaan believes most of the place-names are of Arabic origin but some are probably earlier, and he suggests a philological analysis be done in hopes of shedding more light on the ancient history of Petra.[28]

Canaan devotes an entire chapter to the monuments of Petra having Arabic names and the stories relating to those names. Most of these stories revolve, not surprisingly and given the large, storied ruins of Egypt and their lessons about haughtiness, around the presence of "Pharaoh," his wives and daughters and their actions, the importance of hospitality, and the power of God and necessity of faith in Him.[29] He devotes another chapter to the various contemporary peoples who inhabit Petra, likening them to "their ancestors the Edomites," challenging the Orientalist notion that some of their customs are traceable to the Beni Israel and their various branches, writing that instead such customs are widespread among bedouin populations, including those of Palestine.[30]

Harun/Aaron and Musa/Moses have a crucial role to play in the lives of Petra's contemporary people. Canaan says, "It is to be noted that the Liatneh prefer to give the name of Harun and Musa to their children. They believe that these names bring special 'barakeh' (blessing) to the bearer, as they are taken from the two great local prophets."[31] Stories recognizable to those familiar with the Exodus permeate the lore of Petra and its people, but with important pre-Islamic imagery and Islamic nuances. Significant episodes of the Exodus are believed by locals to have taken place in Petra. An image of Musa striking a rock with his staff and obtaining water for the thirsty Israelites occurs for locals at an extant spring in Petra, and the story of the spring contains numerous elements, such as camel sacrifice, that are familiar from pre-Islamic and Islamic oral and literary traditions. Harun, whose "tomb" sits atop a high mountain in Petra and remains a popular destination for hiking, isn't believed to be buried there at all. In local lore, his spirit, disturbed by thirsty, grumbling camels, flew there to find a quiet place to rest where camels couldn't climb and where the mountains didn't shake violently when it tried to rest. Along the way his spirit created springs for the camels. The Bdul, another group among Petra's contemporary populations, on the other hand, say that a she-camel carried Harun to the base of the mountain when he knew his time was near, and he died having climbed it alone.

The story of the Bdul's origins, at least as some locals tell it, is likewise intimately related to Musa, Harun, and the Beni Israel. They were inhabitants of Petra who surrendered to Musa and Harun after the prophets had subdued the rest of the area. In surrendering to Musa and Harun, they accepted, or "changed" (this is what the root of *bdl* means), their religion, acknowledging them as prophets of God. This distinguishes them from the Thamud, an ancient civilization who, in a tradition familiar to Muslims, failed to submit to God's will, spurned God's messenger Salih, and, much like haughty Pharaoh and his civilization, met God's punishment in their destruction, events related in the Qur'an (see especially 7:73–78) and histories such as that of al-Tabari.[32] The site believed to be at the center of the story is known today as Mada'in Salih, similar to Petra and likewise now a UNESCO World Heritage site close by in the Saudi Hijaz. Associated with a hadith tradition, its remains are noted by the Prophet Muhammad as an example of haughtiness and failure to submit to God's will.[33]

Before their incorporation into synthetic Arabist narratives by virtue of their connection to the pre-Islamic Nabateans and their roots in a deep Arab and Semitic past, places like Petra and its counterpart Mada'in Salih were crucial for spiritual connections to place and historical lessons running much deeper than their value for modern narratives of identity. It was this deep, unquestioned personal value upon which antiquity in historical consciousness depended. In the words of Jordanian archaeologist Suleiman Farajat, himself from the Petra region:

> If Petra was unknown to the Western world until the beginning of the nineteenth century, it was well known for the local population who lived there. They were familiar with the site and its monuments. They feared it, imagined stories, and made parallel histories and even identified themselves with some of its features. But Petra was not only monuments for them. The whole national park was the habitat of several tribes. In it, they lived, used its natural resources, anchored their beliefs, and edified their own history.[34]

While it is unlikely that many early Jordanians ever visited Petra, and certainly not in the way that foreign tourists would have, it is just as unlikely that it failed to have significance in their modern milieu.[35] Swiss Orientalist explorer Johann Burckhardt writes in 1822, "I was particularly desirous of visiting Wady Mousa, of the antiquities of which I had heard the country people speak in terms of great admiration."[36] While such an observation is impossible to verify, it must also be remembered that, as with any archaeological site anywhere, what most visitors understand today as a site and an archaeological park is actually an uncountable number of antiquities sites connected upon a continuously inhabited living landscape. In addition to its religious significance, Wadi Musa, the village by which one could most easily enter Petra, lay close to if not upon the *darb al-hajj al-shami* (the route of the hajj), and was known to caravaneers, pilgrims, and others whose lives and livelihoods bore connection to the hajj throughout the history of Islam. Late Ottoman reforms had incorporated the agricultural villages of the Petra region, albeit with the difficulty that characterized late Ottoman reforms in the rest of southern Transjordan.[37] Wadi Musa was officially designated a *nahiye*, a village of some importance headed by a *mudir*.[38] By 1930, despite a rebellion of the villagers, a road for motor vehicles had been opened linking Wadi Musa to Maʿan for the purposes of aiding the Mandatory administration in tax collection and enhancing ease of tourism to Petra.[39] In 1929, George and Agnes Horsfield had conducted the first excavations in Petra for the Department of Antiquities of Palestine.[40]

The immediacy of Petra's monuments may have meant most to local bedouin and villagers of various tribal affiliations whose connections to the site were articulated by Tawfiq Canaan, but starting in the late Ottoman period, its incorporation into the state, while not unchallenged, was clear. Despite the difficulties faced by Ottoman and emirate authorities to incorporate what became southern Jordan, the fabled ruins of Petra and its living landscape were recognizable to other Jordanians as being within the same boundaries to which they had all been tied first as imperial, and now as nation-state, moderns. Petra as logo of the nation may have served to squelch the agency of local and regional people to articulate their own connections to it in favor of a foreign tourism narrative, but it simultaneously depended upon those visceral connections to create the official narrative. If intellectual Arabist discourse likewise subsumed the local narrative to support or challenge the official narrative, so much the better. Authoritarian delineations and narrations of space depend on these personal connections.

Petra, the most recognizable antiquity of the south, shared its incorporation as a symbol of the state with Jerash, the most recognizable antiquity of the north. Beginning about 1878, the modern town of Jerash was established around the antique city by Circassian settlers, agrarian refugees from Ottoman conflicts with Russia who became part of Istanbul's land initiatives to centralize its southern frontiers.[41] While there seems to have been no ethnographic study of the area similar to Tawfiq Canaan's in the Petra region, similar ties to landscape and multiple layers of tradition engaging with antiquities there should be assumed, as demonstrated by the work of Canaan and others elsewhere in and beyond the region and nationalist poetry such as that of ʿArar, discussed further below. This site was a well-known landmark, and whether people personally and culturally identified with it as a classical city, it must be assumed that they identified with it in myriad ways. Gerald Lankester Harding, British director of Jordan's Department of Antiquities from 1936 to 1956, wrote in 1973, "To this day Arabs as far afield as south Palestine when they wish to speak of something as extremely ruinous say: 'It is like the ruins of Jerash.'"[42] While it is impossible to verify this claim, it can be said that Jerash, a modern late Ottoman town existing in an ancient city and landscape, had been long incorporated into the administrative framework of late Ottoman reforms, and was likewise long connected by roads and socio-economic ties to other towns and regions that came to be included within the borders of the new country.[43] Kimberly Katz's assertion that "the monuments in Jerash may have meant little to a person from Shawbak" in Jordan's south therefore requires additional nuance. People from Shawbak have connections to their own local antiquities in ways that people from Jerash have connections to theirs, connections that are different in specific ways, but understood in the same hermeneutic framework. Transjordan did not, however, deploy Shawbak as its iconography as it did Jerash, since it was not as recognizable outside the borders. The people of Shawbak, meanwhile, certainly recognized that Jerash, its people, and its environs had been part of the same administrative framework to which they had belonged for the previous three decades, even if they hadn't always acquiesced in that framework.[44]

The Department of Antiquities of the government of Transjordan undertook the first excavations at Jerash in 1924. In 1926 the Department of Antiquities of the government of Palestine deemed the site in dire need of conservation work.[45] Due to their easily visible grandeur and their close proximity to Amman, the beautifully preserved ruins of Jerash of the Decapolis continue to be, for foreign tourists, the second most recognizable and most frequently visited archaeological site in Jordan.[46] Archaeologist Philip King calls it "one of the most impressive tourist attractions in the Kingdom of Jordan. Comparable in magnificence to Baalbek, Palmyra, and Petra, Gerasa (Jerash) ranks among the prized monuments in Syria-Palestine."[47]

Jerash and Petra were useful for making the case that a cohesive proto-Transjordan was imaginable and could constitute its own core. Putting Jerash and Petra on its first issue of stamps and currency provided the means of making the connection that was probably most difficult for Transjordan in its early days of nation building to propagate. This essential connection involved incorporating the populations and cultures of disparate regions with differing ways of life and with extensive connections outside the boundaries of the nation-state into one natural entity. The north, west, and central highlands of the young country were traditionally connected to Syria and parts of Palestine. These regions were characterized primarily by village life and had been more easily incorporated into the late nineteenth-century Ottoman framework. The southern and eastern regions, on the other hand, were dominated by pastoral economies, and traditionally bore stronger ties to Iraq, southernmost Palestine, Egypt, and the Hijaz. These territories, moreover, were more recently and problematically incorporated into the administration designed by the Ottomans.[48] Disparate lands had become part of the same core, a Transjordanian nation-state, and its people could now carry a reminder of this in their pockets, or attach it to mail or official paperwork.

Foreigners, furthermore, had demonstrated that Jerash and Petra were important. Many such foreigners had been raised in Europe, where antiquity had long since become a great verifier of legitimacy—of the Bible, of empires, of sovereign nations. Others had been raised in the United States, where antiquities were a means of verifying places' and their people's connections to the places and peoples of the Bible. As for the places and peoples of Transjordan, they had long been categorized in an "east-of-the-Jordan" peripheral context vis-à-vis their ancient neighbors, who constituted a core to the west. Jerash and Petra became for many scholars, explorers, and travelers what defined the land and people east of the River Jordan, what was worth studying and what was worth visiting. For Transjordan to create itself as a core, they became a means of representing that core.

Mandatory Transjordan's first stamp series (1933) featured Jerash's Nymphaeum and the Temple of Artemis. Independent Jordan's first currency (1949) bore an image of Jerash's Oval Forum on the one-dinar bill.[49] Transjordan's first stamp series showcased Petra's *Khazna* (the Treasury) on two stamps, and independent Jordan's first currency carried it on both the five- and ten-dinar bills.[50] The Khazna was the primary subject of archaeological exploration and awe east of the Jordan River for nineteenth- and early twentieth-century foreign explorers and archaeologists.[51] It was made universally famous in the 1989 climax of the *Indiana Jones* trilogy, and is the first structure of the Nabatean city that most visitors to the Petra Park see after a long walk through the narrow Siq. It remains to this day *the* archaeological site most closely associated with modern Jordan.

The colonial paradigm that defined the space east of the river and its historical narrative had informed Mandatory Transjordan's identity, which in turn helped inform the independent Hashemite Kingdom's identity, fit for espousal on its earliest national portraits.[52] The difference was that Transjordan used the elements that defined it as a periphery in terms of the colonial paradigm to affirm that it was a natural core. Within and without the Hashemite *watan*, meanwhile, the audiences of journals such as *al-Muqtataf* could read about these sites of specifically Transjordanian antiquity.[53]

Other Logos of the *Watan*

As is true of other countries in the region and around the world, postage stamps in Jordan have many uses besides indicating payment for postal services.[54] Early laws regarding stamps made them mandatory for use as proof of payment for all official transactions and taxes and were thus affixed to official paperwork.[55] As they have since the earliest days of the state, today postage stamps appear on official documents of the court system and are stuck in the passports of non-Jordanians as proof of payment for a Jordanian visa. Stamps have thus conveyed messages widely to Jordanian audiences by means of their use for official transactions, and to foreigners by means of their placement in passports, attachment to mail, and their appearance on the philatelic market and in international fairs and expositions.[56]

Transjordan's postal service was organized in 1926 and became a member of the Universal Postal Union as a mandatory territory in the same year.[57] Membership legitimized Transjordan's national status among the union's members, allowing for circulation of Transjordanian stamps and acknowledgment that they were proof the right amount of postage had been paid.[58] In 1929 it was announced that Transjordan would produce what would officially be its first series of postage stamps. Appearing in *al-Jarida al-Rasmiyya* (The Official Gazette) and signed by Baz Qawar, Palestine Mandate–appointed director of Transjordan's postal authority, "for pleasing the tourist visiting Transjordan," this item announced the government's intention to print a series of stamps depicting the "best views" in the country and seek an amateur photographer to present such photos to the director-general of the telegraph and post department.[59] The announcement requested any suitable Transjordanian vista, but specifically included the following: the Emirs Abdullah and Talal, Ajloun Castle, Amman (including the Roman Theatre and Bridge), the Allenby Bridge and *Nahr al-Shariʿa* (the Jordan River), the *Khazna Faraʿun* (Pharaoh's Treasury) and al-Dayr (the Monastery) of Petra, an Arab Camp, the Oval Forum, South Temple, the Temple of Artemis of Jerash, Kerak Castle, *al-Naqab* (Negev Desert), and the city of Salt (Transjordan's "first capital").[60] This list is interesting not only for its mix of iconic antiquities, but also for its sites and landscapes related to conceptions of both traditional and modern life and space that lived both within and without paradigmatic narratives of Transjordan. It included both sites and landscapes of "universal value" and those that would have been of acutely Transjordanian value. Taken together as the "best views" in Transjordan, this list represents a highly nuanced vision of a unique core. Salt, *al-Naqab*, and an Arab camp, however, would not grace Transjordan's first stamps.

Yʿaqub Sukkar, a Christian native of Salt, was the artist commissioned to design Jordan's first series of stamps, and would later design the first issue of currency.[61] He designed the frames into which prints made from photographs of the sites were inserted, and included his first initial and last name in the white space between the frame and the perforated edge of the stamp, a subtle touch that ultimately created a good deal of controversy.[62] What Sukkar regarded as works of art met with objections in some quarters that a Christian had been hired to design the first national stamps. Worse, he had signed his own name to these Transjordanian sites, to these first portraits representing Transjordan to itself and to the world.[63] In 1936 Transjordan participated in the Florida International Stamp and Coin Exposition, held at the University of Tampa, where Sukkar's series won a prize for "best pictorial issue" at the event.[64] This only inflamed the controversy surrounding his signature on the stamps and, consequently, they were removed from the market. There are 1,029 sets of these stamps in existence, rendering them incredibly rare and valuable.[65]

Sukkar's series consisted of fourteen stamps of varying values, the highest valued stamp of one Palestine pound bearing a portrait of the Emir Abdullah. These stamps predated Jordan's first currency by seventeen years and clearly provided a template for the design of Jordan's bills. Besides Petra and Jerash, this first stamp series bore images of two sites that nineteenth-century explorers categorized as "desert castles," Qasr al-Mshatta and Qasr Kharanah. Qasr al-Mshatta is located about thirty-five kilometers south of Amman on the grounds of the Queen Alia International Airport. At the time these stamps were produced, however, Qasr al-Mshatta was just off the road linking Amman to Madaba, an earthen path that was upgraded to a modern road in the 1930s.[66] It is believed that the *qasr* is of eighth-century Umayyad construction, was indeed a palace, and was never completed.[67] Qasr al-Mshatta's intricately decorated façade was given as a gift by the Ottoman Empire's Sultan Abdülhamid to Kaiser Wilhelm II of Germany before the First World War, much, as discussed in chapter 3, to the ire of Osman Hamdi.[68] The Hijaz Railway was used to transport the façade to Haifa, to be taken by ship to Berlin, where it remains to this day displayed in the Pergamon Museum.[69] In the late 1960s, Lankester Harding noted that the Department of Antiquities had been actively working to conserve the site, but that many of the stones had been taken and used as building material for the nearby railway station and village.[70] Albeit destructive from the viewpoint of antiquities conservation, these were perhaps more practical and personal uses of the remnants of Qasr al-Mshatta than were Kaiser Wilhelm's, and this was a site of not only international, but domestic importance. However local people may have interacted with the site as part of a living landscape, foreigners—the sultan in Istanbul and the Germans—had realized its value, and so too the other foreigners—the nascent Hashemite state under British Mandate. The choice of the *qasr* as "one of the best views in Transjordan" institutionalized it as part of the state, affirming it as belonging to the long-standing heritage of the state and its peoples.[71]

The inclusion of Mshatta and Kharana in the first series of Transjordanian stamps linked an antiquity of the central part of the country in close proximity to its capital with a site of the eastern *badiyya* (steppe). Along with several other sites, Mshatta and Kharana form a "loop" of so-called—but misnamed—Umayyad desert castles that are an easy day's sightseeing trip from Amman.[72] As such, they are in close proximity to the Wadi Sirhan, an important route for traveling to and from Iraq or the Hijaz, and a zone of contestation between Emir Abdullah and Ibn Saʿud until the British-mediated Hadda Agreement began to resolve outstanding border issues in 1925.[73] Qasr Kharana is an imposing structure on the landscape, tall and fortress-like in appearance. The *qasr* was first published in 1896 by American Gray Hill and was surveyed and excavated by another American, Stephen Urice, in 1979.[74] During those eight decades, the site became a source of controversy among art historians and archaeologists of the early Islamic period. While the building is dated to the seventh century, its exact builders and its precise function remain a matter of some question.[75] It lacks a detectable water source, is not located directly upon a major thoroughfare, yet it lies in close proximity to other antiquities sites of the eastern desert, such as UNESCO World Heritage site Qusayr Amra, that have been used to represent Jordan.[76]

This first Transjordan stamp series also featured Kerak Castle. Subject of much historical and archaeological research from the earliest days of the Emirate, it is the most famous of the antiquities sites of the Kerak Plateau, an area well known and heavily traveled probably long before the age of the biblical Moabites. Bordered on the north by the Wadi Mujib and on the south by the Wadi al-Hasa, for millennia this area has been an important intersection of north-south and east-west routes, and therefore a vital administrative and commercial center. The castle itself has its origins in the Crusader period (mid-twelfth century), but fell into Arab Muslim hands after several sieges by Salah al-Din and his men. It was chiefly the domain of the ruler of whatever administrative body was in charge of matters on the Kerak Plateau, be it Ayyubid, Mamluk, Ottoman, or local. Its last use as a defensive fortification was, perhaps, during the Kerak Revolt of 1910, during which the surviving Ottoman authorities and members of the Ottoman garrison were forced to take refuge within the castle walls.[77] This event may have had repercussions not only for regions farther south in the Ottoman frontier, but also in cities and villages throughout Greater Syria. According to Eugene Rogan, urban adherents to the idea of Arabism rhetorically embraced this tribal incursion against Ottoman authority as part of their own intellectual and political movement.[78] At the very least, the revolt conveniently fit into such a paradigm. The Kerak Revolt has likewise become, for at least some national historians, an important part of Jordanian identity, as it has been viewed as a precursor to a greater part of the Hashemite Jordanian identity, the Arab Revolt.[79] Perhaps the castle, the dominant archaeological feature of the Kerak Plateau's landscape, located in the spot from which so much had been ruled, site of the fall of the Crusaders and site of the besting of the Ottoman Empire, came to represent this important aspect of Jordan's identity. Today Kerak Castle is a popular attraction for tourists, and a museum dedicated to the history of the Kerak Plateau, including the revolt, has been established under the auspices of a major project of the Japanese International Cooperation Agency (JICA).[80]

If Kerak Castle was an important symbol of the center of the state and an important base of its support, Qal'at al-Rabad (Ajloun Castle) was a similarly important site of the northern part of the country. 'Izz al-Din Usama, an emir of Salah al-Din, built the castle as an Ayyubid fortification against Crusader incursions of ca. 1184–85.[81] It is a famous local monument that dominates the skyline for miles around the town of Ajloun that lies below it. Ajloun is only one of the towns in the area known as Jabal Ajloun, which also gave its name to the Ottoman *kaza* (district) of Ajloun, as it came to be known during the Tanzimat reforms. Due to the Ajloun district's proximity to the Hawran and Damascus, it was the earliest focus of Ottoman efforts at incorporating the lands of its Transjordanian frontier.[82]

Another stamp of this first series carries a picture of the Allenby Bridge over the River Jordan (*Nahr al-Shari'a*). It was named for General Allenby when, in the final days of the First World War, British troops in Palestine built it over the Ottoman-era bridge that had linked both sides of the River Jordan for generations.[83] The function of this bridge was radically altered when, with the onset of the Mandate, it came to link Transjordan with Mandatory Palestine, bringing to this sacred, storied zone of interface and borderland the ambiguity of the nation-state context and contestations regarding it.[84] This stamp thus had a multifold purpose. It features the Jordan River, a river of great meaning, fame, and antiquity, and directly connects the new nation-state to it. It likewise acknowledges the British presence and the British role in Transjordan's very existence and history by promoting this bridge named for a British general as one among "the best views in Transjordan." It serves, finally, to demonstrate Transjordan's separate existence from Mandatory Palestine while simultaneously demonstrating the new state's historical and physical connection to it, and perhaps also its emir's desire to incorporate it under his rule. People had been crossing the banks of the River Jordan since time immemorial. For the first time, crossing it meant leaving what was at the moment one nascent country and entering a very much related and coveted, contested other.

From Transjordan to the Hashemite Jordanian Kingdom

In the years between these first stamp series (1933) and Jordan's assumption of control over what it would call the "West Bank" in 1948, Jordan was granted independence from Britain (1946) and monuments of the country's modern history began to appear on postage stamps, a trend that gathered steam as the pace of development in Jordan increased. One of the first issued in the wake of Jordan's independence, a 1947 stamp series commemorated the inauguration of the First National Parliament by featuring the Parliament Building. In 1949, Jordan printed stamps to mark the seventy-fifth anniversary of the Universal Postal Union.[85] One of the stamps depicts the globe in the center surrounded by various means of transport—a ship in the ocean, a plane overhead, and a train chugging along with mountains in the background. The train is clearly representative of the Hijaz Railway where it steams through the port of Aqaba, the ownership of which was still a contested issue between Jordan and Saudi Arabia. Airplanes had been in use in Jordan since the earliest days of the emirate, mainly as part of the British surveillance and security regime.[86] Scenes taken from Jordan's landscape, from the heart of the lore of the Great Arab Revolt, which was and continues to be a great affirmation of the legitimacy of the Hashemite state, thus helped promote its role on the modern world stage.[87] This stamp was printed in the wake of the 1948 war as preparations were under way to issue the first national currency, the highest denomination of which, fifty dinars, depicted an Aqaba seascape. Jordan had lost access to Palestine's ports, by which Jordanian goods, particularly grain, had met the Mediterranean.[88] King Abdullah's unsuccessful bids for access to Gaza or Haifa were a major source of contention during negotiations with Israel in the years following the war, coinciding exactly with the deployment of Aqaba's landscape as Jordanian iconography.[89] Free use of Aqaba port facilities was actually a bargaining chip offered to the Israelis by Abdullah, hoping for similar rights in Haifa.[90] Jordan's long-standing dispute with Saudi Arabia over possession of Aqaba was certainly an immediate concern, and the town's inclusion in the visual fabric of the Hashemite core was a message.[91]

The British occupied the port city in 1925 to protect it from Ibn Sa'ud as the Hashemite kingdom of the Hijaz stood to fall to his forces. Ibn Sa'ud did not give up his claim to Aqaba, and raids by his partisans throughout the early years of the Mandate demonstrated that his territorial ambitions, particularly at Hashemite expense, were not to be taken lightly. In the process, Amman had canceled Aqaba's status as a *baladiyya* (municipality). If controlled by Ibn Saʿud, however, his Arabian territories would have shared a border with the British in Palestine and Egypt, and after 1948, Saudi Arabia would have shared a border with Israel.[92] Under terms of the 1946 treaty, Britain took fortified positions offshore and in the town. And more than a decade after Amman had demoted Aqaba's status, the town was legally reestablished as a *baladiyya*.[93] Jordan's use of Aqaba on a bill thus laid continuing claim to what was now Jordan's only port and its potential for development, and may have been a message to the British and others that, in light of political events—including Israeli threats to occupy the port city—the regional situation would be more stable were its claims to Aqaba maintained.[94]

While issues of new stamp series are frequent, issuing currency is a highly complex and expensive process. For this reason, and for the fact of Transjordan's embedding in the administration of Britain's Palestine Mandate, there had been little impetus for the design and issue of a separate national currency until Jordan's independence, granted in the promulgation of the Anglo-Jordanian Treaty of 25 May 1946.[95] For this reason there have been countless issues of Jordanian stamps across the decades, and only five issues of currency. The Jordan Currency Board, its headquarters in London, was established in 1949, granting the right to determine the design of the currency to the Council of Ministers. The Jordan Currency Board consisted of a president and four members, all appointed from within the Council of Ministers in agreement with the king.[96] On the first of July 1950 the dinar became the official unit of Jordanian currency and on the last day of September of that year the Palestine pound was removed from circulation.[97] Despite the furor over that first series of stamps for the Transjordan Mandate, Yʿaqub Sukkar designed the first issue of currency for the Hashemite kingdom.

In addition to images of Aqaba, Jerash, and Petra, the five banknotes of the 1949 issue of the Jordan Currency Board bore a portrait of King Abdullah I on the obverse.[98] The remaining two motifs depicted on the bills are probably best described as landscape scenes, generally appearing on the reverse of the bill. The five-hundred-fils note (a half-dinar) was the only banknote to depict two landscape scenes. These were the Wadi al-ʿArab irrigation project, likely one of the first irrigation initiatives undertaken in the post-independence era, and a scene of a man tending cattle in the countryside.[99] The message was clear; the new kingdom was a forward-looking country, using new technology to harness its water resources. Together, the nation and the *fellah* (peasant) depicted in this scene improved agricultural output and enhanced each other's lives.[100] Such farmers as this man were the agricultural backbone of the country, tilling the soil and feeding the people, just as their fathers and grandfathers before them. This half-dinar note, being the lowest denomination, was probably one of the most widely circulated, at least domestically.[101] The bill thus showed Jordanians what their nation was doing for them while at the same time presenting them with an image of themselves or someone they knew or had seen, or one of an ideal they were supposed to be, someone to whom they all could relate in what was now depicted as a performance of nationality. At the same time, it elevated the agriculturalist while the state sought to settle the nomad.

Performing *Watan*

This chapter has focused on the Hashemites' project to turn a peripheral space into a national core. It has done so through the lens of the iconography of antiquity on stamps and currency in conjunction with the dissemination of archaeological knowledge and its incorporation into traditional conceptions of antique spaces and artifacts and the narratives of the new and problematic order of nation-states. In so doing, it has offered some possibilities for thinking about how Transjordanians were ideally meant to imagine and historicize their new, smaller *watan* and the possibilities of a larger one, given the competition in which the Hashemites were engaged at home, regionally, and farther abroad. If the amalgamation of archaeological science and traditional modes of understanding history was meant to serve the official narrative of the Hashemite Transjordanian state, however, it stands to reason that, just as a political opposition to it developed based on a number of complex, personal identifications, so those same connections upon which the state depended to support its narrative could serve to articulate challenges to it. Palestinian ethnographer Tawfiq Canaan repeatedly and so well demonstrated that landscape—the severing and cobbling of which created the spaces of new states—was holistically imbued with nonlinear and unquestioned sacrality, history, and identification commensurate with its importance in day-to-day practical life. It is thus reasonable to consider the role that such an understanding of landscape might have played in narratives of identification with the antique spaces of the new state that lay outside the ideal of the official, and thus stood to compete with or be co-opted by it. This chapter concludes with two such examples, one intellectual and one highly personal, that hopefully posit avenues for future consideration. The first involves the career and verse of the celebrated nationalist poet 'Arar (Mustafa Wahbi al-Tal, 1899–1949), and the second an elderly resident's recollection of Dhiban in the early years of Jordanian independence.

The name al-Tal is immediately recognizable to those familiar with Jordan as belonging to a prominent family of Transjordanian descent that has a long-held proximity to the throne and has produced a long line of influential figures, including the controversial assassinated prime minister, Wasfi al-Tal. Among its first famous Transjordanian members was Mustafa Wahbi, better known by his pen name as the poet 'Arar. Born in 1899 in Irbid, the northernmost city in Jordan, 'Arar exemplifies the kind of upwardly mobile late Ottoman citizen described in earlier chapters, and the intellectual and cultural milieu that existed before the war that would prove to be so formative in the decades that followed.[102] 'Arar came from a landowning family of southeastern Bilad al-Sham with means, and while completing secondary studies at the famous Anbar School in Damascus, he engaged actively with the urban political and intellectual scene, adhering to a pre-armistice Arabism that held fast that line between increasing criticism of Istanbul and allegiance to it. His wartime activities got him expelled from school, but he would eventually complete the teachers' course at the Sultaniyyah school in Aleppo. He was among those who engaged the emergent *wataniyya* and joined the struggle against the French in Syria, a mass mobilization as frustrated with Faysal's regime as against French imperialism.[103]

When 'Arar returned to what was now Transjordan, he, his work, and his relationships became emblematic of the multiple layers of identity and the senses of association and dislocation that many intellectuals must have carried into the postwar order. His life as a Transjordanian citizen began as a schoolteacher, where he and thirty-four colleagues faced the daunting challenge of serving a population of a quarter-million people and growing, many of whom were mired in poverty. 'Arar thus joined a small cadre of trained professionals, including many Palestinians, Syrians, and others, tasked with making the institutions of the new state work. He was part of a circle of poet literati that included, among others, Emir Abdullah. The two men emerged as preeminent Jordanian poets, and rivals at that. 'Arar's sardonic political verse and his often allegorical prose brutally took to task the shortcomings of the emir's government and the British, and also of the opposition to it. His sometimes political associations with "nativist" Transjordanian opposition and his unabashed criticism of the government would lead to various episodes of imprisonment, exile, and rehabilitation throughout his short life.

To the extent that he both engaged and eschewed Transjordan's leadership, ideas of a broader Arabism, and the proponents of early chauvinistic Transjordanian nationalism, it was his emphasis on the people of the nation-state *watan*, embedded in his writing—his political works, his love poetry, his prose—that marked him as Jordan's heralded nationalist poet. For 'Arar, everything that lay within Jordan's borders—the landscape, its natural and manmade components, and most importantly its people—constituted a natural, living *watan*. He took everything that lay within the contours of those oddly delineated borders and gave it a reality in verse, etching in words Transjordan's natural existence on the canvas of the mind's eye for those who read or heard his poetry. In so doing, he excoriated outsiders and usurpers, meaning especially the British Mandatory administration, its designated Hashemite emir, and anyone in the political arena who put personal gain ahead of service to the *watan*, demonstrating that the conception of the nation needed no authenticity from them, nor from the new capital at Amman or the *apparati* centered there by which the new state was governed. For many proponents of the new *wataniyya*—at least the history writers who delved into the remote past to articulate the present—people (*al-sha'ab*), not territory, were the decisive element. Intellectuals such as 'Arar may suggest a slight recalibration of that idea: people and their visceral sense of connection, ancient and nonlinear, to locale were the "decisive element" of the *watan*, regardless of a territory's contemporary shape or what ancient manmade monuments it contained.[104]

Characteristic of 'Arar's poetry is the centrality of his conception of landscape and its elements, and the way he comfortably shifts that understanding of space between timelessness and the contemporary moment. Very specific locales in Transjordan, the people who inhabited them, and their ordinary activities frequently served as the centerpiece of 'Arar's poems; against such a backdrop, he deployed blunt opposition politics in language replete with folkloric and religious symbolism. His 1934 poem "Oh Neighborhood of the Ban Tree" is a case in point.[105] In it, he delivers a warning to a "Mr. Abboud," a reference to Sheikh 'Abud al-Najjar, a religious scholar who came with Emir Abdullah to Transjordan and served as his primary court personage. 'Arar saw him as a dangerous sycophant, and takes the opportunity to remind the sheikh that he is not of Transjordan and its people, who yet long for Qahtan, that storied progenitor of the Arabs; it is a clear message to Abdullah about at least some domestic perceptions of his emirate. Sheikh 'Abud had, likely in a sermon, referenced Ridwan, the celestial being who guards heaven's gates. 'Arar proceeds to list a number of places in Jordan where Ridwan has never gone and typically Jordanian activities Ridwan has never experienced as a means to declare that the heaven of Sheikh 'Abud's teachings is no place he wants to go when he dies. Among the experiences Ridwan will never have are drinking from fresh water springs in Irbid, camping in Balqa, sitting under oak trees in Ajloun, hearing birds in the Jordan Valley, shepherding in Salt, and seeing beautiful animals such as gazelle and deer—which can traditionally serve in Arabic poetry as metaphors for women—in places such as Husn and Wadi al-Shita.

'Arar's understanding of people and landscape was indicative of an everyday reality that the iconography emerging in Abdullah's emirate and the paradigms of territory imposed by the West in many ways failed to capture. The Wadi al-Shita never made it onto any postage stamps, but just as people came to understand it as part of Transjordan, so too did they understand the landscapes and monuments that appeared on stamps and currency as belonging within the same borders as did the places of which 'Arar wrote so evocatively. He elegized the contours of the Transjordanian landscape in a paradigm other than that promoted at its center, with the landscape and its inhabitants the source of an inherently understood antiquity. This natural, unconscious interface of landscape, monument, and personal connection, meanwhile, depended on a subtly understood scriptural *longue durée* like that to which many of 'Arar's poems allude, but that was as legible internationally as it was domestically, even if established as the result of a Western paradigm.

'Arar spent much of his short life serving a system that he very publicly rebuked, paying for his indiscretion with exile and imprisonment, and continued to serve the citizens of the *watan* even when not in the role of civil servant. This is not irony, but in fact an important point. While 'Arar contested official narratives of the Hashemite Emirate of Transjordan through his very being, spinning his own early paradigm of a Jordan for Jordanians based on a very natural and timeless concept of connection between land and people, his work was one of the building blocks that ultimately served the official narrative he detested so much. 'Arar's narrative may have brought retribution upon him, but as a resource the new state and its citizens needed, he could be rehabilitated, or even if relapsed, tolerated. While he hurled polemics at the *apparati* of the state, historian Betty Anderson notes, "he also produced positive images of what it meant to be Transjordanian, presaging the emergence of an emotional patriotic tie to this state in which the people now found themselves living."[106] Crucial to that tie was the landscape of their daily lives as holistically understood. A Churchillian map may have initially created an unrecognizable *watan*, but Jordan's springs, valleys, and villages and their timeless and intangible connections to its people were legible. 'Arar imparted them and people's sense of belonging to them into his verse, and they radiated from inside out to realize the borders of Churchill's map, not the other way around. There is a fine line between accepting the territorial borders of the state and the legitimacy of the institutions that govern it. Their relationship contentious but somewhat codependent, with Emir Abdullah holding institutionalized power, the official narrative could co-opt that which contested it. The more 'Arar challenged the status quo, the more he ultimately served it.

'Arar's poetry offers the view of a public figure—an artist, activist, intellectual, and civil servant. How did other Transjordanians of the early emirate, the designated "tribes" of both Arab and international parlance, connect with their landscape and its antiquity?

The way the Liatneh and Bdul of Petra's environs understood and interacted with their landscape and its antiquity, elucidated by Tawfiq Canaan, resembles what I learned of one elderly resident's recollections of Tell Dhiban, the famous modern landscape of the Moabite king Mesha's capital at Dibon, when he was a boy.[107] Abu Dawud is believed to be in his eighties, which means he was likely born around 1930. As a young, unmarried man, he was a workman excavating at Dhiban, later working with British archaeologist Diana Kirkbride at Jerash and Ara'ir. At the time there was no village at Dhiban, only some tents. There were a few buildings on the tell but not many; the most notable was a tomb of someone clearly of local importance, which was probably among those removed by Lankester Harding when he was director of antiquities. People came to picnic on the tell for the powers of the relics of whomever was believed buried at its apex. Abu Dawud mentioned at least one mass burial in the vicinity of the tell, and said there are probably others. Once when he was herding on the tell, he found two stones, one inscribed with stars and another with four keys. He had given them to one of his sons, who had given them away, and their whereabouts were now unknown. He said that he has found a lot of beads and silver over the years, and that if he had known they were precious, he would have never given them to the archaeologists. There were also weird, round stones, he remembers, one that had a map on it (stories of stones and skins with mysterious maps to something equally mysterious are widespread in Jordan and are likewise heard in people's recollections of their villages in Palestine), and both were used as covers for two wells. One of these, sadly not the one with the map, was in the wall around his house. Abu Dawud and his son were also quite well versed in the story of Mesha.

In addition to the archaeological remains that local people find on tells, tells are also known as places where jinn like to reside. They like the early morning, and episodes of things like Bell's palsy that have attacked unwitting archaeologists have been attributed, jokingly and not, to the jinn who reside on the tell. Even today people will pay money for the assistance of Maghribiyeen (Moroccans who apparently use their spices and magic powers) to get rid of these jinn. Christians should not anger Muslim jinn, and vice versa. Abu Dawud referred to a fire in the *wadi*, which was a jinn. Some locals believe that before the Ottomans buried their gold (Ottomans burying their gold in archaeological sites before they left is a widespread story about every archaeological site in Jordan), they sacrificed an animal so as to spill its blood on the gold. This put a blood curse on the gold, serving as a *rasad*, or protection for the treasure. Jinns are also a kind of *rasad*, and can appear as fire or have a very large, black human form. A neighbor of Abu Dawud's had apparently transgressed one of the jinn on the site, who warned him to leave the place. The man did not heed the jinn's warning, and he died. "The jinn hit him," Abu Dawud said, meaning that it killed him. Despite such dire stories, the people of Dhiban have been digging on the tell and will continue to do so. What is officially considered looting serves real purposes for the people of the village, whether they are looking for something in particular that is valuable either to sell or keep, finding building materials or decorations for homes, or enjoying the hunt for the pleasure of sport and pastime.[108]

Much like 'Arar's conception of national space, such identifications with antiquity could serve or compete with official narratives made of the antiquity of Transjordan's landscape. Such identifications and narratives, however, always enable the realization of space; hence their power and the importance of harnessing it.

Britain granted Transjordan's independence in 1946. Jordan was from that moment a Hashemite kingdom, and Abdullah its king. Antiquity and its narratives, along with a range of institutions, had helped create a core out of a periphery with the Hashemites at its head, a national core that had, frankly, no more or less viable or problematic a narrative than any other. The war of 1948 would provide both opportunity and challenge for that Jordan core. After a contentious and manipulated vote west and east of the river, Jordan annexed what lay on its side of the 1948 armistice lines, banning the term "Palestine" and, in a remarkable turnabout of rhetorical and geographical perspective and the relationship between the core and periphery, naming it the "West Bank."[109] Thirty years after leaving the Hijaz for Syria, decades of patient waiting and state building on his side of the river and negotiations with the leadership of the Yishuv, and twenty years after interring his father on the *haram*, King Abdullah's goal of a larger hereditary possession including Jerusalem was realized. He did not live long to enjoy it. On Friday, 21 July 1951, a young Palestinian tailor's assistant became an assassin, shooting the king dead after prayers at al-Aqsa Mosque while in the company of his grandson Hussein, who would succeed him in short order.[110]

King Abdullah's assassination was only the latest in a series of events that had changed the world—again—in previously unimaginable ways. The struggle against colonialism entered a new era with the uncountable cataclysms of the 1948 war, and articulations of *qawmiyya* (increasingly used to refer to pan-nationalism) and *wataniyya* (increasingly used to refer to nation-state nationalism) would become rhetorically loaded in new ways that had important nuances depending on context. Egypt's Free Officers, led by survivors of horrors and humiliations of 1948, were about to show that self-determination could be had without accommodating the Great Powers or the changing dynamics among them, and, at least from appearances at the beginning, without selling out the *sha'ab* (people). His grandfather's assassination was only the first of many such difficult lessons for Hussein, who began his long career embroiled in irreconcilable contradictions. What was a kid who inherited a kingdom won by accommodation with the British and the Zionists, and therefore by unspeakable violence committed against people over whom he was now to rule, supposed to do? How could he compete? How could the periphery that became its own core rule the recognized and coveted core as part of itself?

'Arar passed away in 1949. *Al-Muqtataf's* run of nearly three-quarters of a century ended shortly thereafter. One wonders how the poet might have articulated the expanded borders of the Hashemite Jordanian Kingdom and the baggage that accompanied them, or in what ways the new geopolitical and rhetorical paradigms, those affected by them, and the consequences of the Cold War might have made their way into the contents of the journal of popular science. People like Abu Dawud, meanwhile, would be subject to vigorous settlement programs as part of an ongoing, but nuanced and renewed, modernity. The Hashemite king of Jordan undertook his role in that new phase of modernity as a nationalist, reconciling Jordan's existential contradictions and his family's role in them in carefully nuanced iterations of both *qawmiyya* and *wataniyya*, and making the space of Palestine a periphery to a Jordanian core. The connections of people like Abu Dawud to the ancient landscape upon which he lived, emotive images of that timeless landscape such as those evoked in 'Arar's verse, and the antiquity that gave that landscape historical continuity in the pages of *al-Muqtataf* would be deployed in narratives that were familiar, yet carefully adapted for the competitive context of the 1950s and 1960s.

CHAPTER 6

Antiquity, Pan-National, and Nation-State Narratives in the Expanded Hashemite Kingdom

Nationalists . . . identify for members of the community the historical "lessons" to be learned from the past. From an historical record replete with shining moments and splendid heroes, but also marred by unsatisfactory compromises and ignominious defeats, nationalists stress the former while giving a particular twist to the latter . . . commemoration enables the producers of nationalism to erase or turn into object lessons what they perceive as negative moments and episodes in the national past.[1]

Petra was the great exception in a Jordan core containing little monumental antiquity. It fit within Western paradigms of universal value, but resounded for Arab and non-Arab audiences in different ways. For Petra's locals, the landscape of the site had acute religious and personal meanings, many of which were related to seminal moments in the vast Abrahamic story. Early Western visitors saw both grandeur and lessons of the fall of civilization infused with religious and racial essentialism. Muslims and Arabs could also understand religious lessons in Petra and its nearby counterpart Mada'in Salih (in what is today Saudi Arabia), but the ruin of civilization was not, for them, as a Western audience saw it. It was, rather, evidence of the consequences of refusing to submit to God's will.

Jordan's textbooks narrate Petra for schoolchildren in a way indicative of how the expanded Hashemite kingdom (1950–67) ruled its new Palestine periphery from its core east of the river. While these schoolbooks say little about antiquity generally, they narrate the monumental antiquity of Jordan's core, Petra, less and differently than they narrate that of its periphery, Jerusalem. In owning the narrative of Palestine from Amman, they speak of Jerusalem in terms of its Abrahamic history, presented inseparably from its Semitic-

Arab history. What they say of Petra, meanwhile, is practically devoid of the local or Abrahamic traditions embedded in it. Petra's importance in history and social studies textbooks is that the Nabateans built and inhabited it, and that they were Arabs. Official discourse thus rhetorically divorced local and religious meaning from the discourse of the monumental antiquities site of Hashemite Jordan's core, largely reserving such meanings for Jerusalem and the other parts of Palestine over which Jordan now ruled and the narratives of which it sought to own, further instantiating the paradigm separating the universal value of sacred space from that of antique space. Petra thus became a device for fostering visceral feeling for the Jordanian landscape rooted in the life of the ancient Arab Nabateans and what became, in the narrative of the modern state, their contemporary Jordanian descendants, who played particular important roles in the state's order.

The scientific study of the past had helped realize the Nabateans much as it did other ancient peoples. Despite, and perhaps because of, the obscurities regarding their origins and their world generally, it has been easy for both Arab and foreign scholars to render the Nabateans "Arabs." Nabateans appear in early and medieval Arabic sources, from hadith, to lexicons, histories, and prose.[2] Some Nabateans were known to inhabit parts of Iraq and Bilad al-Sham.[3] Sources suggest that Arab writers considered at least some Nabateans to also be Arabs. A few very early Arabic sources, including some hadith, indicate a strong kin or socioeconomic relationship between the Nabateans and the Quraysh, the tribe of the Prophet and ultimately of the Hashemite family.[4] By extension, this situates the Nabateans in the scientific taxonomy of Arab Semites that developed in the late nineteenth century to parallel the Prophet Muhammad's canonical genealogy. Nabateans as Arabs, Arabs without Nabatean monikers, and Nabateans/Arabs as nomads and as a vast and powerful kingdom based on trade also appear in classical texts such as those of Diodorus Siculus (first century BCE) and Josephus (first century CE).

Upon its expansion, Jordan stopped using textbooks from Lebanon, Syria, Egypt, and Iraq and began producing its own.[5] Jordanian textbooks heavily deployed Palestinian, and particularly Jerusalem, narratives to demonstrate ownership of universally valued space they considered Jordanian and ruled from the capital of the Hashemite core. These textbooks used what was discursively nonsacral antiquity such as Petra, meanwhile, to disseminate pan-national and national narratives to schoolchildren in Jordan's part of a regional competition shaped by the Cold War. For those articulating pan-national narratives, sites like Petra were easily linked to the historicity and continuity of great ancient "Arab" civilization. At the same time, they enabled particularly Jordanian narratives, commemorating the past to be instructive for the present. The antiquity of the Hashemites, the hybrid Semitic-Arab-Abrahamic telos, could be woven through all narratives.

A fifth-grade text called *The Hashemite Reader* (1966) contains among its collection of religious and literary readings and fables a solitary selection on Petra, and one of few references in a textbook to the biblical Edomites. After describing the city as predominantly Greek and Roman, but having some importance to Islamic history, the unnamed author says:

> Petra was the city of the Edomites, who were among the ancient Semitic peoples. Then the Nabateans triumphed over them. They [the Nabateans] were Arabs who came from the west of Iraq, a people of civilization and trade, and the city flourished in their days.[6]

'Adnan Lutfi 'Uthman, who authored the high school text *al-Watan al-'Arabi* (The Arab Nation, 1965, 1967), writes more extensively of the Nabateans, locating their civilization not in Bilad al-Sham but among "civilizations in the south and north of the Arabian Peninsula."[7] He therefore connects the ancient Arab Nabateans to Greater Syria in much the same way that the Hashemites, whose origins were Arabian, were connected to Greater Syria in the present. In their Arabian context, 'Uthman includes the Nabateans among the other pre-Islamic civilizations known for their hydrotechnology, namely the Minaeans, Sabeans, Himyarites, and Ghassanids.[8] About the archaeology of Petra, 'Uthman says:

> We realize the greatness of what the Nabateans brought to it in terms of prosperity and wealth, because the state that has the ability to carve luxurious, elegant houses from rock had engineering as advanced as that of today. Such a state is at the pinnacle of its power, hardiness, and richness.
>
> The geographical location of Petra and its suitability for commerce put its people in a position of control over all ancient trade . . . Petra was at the center of this land trade, and its people at the heart of the transport of goods to the ends of the ancient world, no less than what the greatest ports undertake in the present era.[9]

The ancient Arab citizens of Jordan are instructive for the contemporary citizenry of the expanded Jordan core. Jordan's ancient peoples set a precedent for high civilization, and just like them, modern Jordanians have a strategic role to play on the regional and global stage of power and wealth. Using a different strategy, other textbook authors write that the Nabateans are first attested in the sixth century BCE, when they appear as bedouin in the desert of southern Jordan. They subsequently gave up the bedouin life for a settled life of farming and commerce and established their capital at Petra. The first firm date for them is 312 BCE.[10] Still other authors go a step further, saying, "It is appropriate to mention that the Huwaytat tribe, widespread in southern Bilad al-Sham and Sinai, are among their descendants."[11] While it is difficult to say just how popular the link between the Huwaytat and the Nabateans was, the notion clearly did exist, domestically and internationally, on some level.[12] This message is similar to that embedded in stamps and currency depicting Petra and Jerash to demonstrate that the Hashemites linked Jordanians of disparate regions together into a core under their leadership. In addition to the importance of the Arabian context of Petra and the ancient Nabateans to mirror modern connections between the Hashemites and Greater Syria and Iraq, Petra's meaning has added nuance if, in fact, the famous Huwaytat, considered "true" Arab bedouin and composing a large portion of especially the martial institutions of state, are modern descendants of those ancient Arab Nabateans. The bedouin taxonomy of some Arabs, real or imagined, has provided a romantic ethos for westerners, and therefore proven useful for identity narratives in Jordan. Romanticism for the peoples who lived in and near Petra, Petra's attractiveness as an antiquities site with universal value, and the fact that Jordanians of the region provided many bodies to serve the state in the capacity of the military have rendered Petra's environs and its inhabitants pragmatic for the Hashemites in myriad ways.

Jordan presents Petra to schoolchildren in this scholarly framework because it conveyed simultaneous narratives of both pan-national and nation-state nationalisms. While *wataniyya* could still carry its meaning of a broad Arab nation based on taxonomy of territory, it had also come to refer to a more localized, nation-state nationalism. Pan-nationalism, meanwhile, now frequently took the form of *qawmiyya*, an identity rooted in a taxonomy of people, or *qawm*. How these concepts were deployed, when, and by whom, was highly contextual, fluid, and hybrid. Global competition for resources and narratives in the region had entered an era that was less about questioning the nation-state paradigm and more about seeking national self-determination and forging regional alliances within its framework. The Hashemites thus used antiquities to espouse both national and pan-national narratives in a context fraught with contradictions and existential threats. Egypt's Gamal abd al-Nasser having emerged as the charismatic figurehead of pan-Arabism, Jordan had to show deference to his popular stances and initiatives while simultaneously promoting its own Hashemite vision of leadership as the answer to Arab unity. This meant that against Nasser's support of Cold War non-alignment and his vehement anti-imperial rhetoric and actions, the Hashem-ites had to defend their abject opposition to Communism and their depen-dence on Britain and the United States. In an age of defiant anti-imperialism, the link between Hashemite interests and the family's long relationship with Britain was fraught. Jordan's 1946 treaty with Britain was rightly understood internationally and in the Arab world not as a document guaranteeing Jor-dan's independence, but one firmly rendering Jordan to British servitude for another twenty-five years.[13] The Hashemites lived under the shadow of having colluded with Zionist leaders while Nasser and many of Egypt's Free Officers spent weeks in 1948 taking heavy fire in the trenches of Palestine's battle-fields.[14] While Nasser allied with Syria and rallied the Arab world against Israel, the Hashemites faced sharing an enormous and unstable border with its new national neighbor. Publicly they had to summon support for Pales-tinian national aspirations despite the fact that Jordan had annexed most of what remained of Palestine and its people after 1948, referring to the land as Jordan and the people as Jordanians, and fulfilling a long-held Hashemite aspiration for territorial gain. Having built a Jordanian core from a Holy Land periphery, the Hashemites now sought to rule the Holy Land core of Palestine as its own Jordanian periphery.

This chapter considers how, upon expansion of the borders of the Jordan *watan*, the Hashemites recalibrated the use of antiquities and their narratives to confront the fact that they had finally achieved physical control over Pales-tine's heavily loaded cache of heritage, holistically composed of land, monu-ments, memories, and citizens. As of 1948, the Jordan core they designed included Jerusalem, but it was the crown jewel of what was, in effect, a new physical periphery. To own the Palestine periphery along with their core, the Hashemites set forth to own, in similar fashion as had the British, antiquities designated as having universal value and their narratives. Where the British sought to own antiquities and their narratives to separate these spaces in the postwar nation-state order, Jordan did so to unify them under Hashemite suzerainty from Amman. This was in the context of a multi-nodal competi-tion involving Hussein, Nasser, Syria, Israel, and the Palestinians. In this part of the analysis, I consider phenomena presented in earlier chapters—stamps, currency, the practical development of the discipline of archaeology, the edu-cation system—to discuss Jordan's elevation of the narrative of Palestine's universal value as Jordanian.

The second part of the analysis focuses on Jordan's history and social studies school textbooks of this period to demonstrate the ways in which antiquity, through both history and archaeology, was deployed to address competitive

Hashemite narratives of both *qawmiyya* and *wataniyya*. Given that Jordan's historicity narrative as established through prevailing archaeological syntheses was so similar to, dependent upon, and ultimately subservient to Israel's, in the context of owning Jerusalem, narratives told by history were less problematic for Jordan than those told by archaeology. History and archaeology were thus largely discursively separated. This helped perpetuate binary notions of antiquities for religious versus tourist pilgrimage; in expanded Jordan, historical narratives emphasized the traditional and sacred, while archaeological narratives emphasized the modern and developmental. History was thus particularly useful for expressing narratives of *qawmiyya*, especially as concerned Jerusalem, and archaeology for narratives supporting *wataniyya*, particularly as concerned tourism without universally understood religious value. Given the conflation of Abrahamic and Semitic identity, and the Hashemites' pedigree in the context of that conflation, history more easily supported the Hashemites in the competitive discourse of pan-Arabism, simultaneously challenging the antiquity of Israel's historicity narrative by Arab-izing the Semites and thus the Israelites as one among a long line of related peoples, but certainly not the earliest. Universal value was thus not to be found in antiquities per se, but in the history of their ethnic taxonomy: who could lay earliest claim to them? Archaeology, meanwhile, figured heavily in narratives of contemporary development and its measures, supporting the narrative of Jordan's progress and modernity under Hashemite leadership.

Subsuming Palestine

With the expansion of its borders and population, Jordan immediately set about the task of visually subsuming Palestine to emphasize control by a state centered in Amman. While bespeaking a message of control from Amman, however, the Hashemites perpetuated the British paradigm of narrative ownership, focusing its heritage discourse on Palestine, especially Jerusalem. Under Glubb Pasha's command, the Arab Legion advanced and held its ranks to encompass the West Bank and East Jerusalem in the 1948 war, success that was ultimately questioned as collusion with the Zionists. Between displaced and annexed persons, Jordan's population had more than tripled. If natural ties among peoples had suffered greatly when modern political borders were drawn at the end of the First World War, the war of 1948 was devastating in new ways.[15] Palestinians who now found themselves living in Jordan had had a very different interwar national experience than did their Jordanian counterparts, and Amman's appropriation of Palestine was only the latest, following both England and Israel, which had just demonstrated its martial command of Palestine narratives.

The period of the expanded kingdom was dangerous for all involved. Following a brief period of political liberalization at the beginning of his reign that proved threatening to his throne, King Hussein found himself in a crisis-by-crisis battle to keep it. Jordanians demanded greater popular participation in government, political freedoms, and improved socioeconomic conditions, while those in power demonstrated that they were willing to use force and coercion against them.[16] The ongoing refugee crisis and constant raiding and violence along the Jordan-Israel border underscored conditions in the kingdom. Particularly egregious reprisals from the Israel Defense Forces (IDF), such as that at the West Bank village of Qibya in 1953, resulted in heavy civilian casualties and widespread destruction, highlighting the Arab Legion's problems to maintain security along the border and the fact that its uppermost echelons were composed of British, not Jordanian, officers, including its commander, General John Bagot Glubb (Pasha).[17] By early January 1956, with Nasser having directly intervened to cause the dissolution of Hussein's government and assailing the king from Radio Cairo as the "pygmy of imperialism," Jordan announced that it would not join the unpopular Baghdad Pact, a final British attempt to cobble together an alliance to defend their regional interests against the Soviets. That March, Hussein dismissed Glubb from the kingdom, thus nationalizing the Arab Legion. Nasser had, by the end of the year, nationalized the Suez Canal and would be at the height of his power in the wake of the ensuing colonial conflict. By the end of 1958, Hussein had invoked the Eisenhower Doctrine twice, once during what has been remembered as a coup from within the Arab Legion (1957), and again when a grisly coup wiped the Hashemites out of Iraq, ending plans for a union between Iraq and Jordan to compete with the United Arab Republic (UAR), a union of Egypt and Syria (1958–61). The Palestinian movement, meanwhile, grew so threatening to entrenched powers that Nasser and Hussein collaborated to support the establishment of the Palestine Liberation Organization (PLO) in 1964 in an attempt to control it. Three years later, Israel would deliver Nasser a catastrophic defeat, occupying not just the Sinai but the Golan from Syria and the West Bank, decisively wresting it from Jordan's control.

While Amman issued new stamps bearing Palestine iconography almost immediately after the war, Jordan's use of postage stamps to co-opt Palestinian identity had occurred before it. Following a 1946 Arab League resolution, Jordan, along with other Arab countries, printed the "Palestine Aid" stamp series. These featured widely recognized holy sites of Palestine, including the Dome of the Rock, Hebron's Ibrahimi Mosque, and Acre's Jazzar

Mosque. Revenue that these stamps generated was used to aid development projects for Palestinian Arabs living under the Mandate. In 1951, with the West Bank part of Jordan, an extraordinary session of parliament and a royal decree implemented a temporary law appropriating all revenue from sale of the "Aid" stamps for projects to be undertaken not only in the West Bank but also throughout the kingdom. The subsequent ordinary session of parliament refused to confirm the temporary law, however, and the stamps were instead withdrawn from circulation on the first of the year, 1952.[18]

In 1952, Jordan printed a set of nine stamps commemorating the 1950 unification of what were now the "East and West Banks" of the River Jordan (fig. 6.1).[19] The newly unified kingdom employed its two most recognizable monuments on these stamps, one for each "Bank"—the Dome of the Rock and *al-Khazna*—shown with the river between them. This stamp series provided Jordan the easiest and fastest visual means by which to link these new concepts of the "East" and "West" Banks of its kingdom. Jordan had nationalized Petra on its earliest stamps, shortly after Emir Abdullah and King Faysal had buried Sharif Husayn on the *haram*. Juxtaposing Petra with the Dome of the Rock on a stamp was a logical step in finally nationalizing the latter, and in all of Palestine Jordan had come to control.

The 1952 "unity stamp" marked the beginning of the incorporation of West Bank sites as Jordanian iconography and the trend of juxtaposing East and West Bank landscapes. It was also common for stamp series featuring the Hashemite kingdom's cultural heritage to include a stamp bearing a portrait of the monarch, under whose auspices the two sides of the river now existed as one nation. A 1954 series included Petra's *al-Dayr*, King Hussein, al-Aqsa Mosque, and the Dome of the Rock. The very first Jordanian air mail stamp was issued as part of this series, depicting an airplane flying over the Colonnaded Street of Jerash. This series was issued again in 1955, with a stamp featuring the Dome of the Rock. A watermark was added to each stamp of this series that read, "HKJ," for "Hashemite Kingdom of Jordan," and, in Arabic, "*al-Urdun*," for "Jordan." The sites depicted on these stamps were thus emblazoned with the name of the country to which they belonged.

From the late 1950s until Jordan lost the West Bank in the 1967 war, Jerash was the only East Bank site, and the only site that could not be called a "holy" site, to make another appearance on Jordan's stamps.[20] Jordan utilized Palestinian cultural heritage extensively on stamps of this period. As in British guidebooks of the earlier Mandate era, emphasis in these stamp series in independent, expanded Jordan lay on Christian and Muslim "holy sites" of recognized universal value, all of which were, at that time, located in the West Bank and which Jordan carefully cultivated for religious tourism.[21] Tied

Fig. 6.1. The 1952 "unity stamp," celebrating the unification of the "East" and "West" Banks of the River Jordan as the Hashemite Jordanian kingdom. Copyright Mr. Mansour Mouasher, used by permission. Photo by E. Corbett, August 2013. Stamps generously provided by Mr. Awni Hadidi.

to efforts to develop religious tourism, Jordan created multiple stamp series over a number of years commemorating Pope Paul VI's 1964 visit to the Holy Land (fig. 6.2), conveying messages of Hashemite ownership and guardianship of the holy city and its peace. Each stamp included a portrait of the pontiff in papal attire and a portrait of King Hussein in military dress. These lay atop al-Aqsa Mosque, the Dome of the Rock, and the Churches of the Holy Sepulchre and the Nativity. Another stamp was issued to commemorate, during the Pope's visit, the first meeting between the Latin and Greek patriarchs

Fig. 6.2. 1964 papal visit stamps. Copyright Mr. Mansour Mouasher, used by permission. Photo by E. Corbett, August 2013. Stamps generously provided by Mr. Awni Hadidi.

since the fifteenth century. Set against a Jerusalem cityscape, portraits of the Pope and the Greek patriarch grace the corners of the stamps while a portrait of King Hussein, dressed as a civilian, sits between them, mediator and protector of Jerusalem, for Christian and Muslim holy places alike.[22] A year later, Jordan issued a stamp commemorating the one-year anniversary of the pontiff's visit, featuring a Jerusalem cityscape at its center, flanked by portraits of Pope Paul and King Hussein. Jordan commemorated Pope Paul's visit to the United Nations headquarters in 1966 with a stamp featuring the pontiff, again with the king and the Greek patriarch against the backdrop of Jerusalem.[23]

Jordan also issued gold and silver commemorative coins for the papal visit that, like the currency and some stamp series of this era, sought to blend the "best" of both banks, a visual representation of a united Holy Land under Hashemite leadership. The obverse of these coins featured a portrait of King Hussein. On the reverse of the twenty-five-dinar coin was a portrait of the Dome of the Rock; on that of the ten-dinar coin a portrait of the pontiff and the Gethsemane Church in Jerusalem; the five-dinar coin featured Petra's *al-Khazna* on the reverse; and the two-dinar coin the Oval Forum of Jerash. The silver coins all featured a portrait of King Hussein on the obverse. A Jerusalem cityscape graced the reverse of the one-dinar coin, the Shrine of the Nativity in Bethlehem that of the three-quarter-dinar coin, and one of the "desert castles," Qasr Kharana, was the subject of the reverse of the half-dinar coin.

Digging the Hashemite Holy Land

While all of Jordan was the subject of increasing archaeological interest during this time, stakeholders—scholars, governments, and publics—focused, as they always had, primarily on Palestine. This was reinforced in the West Bank under Hashemite control, but in a way emphasizing the Jordanian national context in which archaeological work occurred. Prior to 1948, the *Quarterly of the Department of Antiquities of Palestine*, a Jerusalem-based publication of the Mandatory British government, carried all archaeological updates on Transjordanian sites. The annexation of the West Bank within the kingdom's borders gave Jordan a new and very important role to play in the biblical archaeology of the coming two decades.[24] The first issue of the *Annual of the Department of Antiquities of Jordan (ADAJ)* was published in 1951. It was "designed to be a successor for East and West Jordan to the *Quarterly of the Department of Antiquities of Palestine*, and sponsored by the Government of the Hashemite Kingdom of Jordan."[25] Gerald Lankester Harding, director of the Transjordan Department of Antiquities and a British employee of Jordan's government since 1936, oversaw the building and opening of the Jordan Archaeological Museum on the Amman Citadel in 1951, and moved the department's offices there.

Harding fell victim to the same purge that exorcised the kingdom of British general Glubb in spring 1956. During the summer and in the midst of Nasser's electrifying showdown with England, France, and Israel over the Suez Canal, Harding was driven out of Jordan in a competitive smear campaign of anti-imperial rhetoric over his purchase and handling of the Dead Sea Scrolls, which he did publicly, legally, and deliberately on Jordan's behalf in his capacity as the head of the Department of Antiquities since their initial discovery in 1946.[26] For the first time, control of Jordan's antiquities and the department that oversaw them went to Jordanian archaeologists and administrators. They continued working closely with foreign scholars, and fieldwork west and east of the river proceeded apace. Peter Parr, then of the British School of Archaeology in Jerusalem (BSAJ), remembers his work in Jordan during this time as based on mutual cooperation and professionalism, devoid of any political baggage.[27]

The second and third volumes of the *ADAJ* were published in 1952 and

1953 before it went on hiatus for seven years. It reappeared in 1960, with a long note at the beginning from the first Jordanian director of antiquities to have a degree in archaeology, Dr. ʿAwni Dajani, who moved the department's offices from their location at the Amman Citadel back to the Roman Theatre.[28] The note was about the nature of administrative and physical reorganization of the department in the novel national context throughout the 1950s, with reference to the difficult years at the end of the decade, which explains the delay in publication.[29] The *ADAJ* was itself undergoing significant developments, as the 1960 issue was the first to include, under the direction of Dajani, an Arabic-language section. Among the items included in the *ADAJ* is a summary of archaeological work in Jordan between 1949 and 1959, and articles about projects on both the East and West Banks, including sites with obvious biblical importance such as Shechem and Jericho, as well as Petra and Azraq. Much of the archaeological work between 1951 and 1967 on both banks of the Jordan seems to have focused on sites of biblical or monumental importance.[30] While non-Jordanian archaeologists conducted most of these projects, the number of Jordanian archaeologists grew, gaining more prominence, working closely with international teams, and undertaking projects of their own for the Department of Antiquities.[31] These archaeologists included Dr. Khair Yassine and Dr. ʿAwni Dajani, among others, and, toward the end of the period, Dr. Fawzi Zayadine. Projects of this period included continued work at Petra, and others with implications for exploring biblical history, such as excavations at Bab edh-Dhra, Jericho, Dhiban, Pella of the Decapolis, Heshbon, Shechem, and Qumran (where the Dead Sea Scrolls were found), and a survey of the Jordan River Valley.[32]

The Challenge of Reconciling History and Archaeology

The nationalization of school textbooks in the early 1950s marked the beginning of efforts to standardize Jordanian primary and secondary education in the expanded national context.[33] Most countries mandate education for children in an attempt not only to ensure their future productivity but also to instill values of citizenship. Such values present a recognizable framework of normative behavior by which the citizens of the community—the nation—conduct themselves. Citizens of the nation must know and accept the spatial and juridical parameters of their state, their origins, and what in the history of their state makes it unique and legitimate. These attributes are what identify them as citizens of their own state vis-à-vis citizens of another.

In this case, the parameters of the state were a Hashemite kingdom with an East Bank core and a West Bank periphery, and what made it unique and legitimate was its role and that of its royal family in a larger, positivist Arab story. Here the projection of state power embedded in education laws meets that embedded in historical narratives of the nation. Curricula are mandated, and textbooks are a vehicle for delivering them. Jordan's Ministry of Education produced both. Since schoolchildren are a captive audience, the presentation of antiquity in textbooks, particularly those written for history and social studies classes, has incredible power for the potential success of the national project, its narratives, and enabling the mind's eye to envision the historical and social landscape of the nation. Textbooks are the verbal counterpart to the visual messages carried in the iconography of stamps and currency.

According to a 1965 elementary and high school teachers' social studies curriculum guide, "The General Goals for Teaching Social Studies" are "striving for the development of the student civically to a level by which it is possible for him to live in a community while preserving his rights and undertaking his duties with a positive and cooperative spirit and sense of responsibility."[34] Social studies specifically seeks to develop "understanding of the students' *milieu* from different perspectives gradually, from the house to the school, to the village or the city, to the municipality or the governorate, to the grand Arab nation."[35] This understanding leads to other important lessons. Among those listed are the good and bad aspects of the contemporary Jordanian and Arab situation, consciousness of the Arab *umma* and Arab unity, the importance of investment, economic development, rights, democracy, the Palestine issue, understanding the Arab past, Arab tradition, Arab heritage, the importance of Arab Islamic civilization, and the importance of thinking about the future.[36] Like history, archaeology, and their interpretation for historical consciousness, the process of educating the citizen is thus unrelentingly contextual and political at the level of its fundamental intentions.

In 1955, Jordan implemented a public education law that went a long step beyond production of new textbooks. Throughout the kingdom, this legislation required

> adoption of textbooks and teaching methods approved by the Jordanian Ministry of Education and the exclusive use of Arabic as the language of instruction. Schools were to close on Fridays and national holidays, including all Muslim holidays, and students, whether Muslim or Christian, were to study only their own religion.[37]

Kimberly Katz writes that King Hussein intervened to extend a degree of leniency with this law vis-à-vis foreign-run religious schools, most of which were in Jerusalem. Approximately ten years later, however, Jordan enacted another public education law affirming anew the provision of the earlier one.[38]

Jordan's model for standardizing education has endured. The Ministry of Education still develops and mandates a uniform curriculum, producing all textbooks and various uniform exams from the first through twelfth grades. Not only public schools in the kingdom, but also private schools and schools run by the United Nations Relief and Works Agency (UNRWA), must be in compliance with the national curriculum. The fact of curriculum standardization is critical to understanding the impact of formulations of history and antiquity as presented in textbooks. Exams, and thus progression from one grade to the next, were and are designed and mandated around the knowledge disseminated in textbooks such as those under discussion. Passing the *tawjihi* and obtaining a certificate of graduation from secondary school means intimately knowing the content of those books.

How did textbooks of this period present Jordan's national narrative in the framework of standardized education and its discourses of history and archaeology? Betty Anderson says that the narrative "follows four interrelated tracks: the Hashemites as vigilant fighters against imperialism; the Hashemites as the leading Arab nationalists in the region; the Hashemites as the sole protectors of the Palestinian people and nation; and, most importantly, the Hashemites as patron-fathers of the Jordanian people."[39]

The irony, of course, is that many people didn't view the Hashemites in either Jordan or Iraq as Arab nationalists, but saw them as collaborators with imperialists and Zionists. Many, moreover, saw the Jordanian Hashemites, having annexed the West Bank and East Jerusalem, co-opted Palestinian imagery and discourse, and banned the use of "Palestine" to describe something other than a part of Jordan, as outright hostile to the aspirations of the Palestinian people and their nation. It was quite a project to assert their legitimate rule, and that from Amman, unabashedly owning a national narrative encompassing an East Bank core and a West Bank periphery as an embodiment of Arabness. To properly serve the cause of national history writing, then, Jordanian schoolbooks of the period under study had to simultaneously promote Arab nationalism and Hashemite Jordanian nationalism, and to defend against Zionism while mitigating the intellectual dissonances created by the political situation described in the introduction to this chapter. The solution was twofold: to speak of ancient Arab history in contemporary terms, and to speak of modern Arab history in their own, Hashemite terms. Gershoni and Jankowski's observations of national commemoration in Egypt are applicable in the Jordan context:

Selected events of the past are reworked, through commemoration, into a purposive, teleological account of history . . . This narrative defines the periodization of the history of the nation, determines the relative importance of the events and individuals that comprise its content, and by exclusion mandates what is trivial and best forgotten.[40]

Jordanian textbooks commemorate the millennia of history in the following basic way: at the hands of the ancient kingdoms of Israel and Judah, and the empires of Greece, Rome, Persia, Byzantium, and the Turks, the Arabs are victims of usurping colonizers. In the Islamic *umma* they find progress in the strength of unity, and heroes in the defenders of the faith, such as those who fought with the Prophet Muhammad and Salah al-Din. The diversity of the *umma* was both its strength and its demise. Diversity was ultimately what left the Arabs susceptible to Turkish oppression in the final decades of the Ottoman Empire. According to the textbooks, it is in those decades that the Hashemite family, of the Prophet's clan of Quraysh, set forth to redefine Arab unity in modern, nationalist terms, strengthening the Arabs against their Ottoman overlords and Arab rights against European and Zionist imperialists who win by deception every time.[41] As for Jordanians themselves, they are nameless, faceless citizens defined only by lifestyle—urbanite, fellahin, bedouin:

The inhabitants of the Kingdom are bedu and settled. The settled work in agriculture, commerce, and industry and live in cities and villages.
  The bedu work in raising livestock, and many work in agriculture. Among the most famous tribes that live in tents are: the Banu Sakhr, Huwaytat, 'Adwan, Banu Hassan, Banu Khaled, al-Sirhan, Banu Hamida, al-Ghazawiyya and al-Balawna.[42]

Uniting the inhabitants is the allegiance they owe to the patriarch-king of their tribe-nation for their national deliverance and for the largesse he bestows upon them.[43]
  While ancient history in general is discussed in the textbooks in a polemical fashion presented as factual detail, archaeology itself, such an important component of the development of national self-consciousness and heralded as a scientific method of history just decades prior, is generally a bland presentation of lists. Archaeology and archaeological sites are frequently mentioned, but without the conviction used to talk about the historical events important to the context of their creation. The following list comes under the heading "Historical Antiquities, Antiquities of the Islamic *Fath*" (Conquest):

> In our country there are a great number of historical remains, among the
> most important: Petra, Jerash, Jerusalem, Jericho, Sebastia, Ascalon, Caesa-
> rea, Shawbak, Rabad and Baʿir Castles, and other marvelous remains . . .
>
> Some of these remains are very old—from the days of the Romans or
> before that—and some of them remain from the days of the Islamic *fath*.
> Our country was a path for the Muslim victors who came from the holy
> country of the Hijaz to conquer Bilad al-Sham. Our forefathers built Arab
> castles on the fringes of the steppe-lands and fortified them. Among the
> most famous are: Qasr Mshatta, Azraq, Baʿir, Amra, and Hallabat. Among
> these remains are many tombs of great leaders . . .
>
> South of Kerak are the graves of the immortal heroes who paved the
> way for the Muslims and met the strength of the Byzantines in the battle of
> Muʾta near Kerak.[44]

With few exceptions, and largely even in the case of Petra, sites and artifacts
are never presented in much detail. The details that *are* presented are generally
simplistic and often wrong, even given the limited amounts of excavation and
research that may have existed at the time of writing.[45]

At first glance this is surprising, given that Jordan went to substantial
lengths to assure that audiences could recognize its visual monumental capital.[46] Stamps and currency, among other measures, ensured that its antiquities
sites were recognizable at home and abroad as being within its borders, and
that in conjunction with one another, they created a composite visual corpus
commemorating the nation. During the period, furthermore, there was no
lack of interest in, coverage of, or awareness of archaeology. *Al-Muqtataf* circulated widely for more than seven decades, and other, similar journals were in
print. Jordan's competition with Israel (in the context of its competition with
Nasser) over the Dead Sea Scrolls, meanwhile, generated a lot of media and
public interest in archaeology both at home and abroad.[47] What Jordan faced
was not lack of knowledge, concern, or awareness of archaeology, but difficulty
to reconcile history and archaeology in its national narrative.

There are a number of interrelated reasons for this difficulty. One is the
instantiated discursive separation between antiquities that were religious and
those that were not. Emir Abdullah sought the establishment of the Department of Antiquities of Transjordan after a visit to Palestine.[48] King Abdullah, for obvious reasons, focused on the religious capital gained by claims
to the holy sites that surrounded and somehow involved Jordan—namely in
Arabia and Palestine. By means of the 1946 constitution upon Jordan's independence from Britain, furthermore, the state had centralized all authority
over *awqaf* (religious endowments, including holy places and assets dedicated

to them), of which the corpus in Palestine and Jerusalem was especially sub-stantive.[49] We thus see not just a discursive, but a physical separation, like that established in scholarly discourse and Mandate policy, of active monumental "holy" sites of veneration and archaeological sites, working in tandem with notions of landscape as a terrain held holistically sacred in different ways by foreigners and locals. King Hussein emulated this discourse. When he talked about archaeological and other heritage sites that are religious in nature, the rhetoric in his published speeches is pure poetry infused with Arabism. In his public speeches he frequently talked about archaeology, but in the context of development. When speaking about sites that have no well-understood, para-digmatic link to religious heritage, especially prior to the loss of Jerusalem and the West Bank in the 1967 war, he talked about them in a way similar to that in which textbooks present them.[50] As the following pages demonstrate, textbook archaeology in this context is not a panegyric to the landscape. It is, rather, a practical discussion of antiquities' importance to the contemporary nation — an economic resource vital to development.

Echoes of Jurji Zaydan's admonitions in the late nineteenth-century pages of *al-Muqtataf* suggest another problem for archaeology in Jordan's historical narrative. Scholars whose names appear in these pages, like Peter Parr, Nelson Glueck, Kathleen Kenyon, and those who deserve more mention than can be given here, such as Paul Lapp and Crystal Bennett, among others, under-took careers full of serious work in Jordan. They were not Arabs, and did not publish in Arabic. Whatever their scholarly or political inclinations or inno-vations, their academic frames of reference, no matter the period in which they worked — from the most remote antiquity to the most modern — were in the first place attributable to the paradigms established by a range of Ori-entalist scholars that had become disciplinary canon. While these paradigms had worked fairly harmoniously for the audiences of *al-Muqtataf*, the West-ern audience for the same scholarship did not approach it with the additional intertextuality as did those embedded in localized and broader-based Islami-cate traditions, whether sympathetic to or dismissive of those traditions. Their capacity for interpretive observations about landscapes, sites, and meanings, therefore, was limited in a way that those of Arab and Muslim professionals might not have been. And such limited interpretive observations had contrib-uted in no small way to the contemporary geopolitical situation.

The education and training of Jordanians — of Palestinian and Jordanian backgrounds alike — to work in antiquities had been underfoot since the earli-est days of the Mandate. In the 1950s and 1960s such professionals were a growing cadre, but still relatively few. At that point, Jordanian archaeologists like ʿAwni Dajani, Kheir Yassine, Fawzi Zayadine, Moawiyyah Ibrahim, and all who have come along since had to obtain their degrees abroad. The *Annual of the Department of Antiquities of Jordan*, first published in 1951 and which from the earliest days featured a section for Arabic-language articles, has always been a publication for a specialist audience, offering progress reports on the past year's excavations and finds. Popular writing about archaeology in Arabic was and remains, unlike in the days of journals such as *al-Muqtataf*, most often produced by journalists.[51] A related limitation is the significant amount of capital required to implement the excavation and development of sites. Since an important component of the story of modern Jordan is in many ways the story of a search for capital in a resource-poor country, it is, perhaps, remarkable that Jordan has directed as many resources as it has for training archaeologists and caring for sites.

A third difficulty in reconciling history and archaeology in the Jordanian narrative is Jordan's perceived lack of archaeology of monumental or universal value. Jordan didn't have such monuments or archives as those found in Mesopotamia or Egypt, or a connection to the landscape of Palestine that was understood by the majority of westerners, who equated it primarily with Jews and were largely responsible for its modern, scientific study—and ultimately its emergence as a modern nation-state in the taxonomic paradigm they created. Early attempts by Western scholars in the nineteenth century to create historicity out of archaeology in the Near East had largely passed by Jordan. Even when they didn't, there were no comprehensive narratives of great ancient civilization upon which to draw, and certainly none that could be spun by anyone for the glory of the modern inhabitants. The Hashemite narrative of legitimacy, which depends heavily upon direct descent from the Prophet of Islam, cannot ultimately be divorced from the broader context of Scripture by which ultimately all Semitic peoples are tied genealogically by their descent from Noah's kin. This was especially problematic given the existence of the State of Israel, and Hashemite control of a large part of Palestine that hadn't been subsumed by it. As for Jordan's monumental sites such as Jerash and the Roman Theatre in Amman, accepted paradigms referred to them as Roman, not Jordanian. Even if the theater was built by proto-Jordanians, it was nevertheless under Roman rule, and could not comfortably be included in nationalist antiquities discourse of this period.

A final consideration regarding the fraught connections between history and archaeology in relating Jordan's national narrative is intimately related to the last: the necessity to define and consciously justify the universal value of antiquities. Before modern knowledge helped taxonomize the landscape, for Palestinians and Jordanians the fact of existing and living in it was natural, and the most important component of claims to it, claims they did not actively have to make on a broad, theoretical basis. Europeans who came to settle those lands had no deep roots in it to draw upon for their claims to settle it, govern it, and forge a citizenry on it. Ancient roots in the land have certainly not been the sole basis of Israel's claim to Palestine, but they have been an important component of it, and have been actively cultivated to strengthen the claim. Both Nadia Abu el-Haj and Raz Kletter discuss the systematic efforts Israel undertook to educate its citizens and imbue them with the sense of connection to the land.[52] Jordan made some similar efforts, but not to the extent that Israel did and not for the entire populace.[53] A major difference between Jordan and Israel was not one of the perception of nation or the perception of citizen. Nor was there any longer doubt about the political power wielded by notions of antiquity. The difference was that what had been natural for Palestinians and Jordanians—living on the land—had to be *made* natural for those Jews who came to settle in Palestine and eventually Israel from abroad. Archaeology was useful for this project because it could support the historicity of the biblical narrative and a justifiable historical consciousness of valuing and owning the land. By this process, simply existing on the land ceases to justify ownership, and everyone is thus compelled to naturalize a claim by means of a historicity narrative that consciously acknowledges widely recognizable universal values in the landscape and its components. Despite essentially sharing a biblical historicity narrative with its new neighbor, however, Hashemite Jordan never overtly challenged Israel for it.

Jordan had great difficulty to create an archaeological arsenal out of its physical landscape to defend its "natural" narrative. To have done so would have implied the unnatural, undermined the discourse of Arab unity, and acknowledged the contemporary political status quo. Jordan could not turn the historicity narrative they shared to compete with Israel because Israel so effectively owned it, and that as a state that came into being only in 1948. To have made a nationalist issue out of Mesha and his stela, for instance, would have acknowledged the taxonomic divisions that had enabled the hegemonic nation-state divisions that were at the root of resistance to imperialism. There were further political implications. The text of the Mesha Stela affirms that the ancient Moabite king soundly defeated the Israelites under King Ahab, dislodging them from Moab and sending them back across the River Jordan. The founder of that Israelite dynasty, however, Ahab's father Omri, had been rendered ethnically Arab in the canonized scholarly paradigm. While this might seem like an appealing solution, as it would appear to enhance the Arab-ization of the ancient Arabs, including the Israelites, in the era under discussion, making a nationalist narrative out of this would have meant using archaeology to demonstrate the historicity of an event in which one ancient

Arab nation went to war against another.[54] That would have further under-mined the discourse of Arab unity at a time when a very vulnerable young monarch was a favorite target of Egypt.

Yet the paradigm of Arab history and its transcendent swath of time and space as presented in Jordanian textbooks relies on the conscious justifica-tion and acknowledgment of that very sensitive ancient relationship between peoples and land and among peoples themselves. Jordan's textbook writers stressed ethnicity as a broader category under which to house the taxonomy of ancient peoples. Taxonomy's value lay in establishing the age and sequence of ancient peoples, and thus universal value in their antiquities lay in antiquities' ability to help determine which ancient peoples came before others. In this re-spect, the authors of Jordan's textbooks wrote about ancient history in much the same way that the authors of Western textbooks did, but with their own specific goals, and with important nuances given the physical and rhetorical challenges posed by Nasser, the international context of the Cold War, and Jordan's having subsumed Palestine in what could be viewed as multiple acts of collaboration. The authors of Jordan's textbooks sought to demonstrate a shared ethnicity for all Arabs, assert historical claims to land that were more ancient than those of Jews, and account for connections between Arabs and Jews. In doing so, some ignored the issue of Jordan's and Israel's shared an-cient ethnicity and historicity narrative, while others confronted it head-on.

Lessons in Ethnicity from the National Ancients

One of the books in the available sample that chooses to ignore the ancient connections between Jews and Arabs is *Mujaz fi Tarikh Filastin mundhu Aqdam al-Azmana hata al-Yawm* (A Concise History of Palestine from the Most Ancient Times to the Present, published 1957), by Mustafa Murad al-Dabbagh.[55] Al-Dabbagh introduces the landscape to his intended sixth-grade audience by putting Palestine, periphery of Hashemite Jordan, at the center of the Arab world:

> Palestine is distinguished by the importance of its geographical position at the crossroads of the Arab world. It is the heart of that world and its center, the singular bridge standing between 25 million Arabs resident in West Asia and 50 million in North Africa, as Palestine is located between the centers of Arab culture: Cairo, Beirut, and Damascus. It is the access point to the sea for the Arab regions lying to its east: East of Jordan, the *badiyya* [steppe-lands], and Iraq.[56]

Al-Dabbagh elucidates the history of this land he defines from its very beginning. For him, Palestine's beginnings are rooted in the Canaanites, whom he describes as Arab tribes that migrated from the Arabian Peninsula and "settled Palestine five thousand years ago."[57] It is from these people, he says, that the land of Canaan gets its name. In al-Dabbagh's paradigm of ancient taxonomy, the Canaanites who had ships were the Phoenicians and settled Palestine's coastal plain, while other Canaanites settled Palestine's highlands. These two groups of Canaanites together established most of the cities still extant in Palestine, many of which retained their original names or a form of them. For these cities, al-Dabbagh provides footnotes detailing their locations and information on shrines and ruins located there, such as the resting place in Gaza of Hashim bin 'Abd Manaf, believed to have been the Prophet's great-grandfather and progenitor of the Hashemite genealogical line of descent.[58]

"Agriculture was the most important work of the Canaanites," writes al-Dabbagh.[59] They cultivated grains, vegetables, and fruits, their agricultural output so vast that their homeland was called "the land gushing forth milk and honey." Grapes, grape derivatives, olives, and olive oil were their most important produce.

The Canaanites of the coast—the Phoenicians—prospered by means of trade and shipping. Their ships sailed beyond the Mediterranean to the European and African shores of the Atlantic, and their industries included shipbuilding and glassmaking.[60] But "the greatest service the Phoenicians presented to knowledge and civilization," writes al-Dabbagh, "is having spread the letters of the alphabet, which they carried by means of commerce to the nations with which they traded, and which became, in time, the source of all the letters of the European alphabet."[61]

Three drawings accompany this passage (figs. 6.3 and 6.4). The first two originate in the Beni Hassan tombs near Minya, Egypt. The caption of the first picture reads, "Canaanite Arab from Palestine driving a pack animal"; the second, "A Canaanite Arab girl from Palestine"; the third, "Canaanite Phoenician teaching the alphabet."[62] "Canaanite Arab" and "Canaanite Arab girl" appear again in later editions of this textbook and in numerous others that discuss Arab origins. The paintings in the Beni Hassan tombs represent ancient Levantine peoples, whom its hieroglyphic caption calls "Asiatic" nomads, on their way to settle in Egypt in the nineteenth century BCE. Scholars have made this determination of the possible ethnicity of the paintings' characters based on their dress, the kinds of pack animals they have, and the kinds of industry they are represented as having. It is thought that these characters represent part of a gradual influx of peoples from southern Palestine who eventually grew powerful enough to rule much of Egypt as the Fifteenth Dy-

عرني كنعاني من فلسطين يسوق دابة

Fig. 6.3. "Canaanite Arab from Palestine driving a pack animal" and "A Canaanite Arab girl from Palestine." From Mustafa Murad al-Dabbagh's *Concise History of Palestine*.

فتاة عربية كنعانية من فلسطين

كنعاني فينيقي يعلم الأنباء

Fig. 6.4. "Canaanite Phoenician teaching the alphabet." From Mustafa Murad al-Dabbagh's *Concise History of Palestine*.

عربية كنعانية	عربية حديثة
قدموس	قديم ، قدماء
طلابا	طيب ، طيبة
داب	دابّة
لاهام	لحم
اوتيك	عتيق
دامور	تُمور او النخل
بصّة	البَصّة (المستنقع)

Fig. 6.5. Chart showing "Canaanite Arabic" words on the right and their "Modern Arabic" equivalents. From Mustafa Murad al-Dabbagh's *Concise History of Palestine*.

nasty (the Hyksos) in the seventeenth–sixteenth centuries BCE. The use of illustrations of the Beni Hassan tomb paintings in these textbooks shows that the writers were well versed in archaeology and in the scholarship of Semitic origins. They had fully claimed the strategy of equating ancient peoples with their modern descendants as their own—here claiming that the "Asiatics" were Canaanite Arabs.

Al-Dabbagh writes that the Canaanites worshipped idols and the sun and moon. They had a concept neither of the "Last Day," nor of judgment for human beings, as they did not believe in life after death. While this rendered them most unlike contemporary Arabs, al-Dabbagh writes that like contemporary Arabs, Canaanites spoke and wrote in Arabic. Any differences between the Arabic of the Canaanites and the Arabic of the twentieth century was attributable to the three millennia that had elapsed between the Canaanites and the Qur'an.[63] A chart containing seven words in their current form and in their "Canaanite Arabic" form is offered as evidence (fig. 6.5).

While the Canaanites had provided the scientific, ethnic connection between the Arabs and the land of Palestine, the prophet Ibrahim, through his son Isma'il, provided the spiritual connection, particularly that between Palestine and Islam. Al-Dabbagh writes that approximately 3,800 years prior, Ibrahim came from Iraq to the land of the Canaanites, settling peacefully among them in Bir al-Saba'a, in which he began propagating *islam* (submission) and near which Isma'il was born.[64] The author cites Qur'an 3:67 (*al-'Imran*), in which Ibrahim is described as neither Jewish nor Christian, but as an upright *muslim* (submitter) unmoved by polytheists. Isma'il was destined to be "the connection between his country, Palestine, the *muslimeen* (submitters), and the Arab prophet."[65] In addition to rebuilding the Ka'aba with his father and sharing the first opportunity to worship God there, Isma'il "was the forebear of the 'Adnaniyeen Arabs; 'Adnan was one of his grandsons, and his lineage leads to the great Prophet."[66] Even if people dismissed their legitimacy in either antiquity or modernity, the additional genealogical connections that extend to the Hashemites were widely known and needed no further elucidation.

Al-Dabbagh writes that the Canaanite Arabs prospered in Palestine for a thousand years until the Jews initiated a protracted period of conflict with them. Valiantly defending their "homelands" (*awtan*) with the help of "their cousins among the inhabitants of Syria," the Canaanites were nonetheless violently crushed by the Jews.[67] Author Dhuqan al-Hindawi relates the same story in his 1966 history of Palestine by quoting *Ancient Times*.[68] Breasted says:

The Hebrews were all originally men of the Arabian Desert, wandering with their flocks and herds and slowly drifting over into their final home in Palestine . . . On entering Palestine the Hebrews found the Canaanites already dwelling there in flourishing towns protected by massive walls . . . by that time these unconquered Palestinian towns possessed a civilization fifteen hundred years old, with comfortable houses, government, industries, trade, writing and religion—a civilization which the rude Hebrew shepherds soon adopted . . . After a time, in appearance, occupation and manner of life, the Hebrews were not to be distinguished from the Canaanites among whom they lived.[69]

In quoting this passage, al-Hindawi is consciously implying that there is no innovation that came at the hands of the Hebrew people.

Al-Hindawi, al-Dabbagh, and others emphasize to their readers that even at the apex of their rule in Palestine, the Jews never gained power over the entire country at once.[70] The strength by which the Jews had conquered Palestine "did not last more than seventy years."[71] This was, say the authors, because they were unable to maintain unity among themselves, some of them living in opulent abundance and others in squalor. Their state thus split into two small states that fought against one another, one in the north with its capital in modern-day Nablus and Samaria-Sebastiyya, and one in the south with its capital in modern-day Jerusalem. The textbook authors contend that continuing discord between these two states eventually wrought their demise. The northern kingdom, Israel, was conquered by the Assyrian Arabs, who originated in the Arabian Peninsula and settled in northern Iraq. Chaldean Arabs, who originated—like the Assyrians and the Canaanites—in the Arabian Peninsula and settled in southern Iraq, were the downfall of the southern state, the Kingdom of Judah.[72] The rest of al-Dabbagh's textbook covers the period from the coming of Christ to the war of 1948. Questions at the end of units and at the end of the book ask students to relate the history of ancient Palestine to the contemporary situation, often by soliciting answers in the form of reactions to *suwar* (chapters) from the Qur'an.

Al-Dabbagh's paradigm of the history of the land of Palestine, and the entirety of the Arab world for that matter, is the standard means by which, for decades, the Jordanian school system approached ancient history. It is a paradigm by which multiple waves of people, Semitic Arabs all, emigrate over the course of ancient time out of the Arabian Peninsula and settle just about everywhere within the boundaries of the contemporary Arab world. There are a few variations in this paradigm. Al-Dabbagh chooses to make the Phoenicians Arab Canaanites while acknowledging that the Philistines were Cretans. Authors of other textbooks tend to share al-Dabbagh's explanation of the identity of the Phoenicians and the Philistines, but others fail to mention the Phoenicians at all.[73] Al-Hindawi et al. maintain that the Hebrews and the Philistines fought one another much like the Hebrews and the Canaanites did, and like the Canaanites, the Philistines were vanquished.[74] Some authors choose to incorporate Canaanite history in the landscape context of Bilad al-Sham more prominently than does al-Dabbagh.[75] Most authors place the origins of the Hebrews in Ur in southern Iraq with Ibrahim, the forefather of all Jews, Christians, and Muslims. There may be some discrepancy from book to book regarding exactly when and how the Hebrews came to Palestine and other related details, and there is certainly cognitive dissonance. The Hebrew patriarchs are beyond reproach, and there is no attempt to reconcile that with the atrocities committed against the Arab Canaanites by the Hebrews as narrated in the textbooks. What is important is that in all narratives, the Canaanites are the original inhabitants of Palestine and the Hebrews are not. Their many good and bad characteristics—prosperity, literacy, idol worship, language—are consistent from one author to another, as are the spiritual foundations and connections attributable to Ibrahim and Isma'il.

Al-Dabbagh's formulation accomplishes two important goals: first, it defines an ethnicity for contemporary Arabs by applying modern notions of ethnic identity—just as Zionism did—to ancient populations who may not have understood their own identity in such a way; second, it establishes a national presence for Arabs and Muslims on the lands of the contemporary Arab world and Palestine that long predates the presence of Jews. There is, however, a fundamental missing piece: in glossing over a united Jewish kingdom under tenth-century BCE kings David and Solomon, al-Dabbagh is denying the very connection of the land to Arabs and Muslims that he so carefully lays out with Ibrahim and Isma'il.[76] While he could just as easily lay claim to Dawud and Suleyman in the same way he does Abraham and Ishmael, he makes a deliberate choice not to do so, as the kingdom united under their rule is the ancient historicity narrative for the origin of the modern state of Israel.

This helps demonstrate the sensitivities in the application of modern notions of ethnicity to ancient peoples, who likely didn't understand their identity the way we are meant to understand ours—or theirs—today. After 1948, Israel worked to Judaize its national landscape in these very terms—that ancient Israelite Jews on the landscape equaled modern Israeli Jews on it.[77] The framework enabling that equation was established as early as the nineteenth century. How were Arabs, then, to contest that claim? The connections of that landscape to Christian and Muslim history, and, most importantly, its connections to the very personal history of the modern individuals who inhabited and were displaced from it were, in the dominant discourse by which nationalism is justified, insignificantly recent when compared with the antiquity of Judaism. Using the biblical narrative in its most literal way to Jordan's advantage, however, was risky. If Mesha the Moabite, who can only be understood in the Arab nationalist paradigm of ancient history to be an Arab (because everyone is an Arab in this paradigm), ever became a Jordanian national symbol of the Arab struggle against Israel, there would be a huge problem for the entire formulation.[78] Omri, king of Israel—the northern kingdom described by al-Dabbagh—who is vanquished by Mesha, survives in the written record as what some scholars describe as an Arab.[79] Mesha versus Omri is thus not at its roots a story of Moabite versus Israelite, Jordanian or Arab versus Israeli, or Muslim versus Jew. Mesha versus Omri is ultimately a story of Arab versus Arab. Only the barest mention of Ammon, Moab, and Edom—the three kingdoms contained within the Hashemite Jordanian core that were, according to Abrahamic tradition, contemporaneous and competitive with those of Israel and Judah in the Hashemite Jordanian periphery—is made in the entire collection of textbooks under review. While archaeological research has not focused on the inhabitants of these kingdoms to the extent that it has the Israelites and Judahites, they had long been part of the taxonomy and Glueck had been publishing about them specifically since the mid-1930s. The exigencies of ideologically competing against Zionism and representing Arab nationalism left no safe space in which to let the proto-Jordanians of the Hashemite core drive the paradigm; they would either compete with other Arabs, or, by their existence, help affirm the antiquity narrative of the state of Israel.

Pan-Semitism, however, *could* safely drive the paradigm, and drove the Arab nationalist narrative of Jordanian textbooks. Developed in the late nineteenth and early twentieth century, pan-Semitism focused on the *Arabness* of ancient Semitic peoples, Jews included. It is most likely that al-Dabbagh doesn't broach the complicated nuances of this subject because his audience ranges from just eleven to thirteen years old. Authors of high school textbooks, writing for an older audience, had more freedom, and perhaps a mandate, to complicate the issues. In his high school text, *al-Watan al-'Arabi* (The Arab Nation, published 1965 and 1967), author 'Adnan Lutfi 'Uthman offers a detailed and competitive formulation of Arab origins for the entirety of the contemporary Arab world and, in fact, that beyond. "Civilization is Semitic, not Aryan," he writes, "and what is Greek civilization except an heir to it, having transplanted from it more than it invented."[80]

To support his conclusion, 'Uthman gives students a detailed description of the antiquity of the "Arab homeland," attributing its countless achievements to the "vigor and clarity" of the "unbroken waves of Arab Semites" who left the Arabian Peninsula and settled its fertile landscape in and beyond the Fertile Crescent and the Nile Valley over the course of about seven thousand years. He notes the importance of archaeology for knowledge of the "first people," who did not have writing. The Arab homeland is old and vast, and included many Semitic peoples among its inhabitants. 'Uthman writes that "included in their numbers are the Akkadians, Babylonians, . . . Assyrians, and Chaldeans," who settled in the eastern portion of the Fertile Crescent, and "the Canaanites, Phoenicians, Amorites, Arameans, and Hebrews," who settled in the western part of it. Beyond that, 'Uthman notes that "Semitic footsteps" can be traced beyond the Suez, the Nile Valley, and the Bab al-Mandab to other parts of Africa. "Perhaps they arrived in Egypt," he writes, "at a time no less ancient than that in which they arrived in the Fertile Crescent."

In all places they went, Semitic peoples were at the very origin of civilization and nations, including in Iraq, Bilad al-Sham, Egypt, and the Arabian Peninsula. They were responsible for every innovation, industry, art, form of organization, discipline, and thought — including writing, commerce, sculpture, government, medicine, and law. Last but not least, Semites were the first monotheists, of which the "last and best," writes 'Uthman, were those of the Islamic Arab conquests. Semitic civilization and its countless innovations was the basis of Greek and Roman civilization, and therefore that of the rest of the world, to which it spread by means of trade, via sea by the Phoenicians and via land by the Arameans.

'Uthman's celebration of Semitic civilization, however, comes with lessons and warnings for the contemporary context in which he writes. The great ancient Arab civilizations didn't last, and he enumerates the reasons for their downfall. These are instructive, particularly in terms of the goals of development in modern times, and include lack of rational thought regarding natural phenomena and thus reliance on superstition; lack of constitutional rule as it exists in the present; lack of a solution to class problems; and the protracted belief of the ancient Arabs in polytheism. 'Uthman presents his formulation of specifically Bilad al-Sham's history similarly, infusing it with all the elements of national glory and national warning discussed by Gershoni and Jankowski.[81] The heading under which he writes the following, "Bilad al-Sham between the Grindstones," reflected the world in which Jordan's schoolchildren lived:

> The ancient inhabitants of Syria were of Arab Semitic origin and came in waves from the Arabian Peninsula beginning about 3000 B.C., ending in the seventh century A.D. when the Islamic Arab wave left to liberate mankind from the oppression of the Romans. . . .

Bilad al-Sham faced in ancient times migrations of non-Arab-Semites, such as the Hittites from Asia Minor, and the Philistines from Crete, Greece, and Rome. Despite their intention of conquest or colonization, they were not able to dye it [Bilad al-Sham] with a non-Arab-Semitic hue.

Bilad al-Sham lived in ancient times a life of urban kingdoms in the days of the Canaanites, Amorites, Phoenicians, and Arameans, until the Hebrews became divided among themselves into two hostile states.

This political situation made Bilad al-Sham like a football seized at the hands of conquerors from Babel, Ashur and Iran in the east, Egypt in the west, and Asia Minor in the north.

The kings between the two rivers were in a constant struggle with the Pharaohs of Egypt for mastery of Bilad al-Sham and control over its strategic location. This strong rivalry between eastern and western powers brought Bilad al-Sham no peace or stability throughout the historical epochs, at the hands of the Semitic nations, nor at the hands of the Aryan empires that followed."[82]

'Uthman's lesson for the 1960s is that the Arabs of Bilad al-Sham have an inherent predisposition for resisting colonization by outsiders. What was true in the Bronze Age thus provides inspiration for modern times. It is only when the Arabs of Bilad al-Sham become divided among themselves, as he notes the Hebrews did, that they have been dominated by others. The point isn't that 'Uthman fails to adhere to a strictly chronological historical narrative—a common feature of this genre—nor does it matter for 'Uthman that both the Hebrews and most of the others mentioned—at least until the coming of the Persians, Greeks, and Romans—are also Arab Semites in this paradigm. Contained herein are three strong messages that 'Uthman, and certainly other textbook writers, wanted to convey about the consequences of division among the Arabs. First, when the Arab people become divided as the Hebrews did, they are likely to fall victim to domination by another power. Second, the Hebrew people have a long history of fomenting division among the Arab people.[83] Finally, domination of one Arab Semitic people over another—Hebrew or Egyptian—is still domination. 'Uthman describes Late Bronze Age pharaonic imperialism in Bilad al-Sham thus: "Despite the system that Tuthmoses III established . . . no sooner did he blink than rebellions rose in Bilad al-Sham, the most important parts of the Empire, costing Egypt the greatest part of its soul, its fortune and materiél."[84] The Hashemite king of Jordan, standing in the crosshairs of Nasser's popularity and propaganda machine and long since rendered without his Hashemite cousins in Iraq, must have felt this most acutely.[85]

Unlike al-Dabbagh, 'Uthman offers in his textbook a detailed history of the Hebrews in Palestine, but drops the use of the term "Hebrews" for "Jews." The Jews, he says, make their first historical appearance when they arrived in Palestine. He alludes to their Arab-ness, placing their origins in a small tribe of Semites that came from Arabia and then Iraq. 'Uthman describes their lifestyle as originally like that of the bedouin, but they adopted the ways of the various people with whom they came in contact, including the worship of Ba'al, one of the Canaanite gods. They were steeped, he says, in the magic and superstition that characterized ancient religious practice, until the time of the Prophets Musa (Moses) and Harun (Aaron). It was Musa who led the Jews to their true, monotheistic religion. When they arrived in Sinai's desert and Moses gave them God's divine instruction, however, they became fractious and insubordinate, worshipping the calf and warring with one another. "This," writes 'Uthman, "is a characteristic that plagued them throughout their ages . . . God punished them; they wandered in the desert for forty years, then entered Palestine." 'Uthman says that the twelve tribes settled in Palestine at the Canaanites' expense. He describes the age of the Judges and that of the Kings, which was founded with Saul, was consolidated under the Prophet Dawud (David), and achieved its apex under the Prophet Suleyman (Solomon), under whose rule the Jews were united, their affairs were organized, and they eliminated the Philistine threat. But after the death of the Prophet Suleyman, 'Uthman says, the old religious and political divisions returned. Jewish unity under Dawud and Suleyman had not lasted more than seventy years, and the union split into northern and southern kingdoms. The northern kingdom of Israel had its capital at Samaria; its people stopped worshipping Yahweh, and reverted to worshipping Ba'al. The southern kingdom of Judah had its capital at Jerusalem. Israel fell to the Assyrians and later Judah fell to the Babylonians, who took many of its people into captivity.

After describing beliefs common to the three Abrahamic faiths that originated with Judaism—such as creation, resurrection, the Last Day, and the existence of angels and the devil—'Uthman discusses the impact of the Babylonian Exile on the Jewish people. He asserts that their history of suffering may, at this point, have reinvigorated their belief in monotheism and the message of their prophets; he specifically mentions Amos, Isaiah, and Jeremiah. They may have understood events from their defeats, the destruction of the Temple, and the Exile as God's punishment for being unfaithful.

When the Persians allowed the Jews to return to Jerusalem from Babel, writes 'Uthman, the effect of the Exile on Jewish identity was palpable. This was particularly true of the priestly class, whose authority increased as it sought to rebuild the Temple and reinvigorate its commitment to the Torah, the prophetic texts, and the Ten Commandments of Mosaic law. 'Uthman says that "it wasn't before 400 B.C. that the Jewish religion reached its final development."

There is no denying that passages found in these textbooks cross the red lines between racism and opposition to colonialism.[86] It is vital to the discussion at hand, however, that for older audiences of schoolchildren, Jewish history and Christian history of Arabs and Muslims is not denied, although the presentation is problematic at multiple levels. Just as the State of Israel was "Juda-izing" and "Israel-izing" the landscape of Palestine and Jewish history to fit its contemporary national context, so this Jordanian textbook author "Arab-ized" the ancient Israelites.[87] Peculiar to Jordan's case, as opposed to that of other Arab states, was that the Hashemite family was on record acknowledging this very history, as its narrative legitimacy was as embedded in it as Israel's. Also like Israel, Jordan had usurped Palestinian national aspirations at both the pan-national and nation-state levels. Given the complication of turning the biblical history of the peoples of its core to a competitive narrative advantage, expanded Hashemite Jordan's historicity narrative focused on its periphery, Arab-izing its history in a way that, without subtlety, reflected the current milieu.

Antiquity and Development Lessons for Modernity

A second group of schoolbooks adds another layer of nuance to the national narrative—Jordan as tourist destination. These books admonish students, as citizens of the nation, to support Jordan's tourism industry by taking responsibility for educating themselves about it. In this regard, Jordan's cultural heritage, especially that which can be discursively separated from religious heritage, is less about the ethos of Arab nationalism and more about that of Jordanian nationalism specifically, particularly as it adheres to accepted development paradigms.

Development in the tourism sector occurred in the context of other development initiatives and the U.S.'s replacement of England as Jordan's primary source of Western aid. From its early years until now, the United States Agency for International Development (USAID) has played a vital role in the development of Jordan's heritage industry, of which antiquities sites have been a key element. USAID began as the American Point IV Program, so-named because its creation came out of the "fourth point" of Harry Truman's inauguration speech in January 1949. Early in the Cold War, Truman envisioned "a program of international development to which all technically advanced nations could contribute, dedicated to helping free people of the world improve their economies based on the premise of 'democratic fair-dealing.'"[88] Having withheld official recognition of the independence of Jordan from 1946 until early 1949, the introduction of Point IV in Jordan along with a substantial security aid package in 1952 was a major turning point in U.S. involvement in the country.[89] U.S. entry was primarily a response to the desperate situation of hundreds of thousands of Palestinian refugees who had been festering since 1948 in deplorable conditions throughout resource-poor Jordan without enough aid, shelter, or employment opportunities.[90] By the end of the 1950s, the Suez war had effectively ended the British initiates in the region. With King Hussein's invocation of the Eisenhower Doctrine in 1957 and again in 1958, the U.S. had assumed the mantle as Jordan's primary Western benefactor.

The first tasks for Point IV, later called the U.S. Operation Mission in Jordan (USOM) and eventually USAID, were a number of infrastructure improvement projects to alleviate the most immediate problems: lack of clean water, lack of irrigation sources, lack of medical clinics and health professionals, lack of schools, lack of roads, and lack of employment opportunities. To this extent, a great number of canals were dug; dams, roads, schools, and clinics built; and trainees graduated from professional programs.[91] Early in these endeavors, Point IV/USOM/USAID also took an interest in the tourist industry, the growth of which was seen as a way of achieving what today would be called "sustainable development." Granting loans to hoteliers was a component of these early industry- and infrastructure-based efforts, the objective being "to expand tourism in Jordan and increase foreign exchange earnings."[92] To this end, from 1953 to 1956, loans were given to nine hotels in Jerusalem and one in Bethlehem—none in the Hashemite Jordanian core—repayable at 4 percent interest per annum for five to ten years.[93]

Hashemite rule may have emphasized the primacy of the East Bank core over the West Bank periphery, but Jordan's extensive use of Palestine iconography was in tandem with the reality that most visitors to Jordan were not visiting the core. In 1959, American contractor George Kovach created the Tourism Plan of Action for Jordan.[94] An undated report, clearly from the 1960s, gives us some indication as to what might have been included in Kovach's plan. It recognizes the issue of East Bank tourism, saying:

> Jordan, whose Holy Places are venerated by followers of three major religions, and with well preserved antiquity sites such as world-renowned Petra, is an "open air museum" without parallel. It offers a tourist potential which until recently has been largely untapped, the currency earning possibilities of

which have been lost neither on representatives of the Government of Jordan nor on USAID personnel. Both are convinced that tourism can be one of Jordan's leading industries; and while little progress was possible during the turmoil of the fifties, the last three years have seen the beginning of a systematic effort to realize this potential.

U.S. assistance has been directed toward the solution of three main problems: first, increasing the number of hotels and rest houses . . . ; second . . . help to the Jordan Tourism Authority to improve the quality of hotels and services rendered to tourists; and third, . . . to restore and develop a wide-range of Jordan's antiquities so that the "package" offered to the prospective tourist can be larger than a visit only to the Holy Places of the West Bank.[95]

There was recognition that antiquities in the Hashemite Jordan core were an underdeveloped resource and could draw tourists whose primary interest was in religious sites of the West Bank periphery. In addition to providing loans to hoteliers, throughout the 1960s Jordanians were sent overseas to hotel and restaurant management projects. USAID also financed tourism promotion campaigns and advised Jordan on obtaining large-scale loans to build higher-class tourist hotels in an effort to attract visitors with more money. By selling U.S. agricultural surplus in local markets, USAID funded the building of rest houses at various sites, restoration and excavation at Petra, Jerash, Kerak, and the Dead Sea, and "'historical marker' signs . . . near interesting places."[96] By the late 1960s, USAID had helped developed a plan for a national park service, to include Amman, the Dibbeen forest near Jerash, and Petra. The over-arching, interrelated goals of these efforts were five-fold: attract more tourists; attract a diversity of tourists; attract tourists who had more money to spend; increase their length of stay; dramatically increase tourism receipts.[97]

Profiting from heritage was certainly not a new or foreign idea. In expanded Jordan, tourism sector development occurred in the context of broader, multi-faceted competition with popular Arab nationalist, Israeli, and Palestinian interests. Having turned the peripheral part of the Holy Land into their own core, the Hashemites had to own the tourism narrative of their Palestine periphery—the recognized Holy Land core—to create a viable narrative to attract tourists to what, by their understanding, was the Holy Land periphery east of the river. Education legislation and schoolbooks, developed to help meet the broader goal of instantiating a complex nationalist narrative in schoolchildren, spoke directly to tourism development and Jordanians' roles in it.

Narrative Maps of the Modernizing *Watan*

God bestowed upon our dear Arab countries the most noble dignities and greatest qualities . . . wherever you turn or wherever you stay in the parts of the large Arab watan, *its sanctity, its features, and its archaeology bedazzle your eyes . . . And in it is holy Jordan, the cradle of Islam and the wellspring of the divine religions . . . Our Arab homeland is the birthplace of divine religion and civilization.*[98]

These lines, appearing under the heading "Tourism in the Arab *Watan*," come from a social studies text for high school students, dating from 1966 and 1968. It is a panegyric to Arabism giving Jordan pride of place in the pan-Arab narrative, intended to demonstrate Jordan's unique role in and special contributions to the important history contained in the books discussed earlier in this chapter. While the virtues of many of the countries in the extensive Arab *watan* are highlighted, Jordan's are first and foremost. Egypt is specifically noted for its archaeology, and the Hijaz for being the Holy Land, but it is Jordan under Hashemite rule and including Jerusalem that is the cradle of Islam, a point clearly emphasizing God's revelation to the Prophet Ibrahim and alluding to all the territorial and genealogical connections that follow. Jordan's location "between its Arab sister states" distinguishes it as a crossroads of the diverse civilizations that settled in it.[99] Within it one finds the cultural imprint and archaeology of many civilizations, including the Arab Nabateans and Ghassanids. On the list of archaeological interests are Petra, Jerash, Arab desert castles, Crusader castles, Jericho, Byzantine churches, and everything included in them. The book tells students that in Jordan, one finds the holy places of Muslims and Christians, such as al-Aqsa, *Masjid al-Sakhra* (The Mosque of the Rock), the Holy Sepulchre, and the Church of the Nativity.[100] Jordan is described as the cradle of Judaism and Christianity. It is the birthplace of noble prophets, and the landscape upon which occurred events such as Moses' Exodus, Jesus' birth and mission, and the Prophet's journey by night.[101]

The authors write that Jordan is also blessed with natural beauty, seen in the mountains and warm locales along the water, such as near the Dead Sea and Aqaba, giving the country status as both a summer and winter resort.[102] All of these things make Jordan attractive to tourists, and the book emphasizes to students that the government goes to great lengths to take care of and promote Jordan's numerous tourist sites. Among the government's initiatives are improvements to tourist roads and facilities, especially at rich archaeological sites like Jerash and Petra, and a foreign pen-pal program intended to promote this heritage abroad.[103] Everyone has a role to play in promoting Jordan.

While al-Hindawi et al. mention "wounded Palestine, land of valor and first *qibla* [direction of prayer] of the Muslims" among the parts of the "dear Arab *watan*," the word "Palestine" never appears among the numerous themes of Jordanian heritage mentioned above.[104] This is the very point. It was one thing to mention that something was amiss in Palestine and to talk about its spiritual and touristic importance; it would have been quite another to insinuate that it was a political entity apart from Hashemite Jordan, or that its citizens were other than Jordanian. Palestine was spiritually distinct, yet nationally indistinct in the context of the Hashemite narrative.

In writing about Jordan this way, not only did official discourse subsume Palestine, but it also co-opted an Arabic literary tradition that delineated Palestine spatially based on sacred geography. Dating to at least the time of the Crusades, the literary genre known as *fada'il al-quds* (the virtues of the holy city) became, over the progression of the eighteenth and nineteenth centuries, a means by which Palestine was delineated and understood as discrete space by its inhabitants. Jordanian textbooks of this period rendered that same space, and the literary tradition that for centuries had verbalized it, "Jordanian."[105] A tactic that remained popular across the decades under study was to send child characters portrayed in textbooks on journeys around the country, creating in the process a kind of narrative map of the *watan* and a genre that could hypothetically be called *fada'il al-urdun*. These were imaginary grand tours of Jordan mimicking programs for camping and scouting that were implemented in the kingdom. A 1953 third-grade social studies textbook entitled *al-Mamlaka al-Urduniyya al-Hashimiyya* (The Hashemite Jordanian Kingdom) says:

> The best way to know a country well is to undertake a number of trips from one end of that country to the other, to personally see its communities, mountains, shores, its rivers, its lakes, its archaeology, its history, and its natural areas.[106]

In this book, five friends—Nabil, Hasan, Nu'uman, Talal, and Ghassan— decide to spend their spring break getting firsthand knowledge of their own country, just as the textbooks exhort real Jordanian students to do. Their adventure begins in the capital, Amman, seat of the monarchy and the nation, which had become "several times what it was in the old days," bustling with commerce, construction, industry, and a growing population on its hilly landscape. Amman, furthermore, "is famous for its ancient, historical archaeology, especially the Roman Theatre and the Citadel, and it also has a train station and an airport."[107] This discourse, whereby the romantic and ancient stands alongside the progressive and modern (much like it did on stamps and currency), is the framework by which the fictional children are to understand the journey around their national homeland.

After describing Amman, the textbook sends its child tour guides their separate ways so that they each can explore a different region of Jordan. All narratives begin and end in Amman, rendering the city the nexus of *fada'il al-urdun*, and requiring a journey back and forth across the river that, for the reader, mentally links its banks together at the central point of the capital. When school is back in session, the boys come together to boast about their respective journeys, which emphasize the shape and contents of Jordan as a modern nation.

The sequence in which the boys visit different parts of Jordan and the length of the description of their journeys mirrors tenets of the broader Hashemite narrative. All of Jordan is one under Hashemite leadership, and while Palestine is sacred and therefore special, there is no distinction between one side of the river and the other. Nu'uman is the only child who mentions the Allenby Bridge, which is, on his trip, en route to something else. He describes it as "the bridge that travelers cross to the West Bank," not to Palestine.[108] The idea of "crossing" anything is completely absent in the subsequent tales of Nabil and Talal, the two boys who go to Palestine. In Nabil's case we are simply told that he traveled from Amman to Jerusalem by car.[109]

The climax of the *fada'il* sequence, however, marks a return from west of the river to the largest and most nostalgically described region of Jordan that any of the boys visit. The first two boys go north; Hasan by way of an eastward loop from the capital and Nu'uman by way of a westward loop. The second two go to Palestine. Nabil leaves Amman for Jerusalem, which serves as the nexus for his tour of the West Bank, longer and more detailed than the tours of either Hasan or Nu'uman. Jerusalem is likewise the nexus of Talal's trip to Palestine, mostly in the coastal plain and therefore outside the confines of the West Bank, and written in hypothetical language (i.e., "if we traveled in the direction of X, we would see Y") that does not characterize the other boys' stories.[110] Ghassan, the final student to tell the story of his spring break journey, takes the reader back to the east bank of the River Jordan and the regions of Kerak and Aqaba.[111] His is the longest of all the boys' stories because he covers the most physical area of Jordan. He covers the most geographical territory, with the exception of the eastern steppelands/desert (visited by none of the boys), but the southern Jordanian highlands contained fewer cities, towns, and villages and were less populated than those regions visited by the other boys. During Ghassan's journey across Jordan's vast landscape south of the capital, he encounters views of the Red Sea, fishermen, fortresses and encampments bearing the memories of two global conflicts and more regional conflicts, the Hijaz Railway, Petra, horses, the final resting place of Muslim heroes, the plains of Moab, and old mosaics. Most importantly, he visits or mentions every major village and region of southern Jordan, describing the geography and topography in great detail along the way. Major cities he visits, such as Aqaba and Ma'an, are of great importance to modern Hashemite national claims. Mentioning Mu'ta and Mazar further links the monarchy to great moments in Arab and Islamic history. Wadi Musa and Shawbak (representing the Edomite highlands), Tafila and Kerak (representing the plains of Moab), and Madaba (representing the Balqa highlands) are vital to long held traditional understandings of the division of the landscape of this region. The late Ottoman Empire in Transjordan organized itself around these distinctions of landscape, as did the early British local governments.[112] The emirate was subsequently established on this framework. The conception of southern Jordan and its people as described by Ghassan thus became vital to the "East Bank" component of the overall character of Hashemite Jordan.

This tour sequence is likewise interesting for its emphasis on the routes the boys take from one place to another. Whether they take a car or a train is a deliberate device to demonstrate something about the map of the landscape: distance, topography, and ease of travel enabled by modernity. As important as the actual stops that the boys make are the details given about the natural landscapes they traverse along the way: every mountain, vista, water source, *wadi* confluence, mineral hot spring, crossing, garden, plain, field, ascent, or descent is a named critical component tying one part of the Hashemite kingdom to the next, ferrying the boys from one part of their journey to another, and tying the whole of the kingdom together.

If Jordanian students were taught that tourism sector development was based on foreigners' desire to visit the country's ancient cultural heritage, the narrative of tourism they were themselves supposed to consume was rooted in Jordan's modernity. The boys stop at very few antiquities sites and say little about them. Never are antiquities presented in the context of any of the history presented in the schoolbooks discussed earlier. Hasan, for instance, visits iconic Ajloun Castle, about which he gives no details except to allude to its height, and the importance of which is that from it, he can see the mountains of Palestine beyond the Jordan River Valley. He says barely more about Jerash: "I had heard from my brothers who went on many scouting trips about the town of Jerash, then I saw it for myself . . . I saw its great archaeology which attracts tourists from all over the world. I was pleased by its marvelous inscriptions, its decorated columns, and its paved streets."[113] Ghassan says about as much of his trip to Petra: "From Wadi Musa I rode a horse carrying me to Petra and I saw amazing things . . . I saw a town that could hold thousands of people dug into the rocks and decorated with marvelous inscriptions and engravings. Among the most beautiful things I saw there were the Pharaoh's Treasury and the Monastery, which are some of the most beautiful of its archaeology." His visit to the most famous antiquity in Madaba, the fifth-century mosaic map, is equally lacking in detail: "I went to the church," he says, "and I saw the map made a very long time ago, depicting the countries of Jordan and Palestine and parts of Egypt."

Of most interest in these journeys are institutions of the modern state: the phosphate industry near Rusayfa, the Jordanian Arab Army in Zarqa, the Iraqi oil company in Mafraq, agriculture in Irbid, the view of the orchards from Salt's citadel, the Hashemites' winter palace at Shuna, water-pumping stations along the rivers for generating electricity, the potash and resort industries along the Dead Sea, agriculture and winter resorts at Jericho, cargo trucks at the rail stations bound for Kerak and Tafila, the air station at Maʿan, the fishing industry and port facilities at Aqaba. This is an *homage* to man's—specifically Jordanian man's—ability to harness nature's bounty to feed the masses, extract minerals, please vacationers, defend the nation, and transport goods. The rich historical and religious value of Salt, the Dead Sea, Beisan, the River Zarqa, Maʿan, and so many other places is entirely absent.

Much of Nabil's and Talal's journeys also focus on modernity. Acknowledging the special character of Jerusalem and other holy cities of Palestine was critical to the Hashemite raison d'être, but this was handled with rhetorical caution and emphasis on economic importance to Jordan from both tourism and agricultural and industrial productivity. Nabil visits al-Quds, Bayt Lahm (Bethlehem), Khalil (Hebron), Nablus, and al-Nasira (Nazareth), visiting the holiest and most important sites, noting the many tourists he sees. In al-Quds, this includes the Dome of the Rock and al-Aqsa Mosque on *al-Haram al-Sharif*, the tomb of the late king Husayn, and the Church of the Holy Sepulchre. In Bayt Lahm, he visits the Church of the Nativity, in Khalil the Ibrahimi *Haram* where Sara, Ishaq (Isaac), Rifqa (Rebecca), Yʿaqub (Jacob), Laʾiqa (Leah), and Yusuf (Joseph) are buried. About Nablus, he mentions the temple of the Samaritans, noting that they are small in number, live only in Nablus, and that their religion is close to Judaism. Nearby, he says, "is the village of Sebastiyya, famous for its historical archaeology, most of it going back to the days of the Romans." The historical and archaeological importance of Sebastiyya actually dates far earlier than Roman times, specifically to the days of the problematic Omri. Of his last stop, al-Nasira, Nabil says it is a holy site because of its centrality to the life of Christ, whose followers are called *al-nasari* (another term for Christian) and visit the town as they visit al-Quds and Bayt Lahm.

While the unique spiritual character of these places is certainly at the center of this story, so are the economics of the international tourist trade—traditional industries such as glass and tanning in Khalil and soap in Nablus, handicrafts like the religious shell and wood implements produced at Bayt Lahm, and agriculture. Nabil never alludes to contestation for ownership of the places he travels—neither between Jordanians and Palestinians nor between Jordanians and Israelis. To do so would have inserted an unnatural element into something that was supposed to be natural. He never mentions Palestinians or Israelis, or Jews and Jewish holy places, even though many, particularly in al-Quds and Khalil, are shared.

Talal's journey is mostly about modern transport, commerce, industry, and agriculture in Palestine outside of the West Bank, and in it, the reader gets the only hint that something is amiss in the land. It is not clear how much traveling he actually does, as he describes many places and the way to them conditionally. Of Bir al-Saba'a (Beer Sheva), he mentions nothing of its connections to the Prophet Ibrahim. Of Qaysariyya (Caesarea), he says only that it was Palestine's most important port in antiquity, and today it is famous for its archaeology. His journey becomes unnatural when he notes that north of Yaffa (Jaffa) is the new Jewish city, Tel Aviv. At no point does he mention the impact of the new capital of the new state on the economic situation of Yaffa that he has described, nor does he mention that there is a new state. He says merely that Tel Aviv is "very advanced in its culture and industry . . . and it connects to the south with the Arab city of Yaffa until the two cities are as one." Is the reader to assume that Talal visits Tel Aviv? He describes the city in some detail, identifying it as a Jewish city having the same positive characteristics as particularly modern and progressive Jordanian cities described in this textbook, and he locates it squarely within the context of Jaffa and the commercial context of essentially all of Palestine. He leaves one more clue, meanwhile, that something is strange in the Hashemite kingdom. In addition to its famous oranges and vegetables, Qalqilya is famous, he says, "for its national struggle [*jihad*]. Its people demonstrated distinguished *wataniyya* and unprecedented bravery." This assumes that the child reader understands the reference, just as it assumes he or she has internalized the binary of natural and unnatural that provides the complex context of not only Talal's journey, but also that of the other boys in the core and periphery.

A book from more than a decade later, a social studies text for fourth grade called *Watani al-Saghir* (My Little Country, published 1966 and 1969), sends child characters on a similar narrative journey across Jordan's national landscape, although the circumstances of the trip reflect greater emphasis on tourism and the extracurricular aspects of development in educating child-citizens, including camps and scouting ventures that put fictional schoolbook journeys around Jordan into rhetorical practice.[114] Given regional developments over the course of that decade and more, the rhetoric and tone of *Watani al-Saghir* is notably less anodyne than that read in the pages of the earlier book, *al-Mamlaka al-Urduniyya al-Hashimiyya*.

Much of this text is a first-person account of a child's journey through Jordan as part of a "scout camp" composed of a "scout team" drawn from his school.[115] It is the narrator's great fortune, he says, to be part of a scout camp just west of the city of Jenin (in the West Bank, a distinction that he doesn't make, for obvious reasons), near the plains of Ibn 'Amar just beyond which is the land that was "seized illegally [also usurped, raped, or conquered] by the Zionist colonizers."[116]

On the second day of camp, the children encounter a "brave officer of the Jordanian Arab Army" on his way to join his company. They go with him and, sitting among the almond trees, he tells them about the situation in the area and the positions of "enemies." On day three of camp, the children take a trip to visit "the most important Jordanian archaeology and to get acquainted with the nature of Jordan." They decide to tour around the whole of the natural *watan*, visiting Sebastiyya, al-Quds, Bayt Lahm, Khalil, Ariha (Jericho), Jerash, Amman, Madaba, Petra, and Aqaba.

The children leave Jenin on public transportation headed south. After the narrator gives a geographical and geological description of the Nablus Mountains, they arrive in Sebastiyya. The boy mentions that there is Roman archaeology—columns and impressive large stones used for building. This is all he tells the reader about the site. In this way, the schoolchildren's experience with archaeology is very similar to that of the schoolchildren in the book previously discussed. They see there, however, a large, foreign tour group. They ask their trip leader about it. He explains:

Tourists come to our country from all ends of the earth. Our country is rich in archaeology because it is the cradle of civilizations and sacred ground for all religions. In it are many holy sites we will see when we arrive in Jerusalem. We'll also see a great many tourists there, as well as at other archaeological sites we'll visit. It is our duty to work with tourists in the best way and to offer them all assistance, and we must preserve our beautiful country to attract many tourists to it. When the tourists come to our country they spend a lot of money to stay and to eat, and they buy gifts, souvenirs, and crafts from touristic places.

Tourism is an important source of wealth for our country. We must take an interest in tourists and their comfort in our country so that one of them returns to his country and talks about the best things he saw in ours, and encourages another to visit it.

After leaving Sebastiyya, the students eat the famous *kunafa* found in Nablus. After passing Ramallah, they see al-Quds, "the spiritual capital of our kingdom."[117] The narrator says, "In al-Quds we felt the awe of the holy city which is the first of the two *qibla*(s) and the third noble holy place." He describes foreign tourists on pilgrimage. The students visit al-Haram al-Sharif, al-Aqsa, and Qubbat al-Sakhra. The narrator mentions that there were a lot of foreign tourists at the Islamic holy places. A visit to the Holy Sepulchre follows, which the trip leader tells them was built by Helena, mother of the Emperor Constantine, and that Christians like to come to it on holidays. After that the students visit the Mosque of ʿUmar and *Bab al-ʿAmud* (the Damascus Gate).

Bethlehem is next. The children visit the Church of the Nativity, which, as the boy mentions, marks the place where Jesus was born. Then it's on to Hebron, where they go to the Ibrahimi *Haram*, which the boy says is a mosque standing on the grave of Ibrahim. There they are met by a shaykh who explains its history. The children notice that the Tourism Authority has made a place in front of the mosque for selling handicrafts. "Seeing these things reminded us a lot of businesses in al-Quds and Bayt Lahm, and brought us to a greater appreciation of tourism as an economic resource for the country." Its revenues bring "not less than 5 million dinar every year," the boy tells his readers.

The children then head for Jericho, where they visit the qasr of the Umayyad caliph Hisham. Of all its archaeology, the boy says that the most beautiful is the tree mosaic, by which he means a particularly famous depiction of the popular tree-of-life motif in which gazelles graze from a tree while another gazelle is eaten by a lion. Again he mentions seeing many foreign tourists. A guide from the Tourism Authority tells the children about the recent excavations at Jericho, which he says show that it is the oldest known city in the world.

Leaving Jericho the children cross the River Jordan over a bridge and find themselves in the Balqa Mountains. They are shown the path to Ajloun, where, they are told, there is a fort built by Salah al-Din. Then the students go to Jerash, where they see "Roman ruins." After Jerash they go to Amman and visit the Roman Theatre, Jabal al-Qalʿa (the Citadel), the Citadel museum, and the "new" mosque on Jabal al-Ashrafiyya. The children spend the night in Amman, "happy with what we had seen and heard."

The following morning the boys head for Madaba to visit its archaeology and see the "mosaic map of Palestine," after which they visit Kerak Castle, Tafila, and Shawbak before arriving in Wadi Musa. The children visit Petra, entering its archaeology "by way of a large crack in the mountains." They see "Pharaoh's Treasury," which the narrator says is a temple built to Zeus carved in beautiful, rose-colored rock. The children also see Petra's theater. At Aqaba they see cargo moving in the port, and then they visit Maʿan.

The boys finally return to their camp near Jenin, where the camp leader asks them to write about their thoughts and memories of their trip. The protagonist shares his essay with readers:

> I am proud of my country and pleased by it. It is a beautiful country with lowlands, highlands and valleys . . . This nature also gives us the chance to grow various crops in different places. My country is really beautiful. Being full of holy places and ancient archaeology increases its importance and beauty. It is really a big museum full of unique works of art and remnants of ancient civilizations who settled in it and created it. The attention of all the world is drawn to it, and people come to visit from all its regions. Commerce is stimulated by what they spend during their stay, increasing the income of my country, growing business and spreading prosperity.[118]

Just two examples of books in this *fadaʾil* genre are discussed here, demonstrating how Jordan's standardized curriculum tried to inculcate a sense of "Jordanian-ness" into some of its younger students. Just as the history and civics books discussed earlier in this chapter use cultural heritage as a means to drive home an ethos of pan-Arabism based on historical consciousness of ancient connections to the landscape, so the two books discussed and quoted above use cultural heritage to support an ethos much closer to home. That ethos was for the wealth and prestige of the modern Jordanian nation embedded in a paradigm of development.

The expanded Hashemite kingdom navigated its very problematic role in the regional competition characterizing this era by both physically controlling Palestine from its eastern core and owning narratives in which Jordanian was its only available identity. Jordan *was*, finally, *the* Holy Land. Commemoration of antiquity and modernity as seen in stamps, the development of archaeology, and the writing of history and social studies for schoolchildren are lenses through which to understand this process. In owning the narrative of the sacred universal value of Palestine as Jordanian, the value of antiquity of the Hashemite core became firmly established in something else. The choice was Arabism, and the ancients were most important for the depth of their roots in the landscape and for being the forebears of modern Jordanians. The antiquity narratives of Jordan's core and periphery thus worked in tandem, enabling complex Hashemite in expressions of both nationalism and pan-nationalism. The cost of investing Jerusalem with the Jordanian nation's universal value, however, would be manifest when the Palestine periphery was severed from the Hashemite core in 1967.

CHAPTER 7

Return to the Core

I have more right to claim the Jewish heritage as my own than a Jew from Europe does. But I can't say that.

JORDANIAN ARCHAEOLOGIST, INTERVIEW WITH
THE AUTHOR, AMMAN, 23 AUGUST 2006

At the end of the archaeological galleries on the first floor of the new Jordan Museum, one of the Dead Sea Scrolls, the Copper Scroll, sits alone on display in its exhibit. Packed away in Amman when the 1967 war erupted, it met a fate different from that of the other scrolls. During the fraught 1950s, Jordan's Council of Ministers had nationalized the contents of Jerusalem's Palestine Archaeological Museum (PAM), where the scrolls were housed. In late 1966, mayor of Jordanian Jerusalem Anwar Khatib spearheaded efforts to nationalize the PAM, which had been left by means of its endowment in international trust since the British withdrawal from Palestine in 1948.[1] What he called "a triumph for Arab nationalism" was, however, short-lived.[2] These acts of nationalization enabled Israel's Foreign and Education Ministries to legally declare the world-famous scrolls and the PAM (henceforth known as the Rockefeller, in honor of John D. Rockefeller, who endowed it during the Mandate) Jordan's national property, therefore captured enemy property, giving them over to Israel's Department of Antiquities.[3]

With the Dead Sea Scrolls, the PAM, Jerusalem, and the "West Bank" went the major part of Jordan's GDP, including that generated by tourism, which had grown substantially in the era of the expanded kingdom.[4] A crucial component of the Hashemite Jordanian narrative since the days of the Arab Revolt was gone. The previous two decades in and beyond Jordan had proven bankrupt. Palestine had been a key component of the general Arab fight against colonialism and for self-determination, regardless of the differences in various visions of *qawmiyya* and *wataniyya*. When the fighting was done, however, the Arab armies had been humiliated again and the rest of Palestine was lost in the process. Without its Palestine periphery, Jordan returned to the configuration of its Hashemite core, and another recalibration of its narrative as told by antiquity would ensue.

The day-to-day realities of the loss of Palestine helped shape this recalibration. There was an entirely new aspect to the ongoing refugee crisis. While many Palestinians living in the occupied West Bank continued to carry Jordanian passports and Jordan still paid government salaries, the River Jordan had become a border in an unprecedented way. Elements of the Palestinian resistance took matters into their own hands. A civil war was fought in Jordan in 1970–71, surviving erroneously in the historical record as a war between Jordanians and Palestinians and establishing "red lines" vis-à-vis the narrative of Jordan's security that have only recently begun to be broadly crossed. During that war, Syrian forces invaded northern Jordan, and upon negotiating a ceasefire to help Hussein, a man he had so publicly vilified for years, Gamal abd al-Nasser suffered a massive heart attack and died. In Jordan, the government and martial institutions of state were purged of suspected *fedayeen* sympathizers, whether of Palestinian or Transjordanian background. Those purged were generally replaced with definitively pro-Hashemite Transjordanians, particularly at the highest levels. While this is a generalization and there were certainly notable exceptions, Jordanians of Palestinian descent were largely relegated to the private sector, where those who could flourished and helped enhance what was already a highly professionalized sector of society. This purging marked a relative "de-Palestinianization" of the government and the identity of the country. While Transjordanian tribes and bedouin, like a range of Transjordanian and Arab professionals and entrepreneurs, had always been important components of the state apparatus for specific reasons, after the events of 1970–71 Transjordanians' own perceptions of security and place vis-à-vis their country, their king, and Palestinians entered a new era of definition and distinction as tribal life and tribal culture, an identity ethos that had emerged in the scholarly paradigms of antiquity as far back as the nineteenth century, were officially promoted as Jordan's identity with renewed vigor.[5] By and large, Transjordanians no longer took part in what were perceived to be "Palestinian" organizations. Some became radical, seeking the elimination of Palestinians from their country. Some became strong supporters of Palestinian nationalism, as the realization of Palestinian national aspirations had grand implications for their own perceptions of Jordanian nationalism under the new conditions that had taken hold in Jordan.[6] In this atmosphere, tribalism, the bedouin lifestyle, and the role of these vis-à-vis tradition and modernity in

Jordan have loomed large in Jordanian discourse.[7] Not far beneath the surface of ordinary day-to-day political life, the fear that Jordan is to be the "substitute homeland" for "the Palestinians" is unabashedly spoken aloud. There is clearly a perception that the Jordan core and its contents are fixed, and Palestine does not figure in that paradigm.

In this context, the new or renewed cultural heritage paradigms by which Jordan has sought to recast and present itself to audiences at home and abroad and attract tourists has focused heavily on notions of tribe and bedouin, tribe and bedouin within the context of heritage sites, and concepts of hospitality embedded in a "tribal," "bedouin," "Arab," and "Jordanian" past. As a life-long resident of Jordan told me, "After the war we were told we were tribes and bedouin. Everything was about tribes and bedouin."[8] Jordan's postage stamps, as well as many of its tourism and cultural heritage initiatives, demonstrate this emphasis on a tribal and bedouin past as a meme for the Jordanian present, as does the work of several scholars cited herein.[9]

As two antiquities sites of recognized universal value, Jerash and Petra have likewise been vital in the recalibration of Jordan's narrative. As they were during the Mandate, they have both been used in ways to appeal to foreign audiences, such as the designation of Petra as a UNESCO World Heritage site (1985), and to domestic audiences, such as the establishment of the Jerash Festival (1981) of local and regional culture and arts. As indicated in the archives of the Department of Antiquities, USAID's Jordan offices, and the U.S. government, furthermore, Wadi Rum, the Azraq Oasis, the so-called desert castles, various locations seen in the 1962 film *Lawrence of Arabia*, and Jordan's mineral waters and therapeutic hot springs, among others, were heritage sites targeted to take on new importance.[10]

Considerations of cultural heritage discourse specifically and identity generally since 1967 have focused, however, extensively on "tribal" and "bedouin" Jordan, while tending to ignore other important cultural heritage initiatives that have served to recalibrate identity narratives of the nation told by antiquity within its post-1967 borders. In the early days of a mid-1980s fiscal crisis that drove Jordan to insolvency by 1989 and a narrative of political and economic "liberalization" in its aftermath, King Hussein, much like the Ottomans a century prior, focused his attention on loci of Muslim religious heritage. He undertook massive renovations at the Shrines and Tombs of the Prophets and Companions (the *Sahaba*, or Companions of the Prophet Muhammad), of which there are several in Jordan, referenced frequently in textbooks cited herein as important sites (fig. 7.1). King Hussein attracted pious donations and appropriated state funds to support these projects, which were meant to benefit local communities while attracting mostly Jordanian

Fig. 7.1. Inside the mosque and shrine of the Prophet's Companion Abu ʿUbayda ibn al-Jarrah in the Northern Ghor, Jordan. Photo by E. Corbett, May 2008.

and non-Jordanian Muslim visitors, Sunni and Shiʿi alike. For Shiʿi visitors, pilgrimage to such sites is a highly ritualized aspect of routine religious observance. These projects enabled Jordan not only to officially express the religious tolerance it has always espoused in the framework of Muslim-Christian and often Jewish relations in the Sunni-Shiʿi sectarian idiom, but also to exert further control over the rural space, propriety, and discourse of Sunni practice, activity, and organization. This occurred in a context in which opposition rooted in influential Islamist political circles became a greater challenge to the monarchy and in which the monarchy's efforts to foster Islamization of urban space were usurped by widespread popular mobilization to do the same.[11]

In tandem with the promotion of the Shrines and Tombs of the Prophets and Companions, Jordan has promoted specifically Islamic religious tourism within the framework of all the Abrahamic faiths. This is in a bit of rhetorical contrast to the presentation of religious antiquity in textbooks discussed in previous chapters. The paradigm for talking about the ancient past as established in the textbooks of the 1950s, for instance, was to focus discursively on the primacy of its Arab, rather than its Islamic, character. It steered around Zionist claims to the ancient past by making Arab-ness the foremost identity of all the region's ancient peoples, including the Hebrews. In keeping with the inclusive needs of Arab nationalism, it tried when possible to discuss Christian and Muslim heritage sites as related, but practically separate entities, while giving a Muslim identity to some locales that might otherwise, particularly in Western taxonomies, be thought of as specifically Jewish. The child characters in the textbooks who take trips throughout the kingdom are of ambiguous backgrounds, but, particularly at Christian heritage sites, one gets the impression that they are outsiders learning about a different type among their fellow Arabs. It is always the children's guide who is at the forefront of their experience at Christian heritage sites, whereas their experiences at Islamic heritage sites are led by a cleric or by their own very personal and poignant experiences.

In most respects—and not surprisingly—the paradigm of Arabism espoused by those textbooks has disappeared. It is still the case that sites believed to have no significance to non-Muslim tourists are far off the beaten path.[12] It is also the case that Christian-centric tourism focuses little on the connection between Christian (and Jewish) antiquity and Islamic antiquity.[13] But within the context of Islamic tourism, sites having significance to all three Abrahamic faiths are promoted in a fairly inclusive way much more akin to the Islamicate milieu detectable in the pages of *al-Muqtataf* a century ago. A booklet published by the Jordan Tourism Board in 2005 is a case in point. Available in Arabic and English, *al-Islam fi al-Urdun: Masira wa Mawaqiă* (Tracing Islam in Jordan) is a twenty-page guide to Islamic sites all over the country.[14] It is indicative of the kind of message and picture of Islam King Abdullah II tries to promote in line with other initiatives, such as the Amman Message.[15] In the guide, the Cave of the Seven Sleepers, Madaba, Mount Nebo, Mukawir, the Bethany Baptism Site (*al-Maghtas*), Jesus, Gadara, Herod, John the Baptist, Noah, the Dead Sea, Kings David and Solomon of Israel, Lot, Jethro, Joshua, Job, Saul, Aaron, and Seth are all woven into a journey encompassing thousands of years of regional religious tradition. The force behind the excavation, interpretation, and renovation of *al-Maghtas* (the site sanctioned by the Vatican as that where John [*Yahya*] baptized Jesus [*'Issa*, the *Masih*, or Messiah], and where there was clearly a very early Christian community conducting baptisms) was Dr. Mohammad Waheeb, a Jordanian Muslim archaeologist. Scholars have expressed a degree of surprise that a Jordanian Muslim archaeologist would have or want expertise in early Christian archaeology; the importance of books such as this is that they can help disabuse such notions and suggest other paradigms for thinking about people's identification with heritage.[16] Administered by a special commission, *al-Maghtas* has become an important locus of identity for Jordanians generally, and is a common place for Christians to be baptized. It has also become a cornerstone of the Christian tourism industry, and Christian communities from all over the world have built or are building churches and monasteries there, blessed in person by their various holy patriarchs. As of late 2013, there is also an initiative, supported by Jordanians of diverse intellectual and religious backgrounds, to have *al-Maghtas* recognized as a UNESCO World Heritage site. This portrait of tolerance and moderation is a self-likeness espoused by Jordan over several decades, and the persona Jordan seems to enjoy internationally.[17] While there are certainly critiques to be made here about globalization and the hegemonic legacy of colonial knowledge, it is possible to view such projects more holistically if we consider the history of Arab interest in archaeology not just as a competition, but as an engagement with modernity, the scientific basis of traditional modes of identification. Jesus and John the Baptist are crucial to Islamic history and tradition; why wouldn't Dr. Waheeb and so many others be invested in a landscape so linked to the lives of these two seminal figures? As a professional tour guide said of the site in the context of a conference paper, "We as Jordanians, Muslim and Christian, are blessed to have Jesus in our country."[18]

As projects such as the Shrines and Tombs of the Prophets and Companions and *al-Maghtas* were completed, opened, and began to draw visitors, the Royal Court threw its weight behind the development of a massive new Amman park dedicated to the late King Hussein's memory.[19] Abutting the moneyed estates at one of the fringes of West Amman, the King Hussein Gardens is visible from all over the city in the form of its mosque, designed to evoke Bilad al-Sham of the Umayyad period, dedicated to the memory of the late king and serving as the state mosque since 2006 (fig. 7.2). Among the park's numerous components, including football fields, cafes, artists' workshops, a go-cart track, and the ultra-sleek Royal Automobile and Children's Museums, is a 488-meter-long wall and promenade known as the Historical Passageway, designed by artist and architect Jamal Joucka.[20] This wall, divided into numerous panels created and installed by artists from Jordan, Syria, and Iraq, is a comprehensive study of the various epochs in Jordan's history. It presents traditionally espoused narratives of Jordan's modern history, such as the Hashemite role in leading the Arab Revolt and protecting Jerusalem's holy sites, its pre-Islamic past as understood through Nabatean

Fig. 7.2. The King Hussein Mosque, Amman, Jordan. Photo by G. J. Corbett, September 2006.

Petra, and its Hellenistic, Christian, and Islamic heritage. But the panels also depict, for the first time, the cultural achievements and artifacts of Jordan's most remote and most sensitive past. These include the Neolithic period (ca. 8500–4500 BCE), by means of the famous Ain Ghazal statues—the oldest known figural representations in the world—and various well-known aspects of desert scripts, murals, and rock art; the Late Bronze Age (ca. 1550–1200 BCE), with famous stelae that have connections to the biblical world; and the controversial Iron Age (ca. 1200–550 BCE) and its Transjordanian peoples, particularly the Ammonites and the Moabites—through the Mesha Stela. All of these ancient peoples are, for the first time, included as part of the national narrative, they and their civilizations meant to be understood as the forebears of the contemporary nation. A physical wooden bridge on the promenade links the premodern sections of the Historical Passageway to the panels that depict traditionally touted great moments in the history of the modern state. It is a visual, positivist, comprehensive narrative linking Jordan's antiquity to its modernity, suggesting that a proto-Jordan has always been there and that history culminates inevitably in the Hashemite dynasty. King Abdullah II thus reigns, just as he should, over a diverse yet united citizenry bound by the continuous prosperity and stability it has enjoyed under the kings' leadership (figs. 7.3 and 7.4).

While the park offers many recreational benefits to sectors of the community that can access it, it is a very different project from those such as the

Fig. 7.3. Near the beginning of the Historical Passageway. Photo by E. Corbett, November 2006.

renovations to shrines and tombs undertaken by King Hussein, and reflects a very different set of circumstances. The renovation of the shrines and tombs, much like the hospitals and schools built at his behest, was a project characteristic of the reign of Hussein, who maintained the legitimacy of his monarchy by attracting and redistributing largesse. King Hussein Gardens is characteristic of Abdullah, who can be seen reacting in ways demonstrating that Jordan's "liberalization" has left him without the ability to do the same. In the early 1970s, Hussein built the renowned medical complex that bears his name next to what is now a park built by his son in his honor. In the first decade of the twenty-first century, the sultan of Oman donated the money for the new state mosque, and elites and gulf entrepreneurs built expensive mega-malls that most Jordanians can't afford to frequent across the street from the park. The Royal Palace, meanwhile, directed the implementation of the Historical Passageway—the monumental paean to itself—that sits among them.

Across town and in the works for more than a decade, the Jordan Museum, known originally as "The National Museum," is nearing completion.[21] Its story spans five decades, the first ideas for a national museum for Jordan on the eastern side of the river having been hatched in the 1960s prior to the war. Its governance is emblematic of Jordan's liberalization and development and the role of Jordan's NGOs as elucidated by Laurie Brand. Brand shows that membership in prestigious institutions, NGOs, and civil society organizations is inextricably bound to the complex and codependent relationship among the royal family, government, and the variety of elite Jordanians who participate in Jordan's institutions and drive the discourse of development and modernity, and by extension, antiquities' role in both.[22] Although the Jordan Museum became "independent" of government and beholden to its own board of trustees in 2005, the board includes more than one member of the royal family and the ministers of Tourism and Antiquities, Planning, and the Greater Amman Municipality, among others. Its very existence is, furthermore, a case study in the link between globalization and cultural heritage. As a subproject of the larger Tourism Sector Development Project, it was financed with a Japanese loan under the auspices of the Japanese International Cooperation Agency (JICA).

The Jordan Museum is one of many cultural heritage projects generally in recent years, and specifically museum projects. Other museums, such as those in Salt, Ma'an, and Aqaba, have local history as their themes. As Irene Maffi has observed, this local history is presented in such a way as to be intimately tied to Hashemite history.[23] The choice of the Abu Jaber House for the new

Fig. 7.4. Along the Historical Passageway. Photo by E. Corbett, November 2006.

museum in Salt, for instance, is indicative of its having been the place from which Emir Abdullah first governed his nascent state.[24] Rami Daher, architect and designer of the project, is, however, as a professional who named his company *Turath*, certainly focused on a range of meaningful aspects of local and national heritage. The Maʿan museum is the house in which Abdullah I stayed when he rode out of the Hijaz to defend his family's claim to an Arab kingdom in the territories at the heart of the Husayn-McMahon/Sykes-Picot debacles. Aqaba's renovated museum was home to Sharif Husayn of Mecca after his ouster from the Hijaz by Ibn Saʿud. Others of the new museums have site-, issue-, or archaeology-specific themes. Among these are the Dead Sea Panorama, which is primarily an environmental museum, the Kerak Castle Museum, and the new museum at Ghor al-Safi near the site known as Lot's Cave. Along with the Jordan Museum, the museums at Salt, Kerak, and the Dead Sea are JICA-funded projects. The Aqaba and Ghor al-Safi Museums were financed at least in part by the European Union.

Maffi views the rash of museum openings in Amman and throughout Jordan over the past two decades in the context of Jordan's efforts at "liberalization" since 1990. The museums have two audiences: international tourists and Jordanians. An audience of international tourists is, as it has always been, important for generating revenue and cultivating a national story and reputation abroad. The domestic audience is, as always, important for helping cultivate the tacit understanding of the performance of being a citizen in a national space. For Maffi, these new museums are intended to further "patrimonial-ize," that is, Hashem-ize, Jordan's historical memory for the twenty-first century. Certainly the Royal Automobile Museum at the King Hussein Gardens, which tells the story of the state by means of the royal family's private collection of cars, is indicative of this trend.

After a debate of more than twenty years, Ras al-Ain, in an old neighborhood in Amman's downtown, was chosen as the location for the museum.[25] Near Amman City Hall, opened in 1998, it is intended to be accessible via a pedestrian path from the Amman Citadel. The building was designed by architect Jaʿafar Touqan, winner of an Aga Khan award, and designer of Amman City Hall. According to a 2006 brochure:

> The general concept of the exhibition plan in the museum is "A Story Telling [*sic*] of Jordan: Land and People": [*sic*] past, present, and an attempt to look into the future. [*sic*] This concept is physically reflected in the exterior finish of the building, where rough and smooth stones symbolize the past and present, while glass symbolizes the future.[26]

The first thing that greets the visitor in the museum is a Nabatean motif, the description of which is, in fact, entitled "Land and People." The text begins with the idea of connection between the two that has been a theme throughout these pages: "The story of humanity on Earth; the result of what seems to us as the 'eternal' interaction between people and land with its geography, fauna, and flora." Like the antiquity presented on the Historical Passageway, collections from the prehistoric and other traditionally neglected periods are important components of the museum's collections. As of early 2014, only the archaeological galleries were open, and visitors can experience themes both familiar and neglected, as discussed in these pages. Between the prehistoric gallery and the historical galleries is a room serving as an interlude about bedouin life, indicating the connection of this national meme with remote antiquity. From this room, one enters the displays of the archaeology of historical periods, beginning in the Bronze Age, highlighting, as did textbooks of the postwar period through the 1970s, Canaanite urbanism in the area and the entry of the Amorites from the Arabian Peninsula. Moving into the Iron Age, the displays emphasize the "national" kingdoms of Ammon, Moab, and Edom, without overt references to the contemporaneous situation on the other side of the river or allusion to its importance for the modern history of the region. Beyond the Iron Age lie the Hellenistic through Byzantine periods, in which the Nabateans are, as usual, rendered Arabs who came to Jordan from the Arabian Peninsula, while archaeology related to Christianity, particularly from the Petra region, emphasizes its existence in Arabia.

The second floor, which focuses on more recent history and "Living History," was not yet open as of early 2014. In the process of creating the museum, archaeologist Dr. "Anonymous Four" gave a lot of thought to the nature of the museum's presentation of this idea. Scenes of "traditional life" and "folklore" as presented in various museums throughout Jordan and in performances at numerous venues as "Jordanian" actually hearken back to the era in which the Arabs lived under Ottoman suzerainty. When Jordanians over a certain age talk about the lives of their grandparents and their great-grandparents, they are talking about memories of the late Ottoman world. The Ottoman period is contentious in modern Arab historiography, yet it represents the foundation of today's Jordan in myriad ways. "The Ottoman Period is a problem both historically *and* archaeologically," Dr. "Anonymous Four" said. To this day, an antiquity, according to the law, remains anything older than 1700 CE, which leaves more than two formative centuries of the Ottoman period missing. During an interview when the "Living History" gallery was in its earliest stages and known as the "Traditional Life" gallery, archaeologist Dr. "Anonymous Five" saw this gallery as a metaphorical bridge, much like the physical bridge that architect and artist Jamal Joucka, designer of the Historical Passageway, built to link the part of the wall that represents Jordan's pre-Hashemite past with those parts depicting the Hashemite present. "In this gallery we are working on the attachment of the present with the past, bridging into that, connecting to before [the] Ottoman [period]."[27] The Jordan Museum thus maintains the long-held discursive separation between archaeological and "living" heritage.

Designed as a modern, multipurpose museum facility, in addition to having numerous amenities for visitors, the museum will help alleviate the general lack of office, storage, laboratory, and library space that has plagued Amman's archaeological professionals for the entirety of the nation's history. The National Museum/Jordan Museum project team has been extremely conscious of building the museum to international standards and making use of new technology. "We don't want a static archaeological museum," said Dr. "Anonymous Five." "We want it to have aspects of science museums," said Dr. "Anonymous Four."

When asked about a correlation between the museum and the various tourism development projects and slogans like "You reap what you sow" and "Jordan First," Dr. "Anonymous Four" agreed. "What's behind these statements? To entice economic development and to strengthen people's identity and sense of respecting cultural heritage . . . It's the idea of economic development hand-in-hand with the development of cultural heritage management."

That the rest of the Dead Sea Scrolls remain in the Shrine of Book in Jerusalem, property of the State of Israel, while the Copper Scroll sits alone in the Jordan Museum, is not for lack of trying. In recent years and with the support of the King Abdullah II Fund for Development, the Jordanian Committee for the Dead Sea Scrolls has been working to study and disseminate knowledge of the scroll texts, which, in the words of Dr. 'Adnan al-Bakhit, "represent a foundational part of the religious and cultural heritage of our countries."[28] In the midst of a Dead Sea Scrolls exhibit at Toronto's Royal Ontario Museum in early 2010, the Jordanian government made official, diplomatic representation to the government of Canada to seize them, citing the Hague Convention of 1954 to which it and Canada are both signatories. There was a simultaneous uptick of popular interest in them, as renowned Jordanian academics published articles in the press, appeared on Arabic-language television, and offered public lectures. This complicated an issue that had already been raised in 2009 when the Palestinian Authority, which challenges both Israeli *and*

Jordanian claims to ownership of the Dead Sea Scrolls, had made its own official representation protesting Israel's use of the Dead Sea Scrolls to the government of Canada. Canada refused any requests to act, referring to the issue of Dead Sea Scrolls ownership as a matter to be resolved among Israel, Jordan, and the Palestinian Authority.

In late 2010, the Israel Antiquities Authority (IAA) announced plans to digitize the Dead Sea Scrolls, publishing them online in partnership with the Israel Museum and Google. The issue of ownership was front and center once again. Jordanian antiquities officials, namely the department's director, very publicly went on record claiming Jordan's ownership of the scrolls, adding to the claim both their discovery and recovery from what were, at that time, Jordanian territories, and their recovery from antique dealers at that time with Jordanian money.

In the meantime, a hyperbolic *National Geographic* television special seemed to tie the ancient copper mines being excavated in Jordan's Wadi Faynan with the completely unrelated discovery of a very early inscription found at Khirbet al-Qeiyafa, a site in Israel that has become central to supporting the historicity of a Davidic/Solomonic United Monarchy.[29] By early 2011, a new story had broken about the "Lead Codices," a collection of small, ring-bound leaves of lead and copper, the contents of which seemed to place them in the context of the earliest followers of Jesus, and, if authentic, would be the earliest Christian texts ever found. Discovered in Jordan, they had apparently been smuggled into Israel, and Jordan's director of antiquities was again a very public face for stating Jordan's intentions to claim ownership of old texts. In the midst of internal political turmoil that characterized the first half of 2011, the director's term came to an end, and the position sat vacant for more than two years. The authenticity of the "Lead Codices" remains suspect, unresolved, and the issue seems to have gone to the ether. The Israel Museum/Google Dead Sea Scrolls partnership went online in early autumn 2011, and almost simultaneously Israel returned some artifacts to Jordan that had been in Israeli custody since the 1967 war. A team of Palestinian archaeologists and cultural heritage experts was, meanwhile, standing ready with an antiquities law for Palestine in the unlikely event the PA's statehood bid at the 2011 UN General Assembly meeting was successful.

A More Complex Canvas than Meets the Eye

In this book I have considered antiquity in the context of competition for narratives related to it and the history, as viewed officially from Jordan, of Jordan and Palestine as contested spaces. Antiquities and the recognizable landscapes they help delineate have, on both sides of the river, played an important role in defining notions of Jordan. The importance of antiquities and their delineated landscapes, even in the Transjordanian frontier, was harnessed by late Ottoman statesmen and Western scholars and explorers alike. In some instances, Ottoman and Western authorities seized upon different antiquities for reasons related to their respective imperial ventures. Istanbul had a reason for cultivating the shrine of the Prophet's Companion Abu ʿUbayda in the Transjordanian frontier. The English, French, and Germans had a reason to fight over the Mesha Stela. In the case of Jerusalem, which has continued—despite the rhetoric of "Jordan First" and its aftermath—to be central to Jordanian Hashemite notions of *qawmiyya* and *wataniyya* and the identity of Jordan's diverse citizens, Istanbul and the European capitals seized on the same antiquities with perhaps the same purpose, although differences in the nuances of meaning were so important, and so lost upon the Western paradigms of knowledge that gained and in most respects maintain such preeminence. Prevailing discourses of antiquity, whether imperial or national ventures, whether rooted in "East" or "West," have been harnessed to cultivate modernity. This has been true as much in Jordan as anywhere else.

As Western scholarship has viewed Jordan's antiquities, Jordan's archaeological heritage has, to its detriment, been defined largely in terms of not being Israel's archaeological heritage, and thus in many ways still has largely to be meaningfully synthesized domestically or regionally in either academic or popular narratives. Not only are regional sensitivities to blame, but also the backgrounds and agendas of scholars themselves and the paradigms of antiquity and modernity they created. Such paradigms helped create maps of nation-states, and Jordan's modern territorial composition has been problematic; the fledging state had no comprehensive narrative of great ancient civilization upon which it could draw to demonstrate the historicity of its modern borders. The stewardship of the Hashemites, furthermore, was likewise problematic in both the present and the past. The historicity narrative of their legitimacy to rule over not just Jordan, but the larger hereditary possession they coveted—including Palestine—was inseparable from the same Abrahamic scriptural narrative upon which Israel depends for the historicity narrative of its state. Social and political sensitivities stemming from this issue, in tandem with the problematic of Jordan's territorial configurations and Hashemite leadership over them, have, at important moments in Jordan's history, served to define antiquities, and how and whether they are included in the language of *qawmiyya* and *wataniyya*—or as part of the national patrimony—at all.

Another goal of this project has been to complicate the discourse of archaeology and antiquity specifically, and cultural heritage more broadly, in Jordan within the framework of the country's history, particularly its expansion and contraction, the prevailing narratives of which have been greatly complicated by other scholars cited within these pages. As competition for archaeology and cultural heritage is so embedded in nationalism, and the nationalist discourse of identity in Jordan is still overwhelmingly couched in a binary of Jordanian and Palestinian, this book also opens new avenues for considering Jordan's archaeology and its role in supporting, challenging, and complicating prevailing discourses of identity. There is much room for further work on this issue.

Over the course of working on this project, I have had many conversations with Jordanians, particularly cultural heritage professionals and enthusiasts, about an array of practical and theoretical issues important to the disciplines related to heritage. Among these issues were questions about their sense of identity and the role of archaeology and cultural heritage in it. Anecdotally and not at all surprisingly, their feelings on such matters are complicated, and logically so given the ideas presented herein. A professional Jordanian archaeologist might identify personally with Jerusalem because he or she is from a family that originated there, because he or she feels a religious connection to it, or because he or she feels connected to the Palestine issue. Simultaneously he or she may feel personally connected with Amman, having been born there, grown up there, gone to school there, and having all his or her family and friends there. He or she may be employed there, maybe in service to the government of the Hashemite state. At the same time, he or she has a professional interest that creates another personal tie to both places, especially as someone educated and trained as a specialist in archaeology and cultural heritage. The archaeologist whose quote opened this chapter, who hails from what would be considered a family of Palestinian origin said, "My life is here [in Amman]. My *rizq* [daily bread] is here."[30] Another archaeologist of a family of Circassian origin said, "If I had it to do over, I would be a biblical archaeologist."[31]

I have never met a Jordanian of any professional, familial, or religious background who has *not* said that he or she feels personally connected to Jerusalem. A young member of Jordan's Friends of Archaeology Society, for instance, said that while he likes and appreciates Petra and intellectually understands its importance, "I feel more personally connected to Jerusalem." He has never been there, has lived all his life in Jordan and comes, like so many Jordanians, from a family with origins in Palestine. Yet, he added, "I feel more Jordanian than Palestinian."[32] Such sentiments would seem to run counter to prevailing narratives in both academic and popular discourse. In light of the ideas presented in this book, however, they should appear normative. They likewise present an anecdotal springboard for further research into the interstices of antiquity and identity in Jordan, Palestine, and the region more broadly.

Speaking with Jordanians who are not connected by profession, hobby, or interest to archaeology or cultural heritage about the interstices of heritage and identity can be difficult and enlightening. In a recent conversation I had with a PhD in another profession about the contents of *al-Muqtataf* discussed herein, she mentioned that she had been to the Egyptian Museum and seen Ramses II's mummy, and that as a devout Muslim, seeing him there was an emotional experience attesting to God's power and the truth of His revelations.[33] Until we had this conversation, she had not thought about this in terms of identity and narratives told by antiquity, as it was a deeply spiritual and personal matter unrelated to matters of archaeology. I would suggest that just such a reaction to witnessing the corpse of Pharaoh is exactly what laid the foundation for the engagement with the science of archaeology—and its embrace as historical consciousness in a rapidly modernizing world—that one can read in the pages of *al-Muqtataf*, and on that basis understand the problematic of archaeology in the nation-state paradigm. Taxonomy served to narrate archaeology and the historicity of nation-states; archaeology in the framework of nation-states has further taxonomized the praxis of archaeology. The context for this is colonialism, and colonialism and its legacies are omnipresent in assigning monetary, academic, and ultimately personal value to antiquity. These forces are responsible for the very imposition of the nation-state itself and continue to influence the interpretation of archaeology. What many in the cultural heritage community both in Jordan and abroad bemoan as the general lack of awareness or concern for antiquity, then, is surely not a simple question. Assigning a bit of ancient heritage to citizens of one country or adherents to one religious tradition while denying it to another on the basis of such parameters is perhaps not a productive avenue for encouraging engagement with heritage, but this is exactly what continues to happen. As the conversation about Ramses II's mummy demonstrates, however, while the lively engagement with innovative knowledge of the past as read in the pages of *al-Muqtataf* may be hard to find these days, that which made it possible in the first place is not, even if it is mired in the arbitrariness of borders, perceptions of value, and the legacies of colonialism. In a time when cultural heritage and disciplines related to its study find themselves under increasing existential threat, may the introspection related to guaranteeing a future for them begin with recognition of that fact.

Notes

Chapter One

1. Interview with Ammar Khammash, 7 November 2006, Amman, Jordan.
2. Dhuqan al-Hindawi, *al-Qadiyya al-Filastiniyya* (The Palestinian Issue) (Amman: Ministry of Education, 1966), 7.
3. Betty S. Anderson, *Nationalist Voices in Jordan: The Street and the State* (Austin: University of Texas Press, 2005).
4. Donald Malcom Reid, *Whose Pharaohs? Archaeology, Museums, and Egyptian National Identity from Napoleon to World War I* (Berkeley: University of California Press, 2002); Elliott Colla, *Conflicted Antiquities: Egyptology, Egyptomania, Egyptian Modernity* (Durham: Duke University Press, 2007); Magnus T. Bernhardsson, *Reclaiming a Plundered Past: Archaeology and Nation Building in Modern Iraq* (Austin: University of Texas Press, 2005); James F. Goode, *Negotiating for the Past: Archaeology, Nationalism, and Diplomacy in the Middle East, 1919–1941* (Austin: University of Texas Press, 2007); Nachman Ben-Yehuda, *The Masada Myth: Collective Memory and Mythmaking in Israel* (Madison: University of Wisconsin Press, 1995); Nadia Abu el-Haj, *Facts on the Ground: Archaeological Practice and Territorial Self-Fashioning in Israeli Society* (Chicago: University of Chicago Press, 2001).
5. Mary C. Wilson, *King Abdullah, Britain and the Making of Jordan* (Cambridge: Cambridge University Press, 1987); Avi Shlaim, *Collusion across the Jordan: King Abdullah, the Zionist Movement, and the Partition of Palestine* (New York: Columbia University Press, 1988); Laurie Brand, *Jordan's Inter-Arab Relations: The Political Economy of Alliance Making* (New York: Columbia University Press, 1994).
6. Linda L. Layne, *Home and Homeland: The Dialogics of Tribal and National Identities in Jordan* (Princeton: Princeton University Press, 1994); Eugene Rogan, *Frontiers of the State in the Late Ottoman Empire: Transjordan, 1850–1921* (Cambridge: Cambridge University Press, 1999); Michael R. Fischbach, *State, Society and Land in Transjordan* (Leiden: Brill, 2000); Joseph A. Massad, *Colonial Effects: The Making of National Identity in Jordan* (New York: Columbia University Press, 2001); Andrew Shryock, *Nationalism and the Genealogical Imagination: Oral History and Textual Authority in Tribal Jordan* (Berkeley: University of California Press, 1997); Anderson, *Nationalist Voices*

in Jordan; Kimberly Katz, *Jordanian Jerusalem: Holy Places and National Spaces* (Gainesville: University Press of Florida, 2005); Yoav Alon, *The Making of Jordan: Tribes, Colonialism and the Modern State* (London, New York: I. B. Tauris, 2007).

Chapter Two

1. MECA/Hogarth Papers, Hogarth to Mother, 20 August 1918.

2. Roger Owen, "British and French Military Intelligence in Syria and Palestine, 1914–1918: Myths and Reality," *British Journal of Middle Eastern Studies* 38, no. 1 (2011); Priya Satia, *Spies in Arabia: The Great War and the Cultural Foundations of Britain's Covert Empire in the Middle East* (Oxford: Oxford University Press, 2008), chapters 3–5.

3. Mark Bradley, ed., *Classics and Imperialism in the British Empire* (Oxford: Oxford University Press, 2010). See also Debbie Challis, *From the Harpy Tomb to the Wonders of Ephesus: British Archaeologists in the Ottoman Empire, 1840–1880* (London: Duckworth, 2008).

4. Bradley, *Classics and Imperialism*.

5. Nadia Abu el-Haj, *Facts on the Ground: Archaeological Practice and Territorial Self-Fashioning in Israeli Society* (Chicago: University of Chicago Press, 2001), 28; Neil Asher Silberman, *Digging for God and Country: Exploration, Archeology, and the Secret Struggle for the Holy Land, 1799–1917* (New York: Alfred A. Knopf, 1982), 123.

6. Silberman, *Digging for God and Country*, 63–69. See also Roberto Mazza, *Jerusalem from the Ottomans to the British* (London: I. B. Tauris, 2009), 52. For more about Latin and Greek Orthodox relations in terms of French and Russian posturing in the Holy Land, the involvement of the Vatican, and the roles and preferences of the various Catholic orders, see Thomas Stransky, "Origins of Western Christian Missions in Jerusalem and the Holy Land," in *Jerusalem in the Mind of the Western World, 1800–1948*, ed. Yehoshua Ben-Arieh and Moshe Davis (Westport: Praeger Press, 1997).

7. Margarita Díaz-Andreu, *A World History of Nineteenth-Century Archaeology* (Oxford: Oxford University Press, 2007), chapters 5 and 6.

8. Silberman, *Digging for God and Country*. Lebanon's governance was separated from that of the rest of Greater Syria and put under French protection in the wake of sectarian violence in 1860. See Ussama Makdisi, *The Culture of Sectarianism: Community, History and Violence in Nineteenth-Century Ottoman Lebanon* (Berkeley, Los Angeles: University of California Press, 2000).

9. Geraldine Chatelard and Jean-Michel de Tarragon, *L'Empire et le Royaume: La Jordanie Vue par l'École Biblique et Archéologique Française de Jérusalem (1893–1935)* (Amman: Institut Française de Proche Orient, 2006).

10. Silberman, *Digging for God and Country*, chapter 7.

11. By speaking of Germany, I am referring to the confluence of German-language scholarship and political, sociocultural, and Protestant affinity that bound the German states long before unification. For the situation of Catholics, both vis-à-vis Protestants and in the late nineteenth-century Holy Land, see Haim Goren, "The German Catholic 'Holy Sepulchre Society': Activities in Palestine," in *Jerusalem in the Mind of the Western World, 1800–1948*, ed. Yehoshua Ben-Arieh and Moshe Davis (Westport: Praeger Press, 1997); Suzanne L. Marchand, *Down from Olympus: Archaeology and*

Philhellenism in Germany, 1750–1970 (Princeton: Princeton University Press, 1996), xxii–xxiii.

12. James R. Moore, *The Post-Darwinian Controversies: A Study of the Protestant Struggle to Come to Terms with Darwin in Great Britain and America, 1870–1900* (Cambridge: Cambridge University Press, 1979); Owen Chadwick, *The Secularization of the European Mind in the Nineteenth Century* (Cambridge: Cambridge University Press, 1990).

13. Marchand, *Down from Olympus*, 188–92.

14. Ibid., 220–23.

15. Richard Elliott Friedman, *Who Wrote the Bible?* (New York: Summit Books, 1987), 24–31; Peter Douglas Feinman, *William Foxwell Albright and the Origins of Biblical Archaeology* (Berrien Springs, MI: Andrews University Press, 2004), 54–64, 90–108.

16. Marchand, *Down from Olympus*, 224–25.

17. Ibid., 220–27; Bruce Kuklick, *Puritans in Babylon* (Princeton: Princeton University Press, 1996), 196–202. Ominously, the deconstruction of the Hebrew Bible and the consolidation of the field of Assyriology were incorporated into the rising tide of German anti-Semitism. Marchand, *Down from Olympus*, 225–27. For a complex perspective on broader German intellectual and social trends with connections to Oriental scholarship, see Jonathan Karp and Adam Sutcliffe, eds., *Philosemitism in History* (Cambridge: Cambridge University Press, 2011). See especially the chapters by Lars Fischer, "Anti-'Philosemitism' and Anti-Antisemitism in Imperial Germany," and Alan T. Levenson, "From Recognition to Consensus: The Nature of Philosemitism in Germany, 1871–1932."

18. Yehoshua Ben-Arieh and Moshe Davis, *Jerusalem in the Mind of the Western World, 1800–1948* (Westport: Praeger Press, 1997). See especially the chapters by Frank Foerster, "German Missions in the Holy Land," and Martin Luckhoff, "Prussia and Jerusalem: Political and Religious Controversies Surrounding the Foundation of the Jerusalem Bishopric."

19. Kuklick, *Puritans in Babylon*, 19.

20. Ibid., 6–7, chapter 1.

21. Moore, *The Post-Darwinian Controversies*, 6–9.

22. Ibid.

23. Silberman, *Digging for God and Country*, 113–17; Rachel S. Hallote, *Bible, Map and Spade: The American Palestine Exploration Society, Frederick Jones Bliss, and the Forgotten Story of Early American Biblical Archaeology* (Piscataway: Gorgias Press, 2006), 51–55.

24. The context of national modernity for this affinity is discussed in Jonathan Karp and Adam Sutcliffe, "Introduction: A Brief History of Philosemitism," in *Philosemitism in History*, ed. Jonathan Karp and Adam Sutcliffe (Cambridge: Cambridge University Press, 2011). See two other essays in this volume, Adam Shear, "William Whitson's Judeo-Christianity: Millenarian and Christian Zionism in Early Enlightenment England," and Yaacov Ariel, "'It's All in the Bible': Evangelical Christians, Biblical Literalism, and Philosemitism in Our Times."

25. Regarding English literature and its confluence with antiquity, imperialism, and capitalism, see esp. chapters 5 and 6 of Saree Makdisi, *Romantic Imperialism: Universal Empire and the Culture of Modernity* (Cambridge: Cambridge University Press, 1998).

26. John Davis, *The Landscape of Belief: Encountering the Holy Land in Nineteenth-Century American Art and Culture* (Princeton: Princeton University Press, 1996), chapter 1.

27. On the appearance of the first British and Americans in the Holy Land in and beyond Palestine, see Hallote, *Bible, Map and Spade*, chapters 2–5; Silberman, *Digging for God and Country*, chapters 3–4; Joseph L. Grabill, *Protestant Diplomacy and the Near East: Missionary Influence on American Policy, 1810–1927* (Minneapolis: University of Minnesota Press, 1971), chapter 1; Ussama Makdisi, *Artillery of Heaven: American Missionaries and the Failed Conversion of the Middle East* (Ithaca: Cornell University Press, 2008), introduction and chapter 1.

28. Neil Asher Silberman, "Desolation and Restoration: The Impact of a Biblical Concept on Near Eastern Archaeology," *Biblical Archaeologist* 54, no. 2 (1991).

29. Quoted in John James Moscrop, *Measuring Jerusalem: The Palestine Exploration Fund and British Interests in the Holy Land* (London: Leicester University Press, 2000), 70–71.

30. Edward Robinson, *Biblical Researches in Palestine, Mount Sinai and Arabia Petraea. A Journal of Travels in the Year 1838, by E. Robinson and E. Smith. Undertaken in Reference to Biblical Geography. Drawn up from the Original Diaries with Historical Illus. by Edward Robinson.* 3 vols. (Boston: Crocker and Brewster, 1841); Thomas W. Davis, *Shifting Sands: The Rise and Fall of Biblical Archaeology* (Oxford, New York: Oxford University Press, 2004), 4–12; Silberman, *Digging for God and Country*, chapter 5; Moscrop, *Measuring Jerusalem*, 18–20; Davis, *The Landscape of Belief*, 34–37; Stephanie Stidham Rogers, *Inventing the Holy Land* (Lanham: Lexington Books, 2011).

31. Stransky, "Origins of Western Christian Missions."

32. Moscrop, *Measuring Jerusalem*, 20; Rogers, *Inventing the Holy Land*, chapter 5.

33. Davis, *Shifting Sands*, 11; Moscrop, *Measuring Jerusalem*, 20; Piers Brendon, *Thomas Cook: 150 Years of Popular Tourism* (London: Secker and Warburg, 1991).

34. William Francis Lynch, *Narrative of the United States' Expedition to the River Jordan and the Dead Sea* (Philadelphia: Lea and Blanchard, 1849); Robert Rook, *The 150th Anniversary of the United States' Expedition to Explore the Dead Sea and the River Jordan* (Amman: American Center of Oriental Research, 1998).

35. H. B. Tristram, *The Land of Israel, a Journal of Travels in Palestine* (London: Society for Promoting Christian Knowledge, 1882; reprint, Gorgias Press, 2002).

36. Moscrop, *Measuring Jerusalem*, 53–58, 66; Silberman, *Digging for God and Country*, 79–86.

37. Silberman, *Digging for God and Country*, 83–84.

38. Moscrop, *Measuring Jerusalem*, 63–67.

39. PEF/MINS, 22.6.1865, as quoted in ibid., 70; Silberman, *Digging for God and Country*, 86.

40. Report of the first meeting at Willis's Rooms, 22 June 1865, *Palestine Exploration Quarterly*, 3. Also quoted in Moscrop, *Measuring Jerusalem*, 70.

41. Moscrop, *Measuring Jerusalem*, 66–72. As for the British Empire as a middle-class enterprise, see Kathryn Tidrick, *Empire and the English Character* (London: I. B. Tauris, 1990), 4.

42. Moscrop, *Measuring Jerusalem*, 66–72.

43. Among the catalysts for the Crimean War were diplomatic machinations between France and the Ottoman Empire to limit Russian inroads in the region by

limiting Russian influence over Jerusalem's holy places. The Indian Rebellion of 1857 had led to British dissolution of the East India Company and Crown takeover of its assets.

44. Moscrop, *Measuring Jerusalem*, 53–60.

45. William Foxwell Albright, "Palestinian Inscriptions," in *Ancient Near Eastern Texts Relating to the Old Testament*, ed. J. B. Pritchard (Princeton: Princeton University Press, 1969).

46. Moscrop, *Measuring Jerusalem*, 90.

47. "Quarterly Statement of Progress (January to March 1869)," *Palestine Exploration Quarterly* 1 (1869).

48. Moscrop, *Measuring Jerusalem*, 72–83.

49. Silberman, *Digging for God and Country*, 101–2.

50. Klein's account of the discovery can be found in Rev. F. A. Klein, "The Original Discovery of the Moabite Stone," *Palestine Exploration Quarterly* (March–June 1870).

51. Silberman, *Digging for God and Country*, 104–5.

52. Warren's account of the stela's saga and correspondence between George Grove and various scholars dating to the first quarter of 1870 is found in Charles Warren, "The Moabite Stone: Captain Warren's First Account of the Inscription from Moab," *Palestine Exploration Quarterly* (1870): 169–82. The *PEQ* notes that most of these letters appeared in the press.

53. Moscrop, *Measuring Jerusalem*, 88; Silberman, *Digging for God and Country*, 105–6.

54. Silberman, *Digging for God and Country*, 106–7.

55. Ibid.

56. Moscrop, *Measuring Jerusalem*, 89.

57. Silberman, *Digging for God and Country*, 108–11, 15. See also accounts and letters published and reprinted from the media in the *Palestine Exploration Quarterly*, Charles Warren, "The Moabite Stone"; Klein, "The Original Discovery of the Moabite Stone."

58. Moscrop, *Measuring Jerusalem*, 90.

59. Ibid., 90–91.

60. Ibid.

61. Ibid.

62. Silberman, *Digging for God and Country*, 111, 15. A tell is a mound that, to the trained eye, is easily discernible as man-made. Tells were early recognized by explorers of the Near East as places where antiquities could be found. By the early twentieth century, Flinders Petrie had developed a methodology for excavating tells stratigrapically, i.e., by layers, the earliest occupation at the bottom of the mound and the most recent at the top. In excavating a tell, one thus excavates the most recent layers of habitation first, working backward through time and moving downward through layers of the mound. The layers provide context for the artifacts found; potsherds and other artifacts assist in dating the layers. This was quickly understood and adopted as the scientific standard.

63. E. H. Palmer, "The Desert of the Tíh and the Country of Moab," *Palestine Exploration Quarterly* (October–December 1869): 72–73.

64. George Grove, "Mr. Grove's Letter to the 'Times,'" *Palestine Exploration Quarterly* (January–March 1870): 170–71.

65. American Congregationalist Selah Merrill, later U.S. consul to Jerusalem, was part of the American expedition to map the territories east of the River Jordan and published his popular book, which mentioned several tells, in 1881. Selah Merrill, *East of the Jordan: A Record of Travel and Observation in the Countries of Moab Gilead and Bashan during the Years 1875–1877* (New York: Charles Scribner's Sons, 1881). Gottlieb Schumacher, a trained engineer and American-born German Evangelical whose family settled in Haifa, surveyed and mapped other areas east of the river in his work on extensions from the Hijaz Railway. His results were published in the journal of the German Oriental Society and in the *Palestine Exploration Quarterly* near the turn of the century. He eventually became an excavator at Megiddo.

66. Palmer, "The Desert of the Tih," 69–70.

67. This logically correlates with what appear to be distinct differences in French and British strategies regarding exploration and acquisition of antiquities. The French government was more hands-on than was the British government, which depended on the initiatives of private individuals working with state support through the vehicle of the British Museum. Challis, *From the Harpy Tomb*, 19–22.

68. Sources relating to mapping before the PEF's surveys include John R. Bartlett, *Mapping Jordan through Two Millennia*, ed. David M. Jacobson, Palestine Exploration Fund Annual (Leeds: Maney, 2008); I. W. J. Hopkins, "Nineteenth-Century Maps of Palestine: Dual-Purpose Historical Evidence," *Imago Mundi* 22 (1968).

69. Conder's original partner was Tyrwhitt Drake, who died of malaria in 1874 while in the field. Extensive accounts of the Western Survey are found in Moscrop, *Measuring Jerusalem*, chapter 4; Silberman, *Digging for God and Country*, chapter 12; David Jacobson, "Introduction to the Palestine Exploration Fund Explorations at Jerusalem, 1867–1870," in *Survey of Western Palestine including a Survey of Eastern Palestine, 1881: Essays to Accompany the Archive Editions Facsimile* (London: Archive Editions in association with the Palestine Exploration Fund, 1999).

70. Silberman, *Digging for God and Country*, 123; Abu el-Haj, *Facts on the Ground*, 28.

71. George W. Stocking, *Victorian Anthropology* (New York: Free Press, 1987); Debbie Challis, "'The Ablest Race': The Ancient Greeks in Victorian Racial Theory," in *Classics and Imperialism in the British Empire*, ed. Mark Bradley (Oxford: Oxford University Press, 2010); Emma Reisz, "Classics, Race, and Edwardian Anxieties about Empire," in *Classics and Imperialism in the British Empire*, ed. Mark Bradley (Oxford: Oxford University Press, 2010).

72. This term, as opposed to *jund al-urdun* (a term denoting the spatial parameters of an early Islamic military district), most accurately reflects the European conception of this space and its meaning. Neither *Oultrejourdain* nor *jund al-urdun* was a territorial precursor to the borders of the nation-state.

73. Moscrop, *Measuring Jerusalem*, 123–25.

74. Hallote, *Bible, Map and Spade*, 53–54. Syrian Protestant College later became the American University of Beirut.

75. Ibid., 52–55.

76. Rachel S. Havrelock, *River Jordan: The Mythology of a Dividing Line* (Chicago: University of Chicago Press, 2011).

77. Hallote, *Bible, Map and Spade*, 52–55; Felicity J. Cobbing, "The American Palestine Exploration Society and the Survey of Eastern Palestine," *Palestine Explo-*

ration Quarterly 137, no. 1 (2005): 11; Moscrop, *Measuring Jerusalem*, 95; Silberman, *Digging for God and Country*, 115–16.

78. See, for instance, the reprints of John Lewis Burckhardt, *Travels in Syria and the Holy Land* (New York: AMS Press, 1983); Selah Merrill, *East of the Jordan: A Record of Travel and Observation in the Countries of Moab, Gilead, and Bashan* (London: Darf, 1986).

79. Moscrop, *Measuring Jerusalem*, 95; Hallote, *Bible, Map and Spade*, 53–55.

80. Moscrop, *Measuring Jerusalem*, 96.

81. Ibid.

82. Marchand, *Down from Olympus*, 191–92.

83. Cobbing, "The American Palestine Exploration Society"; Moscrop, *Measuring Jerusalem*, 129. A comprehensive account of the APES Eastern Survey is found in Hallote, *Bible, Map and Spade*, 57–65.

84. Cobbing, "The American Palestine Exploration Society," 11.

85. Hallote, *Bible, Map and Spade*, 62–65.

86. David Jacobson and Felicity Cobbing, "'A Record of Discovery and Adventure': Claude Reignier Conder's Contributions to the Exploration of Palestine," *Near Eastern Archaeology* 68, no. 4 (2005).

87. Had the Survey of Eastern Palestine been completed and extended over its projected eighteen months as planned, it is likely that more publications would have come of it. There is ample evidence that this was the PEF's intention, especially given its success in publishing the results of the Western Survey. As it was, Conder had only about six months in the field. Yolande Hodson, "An Introduction to the Publication of the Map and Memoirs," in *Survey of Western Palestine including a Survey of Eastern Palestine, 1881: Essays to Accompany the Archive Editions Facsimile* (London: Archive Editions in association with the Palestine Exploration Fund, 1999), 63–67.

88. Rogers, *Inventing the Holy Land*. See especially chapters 3 and 4.

89. Silberman, "Desolation and Restoration."

90. Ibid., 81.

91. Ibid., 82.

92. Marchand, *Down from Olympus*, 222; S. D. Goitein, *Jews and Arabs: Their Contacts through the Ages* (New York: Schocken Books, 1964), 23–25.

93. Barbara McKean Parmenter, *Giving Voice to Stones: Place and Identity in Palestinian Literature* (Austin: University of Texas Press, 1994), 8–15.

94. Rogers, *Inventing the Holy Land*, chapter 3.

95. See the discussion on cultural-historical archaeology in Bruce G. Trigger, *A History of Archaeological Thought* (Cambridge: Cambridge University Press, 1989), chapter 5. See also Rogers, *Inventing the Holy Land*, chapter 4. The role played by Jews in Jerusalem in various eschatological traditions coincided with the rise of anti-Semitism and initiatives for Jewish resettlement in both Zionist and anti-Semitic circles.

96. Kathleen L. Sheppard, "Flinders Petrie and Eugenics at UCL," *Bulletin of the History of Archaeology* 20, no. 1 (2010).

97. Davis, *The Landscape of Belief*. See especially chapter 8. Davis emphasizes the ideological link that bound American nineteenth-century Protestantism, landscape and nature, and notions of firsthand experience, with personal experience of God being the goal.

98. Ezekiel 25:13; Malachi 1:2–5; Obadiah; Jeremiah 49:7–22.
99. Davis, *The Landscape of Belief*, 193–94.
100. Ibid., 196.
101. Kenneth Paul Bendiner, "David Roberts in the Near East: Social and Religious Themes," *Art History* 6 (1983).
102. Joseph A. Massad, *Colonial Effects: The Making of National Identity in Jordan* (New York: Columbia University Press, 2001). See especially pp. 105–11 and the quote from Mark Sykes on p. 106.
103. Kathryn Tidrick, *Heart Beguiling Araby* (London: I. B. Tauris, 1990).
104. Yoav Alon discusses the earliest British attempts to rule east of the river immediately after the war. Yoav Alon, "'Heart Beguiling Araby' on the Frontier of Empire: Early Anglo-Arab Relations in Transjordan," *British Journal of Middle Eastern Studies* 36, no. 1 (2009).
105. Massad, *Colonial Effects*, chapter 3.
106. Betty S. Anderson, *Nationalist Voices in Jordan: The Street and the State* (Austin: University of Texas Press, 2005); Betty S. Anderson, "Writing the Nation: Textbooks of the Hashemite Kingdom of Jordan," *Comparative Studies of South Asia, Africa and the Middle East* 21, nos. 1 and 2 (2001).
107. Kuklick, *Puritans in Babylon*, chapters 5 and 9.
108. Moscrop, *Measuring Jerusalem*, chapter 5.
109. Kuklick, *Puritans in Babylon*, chapter 7.
110. Hallote, *Bible, Map and Spade*, 99–183.
111. Ibid., 65–66.
112. Duncan MacKenzie, "Dibon: The City of King Mesha and of the Moabite Stone," *Palestine Exploration Quarterly* (April 1913): 57–79. Quote is found on p. 77.
113. Moscrop, *Measuring Jerusalem*, chapter 8.
114. Hallote, *Bible, Map and Spade*, 121–47; Moscrop, *Measuring Jerusalem*, chapter 6.
115. Rachel S. Hallote, "Before Albright: Charles Torrey, James Montgomery, and American Biblical Archaeology, 1907–1922," *Near Eastern Archaeology* 74, no. 3 (2011); Kuklick, *Puritans in Babylon*.
116. Brendon, *Thomas Cook*; Rogers, *Inventing the Holy Land*, chapter 2.
117. Feinman, *William Foxwell Albright and the Origins of Biblical Archaeology*.
118. Davis, *The Landscape of Belief*, 88–97.
119. Mustafa Aksakal, *The Ottoman Road to War in 1914: The Ottoman Empire and the First World War* (Cambridge: Cambridge University Press, 2008).
120. Satia, *Spies in Arabia*.
121. MECA/Hogarth Papers, Hogarth to his mother, 20 September 1918. Permission to quote the Hogarth Papers was generously granted by the Hogarth family with the aid of the Middle East Center Archives, St. Antony's, Oxford.
122. Magnus T. Bernhardsson, *Reclaiming a Plundered Past: Archaeology and Nation Building in Modern Iraq* (Austin: University of Texas Press, 2005), 69.

Chapter Three

1. Jens Hanssen, "Imperial Discourses and an Ottoman Excavation in Lebanon," in *Baalbek: Image and Monument, 1898–1998*, ed. Helene Sader, Thomas Scheffler, and Angelika Neuwirth (Beirut: Franz Steiner Verlag, 1998).

2. Wendy K. Shaw, *Possessors and Possessed: Museums, Archaeology and the Visualization of History in the Late Ottoman Empire* (Berkeley, Los Angeles: University of California Press, 2003), 149–56.

3. Ibid., chapters 3, 4, 6.

4. Ibid., 58–70, 110–12, and chapter 6; Selim Deringil, *The Well-Protected Domains: Ideology and the Legitimation of Power in the Ottoman Empire, 1876–1909* (London: I. B. Tauris, 1998); Kemal Karpat, *The Politicization of Islam: Reconstructing Identity, State, Faith and Community in the Late Ottoman State* (Oxford: Oxford University Press, 2001); Niyazi Berkes, *The Development of Secularism in Turkey* (London: Hurst, 1964).

5. Shaw, *Possessors and Possessed*, 89–97, 108–30. See also the discussions in Morag Kersel, "License to Sell: The Legal Trade of Antiquities in Israel" (PhD diss., Lucy Cavendish College, Cambridge University, 2006), 72–76; Suzanne L. Marchand, *Down from Olympus: Archaeology and Philhellenism in Germany, 1750–1970* (Princeton: Princeton University Press, 1996), chapter 6; Alev Koçak, *The Ottoman Empire and Archaeological Excavations: Ottoman Policy from 1840–1906, Foreign Archaeologists, and the Formation of the Ottoman Museum* (Istanbul: Isis Press, 2011).

6. Felicity J. Cobbing and Jonathan N. Tubb, "Before the Rockefeller: The First Palestine Museum in Jerusalem," in *Tutela, Conservazione e Valorizzazione del Patrimonio Culturale della Palestina, Mediterraneum*, ed. F. Maniscalco (Naples: Massa Editore, 2005), 71–72.

7. Shaw, *Possessors and Possessed*, chapter 4; Koçak, *The Ottoman Empire and Archaeological Excavations*.

8. Shaw, *Possessors and Possessed*, chapter 4; Koçak, *The Ottoman Empire and Archaeological Excavations*. See esp. pp. 27–30 regarding the Parthenon Marbles and pp. 77–81 regarding Schliemann and his antics.

9. Shaw, *Possessors and Possessed*, 119.

10. Carl Watzinger, *Theodor Wiegand* (Munich, 1944). Quoted in Marchand, *Down from Olympus*, 188. Theodor Weigand was a German archaeologist and head of the German Archaeological Institute in Izmir. Shaw, *Possessors and Possessed*, 119–21. Johann Strauss, "The Disintegration of Ottoman Rule in the Syrian Territories as Viewed by German Observers," in *The Syrian Land: Processes of Integration and Fragmentation, Bilad al-Sham from the Eighteenth to the Twentieth Century*, ed. Thomas Philipp and Birgit Schaebler (Stuttgart: Franz Steiner Verlag, 1998), 308–13. German engineers were consultants on the Hijaz Railway, and the building of the railway was actually what made the gift of the Mshatta façade possible. Shaw, *Possessors and Possessed*, 132.

11. Koçak, *The Ottoman Empire and Archaeological Excavations*, 147–48.

12. Shaw, *Possessors and Possessed*, chapter 7; Koçak, *The Ottoman Empire and Archaeological Excavations*, 119–23.

13. Shaw, *Possessors and Possessed*, chapters 4 and 6.

14. Koçak, *The Ottoman Empire and Archaeological Excavations*, 119–23.

15. See the discussion in Abigail Jacobson, *From Empire to Empire: Jerusalem be-*

tween Ottoman and British Rule (Syracuse: Syracuse University Press, 2011), 13–15. See also the various contributions in Jens Hanssen, Thomas Philipp, and Stefan Weber, eds., *The Empire in the City: Arab Provincial Capitals in the Late Ottoman Empire* (Beirut: Ergon Verlag Wurzburg, 2002).

16. Debbie Challis, *From the Harpy Tomb to the Wonders of Ephesus: British Archaeologists in the Ottoman Empire, 1840–1880* (London: Duckworth, 2008), 21; Hanssen, "Imperial Discourses."

17. Selim Deringil, "'They Live in a State of Nomadism and Savagery': The Late Ottoman Empire and the Post-Colonial Debate," *Comparative Studies in Society and History* 45, no. 2 (2003); Ussama Makdisi, "Ottoman Orientalism," *American Historical Review* 107, no. 3 (2002); Christoph Herzog, "Nineteenth Century Baghdad through Ottoman Eyes," in *The Empire in the City: Arab Provincial Capitals in the Late Ottoman Empire*, ed. Jens Hanssen, Thomas Philipp, and Stefan Weber (Beirut: Ergon Verlag Wurzburg, 2002); Hanssen, "Imperial Discourses."

18. Such acts of subversion often require acceptance of at least some aspects of the hegemonic narrative. For other examples, see Colla's treatment of Egyptian antiquities, Makdisi's consideration of responses to the 1860 conflict in Lebanon, and Kaicker's consideration of one of the first modern Urdu poems, *Musaddas*, which elevated the Arabs as the inheritors of Classical civilization, preserving them for humankind. Elliott Colla, *Conflicted Antiquities: Egyptology, Egyptomania, Egyptian Modernity* (Durham: Duke University Press, 2007); Ussama Makdisi, "After 1860: Debating Religion, Reform, and Nationalism in the Ottoman Empire," *International Journal of Middle East Studies* 34, no. 4 (2002); Abhishek Kaicker, "Visions of Modernity in Revisions of the Past: Altaf Hussain Hali and the 'Legacy of the Greeks,'" in *Classics and Imperialism in the British Empire*, ed. Mark Bradley (Oxford: Oxford University Press, 2010).

19. Deringil, "They Live in a State of Nomadism and Savagery"; Makdisi, "Ottoman Orientalism."

20. Makdisi, "Ottoman Orientalism," 795.

21. Shaw, *Possessors and Possessed*, 89; Koçak, *The Ottoman Empire and Archaeological Excavations*, 102–19. Despite public awareness campaigns about the importance of antiquities, participation in international expositions, and the development of museums and antiquities laws, Ottoman efforts to institute indigenous archaeological programs to compete with those of the Europeans were expensive and thus stymied.

22. Shaw, *Possessors and Possessed*, 117; Mehmet Özdogan, "Ideology and Archaeology in Turkey," in *Archaeology under Fire: Nationalism, Politics and Heritage in the Eastern Mediterranean and Middle East*, ed. Lynn Meskell (London: Routledge, 1998).

23. Examples include Raz Kletter, *Just Past? The Making of Israeli Archaeology* (London: Equinox, 2006); Asher Kaufman, *Reviving Phoenicia: In Search of Identity in Lebanon* (New York: I. B. Tauris, 2004); Nadia Abu el-Haj, *Facts on the Ground: Archaeological Practice and Territorial Self-Fashioning in Israeli Society* (Chicago: University of Chicago Press, 2001); Donald Malcom Reid, *Whose Pharaohs? Archaeology, Museums, and Egyptian National Identity from Napoleon to World War I* (Berkeley: University of California Press, 2002); Nachman Ben-Yehuda, *The Masada Myth: Collective Memory and Mythmaking in Israel* (Madison: University of Wisconsin Press, 1995); Amatzia Baram, *Culture, History, and Ideology in the Formation of Ba'athist Iraq* (New York: St. Martin's Press, 1991); Israel Gershoni and James Jankowski, *Egypt, Islam and*

the Arabs: The Search for Egyptian Nationhood, 1900–1930 (New York: Oxford University Press, 1986).

24. An example of this in the context of Petra is discussed in chapter 5. For examples from Palestine, see Rochelle Davis, *Palestinian Village Histories* (Stanford: Stanford University Press, 2011), chapter 6; Barbara McKean Parmenter, *Giving Voice to Stones: Place and Identity in Palestinian Literature* (Austin: University of Texas Press, 1994), 21–27; Tawfiq Canaan, "Modern Palestinian Beliefs and Practices Relating to God," *Journal of the Palestine Oriental Society* 14 (1934); Canaan, "The Palestinian Arab House: Its Architecture and Folklore," *Journal of the Palestine Oriental Society* 12 (1932); Canaan, "Water and 'The Water of Life,'" *Journal of the Palestine Oriental Society* 9 (1929); Canaan, "Plant-Lore in Palestinian Superstition," *Journal of the Palestine Oriental Society* 8 (1928); Canaan, "Mohammedan Saints and Sanctuaries in Palestine," *Journal of the Palestine Oriental Society* 7 (1927); and Canaan, "Haunted Springs and Water Demons in Palestine," *Journal of the Palestine Oriental Society* 1 (1921).

25. Parmenter, *Giving Voice to Stones*, 3–7.

26. See Eugene Rogan, *Frontiers of the State in the Late Ottoman Empire: Transjordan, 1850–1921* (Cambridge: Cambridge University Press, 1999); Rogan, "Instant Communication: The Impact of the Telegraph in Ottoman Syria," in *The Syrian Land: Processes of Integration and Fragmentation, Bilad Al-Sham from the Eighteenth to the Twentieth Century*, ed. Thomas Philipp and Birgit Schaebler (Stuttgart: Franz Steiner Verlag, 1998); Michael R. Fischbach, *State, Society and Land in Transjordan* (Leiden: Brill, 2000); Raouf Saʿad Abu Jaber, *Pioneers over Jordan: The Frontier of Settlement in Transjordan, 1850–1914* (London: I. B. Tauris, 1989); Eugene Rogan and Tariq Tell, eds., *Village, Steppe and State: The Social Origins of Modern Jordan* (London: I. B. Tauris, 1995).

27. Greek and Latin Christians in Transjordan were under the umbrella of their respective patriarchates based in Jerusalem. As foreigners vied for space in Jerusalem, the city became the center of many of their activities in the region.

28. Deringil, *The Well-Protected Domains*; Karpat, *The Politicization of Islam*, chapters 10, 11.

29. Hasan Kayalı, *Arabs and Young Turks: Ottomanism, Arabism, and Islamism in the Ottoman Empire* (Berkeley: University of California Press, 1997), 31–32; Michelle U. Campos, *Ottoman Brothers: Muslims, Christians, and Jews in Early Twentieth-Century Palestine* (Stanford: Stanford University Press, 2011), 64–69.

30. Karpat, *The Politicization of Islam*, 223–25.

31. Campos, *Ottoman Brothers*; Jacobson, *From Empire to Empire*; Rashid Khalidi, *Palestinian Identity: The Construction of Modern National Consciousness* (New York: Columbia University Press, 1997). The *millets* were the non-Muslim religious communities as organized within the Ottoman Empire for most of its history. Affairs of taxation and personal status were traditionally handled within the communities themselves, creating a very particular interface between non-Muslim subjects and the state. The process of modernization in the late Ottoman Empire was meant in no small way to provide an alternative mode of identification for non-Muslims and personalize the nature of their interaction with the state.

32. Campos, *Ottoman Brothers*, 12.

33. Khalidi, *Palestinian Identity*, 35.

34. Carter V. Findley, "The Evolution of the System of Provincial Administration

as Viewed from the Center," in *Palestine in the Late Ottoman Period: Political, Social and Economic Transformation*, ed. David Kushner (Jerusalem: Yad Izhak Ben-Zvi Press, 1986), 8.

35. See Campos, *Ottoman Brothers*, chapter 5; Jacobson, *From Empire to Empire*, introduction; Khalidi, *Palestinian Identity*, chapter 3; Kayalı, *Arabs and Young Turks*.

36. Campos, *Ottoman Brothers*, 49–52.

37. Deringil, *The Well-Protected Domains*, 60–63.

38. Karpat, *The Politicization of Islam*, 229–31.

39. Kamal Boullata, *Palestinian Art* (London: Saqi Books, 2009), 71.

40. Kayalı, *Arabs and Young Turks*, 145–46.

41. William Ochsenwald, "Opposition to Political Centralization in South Jordan and the Hijaz, 1900-1914," in *Religion, Economy, and State in Ottoman-Arab History*, ed. William Ochsenwald (Istanbul: Isis Press, 1998), 183–85.

42. Kayalı, *Arabs and Young Turks*, 146.

43. C. Ernest Dawn, *From Ottomanism to Arabism: Essays on the Origins of Arab Nationalism* (Urbana: University of Illinois Press, 1973), 5–7.

44. Dawn reads the appointment of Husayn as a defiant manifestation of the adversarial relationship between Abdülhamid and the CUP (ibid., 3-15). Kayalı sees the appointment as somewhat less dramatic (Kayalı, *Arabs and Young Turks*, 146–49).

45. Dawn, *From Ottomanism to Arabism*, 15–19.

46. Kayalı, *Arabs and Young Turks*, 170-73, 81-200; Dawn, *From Ottomanism to Arabism*, 15-29.

47. Koçak, *The Ottoman Empire and Archaeological Excavations*; Shaw, *Possessors and Possessed*.

48. This is common, for instance, at archaeological sites in Jordan that are largely off the beaten path of foreigners.

49. See the relevant discussions in Morag M. Kersel, "When Communities Collide: Competing Claims for Archaeological Objects in the Marketplace," *Archaeologies: Journal of the World Archaeological Congress* (2011); Kersel, "License to Sell"; Colla, *Conflicted Antiquities*, chapter 1; Shaw, *Possessors and Possessed*, chapter 4.

50. Yoav Di-Capua, *Gatekeepers of the Arab Past: Historians and History-Writing in Twentieth-Century Egypt* (Berkeley: University of California Press, 2009), 52–59; Marwa Elshakry, *Reading Darwin in Arabic, 1860-1950* (Chicago: University of Chicago Press, 2013); Timothy Mitchell, *Colonising Egypt* (Cambridge: Cambridge University Press, 1988), 108–11.

51. Donald Malcolm Reid, "Syrian Christians, the Rags-to-Riches Story, and Free Enterprise," *International Journal of Middle East Studies* 1, no. 4 (1970).

52. Youssef M. Choueiri, *Arab Nationalism: A History* (Oxford: Blackwell, 2000), 70–72.

53. Betty S. Anderson, *The American University of Beirut: Liberal Education and Arab Nationalism* (Austin: University of Texas Press, 2011).

54. Nadia Farag, "The Lewis Affair and the Fortunes of Al-Muqtataf," *Middle Eastern Studies* 8, no. 1 (1972); Reid, "Syrian Christians"; Donald Malcolm Reid, "The Syrian Christians and Early Socialism in the Arab World," *International Journal of Middle East Studies* 5, no. 2 (1974).

55. The literature in this regard is vast. In addition to countless other articles, monographs, and dissertations, some cited herein, the following important works

should be noted: Choueiri, *Arab Nationalism*; James P. Jankowski and Israel Ger-shoni, eds., *Rethinking Nationalism in the Arab Middle East* (New York: Columbia University Press, 1997); Rashid Khalidi, Lisa Anderson, Muhammad Muslih, and Reeva Simon, eds., *The Origins of Arab Nationalism* (New York: Columbia University Press, 1991); Albert Hourani, "Ottoman Reform and the Politics of the Notables," in *The Modern Middle East*, ed. Albert Hourani, Philip S. Khoury, and Mary Wilson (London: I. B. Tauris, 1993); Philip S. Khoury, *Urban Notables and Arab Nationalism: The Politics of Damascus, 1860–1920* (Cambridge: Cambridge University Press, 1983); Albert Hourani, *Arabic Thought in the Liberal Age, 1798–1939* (Cambridge: Cambridge University Press, 1983); Sylvia Haim, ed., *Arab Nationalism: An Anthology* (Berkeley: University of California Press, 1976); Zeine N. Zeine, *The Struggle for Arab Independence: Western Diplomacy and the Rise and Fall of Faisal's Kingdom in Syria* (Beirut: Khayat's, 1960); George Antonius, *The Arab Awakening: The Story of the Arab National Movement* (G. P. Putnam's, 1938).

56. Di-Capua, *Gatekeepers of the Arab Past*, 29–30.

57. Benjamin Fortna, *Learning to Read in the Late Ottoman Empire and the Early Turkish Republic* (New York: Palgrave Macmillan, 2011), 15.

58. For example, Ami Ayalon, *Reading Palestine: Printing and Literacy, 1900–1948* (Austin: University of Texas Press, 2004); chapter 1; Rogan, *Frontiers of the State*, 156; Selçuk Akşin Somel, *The Modernization of Public Education in the Ottoman Empire, 1839–1908* (Leiden: Brill, 2001).

59. Ayalon, *Reading Palestine*, 22.

60. Eugene Rogan, "Aşiret Mektebi: Abdulhamid II's School for Tribes (1892–1907)," *International Journal of Middle East Studies* 28, no. 1 (1996).

61. Ayalon, *Reading Palestine*, 50; Ayalon, "Modern Texts and Their Readers in Late Ottoman Palestine," *Middle Eastern Studies* 38, no. 4 (2002).

62. Ayalon, "Modern Texts and Their Readers," 19, 35–38.

63. Ayalon, *Reading Palestine*, 50, 107.

64. Salim Tamari, *Year of the Locust: A Soldier's Diary and the Erasure of Palestine's Ottoman Past* (Berkeley: University of California Press, 2011), 34.

65. Ayalon, *Reading Palestine*, chapter 3.

66. Ibid., 51–52.

67. Ibid., 107. Ayalon reports that by 1913, the editor of *Filastin* was providing free copies of the paper to Jaffa villages with one hundred residents or more, via the *mukhtar* (headman), who would make them available in communal space.

68. Colla, *Conflicted Antiquities*, 129–36.

69. Deringil, "They Live in a State of Nomadism and Savagery," 317; Bernard Lewis, "Ibn Khaldun in Turkey," in *Studies in Islamic History and Civilization*, ed. M. Sharon (Jerusalem: Cana, 1986).

70. Lewis, "Ibn Khaldun in Turkey"; Mohammad Abdullah Enan, *Ibn Khaldun: His Life and Works* (Kuala Lumpur: The Other Press, 2007).

71. See Colla's discussion of Arabic literary forms, pharaonic monuments, and the character of Pharaoh in Islam. Colla, *Conflicted Antiquities*, chapter 2.

72. Emir Amin Mujid Arslan, "Usul al-Tarikh," *al-Muqtataf* 13 (1888–89). The author is a member of the influential Druze family. See William Cleveland, *Islam against the West: Shakib Arslan and the Campaign for Islamic Nationalism* (Austin: University of Texas Press, 1985).

73. *Isnad* is the means by which to gauge the reliability of sources in Islamic tradition. The reliability of reports depends not just on the proximity or access of the reporter, but on his or her character and piety. Long after the reporter has died, the reliability of the report depends on the chain of transmission and the strength of each person who represents a link in it. It is best known as regards hadith science but also characterizes history-writing. In terms of more recent examples, Rochelle Davis notes this practice in the written histories of Palestinian villages' oral traditions, as does Andrew Shryock in the written histories of the Balga tribes. Davis, *Palestinian Village Histories*, 78–83, fn. 39; Shryock, *Nationalism and the Genealogical Imagination: Oral History and Textual Authority in Tribal Jordan* (Berkeley: University of California Press, 1997), 107–10.

74. Arslan, "Usul al-Tarikh," 810, 12.

75. Regarding Alexander in Islamic tradition, see Z. David Zuwiyya, *Islamic Legends concerning Alexander the Great: Taken from Two Medieval Arabic Manuscripts in Madrid* (Binghamton: Global Publications, 2001). About the discovery of the tomb in question, see Hanssen, "Imperial Discourses"; and Koçak, *The Ottoman Empire and Archaeological Excavations*. Regarding the issue of Alexander's tomb in general in both the historic and modern perspectives, see Andrew Michael Chugg, *The Lost Tomb of Alexander the Great* (London: Periplus, 2005). Arslan uses this example to take a very public swipe at Heinrich Schliemann, excavator of Troy, who had been in trouble with the Ottoman authorities numerous times for his illegal shipments of artifacts out of the empire. Given his interest in Alexander the Great's relationship to Troy, Schliemann was apparently seeking his sarcophagus in Alexandria. Arslan writes that given the discoveries in Sidon, all of Schliemann's efforts could be for naught.

76. Arslan, "Usul al-Tarikh," 812.

77. Colla, *Conflicted Antiquities*, 76–80. Regarding Moses in Islamic tradition, see Brannon Wheeler, *Moses in the Quran and Islamic Exegesis* (London: Routledge, 2002). See also B. Heller and D. B. MacDonald, "Musa," in *Encyclopedia of Islam*, ed. P. Bearman et al., 2nd ed. (Brill Online, 2012). Moses is intimately connected to the Alexander Romance in Islam, mentioned and cited above. These figures are also linked to the figure of *al-Khidr*, "the Green Man" of ancient and Islamicate lore. See A. J. Wensinck, "Al-Khidr," in *Encyclopedia of Islam*, ed. P. Bearman et al., 2nd ed. (Brill Online, 2012).

78. Marchand, *Down from Olympus*, 16–24, 188–92.

79. Qur'an 3:67. Regarding Joktan, see Richard Hess, "Joktan," in *The Anchor Bible Dictionary*, ed. David Noel Freedman (Bantam Doubleday Dell, 1992). See also A. Fischer, "Kahtan," in *Encyclopedia of Islam*, ed. P. Bearman et al., 2nd ed. (Brill Online, 2012).

80. This has implications for understanding various Hashemite narratives of legitimacy, discussed further in chapters 5 and 6. Details of the genealogical connections can be found in Daniel Martin Varisco, *Reading Orientalism: Said and the Unsaid* (Seattle: University of Washington Press, 2007), 69–73; Varisco, "Metaphors and Sacred History: The Genealogy of Muhammad and the Arab 'Tribe,'" *Anthropological Quarterly* 68, no. 3 (1995).

81. Semitic Wave Theory, the desert origins of the Semites, and their cycles of nomadic and settled civilization are further discussed in chapters 4 and 6, particularly as pertains to James Henry Breasted's synthesis of these phenomena in his book *An-*

cient Times, and its incorporation into Arab nationalist discourses. Breasted, *Ancient Times: A History of the Early World*, 2nd ed. (Boston: Ginn, 1944).

82. Consider here the Table of Nations in Genesis 10, for instance.

83. Salim Tamari, "Factionalism and Class Formation in Recent Palestinian History," in *Studies in the Economic and Social History of Palestine in the Nineteenth and Twentieth Centuries*, ed. Roger Owen (Carbondale: Southern Illinois University Press, 1982).

84. Davis, *Palestinian Village Histories*, 187. See also F. G. Peake, *A History of Jordan and Its Tribes* (Coral Gables: University of Miami Press, 1958).

85. See for instance the forty-volume translation of Abu Jʿafar Muhammad bin Jarir bin Yazid al-Tabari's *History of the Prophets and Kings*, published by SUNY Press.

86. Arslan, "Usul al-Tarikh," 813. Arslan mentions Homer and makes the connection between him and al-Lakhmi, likely the third century CE king appointed by the Persians over the Arabs of Iraq. Herodotus is mentioned in the letters to the editor of *al-Muqtataf* (see below).

87. Interview with Mr. Anonymous One, Amman, 31 May 2006. Quoted in Elena D. Corbett, "History Lessons in the City of Dawud: Jordan's Past and Complexities of Identity beyond Silwan," *Middle Eastern Studies* 47, no. 4 (2011): 589-90.

88. Arab interest in Egypt was further served by the fact that Syrian Christians who edited popular journals had their base of operations in Cairo. Additionally, Salim Tamari argues that the idea of the national union of Bilad al-Sham, popularized after the war, belies the assumption for many in what might be considered the southern reaches of that territory during the war (in Palestine, for instance) that they would federate with Egypt. Not only did this reflect territorial conceptions depicted in late Ottoman maps, but journals and newspapers circulating in Palestine, for example, came mainly from Egypt. Tamari, *Year of the Locust*, 30-35.

89. Anonymous, "Musa wa al-Faraʿun wa Banu Israʾil," *al-Muqtataf* 11 (1886-87).

90. Ahmad Effendi Fahmy, *al-Muqtataf* 27 (1902): 1125.

91. Salim Effendi al-Taneer, *al-Muqtataf* 10 (1886): 316.

92. Nicola Khuri Suleyman, *al-Muqtataf* 55 (1919): 346.

93. This *could* be Mlayh, near Madaba, in Jordan, but it is difficult to know for certain. ʿAbd al-Malik Effendi Kiriakus, *al-Muqtataf* 39 (1911): 201.

94. Ayalon, "Modern Texts and Their Readers," 26-30. See Ayalon's description of the phrases "*wa minhu*" and "*wa minha*" on p. 29.

95. Anonymous, "al-Naqb ʿan Athar Filastin" (The Search for the Archaeology of Palestine), *al-Muqtataf* 31 (1906).

96. Nadav Naʿaman, "Amarna Letters," in *The Anchor Bible Dictionary*, ed. David Noel Freedman (Bantam Doubleday Dell, 1992); Donald Redford, "Mernptah," in *The Anchor Bible Dictionary*, ed. David Noel Freedman (Bantam Doubleday Dell, 1992).

97. "al-Athar al-Suriya" (Syrian Archaeology), *al-Muqtataf* 21 (1897).

98. As the notion of race was more commonly incorporated into intellectual discourse and played a growing role in ideas of Turkish and Arab identity, and given the critical view of the contemporary Ottoman milieu held by the editors of *al-Muqtataf*, it is tempting to read such details and conclusions in *al-Muqtataf* in light of Ussama Makdisi's "multiple Orientalist discourses." He notes that these persist well beyond the end of the Ottoman Empire. The Hittites would later dominate nationalist narratives

of antiquity in Turkey, just as the ancient peoples known to have thrived and fallen on the landscapes of the Arab world would be Arabized to do the same.

99. Genesis 10.

100. George Mendenhall, "Amorites," in *The Anchor Bible Dictionary*, ed. David Noel Freedman (New York: Bantam Doubleday Dell, 1992).

101. Articles related to this topic include Anonymous, "Musa wa al-Faraʿun wa Banu Israʾil" (Moses, the Pharaohs, and the Beni Israel), *al-Muqtataf* 11 (1886–87): 705–9; Anonymous, "Athar al-Amuriyyeen fi Filastin" (Archaeology of the Amorites in Palestine), *al-Muqtataf* 15 (1890–91): 90–91; Anonymous, "Araʾ al-ʿUlamaʾ" (Views of the Scholars), *al-Muqtataf* 20 (1896): 476; Anonymous, "Kharuj Bani Israʾil wa ʾAdaduhum" (The Exodus of the Israelites and Their Numbers), *al-Muqtataf* 31 (1906): 538–41.

102. The Jebusites would have been the original inhabitants of what became Jerusalem defeated by David as described in Second Samuel and First Chronicles. Genesis 10 describes them as descendants of Canaan, and scholars relate them to the Hurrians or Hittites, thus *al-maguhl* and certainly not Semites. Stephen A. Reed, "Jebusites," in *The Anchor Bible Dictionary*, ed. David Noel Freedman (Bantam Doubleday Dell, 1992). "Phoenician" is a Greek term used to refer to the coastal Canaanite cities of the Levant, many of which are referenced in the Hebrew Bible and distinguished from the cities of Israel and Judah. No one knows whether the Phoenicians may have referred to themselves as Phoenicians. Brian Peckham, "Phoenicians," in *The Anchor Bible Dictionary*, ed. David Noel Freedman (New York: Bantam Doubleday Dell, 1992); Glenn Markoe, *Phoenicians* (London: British Museum Press, 2000), 10–13. The Philistines enter this larger story later as the migrants who came by sea, were defeated by the Egyptians, and were settled by them in the coastal towns of Palestine by the end of the thirteenth century BCE. There are many biblical allusions to their struggles with the Israelites, sometimes as part of alliances with the Edomites and Arabs. H. J. Katzenstein, "Philistines," in *The Anchor Bible Dictionary*, ed. David Noel Freedman (New York: Bantam Doubleday Dell, 1992).

103. While Abraham is said to have come from Ur of the Chaldeans, there is no clear indication as to who the Chaldeans were until about the ninth century BCE (long after the origins of the Abraham story). Richard Hess, "Chaldeans," in *The Anchor Bible Dictionary*, ed. David Noel Freedman (New York: Bantam Doubleday Dell, 1992). The Elamites seem to have been a Persian people who invaded Mesopotamia around 2000 BCE. François Vollat, "Elamites," in *The Anchor Bible Dictionary*, ed. David Noel Freedman (New York: Bantam Doubleday Dell, 1992).

104. Physical characteristics were thus already embedded in the taxonomy of language-based ethnies.

105. Anonymous, "Musa wa al-Faraʿun," 706.

106. As with many other such terms, *hapiru* is a very old Semitic term used by many people to refer to many ways of life, from that of brigands to that of mercenaries. And as with other such terms, scholars have tried to make it an ethnie. There has been extensive controversy over its resemblance to the term "Hebrew," but the terms are likely unrelated. Robert B. Coote, "Hapiru, Apiru," in *Eerdmans Dictionary of the Bible*, ed. David Noel Freedman (Grand Rapids: William B. Eerdmans, 2000).

107. Many of the dates initially proposed for lines of evidence upon their discovery

and reported in the pages of *al-Muqtataf* have been revised by scholars over time. A date of approximately 1500 BC was given for the Amarna Letters in *al-Muqtataf* in 1897, but about 1350 BCE is the accepted date now. The Merneptah Stela was likewise given a date in *al-Muqtataf* of approximately 1200 BC (which is correct, the date being 1207). The nature of the entity called "Israel" to which it refers remains, however, controversial.

108. See the brief discussion of this inscription at Silwan in chapter 2.

109. Elshakry, *Reading Darwin in Arabic*, 86–91.

110. Jurji Zaydan, "al-ʿArab qabl al-Islam," *al-Muqtataf* 33 (1908).

111. Anonymous, "Athar al-Amuriyyeen fi Filastin," *al-Muqtataf* 15 (1890–91): 91.

112. Ibid.

113. Anonymous, "Muzah al-Samiyyeen wa Badahatuhum," *al-Muqtataf* 17 (1893): 434.

114. Ibid., 437.

115. There are other examples of the extreme interest in similarities among the Semitic languages, particularly between Arabic and Hebrew. A good example includes "al-ʿAbraniyya wa al-ʿArabiyya," *al-Muqtataf* 41 (1912).

116. Regarding the details of this incident and the fallout from it, especially in the public sphere and the Arab press, see Suhaila S. Shalabi and Shadia H. al-ʿIdwan, "al-Masuhat wa al-Tanqibat al-Athariyya fi Filastin wa al-Waʿi li Abʿadiha mundhu Muntasaf al-Qarn al-Tasiʿa ʿAshar hata al-Harb al-ʿAlamiyya al-Ula" (Archaeological Surveys and Excavations in Palestine and Awareness of Their Dimensions from the Middle of the Nineteenth Century until the First World War), *al-Majala al-Urduniyya li-l-Tarikh wa al-Athar* (Jordanian Journal for History and Archaeology) 5, no. 4 (2011): 40–53. For the details as presented to the audience of *PEQ*, see Gustav Dalman, "The Search for the Temple Treasure at Jerusalem," *Palestine Exploration Fund Quarterly* (January 1912).

117. Shalabi and al-ʿIdwan, "al-Masuhat wa al-Tanqibat al-Athariyya fi Filastin," 40–53.

118. Ibid., 45–48.

119. Abu el-Haj, *Facts on the Ground*.

120. Shalabi and al-ʿIdwan, "al-Masuhat wa al-Tanqibat al-Athariyya fi Filastin," 48–49.

121. Ibid.

122. Michael R. Marrus, *The Unwanted: European Refugees from the First World War through the Cold War* (Philadelphia: Temple University Press, 2002), 40–50.

123. Benjamin Fortna, *Imperial Classroom: Islam, the State, and Education in the Late Ottoman Empire* (Oxford: Oxford University Press, 2002), 184–91.

124. Rogan, *Frontiers of State*, chapter 7.

125. Ibid., 151–54.

126. Ibid., chapter 5; Geraldine Chatelard and Jean-Michel de Tarragon, *L'Empire et le Royaume: La Jordanie Vue par l'École Biblique et Archaéologique Française de Jérusalem (1893–1935)* (Amman: Institut Française de Proche Orient, 2006).

127. Rogan, "Aşiret Mektebi," 86–95.

128. Ibid., 100–104.

129. Karpat, *The Politicization of Islam*, chapters 8, 10.

130. Rogan, "Aşiret Mektebi," 84–86.

131. Rogan, *Frontiers of State*, 151–59; Deringil, *The Well-Protected Domains*, chapters 2–5; Karpat, *The Politicization of Islam*, chapters 8–11.

132. Rogan, *Frontiers of State*, chapter 7; Michael Provence, *The Great Syrian Revolt and the Rise of Arab Nationalism* (Austin: University of Texas Press, 2005), chapter 2. See also Munib al-Madi and Suleyman Musa, *Tarikh al-Urdun fi al-Qarn al-'Ashreen, 1900–1959* (The History of Jordan in the Twentieth Century, 1900–1959) (Amman: Maktabat al-Muhtasab, 1959; reprint, 1988).

Chapter Four

1. FO 608/116/6, Foreign Office minutes (author's name is illegible), 24 March 1919. Arthur Evans excavated Knossos on Crete and developed the concept of Minoan civilization.

2. Harry Charles Luke and Edward Keith-Roach, eds., *The Handbook of Palestine and Trans-Jordan* (London: MacMillan, 1934), xv–xvi.

3. Ibid. Previous editions were published in 1922 and 1930, respectively.

4. Ibid., 439.

5. *Cook's Traveller's Handbook to Palestine, Syria and 'Iraq* (London: Simpkin Marshall, 1934).

6. Ibid., 257–79.

7. The quote is from Luke and Keith-Roach, *The Handbook of Palestine and Trans-Jordan*, 446. The Naval Intelligence Division's *Palestine and Transjordan* has a similar format as the handbooks mentioned above, with nearly four hundred of about six hundred pages dedicated to Palestine. Historical sites it notes date from the third century BC until the twelfth century AD. *Palestine and Transjordan*, ed. Naval Intelligence Division (London: Kegan Paul, 2006), 540.

8. Abigail Jacobson, *From Empire to Empire: Jerusalem between Ottoman and British Rule* (Syracuse: Syracuse University Press, 2011). See especially chapter 4.

9. Yoav Alon, "'Heart Beguiling Araby' on the Frontier of Empire: Early Anglo-Arab Relations in Transjordan," *British Journal of Middle Eastern Studies* 36, no. 1 (2009).

10. Alon, *The Making of Jordan: Tribes, Colonialism and the Modern State* (London, New York: I. B. Tauris, 2007), chapter 1.

11. Mary C. Wilson, *King Abdullah, Britain and the Making of Jordan* (Cambridge: Cambridge University Press, 1987), 58.

12. Ibid., 51–53; Alon, *Making of Jordan*, 38–40.

13. Wilson, *King Abdullah, Britain and the Making of Jordan*, 51–53; Jacobson, *From Empire to Empire*.

14. R. H. A. Storrs, *Orientations*, 2nd ed. (London: Ivor Nicholson and Watson, 1945), facing p. 310.

15. Ibid.

16. Michelle U. Campos, *Ottoman Brothers: Muslims, Christians, and Jews in Early Twentieth-Century Palestine* (Stanford: Stanford University Press, 2011), chapter 5. See also Jacobson, *From Empire to Empire*, chapters 1 and 2.

17. Storrs, *Orientations*, 312.

18. T161/56, Samuel to Curzon, 24 August 1920. Storrs folded the Pro-Jerusalem Society when he left for Cyprus. It did not enjoy the success in later years that it had in its early life. Storrs, *Orientations*, 438–39.

19. Jacobson, *From Empire to Empire*, chapter 4. The 1922 Mandate for Palestine required Britain to maintain the status quo at holy places until such time that a study commission, also required by terms of the Mandate, could report as to the rights of each religious community at various sites. As of 1943, this had yet to be done, as by terms of an Order in Council of 1924, disputes and claims regarding religious sites were removed from the jurisdiction of Palestine's courts. *Palestine and Transjordan*, 534. See also the Palestine Mandate of the League of Nations.

20. Kamal Boullata, *Palestinian Art* (London: Saqi Books, 2009), 81.

21. Storrs, *Orientations*.

22. Michael Given, "Inventing the Eteocypriots: Imperialist Archaeology and the Manipulation of Ethnic Identity," *Journal of Mediterranean Archaeology* 11, no. 1 (1998).

23. FO 608/82/2, Richmond to Egypt Expeditionary Force, 3 December 1918.

24. Bernard Wasserstein, *The British in Palestine: The Mandatory Government and the Arab-Jewish Conflict, 1917–1929*, 2nd ed. (Oxford: Basil Blackwell, 1991), 247–48.

25. Ibid., 143.

26. FO 608/82/2, Richmond to Egypt Expeditionary Force, 3 December 1918.

27. Ibid.

28. Here may be one of the earliest examples of a development scheme involving the cultural heritage/tourism industry. This idea would have been in line with Ashbee's craft guild initiatives in London.

29. FO 608/82/2, Richmond to Egypt Expeditionary Force, 3 December 1918.

30. Ibid.

31. FO 608/82/2, Hogarth memo, 20 December 1918.

32. Ibid.

33. FO 608/82/2, Ormsby-Gore memo, 20 January 1919.

34. See, for instance, Herbert Samuel's preface to the first edition of the *Handbook of Palestine* (1922), included in the third edition. Luke and Keith-Roach, *The Handbook of Palestine and Trans-Jordan*. See also the accounts of Thomas Cook and Son's early tourism forays into the Holy Land, Piers Brendon, *Thomas Cook: 150 Years of Popular Tourism* (London: Secker and Warburg, 1991).

35. Luke and Keith-Roach, *The Handbook of Palestine and Trans-Jordan*. This is a new edition of the original, published in 1943 by the Naval Intelligence Division.

36. Boullata, *Palestinian Art*, 86.

37. Ibid., 83.

38. FO 608/82/3, Turner to Curzon, 25 February 1919.

39. FO 608/82/3, Adams's minute, 5 March 1919.

40. Ibid.

41. FO 608/82/3, Toynbee's minute, 6 March 1919.

42. Jacobson, *From Empire to Empire*.

43. FO 608/82/3, minutes of R.V. and Louis Mallet.

44. FO 608/82/2, Richmond to Egypt Expeditionary Force, 18 March 1918. FO 608/82/2, minute of Ormsby-Gore, January 1919. It is interesting to note that in his minute, Ormsby-Gore refers to "TransJordania" as part of Syria, indicating not only the official, but also his personal, perception of the territorial separations to take hold

in the mandates. By this time, many Arabs may have shared this territorial view (without the mandate and independent, of course), but such may have been a more recent occurrence and just one among a diversity of views on federation and separation among various Arab regions. See Salim Tamari, *Year of the Locust: A Soldier's Diary and the Erasure of Palestine's Ottoman Past* (Berkeley: University of California Press, 2011), 26–35.

45. FO 608/82/2.

46. FO 608/82/3, spring 1919, "Removal of Antiquities in Asia Minor by Germans and Austrians," British Military Representative at Smyrna to the FO, 21 May 1919.

47. Jacobson, *From Empire to Empire*, chapter 4.

48. Magnus T. Bernhardsson, *Reclaiming a Plundered Past: Archaeology and Nation Building in Modern Iraq* (Austin: University of Texas Press, 2005), 91.

49. Ibid.

50. Ibid., 94.

51. Ibid.

52. FO 608/82/3, Sir Frederick Kenyon's memo, 11 January 1919, "Memorandum of the Archaeological Joint Committee on the Proposal for the International Control of Antiquities Existing in Countries under Turkish Rule."

53. Bernhardsson, *Reclaiming a Plundered Past*, 72.

54. FO 608/82/3, Kenyon memo, 11 January 1919, "Memorandum for the Foreign Office on the Service of Antiquities of the Egyptian Government."

55. Sir Frederick Kenyon was the father of Kathleen Kenyon. Kathleen Kenyon is one of the most important archaeological figures of the twentieth century, having excavated Jericho and developed with Mortimer Wheeler a method for excavating that bore their names. For more about Sir Frederick and his role in the career of his daughter Kathleen, see Miriam C. Davis, *Dame Kathleen Kenyon: Digging up the Holy Land* (Walnut Creek: Left Coast Press, 2008).

56. FO 608/82/3, Kenyon memorandum on behalf of the Joint Archaeological Committee, 11 January 1919.

57. Wendy K. Shaw, *Possessors and Possessed: Museums, Archaeology and the Visualization of History in the Late Ottoman Empire* (Berkeley, Los Angeles: University of California Press, 2003), 117–44.

58. Bernhardsson, *Reclaiming a Plundered Past*, 79–84, 115.

59. FO 608/82/3, Kenyon memo, 11 January 1919, "Memorandum of the Archaeological Joint Committee on the Proposal for the International Control of Antiquities Existing in Countries under Turkish Rule." See also FO 608/82/3, memos and minutes, February 1919, "The Administration of Antiquities in Turkish Territories"; FO 608/82/3, "Proposed Commission to Report on Protection of Antiquities in Near East."

60. FO 608/82/3, "Proposed Commission to Report on Protection of Antiquities in Near East."

61. FO 608/82/3, Kenyon memo, 11 January 1919, "Memorandum of the Archaeological Joint Committee on the Proposal for the International Control of Antiquities Existing in Countries under Turkish Rule."

62. FO 608/82/3, memos, minutes and enclosures, July 1919, "Mesopotamian Antiquities Removed by Germans and Now Lying at Lisbon." See also Bernhardsson, *Reclaiming a Plundered Past*, 84–87.

63. FO 608/82/2.

64. FO 608/82/3, Kenyon memo, 11 January 1919, "Memorandum of the Archaeological Joint Committee on the Proposal for the International Control of Antiquities Existing in Countries under Turkish Rule."

65. Jens Hanssen, "Imperial Discourses and an Ottoman Excavation in Lebanon," in *Baalbek: Image and Monument, 1898–1998*, ed. Helene Sader, Thomas Scheffler, and Angelika Neuwirth (Beirut: Franz Steiner Verlag, 1998), 165–69. The landowner reported the find to the local authorities, who reported to the next officials in their chain of command, and professionals with proper training were quickly dispatched. This is the find of which the "Alexander Sarcophagus," discussed in the previous chapter, was a part.

66. Bernhardsson, *Reclaiming a Plundered Past*, 124.

67. Ibid.

68. Ibid., 125.

69. Ibid., 128–29.

70. Shimon Gibson, "British Archaeological Institutions in Mandatory Palestine, 1917–1948," *Palestine Exploration Quarterly* 131 (1999): 115–16.

71. T161/56, Draft of "Antiquities Ordnance for Palestine, 1920." The introductory clause notes this instruction is contained in an annex to Article 421 of the Treaty of Peace between the Allied Powers and Turkey. See also James F. Goode, *Negotiating for the Past: Archaeology, Nationalism, and Diplomacy in the Middle East, 1919–1941* (Austin: University of Texas Press, 2007), 33–34.

72. T161/56, Samuel to Curzon, 24/8/20. See also Gibson, "British Archaeological Institutions in Mandatory Palestine, 1917–1948," 118.

73. T161/56, draft of "Antiquities Ordnance for Palestine, 1920."

74. T161/56, minute of Mr. Ryan, April 1925, Garstang to Government Offices Jerusalem, 30 October 1924.

75. T161/56, minute of Mr. Ryan, April 1925.

76. Ibid., Stein to Laithwaite (India Office), 6 November 1925. Also Garstang to Government Offices Jerusalem, 30 October 1924.

77. T161/56, Garstang to Government Offices Jerusalem, 30 October 1924. The funding situation is exactly the same in contemporary Jordan.

78. Alon, *Making of Jordan*, 58.

79. Wilson, *King Abdullah, Britain and the Making of Jordan*, 82–83.

80. Gibson, "British Archaeological Institutions in Mandatory Palestine, 1917–1948," 121. There is not a comprehensive account of the establishment of Jordan's antiquities department. There are only a few brief secondary historical accounts that are accessible as photocopies in the JDOA files dealing with the department's origins but without source citations. These include Samer al-Hibahiba, *"Lamha Tarikhiyya"* (A Historical Glance) and Maʿan Abu Nowar, "The Early History of the Department of Antiquities of Jordan." The most easily accessible documents that provide any clues are from the National Archives at Kew Gardens, London. Any attempt to construct such an account therefore remains piecemeal. Early documents from Transjordan's DOA may have been lost in incidents of flooding of the River Zarqa in Amman.

81. *al-Jarida al-Rasmiyya* (The Official Gazette), Law No. 16, 10 September 1923. As for governance in Transjordan in 1923 and after, see Alon, *Making of Jordan*, 3–5.

82. JDOA files, Abu Nowar, "The Early History of the Department of Antiquities of Jordan."

83. MECA/Philby journals and JDOA files, Abu Nowar, "The Early History of the Department of Antiquities of Jordan," 302.

84. JDOA files, Abu Nowar, "The Early History of the Department of Antiquities of Jordan," 302.

85. T 161/56, memos and correspondences related to the Antiquities Ordinances for Palestine and Transjordan. See also JDOA files, Abu Nowar, "The Early History of the Department of Antiquities of Jordan," 302.

86. JDOA files, Abu Nowar, "The Early History of the Department of Antiquities of Jordan," 302–3.

87. Ibid., 303. On the delineation of the borders and the long road thereto, see Alon, *Making of Jordan*, 75–80.

88. JDOA files, Abu Nowar, "The Early History of the Department of Antiquities of Jordan," 303. Also MECA/Philby/box 2/fonds 1 and 2. This venture bore little positive fruit in Philby's time, largely due to the fact that the first to take these tours from Jerusalem to Petra were mostly British officials who were able to go for free. Philby resigned as British resident in Transjordan before the business progressed much further.

89. Tawfiq Canaan, *Notes on Studies in the Topography and Folklore of Petra* (Jerusalem: Beyt ul-Makdes Press, 1930). See also Salim Tamari, *Mountain against the Sea: Essays on Palestinian Culture and Society* (Berkeley: University of California Press, 2009), chapter 6.

90. JDOA files, Abu Nowar, "The Early History of the Department of Antiquities of Jordan," 302–3.

91. JDOA files, Samer al-Hibahiba, "Lamha Tarikhiyya" (A Historical Glance), *Athar* (Archaeology).

92. CO 733/133/9, memo of 11 March 1927.

93. Details of the reorganization are contained in CO 733/157/4 and CO 733/172/4.

94. JDOA files, *"Da'irat al-Athar al-'Amma, Mudara' wa Munjazat"* (General Directorate of Antiquities, Directors and Achievements). Anonymous, undated.

95. JDOA files, "Excavation at Amman of the Italian Archaeological Expedition," by Renato Bartoccini, 1930.

96. Ibid.

97. JDOA files, Amman Citadel reports, "Accounts of the Excavations Initiated by the Italian Archaeological Expedition on the Acropolis, Amman." Anonymous, undated.

98. Abd al-Rahman Munif, *Story of a City: A Childhood in Amman*, trans. Samira Kawar (London: Quartet Books, 1996); Shatha Abu-Khafaja, "Meaning and Use of Cultural Heritage in Jordan: Towards a Sustainable Approach" (PhD diss., Newcastle University, 2007); Shatha Abu-Khafaja and Rama al Radady, "The 'Jordanian' Roman Complex: Reinventing Urban Landscape to Accommodate Globalization," *Near Eastern Archaeology* 76, no. 3 (2013).

99. See Nelson Glueck, *The Other Side of the Jordan* (Cambridge: American Schools of Oriental Research, 1970). The first edition was published in 1940.

100. Quoted in Binyamin Mazar, ed., *Journal of the Israel Exploration Society*, Nelson Glueck Memorial Volume (Jerusalem: Israel Exploration Society, 1975), x, reprinted in Jonathan M. Brown and Laurence Kutler, *Nelson Glueck: Biblical Archaeologist and President of the Hebrew Union College-Jewish Institute of Religion* (Cincinnati: Hebrew Union College Press, 2006), 221.

101. Brown and Kutler, *Nelson Glueck*.

102. Eric M. Meyers, "American Schools of Oriental Research," in *The Oxford Encyclopedia of the Ancient Near East*, ed. E. Meyers (Oxford: Oxford University Press, 1997), 95. Meyers suggests the former. Peter Douglas Feinman, *William Foxwell Albright and the Origins of Biblical Archaeology* (Berrien Springs, MI: Andrews University Press, 2004). Feinman suggests the latter.

103. Brown and Kutler, *Nelson Glueck*, chapters 4–15. For more about the life of William F. Albright, see Feinman, *William Foxwell Albright and the Origins of Biblical Archaeology*.

104. Brown and Kutler, *Nelson Glueck*, 54.

105. Ibid., 62–64. See also chapter 4.

106. Glueck, *The Other Side of the Jordan*. See especially chapter 1, "What Is Biblical Archaeology?"

107. Brown and Kutler, *Nelson Glueck*, 69.

108. Gerald Lankester Harding succeeded George Horsfield as chief inspector of antiquities in 1936. The position was changed to director of the Department of Antiquities in 1938. He served until 1956, when he was expelled in the wake of the Suez War.

109. Brown and Kutler, *Nelson Glueck*, 79–80.

110. Glueck, *The Other Side of the Jordan*, 239–43.

111. Nelson Glueck, *Deities and Dolphins: The Story of the Nabataeans* (New York: Farrar, Straus and Giroux, 1965).

112. The dating of these periods is taken from Amihai Mazar, *Archaeology of the Land of the Bible, 10,000–586 B.C.E.* (New York: Doubleday, 1990). Scholars from various schools of thought tend to locate these dates a century or two in either direction for a variety of reasons having to do with determining who was the Pharaoh of the Exodus, whether various shadowy biblical peoples can be equated with Joshua's army, and whether this can be seen in the archaeological record. This presupposes belief in the Exodus. Those who think settlement patterns visible in the archaeological record are evidence of the biblical Exodus or at least the Exodus tradition tend to give the Exodus a "late date" in this early Iron Age (1200–1000 BCE), also called the Iron I. James K. Hoffmeier, *Israel in Egypt* (New York, Oxford: Oxford University Press, 1996), 122–26.

113. Glueck, *The Other Side of the Jordan*, 11.

114. Alon, *Making of Jordan*; Joseph A. Massad, *Colonial Effects: The Making of National Identity in Jordan* (New York: Columbia University Press, 2001), chapters 3 and 4.

115. James A. Sanders, ed., *Near Eastern Archaeology in the Twentieth Century: Essays in Honor of Nelson Glueck* (Garden City: Doubleday, 1970), xx.

116. Glueck, *The Other Side of the Jordan*, 126–27.

117. Brown and Kutler, *Nelson Glueck*, 82–88.

118. Ibid., 84.

119. Ibid., 158–64.

120. Ibid., 104.

121. Ibid., chapters 10 and 11.

122. James A. Sauer, "Transjordan in the Bronze and Iron Ages: A Critique of Glueck's Synthesis," *Bulletin of the American Schools of Oriental Research (BASOR)* 263 (1986).

123. Sauer, "Syro-Palestinian Archaeology, History and Biblical Studies," *Biblical Archaeologist* 45, no. 4 (1982).

124. Sauer, "Transjordan in the Bronze and Iron Ages," 4–9.

125. Ibid., 17–20.

126. Nelson Glueck's paradigm of Jordan's archaeology has received renewed interest in recent years. Based on his excavation of one of the largest field projects currently in Jordan—the Iron Age copper mines and mining communities of Wadi Faynan (what would be considered the Edomite lowlands)—Dr. Thomas Levy has proposed that Glueck's original dates for the biblical kingdoms of Iron Age Jordan are perhaps more correct than critics have assumed. He argues, as Glueck did, that there is evidence of a highly organized Edomite kingdom as early as the tenth century BCE. This potentially gets touchy, especially regarding the historicity of the Bible. If the argument can be made that the Transjordanian kingdoms were realities so early or at all, then the argument can potentially be extended to the early and actual existence of the Israelite kingdom of David and Solomon. The reality of that Israelite kingdom as described in the Bible is something from which many scholars have shied away in recent decades, sparking what is known in biblical archaeology circles as the Tenth Century Debate. As Zionist claims to Palestine that rely on antiquity locate those claims in the united Israelite monarchy of David and Solomon in the tenth century, regional politics is embedded in this discussion. See Judy Siegel-Itzkovich, "Digs May Help Decide If 'King Solomon's Mines' Was a Misnomer," *Jerusalem Post*, 29 January 2009.

127. Sylvia Haim, ed., *Arab Nationalism: An Anthology* (Berkeley: University of California Press, 1976), 83–88; Hasan Kayalı, *Arabs and Young Turks: Ottomanism, Arabism, and Islamism in the Ottoman Empire* (Berkeley: University of California Press, 1997), 186–87; Youssef M. Choueiri, *Arab Nationalism: A History* (Oxford: Blackwell, 2000), 79–82.

128. Daniel Martin Varisco, "Metaphors and Sacred History: The Genealogy of Muhammad and the Arab 'Tribe,'" *Anthropological Quarterly* 68, no. 3 (1995): 144–50.

129. C. Ernest Dawn, "The Formation of Pan-Arab Ideology in the Interwar Years," *International Journal of Middle East Studies* 20 (1988): 70.

130. Elena D. Corbett, "History Lessons in the City of Dawud: Jordan's Past and Complexities of Identity beyond Silwan," *Middle Eastern Studies* 47, no. 4 (2011): 591.

131. Ibid., 592.

132. Dawn, "The Formation of Pan-Arab Ideology in the Interwar Years."

133. *Al-Muqtataf* is once again instructive. Examples of this presentation of archaeology include John Peters, "Mahd al-Samiyyeen" (Cradle of the Semites), *al-Muqtataf* 56 (1920); "al-Haram al-Qudsi" (The Holy Sanctuary [Jerusalem]), *al-Muqtataf* 63 (1923); "Athar Hawran" (The Archaeology of the Hawran), *al-Muqtataf* 65 (1924); O. G. S. Crawford, "Fi Janub Bilad al-'Arab" (In the South of the Country of the Arabs), *al-Muqtataf* 69 (1926); "al-'Arab fi al-Tarikh" (The Arabs in History, Part 2), *al-Muqtataf* 69 (1926); and "Mafakhir Ur al-Kaldaniyyeen" (The Wonders of Ur of the Chaldeans), *al-Muqtataf* 76 (1930). The article by Peters is a translation of an article that appeared in the Bulletin of the American Schools of Oriental Research (BASOR), and that by Crawford is a translation from an article from the *Journal of the American Geographic Society*.

134. James Henry Breasted, *Ancient Times: A History of the Early World*, 2nd ed. (Boston: Ginn, 1944).

135. Ibid., 136–39.

136. George Aaron Barton, *Semitic and Hamitic Origins, Social and Religious* (Philadelphia: University of Pennsylvania Press, 1934), 5.

137. *'Arab* is both singular and plural, and this is how I am using the term. For different views on this issue, see Jan Retsö, *The Arabs in Antiquity: Their History from the Assyrians to the Umayyads* (London: Routledge, 2003), 107–13; Robert G. Hoyland, *Arabia and the Arabs: From the Bronze Age to the Coming of Islam* (London: Routledge, 2001), 5–8.

138. On the word *'arab*, see the brief discussion by Bernard Lewis, *The Arabs in History* (London: Hutchinson University Library, 1966), 10–13. On the conflation of bedouin with biblical patriarchs, see S. D. Goitein, *Jews and Arabs: Their Contacts through the Ages* (New York: Schocken Books, 1964), 23–25. For a more contemporary synthesis, see Retsö, *The Arabs in Antiquity*.

139. Goitein, *Jews and Arabs*, 24.

140. Barton, *Semitic and Hamitic Origins*, 5. Barton here is describing the work of Dutch Orientalist scholar Michael Jan De Goeje.

141. Corbett, "History Lessons in the City of Dawud," 593.

142. Nimrod Hurvitz, "Muhibb al-Din al-Khatib's Semitic Wave Theory and Pan-Arabism," *Middle Eastern Studies* 29, no. 1 (1993): 120.

143. Jacobson, *From Empire to Empire*, 112–13.

144. Dawn, "The Formation of Pan-Arab Ideology in the Interwar Years," 68.

145. 'Umar al-Salih al-Barghuthi and Khalil Tutah, *Tarikh Filastin* (al-Quds: Matb'a Bayt al-Maqdis, 1923).

146. Tamari, *Mountain against the Sea*, 98.

147. Tawfiq Canaan, "Haunted Springs and Water Demons in Palestine," *Journal of the Palestine Oriental Society* 1 (1921); Canaan, "Mohammedan Saints and Sanctuaries in Palestine," *Journal of the Palestine Oriental Society* 4 (1924); Canaan, "Plant-Lore in Palestinian Superstition," *Journal of the Palestine Oriental Society* 8 (1928); Canaan, "Water and 'The Water of Life,'" *Journal of the Palestine Oriental Society* 9 (1929); Canaan, "The Palestinian Arab House: Its Architecture and Folklore," *Journal of the Palestine Oriental Society* 12 (1932); Canaan, "The Saqr Bedouin of Bisan," *Journal of the Palestine Oriental Society* 16 (1936).

148. 'Arif al-'Arif, *Tarikh Bir al-Sab'a wa Qaba'iluhu* (The History of Bir Sab'a and Its Tribes) (al-Quds: Matb'a Bayt al-Maqdis, 1934).

149. Tamari, *Mountain against the Sea*, 100–102; Stephan Hanna Stephan, "Modern Palestinian Parallels to the Song of Songs," *Journal of the Palestine Oriental Society* 2 (1922); Hanna, "Palestinian Animal Stories and Fables," *Journal of the Palestine Oriental Society* 3 (1923); Hanna, "Studies in Palestinian Customs and Folklore," *Journal of the Palestine Oriental Society* 8 (1928); Hanna, "Animals in Palestinian Superstition," *Journal of the Palestine Oriental Society* 9 (1929).

150. Charles Breasted, *Pioneer to the Past: The Story of James Henry Breasted, Archaeologist* (New York: Charles Scribner's Sons, 1943), 231–32; Dawn, "The Formation of Pan-Arab Ideology in the Interwar Years," 69.

151. Choueiri, *Arab Nationalism*, 23–40; Dawn, "The Formation of Pan-Arab Ideology in the Interwar Years"; Muhammad 'Izzat Darwaza, "Durus al-Tarikh al-'Arabi min Aqdam al-Azmina hata Alan" (Lessons of Arab History from Antiquity to Present Times), in *Mukhtarat Qawmiyya li Muhammad 'Izzat Darwaza* (Nationalist

Selections by Muhammad 'Izzat Darwaza), ed. Naji 'Alush (Beirut: Markaz Dirasat al-Wihda al-Arabiyya, 1988).

152. How Islamist thinkers tackled antiquity is an interesting issue that unfortunately is beyond the scope of this discussion. For a fascinating consideration of Egyptian antiquity in the thought and work of Hasan al-Banna and Sayyid Qutb, please see Elliott Colla, *Conflicted Antiquities: Egyptology, Egyptomania, Egyptian Modernity* (Durham: Duke University Press, 2007), chapter 5.

153. Boullata, *Palestinian Art*, 77–79.

154. Dawn, "The Formation of Pan-Arab Ideology in the Interwar Years."

Chapter Five

1. Philip P. Graves, ed., *Memoirs of King Abdullah of Transjordan* (London: Jonathan Cape, 1950). From the introduction, by R. J. C. Broadhurst.

2. Neil Caplan, *Palestine Jewry and the Arab Question, 1917–1925* (London: Frank Cass, 1978), 179–82.

3. Ibid., 180.

4. Graves, *Memoirs of King Abdullah of Transjordan*, 38–40.

5. Ibid.

6. Hasan Kayalı, *Arabs and Young Turks: Ottomanism, Arabism, and Islamism in the Ottoman Empire* (Berkeley: University of California Press, 1997), 150–51; Graves, *Memoirs of King Abdullah of Transjordan*, chapter 4.

7. Graves, *Memoirs of King Abdullah of Transjordan*, chapter 7.

8. Kayalı, *Arabs and Young Turks*, 169.

9. Graves, *Memoirs of King Abdullah of Transjordan*, chapters 7 and 8.

10. Mary C. Wilson, *King Abdullah, Britain and the Making of Jordan* (Cambridge: Cambridge University Press, 1987), 26.

11. Ernest C. Dawn, *From Ottomanism to Arabism: Essays on the Origins of Arab Nationalism* (Urbana: University of Illinois Press, 1973), chapter 2, 68; Wilson, *King Abdullah, Britain and the Making of Jordan*, 26.

12. Wilson, *King Abdullah, Britain and the Making of Jordan*, 28–38.

13. Ihsan Turjman's diary demonstrates his support for the revolt, although he refers to the Hashemites' partisans as "bedouin" and sees in it the Hashemites' protection of their own interests. Salim Tamari, *Year of the Locust: A Soldier's Diary and the Erasure of Palestine's Ottoman Past* (Berkeley: University of California Press, 2011), 47 and chapter 2.

14. Michael Provence, "Ottoman Modernity, Colonialism, and Insurgency in the Interwar Arab East," *International Journal of Middle East Studies* 43, no. 2 (2011); James Gelvin, *Divided Loyalties: Nationalism and Mass Politics in Syria at the Close of Empire* (Berkeley: University of California Press, 1998).

15. Gelvin, *Divided Loyalties*.

16. Yoav Alon, "'Heart Beguiling Araby' on the Frontier of Empire: Early Anglo-Arab Relations in Transjordan," *British Journal of Middle Eastern Studies* 36, no. 1 (2009).

17. Kimberly Katz, *Jordanian Jerusalem*: Postage Stamps and Identity Construction," *Jerusalem Quarterly* no. 5 (1999): 31–33.

18. Oleg Grabar, "Kubbat Al-Sakhra," in *Encyclopedia of Islam*, ed. P. Bearman

et al., 2nd ed. (Brill Online, 2010), 298; A. Elad, "Why Did ʿAbd al-Malik Build the Dome of the Rock? A Re-Examination of Muslim Sources," in *Bayt Al-Maqdis: ʿAbd Al-Malik's Jerusalem*, ed. J. Raby and J. Johns (Oxford: Oxford University Press, 1992); Hershel Shanks, *Jerusalem's Temple Mount from Solomon to the Golden Dome* (New York: Continuum, 2007), 9–31.

19. Daniel Martin Varisco, "Metaphors and Sacred History: The Genealogy of Muhammad and the Arab 'Tribe,'" *Anthropological Quarterly* 68, no. 3 (1995).

20. Kimberly Katz, *Jordanian Jerusalem: Holy Places and National Spaces* (Gainesville: University Press of Florida, 2005), 31–33.

21. Benedict Anderson, *Imagined Communities*, rev. ed. (New York: Verso Press, 1991), 170–78.

22. Michael R. Fischbach, *State, Society and Land in Transjordan* (Leiden: Brill, 2000), 198.

23. Ibid., chapters 6 and 7.

24. Elena D. Corbett, "Jordan First: A History of the Intellectual and Political Economy of Jordanian Antiquity" (PhD diss., University of Chicago, 2009), chapter 3.

25. Tawfiq Canaan, *Notes on Studies in the Topography and Folklore of Petra* (Jerusalem: Beyt ul-Makdes Press, 1930).

26. Ibid., 2.

27. Ibid., 3.

28. Ibid., 5–6.

29. Ibid., chapter 2.

30. Ibid., 63–66.

31. Ibid., 69.

32. Abu Jʿafar Muhammad bin Jarir bin Yazid al-Tabari, *Tarikh al-Rusul wa al-Muluk* (The History of the Prophets and Kings), vol. 2, *Prophets and Patriarchs* (Albany: State University of New York Press).

33. See *Sahih Bukhari* 4:560–64.

34. Suleiman Farajat, "The Participation of Local Communities in the Tourism Industry at Petra," in *Tourism and Archaeological Heritage Management at Petra: Driver to Development of Destruction?* ed. Douglas Comer (New York: Springer Verlag, 2012), 149.

35. Many contemporary Jordanians have not been to Petra. In years when tourism has taken a hit due to regional instability, the government has offered heavily subsidized trips for Jordanians, who have taken advantage of the opportunity. Patricia Bikai, personal communication, January 2005.

36. John Lewis Burckhardt, *Travels in Syria and the Holy Land* (New York: AMS Press, 1983), 418.

37. Eugene Rogan, "Bringing the State Back: The Limits of Ottoman Rule in Transjordan, 1840–1910," in *Village, Steppe and State: The Social Origins of Modern Jordan*, ed. Eugene Rogan and Tariq Tell (London: British Academic Press, 1994), 41–42, 53–57.

38. Eugene Rogan, *Frontiers of State in the Late Ottoman Empire: Transjordan, 1850–1921* (Cambridge: Cambridge University Press, 1999), 52–55.

39. Vartan Amadouny, "Infrastructural Development under the British Mandate," in *Village, Steppe and State: The Social Origins of Modern Jordan*, ed. Eugene Rogan and Tariq Tell (London: British Academic Press, 1994), 146.

40. Philip C. Hammond, "Petra," in *The Oxford Encyclopedia of Archaeology in the Near East*, ed. E. Meyers (Oxford: Oxford University Press, 1997).

41. Regarding Jerash and its Circassian settlement, see the following: Norman N. Lewis, *Nomads and Settlers in Syria and Jordan, 1800–1980*, Cambridge Middle East Library (Cambridge: Cambridge University Press, 1987); Rogan, *Frontiers of the State*; Fischbach, *State, Society and Land in Transjordan*.

42. G. Lankester Harding, *Jerash, a Brief History* (Amman: Jordan Distribution Agency, 1973). Harding was buried in Jerash when he died in 1979. Philip J. King, *American Archaeology in the Mideast: A History of the American Schools of Oriental Research* (Philadelphia: American Schools of Oriental Research, 1983), 119.

43. Rogan, *Frontiers of the State*; Rogan, "Bringing the State Back," 49.

44. Katz, *Jordanian Jerusalem*, 36. For more about Shawbak prior to the establishment of Transjordan, see Rogan, *Frontiers of the State*; and Fischbach, *State, Society and Land in Transjordan*. Shawbak is a town of the southern highlands of Jordan having evidence of continuous settlement since prehistoric times, and certainly no less so in the modern era.

45. Melissa M. Aubin, "Jerash," in *The Oxford Encyclopedia of Archaeology in the Near East*, ed. E. Meyers (New York: Oxford University Press, 1997), 215–19; Alison Mc-Quitty, "George Horsfield," in *The Oxford Encyclopedia of Archaeology in the Near East*, ed. E. Meyers (New York: Oxford University Press, 1997); John Garstang, "Government of Trans-Jordan Antiquities Bulletin No. 1" (Department of Antiquities, Trans-Jordan, 1926); George Horsfield, *Official Guide to Jerash with Plan* (Government of Transjordan Department of Antiquities, 1930).

46. Between 1954 and 1965, which are the earliest dates for which tourism statistics are currently available to me, the number of tourists to Jerash outnumbered that of tourists to Petra. Jerash and Petra were the only East Bank sites for which statistics appear to have been kept, and Jerash was often second or third in number of visitors when compared with the Palestine Archaeological Museum in Jerusalem or Jericho. There are currently no statistics available between 1966 and 1988. Between 1989 and 2004, the number of tourists to Petra outnumbered that of tourists to Jerash, but Jerash was the second most frequently visited site in the country. Hashemite Kingdom of Jordan Ministry of National Economy, *Statistical Yearbook 1958*, vol. 9 (Jerusalem: Greek Convent Press); Hashemite Kingdom of Jordan Department of Statistics, *Statistical Yearbook 1964*, vol. 15 (Amman: Department of Statistics Press); Hashemite Kingdom of Jordan Department of Statistics, *Statistical Yearbook 1965*, vol. 16 (Amman: Department of Statistics Press). Information and Statistics Department of the Ministry of Tourism and Antiquities, personal communication, February 2006.

47. Philip King, *American Archaeology in the Mideast: A History of the American Schools of Oriental Research* (Philadelphia: American Schools of Oriental Research, 1983), 87.

48. Wilson, *King Abdullah, Britain and the Making of Jordan*, 53–59.

49. The circulation of various denominations is a crucial factor. While the situation is changing, Jordan remains a primarily cash-based economy and most incomes are low. In such an environment, small bills, particularly halves, ones, and fives, will enjoy the widest circulation. Katz, *Jordanian Jerusalem*, 64.

50. Corbett, "Jordan First," 225–37.

51. E. H. Palmer, "The Desert of the Tíh and the Country of Moab," *Palestine Ex-*

ploration Quarterly (1871); Gray Hill, "A Journey to Petra—1896," *Palestine Exploration Quarterly* (January–April 1897).

52. For an in-depth analysis of the far-reaching implications of this phenomenon in Jordan, see Joseph A. Massad, *Colonial Effects: The Making of National Identity in Jordan* (New York: Columbia University Press, 2001).

53. "Athar al-Bitra: Madina Manhuta fi al-Sakhr" (The Archaeology of Petra: A City Carved in Stone), *al-Muqtataf* 68 (1926); "Athar Jarash al-Fakhma" (The Splendid Archaeology of Jerash), *al-Muqtataf* 82 (1933).

54. The Jordan Postal Museum has been defunct for years. All information pertaining to the physical appearance, dates of issue, and values of the stamps discussed herein were found in *Stanley Gibbons Stamp Catalogue, Part 19, Middle East*, 6th ed. (London: Stanley Gibbons, 2005); K. C. R. Souan, *Philatelic History of Jordan, Diamond Jubilee, 1920–1980* (Kuwait: Author); Souan, *Philatelic History of Jordan, Stampexo Jubilee, 1920–1995* (Kuwait: Author). The most famous book on Jordan stamps is R. T. Ledger, *Philatelic History of Jordan, 1922–1953* (Amman, 1953). I thank the staff of the Philatelic Section of Jordan Post for providing access to materials and for helping me contact Jordan's philatelic experts. Information from this discussion with images provided by Jordan Post was previously published in Elena D. Corbett, "Leaving a Stamp on History," *Emerging Jordan, 2006* (Oxford Business Group: 2006).

55. Katz, *Jordanian Jerusalem*, 36.

56. Even the first Transjordanian stamps were canceled with hand-stamps enticing foreigners to visit the country's ancient attractions. Ibid., 38.

57. Saʿad ʿAbu Diyya, *al-Biʾa al-Siyasiyya wa Tatawwur ʿAmal al-Barid fi al-Urdun* (The Political Climate and the Development of Postal Operations in Jordan) (Amman: Lajnat al-Tarikh al-Urdun, 1993), 13; Katz, *Jordanian Jerusalem*, 35–36. The Universal Postal Union (UPU) was established in 1874 under the auspices of Prussian postal minister Heinrich von Stephan. The greatest benefit to a member country was that its stamps alone were required for sending international mail. An additional benefit for Transjordan was that membership in the UPU constituted a form of international recognition of it as a country and a functioning, legitimate bureaucracy.

58. Katz, *Jordanian Jerusalem*, 36; Ami Ayalon, "The Hashemites, T. E. Lawrence and the Postage Stamps of the Hijaz," in *The Hashemites in the Modern Arab World: Essays in Honour of the Late Professor Uriel Dann*, ed. Asher Susser and Aryeh Shmuelevitz (London: Frank Cass, 1995), 17–18.

59. *al-Jarida al-Rasmiyya*, no. 244 (1929).

60. Ibid. I assume, as does Katz, that "Arab Camp" refers to a Bedouin camp. The Naqab (Negev) Desert was not part of Transjordan, and thus its appearance on a list of "the best views of Transjordan" is interesting. Incidentally, it never would appear as a stamp. Salt, the capital of the Balqa region of Transjordan in the late Ottoman period, would not appear in any form on a stamp until the 1980s. This is logical as Emir Abdullah had early chosen Amman over Salt to be the capital of Hashemite Transjordan. To honor Salt would have served only to compromise Amman's and the Hashemites' consolidation of power.

61. Katz, *Jordanian Jerusalem*, 160, fn. 57.

62. I thank Mr. Ramzi Shuwayhat, president of the Jordan Philatelic Club, for an interview in Amman on 21 December 2005.

63. Ibid.

64. Katz, *Jordanian Jerusalem*, 38–39.

65. Shuwayhat interview, Amman, 21 December 2005. The removal of the Transjordan series from the market seems to directly contradict the high sales figures for the series as presented in Katz, *Jordanian Jerusalem*, 162, fn. 84. She is citing Ledger's sales figures for the series, although his figures may reflect combined sales of both the Emir Abdullah and the Transjordan series. As a final note on Sukkar, despite the furor over his first stamps, he went on to design the 1949 currency and is honored in later issues of Jordanian stamps.

66. Vartan Amadouny, "Infrastructural Development under the British Mandate," in *Village, Steppe and State: The Social Origins of Modern Jordan*, edited by Eugene Rogan and Tariq Tell (London: British Academic Press, 1994), 146–47.

67. G. Lankester Harding, *The Antiquities of Jordan*, rev. ed. (New York: Praeger, 1967), 162–63.

68. Ibid., 163; Mohammad al-Asad, "Al-Mushatta Facade at Berlin," in *The Umayyads: The Rise of Islamic Art*, ed. Ina Kehrberg (Amman: al-Faris, 2000), 117.

69. al-Asad, "Al-Mushatta Facade at Berlin," 117. It should be remembered that Kaiser Wilhelm had more than a passing interest in archaeology and antiquities. Neil Asher Silberman, *Digging for God and Country: Exploration, Archeology, and the Secret Struggle for the Holy Land, 1799–1917* (New York: Alfred A. Knopf, 1982), chapter 15. See also Suzanne L. Marchand, *Down from Olympus: Archaeology and Philhellenism in Germany, 1750–1970* (Princeton: Princeton University Press, 1996), chapter 6.

70. Harding, *The Antiquities of Jordan*, 162–64.

71. I have chosen the word *qasr* when speaking generally of these sites because there is no English word by which they can properly be referred. *Qasr* literally means "palace." Many of the structures and archaeological sites throughout the Middle East that are referred to formally as *qusur* (plural of *qasr*), however, were not palaces, nor does their designation as *qusur* indicate that they all served the same functions.

72. The Umayyads are often understood as a Syrian symbol, as Damascus was the seat of the Umayyad caliphate and modern Syria contained numerous monuments such as the Great Umayyad Mosque and many of its own structures of the "desert castle" variety. Not only Jordan's "desert castles," but also its new state mosque and other recent monuments, would seem to challenge Syrian claims to the Umayyads. See Elena D. Corbett, "Hashemite Antiquity and Modernity: Iconography in Neoliberal Jordan," *Studies in Ethnicity and Nationalism* 11, no. 2 (2011). At the same time, the desert site of Humayma in southern Jordan is readily touted as the estate of the Abbasid family, from whence they planned and staged their overthrow of the Umayyads in the eighth century. The Umayyads did not share kinship ties to the Prophet Muhammad as the Abbasids did, but the Abbasids could also be viewed as dynastic usurpers. As importantly, because they ushered in the age of high Islamicate civilization from their seat in Baghdad, Iraq gets to claim them.

73. For details of the extensive border issues, competing claims, and the Hadda Agreement, see Jane Priestland, ed., *Records of Jordan*, vols. 2–4 (Southampton: Hobbes of Southampton, 1996).

74. Stephen Urice, "The Qasr Kharana Project, 1979," *Annual of the Department of Antiquities of Jordan* 25 (1981); Mohammed al-Asad et al., *The Umayyads: The Rise of Islamic Art*, Museum with No Frontiers, Islamic Art in the Mediterranean (Amman:

al-Faris, 2000), 118–20; Rami Khouri, *The Desert Castles: A Brief Guide to the Antiquities* (Amman: al-Kutba, 1988), 18–21.

75. al-Asad et al., *The Umayyads*, 118–20.

76. Harding, *The Antiquities of Jordan*, 161; Urice, "The Qasr Kharana Project, 1979"; al-Asad et al., *The Umayyads*, 118–20; Khouri, *The Desert Castles*, 18–21.

77. Rogan, *Frontiers of the State*, 198. For a full discussion of the Kerak Revolt, see ibid., 184–217.

78. Ibid., 215–17.

79. Ibid., 216; Munib al-Madi and Suleyman Musa, *Tarikh al-Urdun fi al-Qarn al-'Ashreen, 1900–1959* (The History of Jordan in the Twentieth Century) (Amman: Maktabat al-Muhtasab, 1959; reprint, 1988), 26.

80. This museum focuses on Kerak's geopolitical importance over time, through such subthemes as, for instance, the Moabite language and the 1910 Kerak Revolt.

81. C. N. Johns, *Pilgrim's Castle ('Atlit), David's Tower (Jerusalem) and Qal'at Ar-Rabad (Ajloun): Three Middle Eastern Castles from the Time of the Crusades*, ed. Denys Pringle (Aldershot: Ashgate Variorum, 1997), 23.

82. Rogan, *Frontiers of the State*, 41.

83. "Crossing the River Jordan" (The Jordan River Foundation, undated), 12. The Allenby was destroyed as a result of the 1967 war. The King Hussein Bridge replaced it a year later. The most recent renovation of the bridge was carried out with Japanese aid.

84. Rachel S. Havrelock, *River Jordan: The Mythology of a Dividing Line* (Chicago: University of Chicago Press, 2011).

85. An agreement regarding postal exchange was reached in Paris between independent Jordan and the Universal Postal Union in July 1947. *Al-Jarida al-Rasmiyya*, no. 987 (1949).

86. See Rogan's reference to British use of air power in Transjordan, Eugene Rogan, "The Making of a Capital: Amman 1918–1928," in *Amman: Ville et Société, the City and Its Society*, ed. Jean Hannoyer and Seteny Shami (Beirut: Centre d'Études et de Recherches sur le Moyen-Orient Contemporain, 1996), 96. British colonial authorities introduced air transport to Transjordan from the first and relied on it heavily. Jane Priestland, *Records of Jordan*, vols. 1–5. See also Priya Satia, *Spies in Arabia: The Great War and the Cultural Foundations of Britain's Covert Empire in the Middle East* (Oxford: Oxford University Press, 2008).

87. Incidentally, there has been a Hijaz Railway tourist train from Wadi Rum to Aqaba, along the very route depicted on this late 1940s stamp. It has had sporadic outings. Personal communication, Fawwaz Zoubi, manager of the Jerash chariot reenactments, Amman, 27 August 2006. Mr. Zoubi was responsible for the Rum-Aqaba train reenactment.

88. Rogan, "Bringing the State Back," 50.

89. Avi Shlaim, *Collusion across the Jordan: King Abdullah, the Zionist Movement, and the Partition of Palestine* (New York: Columbia University Press, 1988).

90. Wilson, *King Abdullah, Britain and the Making of Jordan*, 202.

91. It is possible that the fifty-dinar note did not circulate widely. The second issue of Jordanian currency, in fact, would not include such a large bill. While Aqaba remained at that time an underdeveloped resource, this was, as Katz says, "perhaps the most politically charged message" in the first currency issue. Its appearance on a high-

denomination bill speaks to its importance, especially at the international level, where most transactions involving a bill of such denomination would likely have taken place. Katz, *Jordanian Jerusalem*, 62.

92. Wilson, *King Abdullah, Britain and the Making of Jordan*, 100. For more on the importance of this border issue, see Shlaim, *Collusion across the Jordan*, 520–33.

93. Michael J. Reimer, "Becoming Urban: Town Administrations in Transjordan," *International Journal of Middle East Studies* 37 (2005), 203.

94. For details regarding the border situation in this period, please see Ma'an Abu Nowar, *The Jordanian-Israeli War, 1948–1951: A History of the Hashemite Kingdom of Jordan* (Reading: Ithaca Press, 2002), 230. The matter of the dispute over Aqaba was settled in the mid-1960s, when Jordan and Saudi Arabia swapped stretches of territory, ultimately allowing for the expansion of Aqaba port.

95. *Jordan Currency* (Amman: Central Bank of Jordan, undated), 21; *Qanun Mu'waqat li-l-Naqd al-Urduni*, 35; *al-Jarida al-Rasmiyya*, no. 987 (1949). In Transjordan from 1927 to 1946, and Jordan from 1946 to 1950, the official currency in circulation was the Palestine pound, issued by the Palestine Currency Board. Palestinian currency circulated in Transjordan because of the overlap in its administration with that of Mandatory Palestine, especially in financial matters. Jordanian coins are not included in this discussion. Jordan's coins are plain, generally bearing only the head of the monarch and the value of the coin.

96. *Jordan Currency*, 21, *Qanun Mu'waqat li-l-Naqd al-Urduni*. The text of this law makes no mention of the Jordan Currency Board's relationship to the British colonial administration. If the relationship between the Colonial Office in London and the Palestine Currency Board is any indication, the members of the board worked in consultation with Mandatory officials. The currency of Mandatory Palestine and independent Jordan was printed by Thomas de la Rue and Co., London. Any information that Thomas de la Rue and Co. may have regarding the Jordan Currency Board is considered sensitive and is therefore classified. Katz, *Jordanian Jerusalem*, 166, fn. 69.

97. *Jordan Currency*, 21.

98. After King Abdullah's assassination in July 1951, the portrait was not changed until King Hussein assumed the throne. I have not found evidence that a bill of that era was ever meant to include a portrait of King Talal. A stamp bearing Talal's image was minted but never circulated. Most were destroyed upon his removal from the throne. Shuwayhat interview, Amman, 21 December 2005.

99. With the exception of a project in the Wadi al-Hasa, no other major irrigation projects were undertaken during the Mandate. See Amadouny, "Infrastructural Development under the British Mandate," 128–61; Ian R. Manners, "The Development of Irrigation Agriculture in the Hashemite Kingdom of Jordan, with Particular Reference to the Jordan Valley" (PhD diss., Oxford University, 1969), 572 and chapter 6.

100. This theme of peasants as beneficiaries of irrigation projects also appears on Egyptian stamps. See Donald Malcolm Reid, "The Symbolism of Postage Stamps: A Source for the Historian," *Journal of Contemporary History* 19, no. 2 (1984): 234; Reid, "Egyptian History through Stamps," *Muslim World* 62, no. 3 (1972): 222–23, 228.

101. Katz, *Jordanian Jerusalem*, 64.

102. Details of the life and work of Mustafa Wahbi al-Tal are found in Abdullah Radwan and Sadik I. Odeh, *Arar: The Poet and Lover of Jordan* (Amman: Greater Am-

man Municipality, 1999); and Richard Loring Taylor, *Mustafa's Journey: Verse of 'Arar, Poet of Jordan* (Irbid: Yarmouk University, 1988).

103. Gelvin, *Divided Loyalties*.

104. Ernest C. Dawn, "The Formation of Pan-Arab Ideology in the Interwar Years," *International Journal of Middle East Studies* 20, (1988): 69.

105. 'Arar (Mustafa Wahbi al-Tal, 1899–1949), "O Neighborhood of the Ban Tree," translated in Taylor, *Mustafa's Journey*, 101–4. See also the translation of the same poem and notes in Radwan and Odeh, *Arar*, 101–5. There are important differences in both translation and interpretation between these two sources.

106. Betty S. Anderson, *Nationalist Voices in Jordan: The Street and the State* (Austin: University of Texas Press, 2005), 47. See Anderson's discussion of 'Arar in its entirety, pp. 42–52.

107. I interviewed Abu Dawud (a pseudonym) at his home in Dhiban on 5 July 2010. This meeting was facilitated by Firas al-Kawamlha, to whom I owe my deepest gratitude.

108. This is in line with the findings of Morag Kersel's work. Morag Kersel, "When Communities Collide: Competing Claims for Archaeological Objects in the Marketplace," *Archaeologies: Journal of the World Archaeological Congress* 7, no. 3 (2011): 518–37; Kersel, "License to Sell: The Legal Trade of Antiquities in Israel" (PhD diss., Lucy Cavendish College, Cambridge University, 2006).

109. Katz, *Jordanian Jerusalem*, 184, fn. 43.

110. Abdullah was actually succeeded briefly by his son (and Hussein's father) Talal. After a troubled reign, Talal was removed and Hussein installed under the regency of his mother, Zein, until he reached majority. Talal was officially removed because of mental instability. The alternative historical narrative, very much alive, is that he was sympathetic to left-leaning nationalist movements and to groups such as Egypt's Free Officers, sympathies that the British could not abide.

Chapter Six

1. Israel Gershoni and James Jankowski, *Commemorating the Nation: Collective Memory, Public Commemoration and National Identity in Twentieth-Century Egypt* (Chicago: Middle East Documentation Center, 2004), 8.

2. Mohammad Abdul-Latif Abdul-Karim, "Lexical, Historical and Literary Sources of the Nabateans in the Arab Tradition," *ARAM* 12, nos. 1–2 (1990): 421.

3. Ibid., 422–23, 424.

4. Ibid., 422.

5. Betty S. Anderson, "Writing the Nation: Textbooks of the Hashemite Kingdom of Jordan," *Comparative Studies of South Asia, Africa and the Middle East* 21, nos. 1 and 2 (2001); Riad M. Nasser, *Palestinian Identity in Jordan and Israel: The Necessary "Other" in the Making of a Nation* (New York, Oxon: Routledge, 2005). My thanks to Betty Anderson for drawing my attention to the collection of Jordanian schoolbooks held in the library of the Truman Center at Hebrew University, Jerusalem. The collection of Jordanian textbooks at the Truman Center contains thirteen textbooks from the 1950s and another sixty-two ranging from the 1960s until the early 1980s. The contents of

the collection are primarily history, geography, and social studies books, with a few literature and religious studies books. A majority of the textbooks of the 1960s and 1970s are later editions of those published earlier. Unless otherwise noted, all textbook translations presented in this chapter are mine. In all cases, I have tried not to take literary license with the translations.

6. Ibrahim al-Fatan, Husni Fariz, Sayyah al-Rusan, and Sa'id Dura, *al-Qira'a al-Hashimiyya* (The Hashemite Reader) (Amman: Ministry of Education, 1966), 58–59.

7. 'Adnan Lutfi 'Uthman, *al-Watan al-'Arabi* (The Arab Nation) (Amman: Ministry of Education, 1965, 1967), 58.

8. Ibid.

9. Ibid., 58–59.

10. Sa'id al-Dura, 'Abbas al-Kurd, Sadiq 'Awda, Muhammad 'Ali al-Shami, and Khalil Zeki al-Dajani, *Tarikh al-Hadara al-'Arabiyya al-Islamiyya* (The History of Islamic Arab Civilization) (Amman: Ministry of Education, 1965), 24.

11. 'Abbas al-Kurd, Radi 'Abd al-Hawi, and 'Abd al-Rahman Jaber, *al-Hadarat al-Qadima fi al-Sharq wa al-Gharb* (The Ancient Civilizations in the East and West) (Amman: Ministry of Education, 1968), 31.

12. Peake Pasha, founder of the Transjordanian Frontier Force, later the Arab Legion, references this idea from the *Arabian Handbook*. F. G. Peake, *A History of Jordan and Its Tribes* (Coral Gables: University of Miami Press, 1958), 210.

13. Among other things, the treaty established the unlimited stationing and quartering of British forces in Jordan and most-favored nation commercial privileges between Jordan and all parts of the British Empire. It was thus similar to treaties the British struck with other regional and colonial possessions. See *Trans-Jordan No. 1 (1946) Treaty of Alliance between His Majesty in Respect of the United Kingdom and His Highness the Amir of Trans-Jordan*. Available in Jane Priestland, ed., *Records of Jordan*, vols. 5 and 6 (Southampton: Hobbs, 1996).

14. Avi Shlaim, *Collusion across the Jordan: King Abdullah, the Zionist Movement, and the Partition of Palestine* (New York: Columbia University Press, 1988). Weapons used by Egyptian troops during the 1948 war were faulty and alarmingly prone to malfunction. These weapons were supplied by the British, and the Egyptian king was essentially a British puppet.

15. A. Shboul, "Trade Routes and Socio-Cultural Networks in Jordan in the Broader Regional Context" (paper presented at the Ninth International Conference in the History and Archaeology of Jordan, Petra, Jordan, 23–27 May 2004). Dr. Shboul recounts his childhood in a village on the Yarmouk River directly between Akka and Damascus. For his village, Damascus remained a commercial center and Irbid remained an administrative center until the mid-1950s, although there was transportation to everywhere imaginable and social connections among the villagers as far away as Ma'an.

16. Betty S. Anderson, *Nationalist Voices in Jordan: The Street and the State* (Austin: University of Texas Press, 2005), 147–56.

17. For more about Qibya, see Trevor Royle, *Glubb Pasha: The Life and Times of Sir John Bagot Glubb, Commander of the Arab Legion* (London: Abacus, 1992), chapter 12; Priestland, *Records of Jordan*, vols. 7 and 8.

18. Kimberly Katz, "Jordanian Jerusalem: Postage Stamps and Identity Construc-

tion," *Jerusalem Quarterly*, no. 5 (1999); Katz, *Jordanian Jerusalem: Holy Places and National Spaces* (Gainesville: University Press of Florida, 2005).

19. This use of stamps for institutionalizing Jerusalem and the rest of the West Bank as part of Jordan has been discussed extensively by Katz, *Jordanian Jerusalem*, 55–59, and "Jordanian Jerusalem."

20. A 1965 series of stamps entitled "Jerash Antiquities" bore images of eight of the more recognizable ruins of Jerash.

21. Katz, *Jordanian Jerusalem*, chapter 5. Examples of such stamp series included the 1963 "Holy Places (Church of the Virgin's Tomb [Jerusalem], Basilica of the Agony [Gethsemane], Holy Sepulchre [Jerusalem], Nativity Church [Bethlehem], Haram of Ibrahim [Hebron], Dome of the Rock [Jerusalem], Omar al-Khattab Mosque [Jerusalem] and al-Aqsa Mosque [Jerusalem])"; the 1965 "Dead Sea (Dead Sea seascape, the Qumran Caves, and the Dead Sea Scrolls)"; the 1965 "Dome of the Rock Inauguration" commemorating the completion of a Hashemite-led restoration of the Dome of the Rock; the 1966 "Christ's Passion" depicting all fourteen Stations of the Cross; and the 1966 "Christmas (the Three Kings, the Presentation of the Magi, the Flight to Egypt)."

22. King Hussein published an article in *National Geographic* shortly after the pontiff's visit. See King Hussein of Jordan, "Holy Land, My Country," *National Geographic*, December 1964.

23. This paragraph draws heavily on Katz, "Jordanian Jerusalem," and *Jordanian Jerusalem*. Katz notes that the papal visit marked the first time that King Hussein appeared on stamps with the holy sites, although both King and sites had appeared separately on many stamps. Katz, *Jordanian Jerusalem*, 125. She also notes that this series was widely consumed in Italy. Katz, *Jordanian Jerusalem*, 183, fn. 37.

24. William G. Dever, "Biblical Archaeology," in *The Oxford Encyclopedia of Archaeology in the Near East*, ed. E. Meyers (Oxford: Oxford University Press, 1997), 315.

25. G. Lankester Harding, "News and Notes," *Annual of the Department of Antiquities of Jordan* 1 (1951): 5.

26. A full account of the Jordanian experience with the Dead Sea Scrolls is found in Elena D. Corbett, "Jordan First: A History of the Intellectual and Political Economy of Jordanian Antiquity" (PhD diss., University of Chicago, 2009).

27. Parr, personal communication, 25 August 2003. Prof. Parr had a long and distinguished career as an archaeologist connected to the BSAJ.

28. Dajani had actually taken his degree under the guidance of Dame Kathleen Kenyon at Cambridge.

29. 'Awni Dajani, "Note," *Annual of the Department of Antiquities of Jordan* 4 (1960): 5. No doubt that any upheaval within Jordan's antiquities department was directly related to the immense changes undergone by the country throughout the 1950s.

30. Dever, "Biblical Archaeology"; J. Sauer and L. A. Willis, "History of the Field: Archaeology in Jordan," in *Oxford Encyclopedia of the Ancient Near East*, ed. E. Meyers (Oxford: Oxford University Press, 1997).

31. Please refer to the *ADAJ* of these years for further details.

32. Farah S. Ma'ayeh, "'Amaliat al-Athar fi al-Urdun, 1949–1959" (Archaeological Projects in Jordan), *Annual of the Department of Antiquities of Jordan* 4 and 5 (1960).

33. Katz, *Jordanian Jerusalem*, 97. Katz cites a 1953–54 annual report of the Ministry of Information (precursor to the Jordanian Ministry of Education) stating that

the nationalization of school textbooks was currently under way. This must have been the case as early as 1951, the date of the earliest Jordanian national textbook in the available collection.

34. Anonymous, *Manhaj al-Ijtima'iyya li-l Marhala al-Ilzamiyya, al-Ibtida'iyya wa al-I'dadiyya* (Social Studies Curriculum for the Compulsory Stage, Elementary and Preparatory) (Amman: Ministry of Education, 1965), 5.

35. Ibid.

36. Ibid., 6.

37. Katz, *Jordanian Jerusalem*, 97. A text of the law and State Department correspondences regarding U.S. concerns over it can be found in NARA II 885.43/1-1255.

38. Ibid., 97–99.

39. Anderson, "Writing the Nation," 10.

40. Gershoni and Jankowski, *Commemorating the Nation*, 8.

41. This is based on my reading of all of the books under discussion, a few of which will be presented in greater detail in the following pages. Among those that I do not discuss further but are indicative of the paradigms I have discussed are Sa'id al-Dura, 'Abd al-Rahim Mur'ib Sadiq 'Awda, and 'Abd al-Bari al-Shaykh Dura, *al-Tarikh al-'Arabi al-Hadith* (Modern Arab History) (Amman: Ministry of Education, 1973); 'Abbas al-Kurd, *Tarikh al-'Arab wa al-Muslimin* (The History of the Arabs and the Muslims) (Amman: Ministry of Education, 1970); Mahmud Tawalbeh and Hassan Riyan, *Mudhakkirat fi Tarikh al-'Arab al-Hadith* (Remarks on the Modern History of the Arabs) (Amman: Ministry of Education, 1979).

42. Wasfi 'Anabtawi, Sa'id Dura, Sa'id al-Sabagh, and Husni Fariz, *al-Mamlaka al-Urduniyya al-Hashimiyya* (The Hashemite Jordanian Kingdom) (Amman: Istiqlal Library, 1953), 79–80.

43. Anderson, "Writing the Nation"; Anderson, *Nationalist Voices in Jordan*.

44. 'Anabtawi et al., *al-Mamlaka al-Urduniyya al-Hashimiyya*, 77–79.

45. This trend has begun to be rectified only in recent textbooks, as archaeological heritage has been, to a certain extent, the subject of more attention in the school curriculum in recent years. My reading of more recent textbooks, facilitated by friends with children in primary and secondary school, suggests that the treatment of archaeology remains rather limited and noncontextual. Other scholars have reached the same conclusion. See Arwa Badran, "The Excluded Past in Jordanian Formal Education: The Introduction of Archaeology," in *New Perspectives in Global Public Archaeology*, ed. K. Okamura and A. Matsuda (New York: Springer Science+Business Media, 2001), 198–99.

46. Benedict Anderson, *Imagined Communities*, rev. ed. (New York: Verso Press, 1991). This is a play on Anderson's ideas regarding "print capital."

47. Corbett, "Jordan First."

48. Shimon Gibson, "British Archaeological Institutions in Mandatory Palestine, 1917–1948," *Palestine Exploration Quarterly* 131 (1999): 121.

49. Michael J. Reimer, "Control of Urban Waqfs in al-Salt, Transjordan," in *Held in Trust: Uses of Waqf in the Muslim World*, edited by Pascale Ghazaleh (Cairo: American University in Cairo, 2011), 117.

50. Ibrahim Ahmad Zahran and Ibrahim Muhammad al-Fa'uri, eds., *al-Nutq al-Sami li Jalalat al-Malik al-Husayn bin Talal al-Mu'atham: Hawal Shu'un al-Urdun al-Ijtima'iyya* (The Royal Speech of His Majesty King Hussein bin Talal the Great: Regarding the Social Conditions of Jordan) (Amman: Unlisted, 2000).

51. Journalist Rami Khouri wrote a series called *Our Ancient Heritage* for the *Jordan Times* in the late 1990s and early 2000s.

52. See Nadia Abu el-Haj, *Facts on the Ground: Archaeological Practice and Territorial Self-Fashioning in Israeli Society* (Chicago: University of Chicago Press, 2001), chapter 3; Raz Kletter, *Just Past? The Making of Israeli Archaeology* (London: Equinox, 2006), chapter 2.

53. Beginning in the 1950s, Jordan established youth summer camps, some with U.S. financial assistance, that were intended to provide physical activity, some military training, national education, and avenues for participation in national and political projects for schoolchildren who would not otherwise have access to affordable summer activities (NARA II 885.432/5-362). Camps in the context of schoolbooks are discussed later in this chapter.

54. Interview with Dr. Anonymous One, Amman, 19 August 2006.

55. Mustafa Murad al-Dabbagh, *al-Mujaz fi Tarikh Filastin mundhu Aqdam al-Azmana hata al-Yawm* (A Concise History of Palestine from the Most Ancient Times to the Present), 2nd ed. (Beirut: Ministry of Education, 1957).

56. Ibid., 5, 8.

57. Ibid., 9.

58. Ibid., 9–13.

59. al-Dabbagh, *al-Mujaz fi Tarikh Filastin*, 14.

60. Ibid., 14–15.

61. Ibid., 14. The civil war in Lebanon (1975–90) gave an ideological boost to Phoenicianism—a formulation of the history of Lebanon by which some Lebanese, particularly Christians, explained contemporary political divides by claiming descent from Greek Phoenicians as opposed to ancient Arabs. See Asher Kaufman, *Reviving Phoenicia: In Search of Identity in Lebanon* (New York: I. B. Tauris, 2004).

62. Ibid., 10–14.

63. Ibid., 16.

64. Today this is Beer Sheva.

65. al-Dabbagh, *al-Mujaz fi Tarikh Filastin*, 17–18.

66. Ibid., 18–19.

67. Ibid., 20. The "Syrian cousins" are described by al-Dabbagh in a footnote as the Philistines. He says that the Philistines came to Palestine from Crete in the early twelfth century BCE, settling the Palestine coast from Karmil to Gaza and thus bestowing their name upon the country.

68. Dhuqan al-Hindawi, *al-Qadiyya al-Filastiniyya* (The Palestinian Issue) (Amman: Ministry of Education, 1966), 8.

69. James Henry Breasted, *Ancient Times: A History of the Early World*, 2nd ed. (Boston: Ginn, 1944), 200–202.

70. 'Uthman, *al-Watan al-'Arabi*; al-Kurd et al., *al-Hadarat al-Qadima*.

71. al-Dabbagh, *al-Mujaz fi Tarikh Filastin*, 22. The authors of the history textbooks tend to use the terms "Jews" and "Hebrews" interchangeably, and do not seem to prefer one term over the other, most of them opting to use both within the same text. What is less frequently part of or simply removed from the discourse by this time, for what should be obvious reasons, are references to the "Banu Isra'il" or the "Isra'iliyeen," as these terms now carried a meaning more akin to "Israeli" than "Israelite," as previously.

72. Ibid., 20–22.

73. An example of the first is al-Kurd et al., *al-Hadarat al-Qadima*, 81. An example of the second is al-Hindawi, *al-Qadiyya al-Filastiniyya*, 8–10.

74. Ibid.

75. 'Uthman, *al-Watan al-'Arabi*; al-Hindawi, *al-Qadiyya al-Filastiniyya*.

76. An entirely different approach would be published by American University of Beirut historian Kamal Salibi in the 1980s. Instead of asserting that waves of Semitic Arabs came out of the Arabian Peninsula and settled in biblical Palestine of the Mediterranean coast, he argues, based on his analysis of Arabian toponyms and the Hebrew Bible, that the biblical Palestine was actually geographically located in the western Arabian Peninsula. Kamal Salibi, *The Bible Came from Arabia* (London: Jonathan Cape, 1985). Salibi and others pursued this paradigm. See Salibi, *Khafiya al-Tura wa Asrar Sha'ab Isra'il* (Secrets of the Torah and the People of Israel) (London: Dar al-Saqi, 1988); Firas al-Sawah, *al-Hadath al-Turati wa al-Sharq al-Adna al-Qadim* (The Phenomenon of the Torah and the Ancient Near East) (Damascus: Dar 'Ala' al-Din, 1999). Others would seek a path establishing pre-Hebraic roots in Jerusalem by pursuing the murky Yabus (Jebusite) heritage. See Salim Tamari, *Mountain against the Sea: Essays on Palestinian Culture and Society* (Berkeley: University of California Press, 2009), 98–99, 110–11. For an example referring specifically to the Jebusite Arabs, see Ra'if Yusuf Najam, *al-Hafriyyat al-Athariyya fi al-Quds* (Archaeological Excavations in Jerusalem) (Amman: Dar al-Furqan, 2009). For a synthesis in line with mainstream scholarship, see Moawiyya Ibrahim, *Dirasat fi Athar Filastin* (Studies in the Archaeology of Palestine) (Amman: Dar al-Baraka, 2010).

77. Abu el-Haj, *Facts on the Ground*.

78. In the Hebrew scriptures, the Moabites and Ammonites are considered the descendents of Lot from his seduction by his two daughters after the destruction of Sodom. As incest is in direct violation of law (see Leviticus 18, for instance), this not only provides a geneaological connection among these peoples but also is a way of explaining much about their antagonistic relationship with one another at the time of writing. Lot is a Muslim prophet, and his "cave" just south of the Dead Sea in Jordan is a shrine. The Edomites, by contrast, are believed to have been descended from Esau.

79. Winfried Thiel, "Omri," in *The Anchor Bible Dictionary*, ed. D. N. Freedman (New York: Doubleday, 1992); Jan Retsö, *The Arabs in Antiquity: Their History from the Assyrians to the Umayyads* (London: Routledge, 2003), 144.

80. 'Adnan Lutfi 'Uthman, *al-Watan al-'Arabi* (The Arab Nation) (Amman: Ministry of Education, 1965, 1967), 52–54.

81. See Gershoni and Jankowski, *Commemorating the Nation*.

82. 'Uthman, *al-Watan al-'Arabi*, 45–46.

83. This paradigm is taken even further by al-Kurd et al., *al-Hadarat al-Qadima*, 204. Talking about the Jews under Roman rule, the author says that Rome gave them freedom of religion and granted them self-rule. The Jews, however, launched many rebellions against them until finally Titus destroyed Jerusalem in AD 70. This was "the end of an era for a Jewish political entity in part of our land." Throughout the rest of history the inhabitants are said to have been Arab.

84. 'Uthman, *al-Watan al-'Arabi*, 46–47.

85. 'Uthman's discussion of Tuthmoses III concludes, "Just as parts of the Empire resisted the Hittite invasions from the north and the tribes of desert Bedu from the

south, known as the *al-Khabiri*," 46–47. The *al-Khabiri* is a reference to the peoples known among scholars as the Hapiru, mentioned in chapter 3.

86. Ibid., 63. ʿUthman's sections on Christ and Christianity are particularly laden with rhetoric that speaks unfavorably of Jews regarding Jesus' crucifixion at the hands of the Romans.

87. For older works that deal with the use of scripture and Biblical scholarship to lend legitimacy to the modern State of Israel, see Keith W. Whitelam, *The Invention of Ancient Israel: The Silencing of Palestinian History* (London: Routledge, 1996); Nachman Ben-Yehuda, *The Masada Myth: Collective Memory and Mythmaking in Israel* (Madison: University of Wisconsin Press, 1995); Robert B. Coote and Keith W. Whitelam, *The Emergence of Early Israel in Historical Perspective* (Sheffield: Almond Press, 1987).

88. JoUSAID files, "From 1920 to the Twenty-First Century: Decisive Dates for the Hashemite Kingdom of Jordan and Its Partnership with USAID." Anonymous, undated.

89. About withholding of U.S. recognition of Jordan, see Uriel Dann, "The United States and the Recognition of Transjordan, 1946-1949," in *Studies in the History of Transjordan, 1920–1949: The Making of a State* (Boulder: Westview Press, 1984). See also the Congressional Record of the U.S. Senate and correspondence between the U.S. Department of State and the Foreign Office, contained in CO 537/1849 and CO 537/1845. Reproduced in Priestland, *Records of Jordan*, vol. 5.

90. For some idea of the plight of refugees, see records of 1951 contained in FO 371/91399, FO 371/91808, FO 371/91210, and FO 371/98871. Reproduced in Priestland, *Records of Jordan*, vol 7.

91. JoUSAID files, "From 1920 to the Twenty-First Century."

92. JoUSAID files, "U.S.A.I.D. Program in Jordan," vol. 4, *Tourism, Industry, Transportation and Public Administration*. Anonymous, undated.

93. Ibid.

94. Katz, *Jordanian Jerusalem*, 120–21. It is my suspicion that Kovach is the unnamed "American tourism advisor" to which the report cited above refers. This adviser was appointed to Jordan for some time and worked with the director of the Tourism Authority and with the director of the Department of Antiquities. He would have thus worked under two antiquities directors—Saʿid Dura, who is an author of children's history textbooks presented herein, and ʿAwni Dajani.

95. Ibid.

96. JoUSAID files, "U.S.A.I.D. Program in Jordan."

97. Ibid.

98. Dhuqan al-Hindawi, Musa ʿAli al-Ghul, and Salam al-Khuri, *al-Jiyughrafiyya al-Iqtisadiyya* (Economic Geography) (Amman: Ministry of Education, 1966, 1968), 153.

99. Ibid., 153–54.

100. Ibid., 154.

101. Ibid.

102. Ibid.

103. Ibid., 154–55.

104. Ibid., 153–55.

105. Rashid Khalidi, *Palestinian Identity: The Construction of Modern National Con-*

sciousness (New York: Columbia University Press, 1997), 29–30, 151, 254, fn. 25. For more on the *fada'il* genre, and in particular its links to antiquities, see Elliott Colla, *Conflicted Antiquities: Egyptology, Egyptomania, Egyptian Modernity* (Durham: Duke University Press, 2007), chapter 2.

106. 'Anabtawi et al., *al-Mamlaka al-Urduniyya al-Hashimiyya*, 20.

107. Ibid., 20–21.

108. Nu'uman's narrative is contained in ibid., 28–34.

109. Nabil's narrative is contained in ibid., 35–43.

110. Talal's narrative in contained in ibid., 44–52.

111. Ghassan's narrative is contained in ibid., 52–62.

112. Yoav Alon, *The Making of Jordan: Tribes, Colonialism and the Modern State* (London, New York: I. B. Tauris, 2007), 20–36.

113. Hasan's narrative is contained in 'Anabtawi et al., *al-Mamlaka al-Urduniyya al-Hashimiyya*, 22–28.

114. Y'aqub al-Dajani, Yunis al-Suqi, 'Abd al-Latif al-Barguthi, 'Issa Abu Shaykha, 'Adnan Lutfi, Nimr al-Madi, and Ibrahim 'Uthman, *Watani al-Saghir* (My Little Country) (Amman: Ministry of Education, 1966, 1969).

115. I have yet been unable to find anyone who participated in one of these as a schoolchild in the 1960s. I have heard an account of someone who, as a schoolchild in the 1950s, participated in what may have been a precursor to the kind of organized activity described in this book. As part of a small group of schoolboys—only boys—he was dropped in the Jordan Valley to camp there until someone came to retrieve them. The U.S. helped finance work and camping programs for Jordanian youth (NARA II 885.432/5-362). While the fictional child in this account tells the story in a gender-neutral way and some of the books do contain female characters who travel with their brothers, I am assuming that the child in this story is a boy.

116. al-Dajani et al., *Watani al-Saghir*. The "scout camp" sequence is told on pp. 37–55.

117. Ibid., 42.

118. Ibid., 53–55.

Chapter Seven

1. Elena D. Corbett, "Jordan First: A History of the Intellectual and Political Economy of Jordanian Antiquity" (PhD diss., University of Chicago, 2009), chapter 5.

2. Patrick Seale, "Jordan Calms Fears for Scrolls," *Observer*, 4 December 1966.

3. Neil Asher Silberman, *The Hidden Scrolls: Christianity, Judaism, and the War for the Dead Sea Scrolls* (New York: G. P. Putnam's Sons, 1994), 154.

4. The growth of tourism between 1950 and 1967 was an important issue in social studies textbooks. See 'Abbas al-Kurd, Yusuf Jum'a, 'Abd al-Hassan Jaber, and Husni 'Aish, *al-Mujtam'a al-'Arabi al-Urduni* (The Jordanian Arab Society) (Amman: Ministry of Education, 1967), 119–21.

5. Yoav Alon, *The Making of Jordan: Tribes, Colonialism and the Modern State* (London, New York: I. B. Tauris, 2007). See especially chapter 5 and his conclusion.

6. Adnan Abu-Odeh, *Jordanians, Palestinians and the Hashemite Kingdom in the*

Middle East Peace Process (Washington, DC: United States Institute of Peace Press, 1999), 190–92.

7. Linda L. Layne, *Home and Homeland: The Dialogics of Tribal and National Identities in Jordan* (Princeton: Princeton University Press, 1994).

8. Ms. Anonymous Two, personal communication, Amman, 14 June 2006.

9. Corbett, "Jordan First," chapters 2 and 3. See also Salam Mahadin, "An Economy of Legitimating Discourses: The Invention of the Bedouin and Petra and National Signifiers in Jordan," *Critical Arts* 21, no. 1 (2007); Joseph A. Massad, *Colonial Effects: The Making of National Identity in Jordan* (New York: Columbia University Press, 2001); Andrew Shryock, *Nationalism and the Genealogical Imagination: Oral History and Textual Authority in Tribal Jordan* (Berkeley: University of California Press, 1997); Layne, *Home and Homeland*.

10. For some recent takes on the issue of tourism and branding in the post-'67 era, and particularly since the 1990s, see Waleed Hazbun, *Beaches, Ruins, Resorts: The Politics of Tourism in the Arab World* (Minneapolis: University of Minnesota Press, 2008); Rami Farouk Daher, "Tourism, Heritage, and Urban Transformations in Jordan and Lebanon: Emerging Actors and Global-Local Juxtapositions," in *Tourism in the Middle East: Continuity, Change and Transformation*, ed. Rami Farouk Daher (Clevedon, Buffalo, Toronto: Channel View Publications, 2007); Salam Mahadin, "Tourism and Power Relations in Jordan: Contested Discourses and Semiotic Shifts," in *Tourism in the Middle East: Continuity, Change and Transformation*, ed. Rami Farouk Daher (Clevedon, Buffalo, Toronto: Channel View Publications, 2007); and Irene Maffi, "New Museographic Trends in Jordan: The Strengthening of the Nation," in *Jordan in Transition*, ed. George Joffe (New York: Palgrave, 2002).

11. Eugene Rogan, "The Physical Islamization of Amman," *Muslim World* 76 (1986).

12. Erin Addison, "The Roads to Ruins: Accessing Islamic Heritage in Jordan," in *Marketing Heritage: Archaeology and the Consumption of the Past*, ed. Yorke Rowan and Uzi Baram (Walnut Creek: AltaMira Press, 2004).

13. Jordan Tourism Board, "Biblical Jordan at a Glance" (Amman: Author, 2005).

14. Jordan Tourism Board, *"Al-Islam fi al-Urdun: Masira wa Mawaqi'a"* (Tracing Islam in Jordan) (Amman, 2005).

15. Interview with official of Jordan's Ministry of Religious Endowments, Amman, 14 November 2006. The Amman Message is an all-inclusive clerical consensus reached among the leading Sunni and Shi'i authorities on contentious points such as Muslim identity, apostasy, and the issuance of legal rulings. It was written, discussed, and signed over two years between 2004 and 2006 at the initiative of King Abdullah II. It is clearly intended to demonstrate a broad Islamic consensus of toleration among recognized Muslim scholars and leaders and to showcase King Abdullah's qualities of leadership. This is not meant to be a cynical observation; on the contrary, the Amman Message and its story are remarkable. The website is available in English and Arabic: http://www.ammanmessage.com.

16. Sandra Schamm, "Disinheriting Heritage: Explorations in the Contentious History of Archaeology in the Middle East," in *Archaeology and the Postcolonial Critique*, ed. Matthew Liebmann and Uzma Z. Rizvi (Lanham: AltaMira Press, 2008), 174–75.

17. In the days following the suicide hotel bombings of 9 November 2005, the *Jordan Times* published numerous letters from Americans expressing condolences. The letters were replete with images of Jordan as a bastion of "human rights" and "tolerance."

18. Mr. Youssef Hilo, "Jordan, a Holy Land: The Case of Bethany beyond the Jordan of Perea (or the Wilderness?)," paper presented at the Ninth International Conference on the History and Archaeology of Jordan, Petra, 23–27 May 2004.

19. For a comprehensive consideration of the King Hussein Gardens, please see Elena D. Corbett, "Hashemite Antiquity and Modernity: Iconography in Neoliberal Jordan," *Studies in Ethnicity and Nationalism* 11, no. 2 (2011).

20. Interview with Mr. Jamal Joucka, Amman, 7 September 2006.

21. "The National Museum" was established by law at the declaration of the king in *al-Jarida al-Rasmiyya* (The Official Gazette), no. 4608, on 1 July 2003.

22. Laurie Brand, "Development in Wadi Rum? State Bureaucracy, External Funders and Civil Society," *International Journal of Middle East Studies* 33, no. 4 (2001); Brand, "'In the Beginning Was the State . . .': The Quest for Civil Society in Jordan," in *Civil Society in the Middle East*, ed. A. R. Norton (Leiden: E. J. Brill, 1995). See also Andre Bank and Oliver Schlumberger, "Jordan: Between Regime Survival and Economic Reform," in *Arab Elites: Negotiating the Politics of Change*, ed. Volker Perthes (Boulder: Lynne Rienner, 2004).

23. Irene Maffi, *Pratiques du Patrimoine et Politiques de la Mémoire en Jordanie: Entre Histoire Dynastique et Récits Communautaires* (Lausanne: l'Université de Lausanne, 2003); Maffi, "New Museographic Trends in Jordan."

24. The Jordanians involved in the Salt Museum initiative, however, clearly have broader meanings in mind. Rami Farouk Daher, "Urban Regeneration/Heritage Tourism Endeavours: The Case of Salt, Jordan. 'Local Actors, International Donors, and the State,'" *International Journal of Heritage Studies* 11, no. 4 (2005): 289–307.

25. Dr. Anonymous Four (Jordan Museum official), personal communication, Amman, 2004.

26. *What Is the Jordan Museum?* ed. Mathaf al-Urdun (Amman: Jordan Museum, 2006).

27. Interview with Dr. Anonymous Five, Amman, 20 December 2004.

28. Muhammad ʿAdnan al-Bakhit, "Taqdim" (Introduction), in *Dirasat fi Makhtutat al-Bahr al-Mayt* (Studies in the Dead Sea Scrolls), ed. ʿUmar al-Ghul (Amman: al-Lajna al-Urduniyya li Makhtutat al-Bahr al-Mayt, Wizarat al-Taʿalim al-ʿAli wa al-Bahth al-ʿIlmi [Jordanian Committee for the Dead Sea Scrolls, the Ministry of Higher Education and Scientific Research], 2012).

29. Gerard Leval, "Ancient Inscription Refers to Birth of Israelite Monarchy," *Biblical Archaeology Review* 38, no. 3 (2012); Robert Draper, "Archaeologists Dig up Controversy as They Dig into the Kings," *National Geographic* 218, no. 6 (2010).

30. Dr. Anonymous Two, personal communication, Amman, 4 November 2006.

31. Interview with Dr. Anonymous Three, Amman, 22 August 2006.

32. Interview with Mr. Anonymous Two, Amman, 19 December 2004.

33. Dr. Anonymous Six, personal communication, Amman, 3 November 2012.

Bibliography

Archival Sources and Abbreviations

Gerald Lankester Harding (GLH) Papers, Morton-on-Marsh, Oxfordshire
Jordan Department of Antiquities Archives, Amman (JDOA)
Jordan National Library, Amman
Library of Congress Middle East Reading Room, Washington, DC
Middle East Center Archives of St. Antony's College, Oxford (MECA):
    The Philby Papers
    The Hogarth Papers
National Archives at College Park, MD (NARA II)
National Archives at Kew Gardens, London:
    Foreign Office (FO) documents
    Colonial Office (CO) documents
    Treasury (T) documents
Palestine Exploration Fund Archives, London (PEF)
Truman Center Library, Hebrew University, Jerusalem
University of Jordan Library Newspaper Department, Amman
USAID office archives, Amman (JoUSAID)

Published Archive Editions

Priestland, Jane, ed. *Records of Jordan*. Cambridge Archive Editions. 14 vols. Southampton: Hobbes of Southampton, 1996.

Periodicals and Abbreviations (General)

Annual of the Department of Antiquities of Jordan (*ADAJ*)
Athar
Biblical Archaeology Review

al-Difāʿa
Filastin
al-Jarida al-Rasmiyya
Jerusalem Post
Jordan Times
Journal of the Palestine Oriental Society (JPOS)
al-Muqtataf
National Geographic
Palestine Exploration Quarterly (PEQ)
Statistical Yearbook (Department of Statistics, Ministry of the National Economy, HKJ)
Time

Secondary Materials

Abdul-Karim, Mohammad Abdul-Latif. "Lexical, Historical and Literary Sources of the Nabateans in the Arab Tradition." *ARAM* 12, nos. 1–2 (1990): 412–24.

ʿAbu Diyya, Saʿad. *al-Biʾa al-Siyasiyya wa Tatawwur ʿAmal al-Barid fi al-Urdun* (The Political Climate and the Development of Postal Operations in Jordan). Amman: Lajnat al-Tarikh al-Urdun, 1993.

Abu el-Haj, Nadia. *Facts on the Ground: Archaeological Practice and Territorial Self-Fashioning in Israeli Society.* Chicago: University of Chicago Press, 2001.

Abu Jaber, Raouf Saʿad. *Pioneers over Jordan: The Frontier of Settlement in Transjordan, 1850–1914.* London: I. B. Tauris, 1989.

Abu-Khafaja, Shatha. "Meaning and Use of Cultural Heritage in Jordan: Towards a Sustainable Approach." PhD diss., Newcastle University, 2007.

Abu-Khafaja, Shatha, and Rama al-Rabady. "The 'Jordanian' Roman Complex: Reinventing Urban Landscape to Accommodate Globalization." *Near Eastern Archaeology* 76, no. 3 (2013).

Abu Nowar, Maʿan. *The Jordanian-Israeli War, 1948–1951: A History of the Hashemite Kingdom of Jordan.* Reading: Ithaca Press, 2002.

Abu-Odeh, Adnan. *Jordanians, Palestinians and the Hashemite Kingdom in the Middle East Peace Process.* Washington, DC: United States Institute of Peace Press, 1999.

Addison, Erin. "The Roads to Ruins: Accessing Islamic Heritage in Jordan." In *Marketing Heritage: Archaeology and the Consumption of the Past*, edited by Yorke Rowan and Uzi Baram, 229–47. Walnut Creek: AltaMira Press, 2004.

Aksakal, Mustafa. *The Ottoman Road to War in 1914: The Ottoman Empire and the First World War.* Cambridge: Cambridge University Press, 2008.

Albright, William Foxwell. "Palestinian Inscriptions." In *Ancient Near Eastern Texts Relating to the Old Testament*, edited by J. B. Pritchard, 320–22. Princeton: Princeton University Press, 1969.

Alon, Yoav. "'Heart Beguiling Araby' on the Frontier of Empire: Early Anglo-Arab Relations in Transjordan." *British Journal of Middle Eastern Studies* 36, no. 1 (2009): 55–72.

———. *The Making of Jordan: Tribes, Colonialism and the Modern State.* London, New York: I. B. Tauris, 2007.

'Alush, Naji, ed. *Mukhtarat Qawmiyya li Muhammad 'Izzat Darwaza*. Beirut: Markaz Dirasat al-Wihda al-Arabiyya, 1988.

Amadouny, Vartan. "Infrastructural Development under the British Mandate." In *Village, Steppe and State: The Social Origins of Modern Jordan*, edited by Eugene Rogan and Tariq Tell, 128–61. London: British Academic Press, 1994.

'Anabtawi, Wasfi, Sa'id Dura, Sa'id al-Sabagh, and Husni Fariz. *al-Mamlaka al-Urduniyya al-Hashimiyya* (The Hashemite Jordanian Kingdom). Amman: Istiqlal Library, 1953.

Anderson, Benedict. *Imagined Communities*. Rev. ed. New York: Verso Press, 1991.

Anderson, Betty S. *The American University of Beirut: Liberal Education and Arab Nationalism*. Austin: University of Texas Press, 2011.

———. *Nationalist Voices in Jordan: The Street and the State*. Austin: University of Texas Press, 2005.

———. "Writing the Nation: Textbooks of the Hashemite Kingdom of Jordan." *Comparative Studies of South Asia, Africa and the Middle East* 21, nos. 1 and 2 (2001): 5–14.

Antonius, George. *The Arab Awakening: The Story of the Arab National Movement*. New York: Simon, 1939.

al-'Arif, 'Arif. *Tarikh Bir Sab'a wa Qaba'ilu* (The History of Bir Saba'a and Its Tribes). al-Quds: Matb'a Bayt al-Maqdis, 1934.

al-Asad, Mohammad. "al-Mushatta Facade at Berlin." In *The Umayyads: The Rise of Islamic Art*, edited by Ina Kehrberg, 117. Museum with No Frontiers, Islamic Art in the Mediterranean. Amman: al-Faris, 2000.

al-Asad, Mohammed, Ghazi Bisheh, Ina Kehrberg, Lara G. Tohme, Fawzi Zayadine, and Bill Lyons. *The Umayyads: The Rise of Islamic Art*. Museum with No Frontiers, Islamic Art in the Mediterranean. Amman: al-Faris, 2000.

Aubin, Melissa M. "Jerash." In *The Oxford Encyclopedia of Archaeology in the Near East*, edited by E. Meyers et al., 215–19. New York: Oxford University Press, 1997.

Ayalon, Ami. "The Hashemites, T. E. Lawrence and the Postage Stamps of the Hijaz." In *The Hashemites in the Modern Arab World: Essays in Honour of the Late Professor Uriel Dann*, edited by Asher Susser and Aryeh Shmuelevitz, 15–30. London: Frank Cass, 1995.

———. "Modern Texts and Their Readers in Late Ottoman Palestine." *Middle Eastern Studies* 38, no. 4 (2002): 17–40.

———. *Reading Palestine: Printing and Literacy, 1900–1948*. Austin: University of Texas Press, 2004.

Badran, Arwa. "The Excluded Past in Jordanian Formal Education: The Introduction of Archaeology." In *New Perspectives in Global Public Archaeology*, edited by K. Okamura and A. Matsuda, 197–215. New York: Springer Science+Business Media, 2001.

al-Bakhit, Muhammad 'Adnan. "Taqdim" (Introduction). In *Dirasat fi Makhtutat al-Bahr al-Mayt* (Studies in the Dead Sea Scrolls), edited by 'Umar al-Ghul. Amman: al-Lajna al-Urduniyya li Makhtutat al-Bahr al-Mayt, Wizarat al-T'alim al-'Ali wa al-Bahth al-'Ilmi (Jordanian Committee for the Dead Sea Scrolls, Ministry of Higher Education and Scientific Research), 2012.

Bank, Andre, and Oliver Schlumberger. "Jordan: Between Regime Survival and Economic Reform." In *Arab Elites: Negotiating the Politics of Change*, edited by Volker Perthes, 35–60. Boulder: Lynne Rienner, 2004.

Baram, Amatzia. *Culture, History, and Ideology in the Formation of Ba'athist Iraq*. New York: St. Martin's Press, 1991.

al-Barghuthi, 'Umar al-Salih, and Khalil Tutah. *Tarikh Filastin*. al-Quds: Matb'a Bayt al-Maqdis, 1923.

Bartlett, John R. *Mapping Jordan through Two Millennia*, edited by David M. Jacobson, Palestine Exploration Fund Annual. Leeds: Maney, 2008.

Barton, George Aaron. *Semitic and Hamitic Origins, Social and Religious*. Philadelphia: University of Pennsylvania Press, 1934.

Ben-Arieh, Yehoshua, and Moshe Davis. *Jerusalem in the Mind of the Western World, 1800–1948*. Westport: Praeger Press, 1997.

Bendiner, Kenneth Paul. "David Roberts in the Near East: Social and Religious Themes." *Art History* 6 (1983): 67–81.

Ben-Yehuda, Nachman. *The Masada Myth: Collective Memory and Mythmaking in Israel*. Madison: University of Wisconsin Press, 1995.

Berkes, Niyazi. *The Development of Secularism in Turkey*. London: Hurst, 1964.

Bernhardsson, Magnus T. *Reclaiming a Plundered Past: Archaeology and Nation Building in Modern Iraq*. Austin: University of Texas Press, 2005.

Boullata, Kamal. *Palestinian Art*. London: Saqi Books, 2009.

Bradley, Mark, ed. *Classics and Imperialism in the British Empire*. Oxford: Oxford University Press, 2010.

Brand, Laurie. "Development in Wadi Rum? State Bureaucracy, External Funders and Civil Society." *International Journal of Middle East Studies* 33, no. 4 (2001): 571–90.

———. "'In the Beginning Was the State . . .': The Quest for Civil Society in Jordan." In *Civil Society in the Middle East*, edited by A. R. Norton, 148–85. Social, Economic and Political Studies of the Middle East. Leiden: E. J. Brill, 1995.

———. *Jordan's Inter-Arab Relations: The Political Economy of Alliance Making*. New York: Columbia University Press, 1994.

Breasted, Charles. *Pioneer to the Past: The Story of James Henry Breasted, Archaeologist*. New York: Charles Scribner's Sons, 1943.

Breasted, James Henry. *Ancient Times: A History of the Early World*. 2nd ed. Boston: Ginn, 1944.

Brendon, Piers. *Thomas Cook: 150 Years of Popular Tourism*. London: Secker and Warburg, 1991.

Brown, Jonathan M., and Laurence Kutler. *Nelson Glueck: Biblical Archaeologist and President of the Hebrew Union College-Jewish Institute of Religion*. Cincinnati: Hebrew Union College Press, 2006.

Burckhardt, John Lewis. *Travels in Syria and the Holy Land*. New York: AMS Press, 1983.

Campos, Michelle U. *Ottoman Brothers: Muslims, Christians, and Jews in Early Twentieth-Century Palestine*. Stanford: Stanford University Press, 2011.

Canaan, Tawfiq. "Haunted Springs and Water Demons in Palestine." *Journal of the Palestine Oriental Society* 1 (1921).

———. "Modern Palestinian Beliefs and Practices Relating to God." *Journal of the Palestine Oriental Society* 14 (1934).

————. "Mohammedan Saints and Sanctuaries in Palestine." *Journal of the Palestine Oriental Society* 7 (1927).

————. *Notes on Studies in the Topography and Folklore of Petra.* Jerusalem: Beyt ul-Makdes Press, 1930.

————. "The Palestinian Arab House: Its Architecture and Folklore." *Journal of the Palestine Oriental Society* 12 (1932).

————. "Plant-Lore in Palestinian Superstition." *Journal of the Palestine Oriental Society* 8 (1928).

————. "The Saqr Bedouin of Bisan," *Journal of the Palestine Oriental Society* 16 (1936).

————. "Water and 'The Water of Life.'" *Journal of the Palestine Oriental Society* 9 (1929).

Caplan, Neil. *Palestine Jewry and the Arab Question, 1917–1925.* London: Frank Cass, 1978.

Chadwick, Owen. *The Secularization of the European Mind in the Nineteenth Century.* Cambridge: Cambridge University Press, 1990.

Challis, Debbie. "'The Ablest Race': The Ancient Greeks in Victorian Racial Theory." In *Classics and Imperialism in the British Empire,* edited by Mark Bradley, 94–120. Oxford: Oxford University Press, 2010.

————. *From the Harpy Tomb to the Wonders of Ephesus: British Archaeologists in the Ottoman Empire, 1840–1880.* London: Duckworth, 2008.

Chatelard, Géraldine, and Jean-Michel de Tarragon. *L'Empire et le Royaume: La Jordanie Vue par l'École Biblique et Archaéologique Française de Jérusalem (1893–1935).* Amman: Insitut Française de Proche Orient, 2006.

Choueiri, Youssef M. *Arab Nationalism: A History.* Oxford: Blackwell, 2000.

Chugg, Andrew Michael. *The Lost Tomb of Alexander the Great.* London: Periplus, 2005.

Cleveland, William. *Islam against the West: Shakib Arslan and the Campaign for Islamic Nationalism.* Austin: University of Texas Press, 1985.

Cobbing, Felicity J. "The American Palestine Exploration Society and the Survey of Eastern Palestine." *Palestine Exploration Quarterly* 137, no. 1 (2005): 9–21.

Cobbing, Felicity J., and Jonathan N. Tubb. "Before the Rockefeller: The First Palestine Museum in Jerusalem." In *Tutela, Conservazione e Valorizzazione del Patrimonio Culturale della Palestina, Mediterraneum,* edited by F. Maniscalco, 69–79. Naples: Massa Editore, 2005.

Colla, Elliott. *Conflicted Antiquities: Egyptology, Egyptomania, Egyptian Modernity.* Durham: Duke University Press, 2007.

Cook's Traveller's Handbook to Palestine, Syria and Iraq. London: Simpkin Marshall, 1934.

Coote, Robert B. "Hapiru, Apiru." In *Eerdmans Dictionary of the Bible,* edited by David Noel Freedman, 549–51. Grand Rapids: William B. Eerdmans, 2000.

Coote, Robert B., and Keith W. Whitelam. *The Emergence of Early Israel in Historical Perspective.* Sheffield: Almond Press, 1987.

Corbett, Elena D. "Hashemite Antiquity and Modernity: Iconography in Neoliberal Jordan." *Studies in Ethnicity and Nationalism* 11, no. 2 (2011): 163–93.

————. "History Lessons in the City of Dawud: Jordan's Past and Complexities of Identity beyond Silwan." *Middle Eastern Studies* 47, no. 4 (2011): 587–603.

————. "Jordan First: A History of the Intellectual and Political Economy of Jordanian Antiquity." PhD diss., University of Chicago, 2009.

————. "Leaving a Stamp on History." *Emerging Jordan, 2006*. Oxford Business Group, 2006. 155–57.

al-Dabbagh, Mustafa Murad. *al-Mujaz fi Tarikh Filastin mundhu Aqdam al-Azmana hata al-Yawm* (A Concise History of Palestine from the Most Ancient Times to the Present). 2nd ed. Beirut: Ministry of Education, 1957.

Daher, Rami Farouk. "Tourism, Heritage, and Urban Transformations in Jordan and Lebanon: Emerging Actors and Global-Local Juxtapositions." In *Tourism in the Middle East: Continuity, Change and Transformation*, edited by Rami Farouk Daher, 263–307. Clevedon, Buffalo, Toronto: Channel View Publications, 2007.

————. "Urban Regeneration/Heritage Tourism Endeavours: The Case of Salt, Jordan. 'Local Actors, International Donors, and the State.'" *International Journal of Heritage Studies* 11, no. 4 (2005): 289–307.

al-Dajani, Yʻaqub, Yunis al-Suqi, ʻAbd al-Latif al-Barguthi, ʻIssa Abu Shaykha, ʻAdnan Lutfi, Nimr al-Madi, and Ibrahim ʻUthman. *Watani al-Saghir* (My Little Country). Amman: Ministry of Education, 1966, 1969.

Dalman, Gustav. "The Search for the Temple Treasure at Jerusalem." *Palestine Exploration Quarterly* (January 1912): 35–39.

Dann, Uriel. "The United States and the Recognition of Transjordan, 1946–1949." In *Studies in the History of Transjordan, 1920–1949: The Making of a State*, 93–116. Boulder: Westview Press, 1984.

Darwaza, Muhammad ʻIzzat. "Durus al-Tarikh al-ʻArabi min Aqdam al-Azmina hata Alan" (Studies in Arab History from the Most Ancient Epochs to the Present). In *Mukhtarat Qawmiyya li Muhammad ʻIzzat Darwaza* (Nationalist Selections by Muhammad ʻIzzat Darwazeh), edited by Naji ʻAlush, 55–221. Beirut: Markaz Dirasat al-Wihda al-Arabiyya, 1988.

Davis, John. *The Landscape of Belief: Encountering the Holy Land in Nineteenth-Century American Art and Culture*. Princeton: Princeton University Press, 1996.

Davis, Miriam C. *Dame Kathleen Kenyon: Digging up the Holy Land*. Walnut Creek: Left Coast Press, 2008.

Davis, Rochelle. *Palestinian Village Histories*. Stanford: Stanford University Press, 2011.

Davis, Thomas W. *Shifting Sands: The Rise and Fall of Biblical Archaeology*. Oxford, New York: Oxford University Press, 2004.

Dawn, C. Ernest. "The Formation of Pan-Arab Ideology in the Interwar Years." *International Journal of Middle East Studies* 20 (1988): 67–91.

————. *From Ottomanism to Arabism: Essays on the Origins of Arab Nationalism*. Urbana: University of Illinois Press, 1973.

Deringil, Selim. "'They Live in a State of Nomadism and Savagery': The Late Ottoman Empire and the Post-Colonial Debate." *Comparative Studies in Society and History* 45, no. 2 (2003): 311–42.

————. *The Well-Protected Domains: Ideology and the Legitimation of Power in the Ottoman Empire, 1876–1909*. London: I. B. Tauris, 1998.

Dever, William G. "Biblical Archaeology." In *Oxford Encyclopedia of the Ancient Near East*, edited by E. Meyers, 315–19. Oxford: Oxford University Press, 1997.

Díaz-Andreu, Margarita. *A World History of Nineteenth-Century Archaeology*. Oxford: Oxford University Press, 2007.

Di-Capua, Yoav. *Gatekeepers of the Arab Past: Historians and History-Writing in Twentieth-Century Egypt*. Berkeley: University of California Press, 2009.

al-Dura, Sa'id, 'Abd al-Rahim Mur'ib, Sadiq 'Awda, and 'Abd al-Bari al-Shaykh Dura. *al-Tarikh al-'Arabi al-Hadith* (Modern Arab History). Amman: Ministry of Education, 1973.

Elad, A. "Why Did 'Abd al-Malik Build the Dome of the Rock? A Re-Examination of Muslim Sources." In *Bayt al-Maqdis: 'Abd al-Malik's Jerusalem*, edited by J. Raby and J. Johns, 33–58. Oxford: Oxford University Press, 1992.

Elshakry, Marwa. *Reading Darwin in Arabic, 1860–1950*. Chicago: University of Chicago Press, 2013.

Enan, Mohammad Abdullah. *Ibn Khaldun: His Life and Works*. Kuala Lumpur: The Other Press, 2007.

Farag, Nadia. "The Lewis Affair and the Fortunes of al-Muqtataf." *Middle Eastern Studies* 8, no. 1 (1972): 73–83.

Farajat, Suleiman. "The Participation of Local Communities in the Tourism Industry at Petra." In *Tourism and Archaeological Heritage Management at Petra: Driver to Development of Destruction?* edited by Douglas Comer, 145–65. New York: Springer Verlag, 2012.

al-Fatan, Ibrahim, Husni Fariz, Sayyah al-Rusan, and Sa'id Dura. *al-Qira'a al-Hashimiyya* (The Hashemite Reader). Amman: Ministry of Education, 1966.

Feinman, Peter Douglas. *William Foxwell Albright and the Origins of Biblical Archaeology*. Berrien Springs, MI: Andrews University Press, 2004.

Findley, Carter V. "The Evolution of the System of Provincial Administration as Viewed from the Center." In *Palestine in the Late Ottoman Period: Political, Social and Economic Transformation*, edited by David Kushner, 3–29. Jerusalem: Yad Izhak Ben-Zvi Press, 1986.

Fischbach, Michael R. *State, Society and Land in Transjordan*. Leiden: Brill, 2000.

Fischer, A. "Kahtan." In *Encyclopedia of Islam*, edited by P. Bearman, Th. Bianquis, C. E. Bosworth, E. Van Donzel, and W. P. Heinrichs. 2nd ed. Brill Online, 2012.

Fortna, Benjamin. *Imperial Classroom: Islam, the State, and Education in the Late Ottoman Empire*. Oxford: Oxford University Press, 2002.

———. *Learning to Read in the Late Ottoman Empire and the Early Turkish Republic*. New York: Palgrave Macmillan, 2011.

Friedman, Richard Elliott. *Who Wrote the Bible?* New York: Summit Books, 1987.

Garstang, John. "Government of Trans-Jordan Antiquities Bulletin No. 1." Amman: Department of Antiquities, Trans-Jordan, 1926.

Gelvin, James. *Divided Loyalties: Nationalism and Mass Politics in Syria at the Close of Empire*. Berkeley: University of California Press, 1998.

Gershoni, Israel, and James Jankowski. *Commemorating the Nation: Collective Memory, Public Commemoration and National Identity in Twentieth-Century Egypt*. Chicago: Middle East Documentation Center, 2004.

———. *Egypt, Islam and the Arabs: The Search for Egyptian Nationhood, 1900–1930*. New York: Oxford University Press, 1986.

Gibson, Shimon. "British Archaeological Institutions in Mandatory Palestine, 1917–1948." *Palestine Exploration Quarterly* 131 (1999): 115–43.

Given, Michael. "Inventing the Eteocypriots: Imperialist Archaeology and the Manipulation of Ethnic Identity." *Journal of Mediterranean Archaeology* 11, no. 1 (1998): 3-29.

Glueck, Nelson. *Deities and Dolphins: The Story of the Nabataeans.* New York: Farrar, Straus, and Giroux, 1965.

———. *The Other Side of the Jordan.* Cambridge: American Schools of Oriental Research, 1970.

Goitein, S. D. *Jews and Arabs: Their Contacts through the Ages.* New York: Schocken Books, 1964.

Goode, James F. *Negotiating for the Past: Archaeology, Nationalism, and Diplomacy in the Middle East, 1919-1941.* Austin: University of Texas Press, 2007.

Goren, Haim. "The German Catholic 'Holy Sepulchre Society': Activities in Palestine." In *Jerusalem in the Mind of the Western World, 1800-1948,* edited by Yehoshua Ben-Arieh and Moshe Davis, 155-72. Westport: Praeger Press, 1997.

Grabar, Oleg. "Kubbat al-Sakhra." In *Encyclopedia of Islam,* edited by P. Bearman, Th. Bianquis, C. E. Bosworth, E. van Donzel, and W. P. Heinrichs. 2nd ed. Brill Online, 2010.

Grabill, Joseph L. *Protestant Diplomacy and the Near East: Missionary Influence on American Policy, 1810-1927.* Minneapolis: University of Minnesota Press, 1971.

Graves, Philip P., ed. *Memoirs of King Abdullah of Transjordan.* London: Jonathan Cape, 1950.

Grove, George. "Mr. Grove's Letter to the 'Times.'" *Palestine Exploration Quarterly* (1870): 170-71.

Haim, Sylvia, ed. *Arab Nationalism: An Anthology.* Berkeley: University of California Press, 1976.

Hallote, Rachel S. "Before Albright: Charles Torrey, James Montgomery, and American Biblical Archaeology, 1907-1922." *Near Eastern Archaeology* 74, no. 3 (2011): 156-69.

———. *Bible, Map and Spade: The American Palestine Exploration Society, Frederick Jones Bliss, and the Forgotten Story of Early American Biblical Archaeology.* Piscataway: Gorgias Press, 2006.

Hammond, Philip C. "Petra." In *The Oxford Encyclopedia of Archaeology in the Near East,* edited by E. Meyers, 303-6. Oxford: Oxford University Press, 1997.

Hanssen, Jens. "Imperial Discourses and an Ottoman Excavation in Lebanon." In *Baalbek: Image and Monument, 1898-1998,* edited by Helene Sader, Thomas Scheffler, and Angelika Neuwirth, 157-72. Beirut: Franz Steiner Verlag, 1998.

Hanssen, Jens, Thomas Philipp, and Stefan Weber, eds. *The Empire in the City: Arab Provincial Capitals in the Late Ottoman Empire.* Beirut: Ergon Verlag Wurzburg, 2002.

Harding, G. Lankester. *The Antiquities of Jordan.* Rev. ed. New York: Praeger, 1967.

———. *Jerash, a Brief History.* Amman: Jordan Distribution Agency, 1973.

Hashemite Kingdom of Jordan Ministry of National Economy. *Statistical Yearbook 1958.* Vol. 9. Jerusalem: Greek Convent Press.

———. *Statistical Yearbook 1964.* Vol. 15. Amman: Department of Statistics Press.

———. *Statistical Yearbook 1965.* Vol. 16. Amman: Department of Statistics Press.

Havrelock, Rachel S. *River Jordan: The Mythology of a Dividing Line.* Chicago: University of Chicago Press, 2011.

Hazbun, Waleed. *Beaches, Ruins, Resorts: The Politics of Tourism in the Arab World*. Minneapolis: University of Minnesota Press, 2008.

Heller, B., and D. B. MacDonald. "Musa." In *Encyclopedia of Islam*, edited by P. Bearman, Th. Bianquis, C. E. Bosworth, E. Van Donzel, and W. P. Heinrichs. 2nd ed. Brill Online, 2012.

Herzog, Christoph. "Nineteenth Century Baghdad through Ottoman Eyes." In *The Empire in the City: Arab Provincial Capitals in the Late Ottoman Empire*, edited by Jens Hanssen, Thomas Philipp, and Stefan Weber, 311-28. Beirut: Ergon Verlag Wurzburg, 2002.

Hess, Richard. "Chaldeans." In *The Anchor Bible Dictionary*, edited by David Noel Freedman, 886-87. New York: Bantam Doubleday Dell, 1992.

———. "Joktan." In *The Anchor Bible Dictionary*, edited by David Noel Freedman, 935. New York: Bantam Doubleday Dell, 1992.

Hill, Gray. "A Journey to Petra—1896." *Palestine Exploration Quarterly* (January–April 1897): 35-44, 134-44.

al-Hindawi, Dhuqan. *al-Qadiyya al-Filastiniyya* (The Palestinian Issue). Amman: Ministry of Education, 1966.

al-Hindawi, Dhuqan, Musa 'Ali al-Ghul, and Salam al-Khuri. *al-Jiyughrafiyya al-Iqtisadiyya* (Economic Geography). Amman: Ministry of Education, 1966, 1968.

Hodson, Yolande. "An Introduction to the Publication of the Map and Memoirs." In *Survey of Western Palestine including a Survey of Eastern Palestine, 1881: Essays to Accompany the Archive Editions Facsimile*, 33-71. London: Archive Editions in association with the Palestine Exploration Fund, 1999.

Hoffmeier, James K. *Israel in Egypt*. New York, Oxford: Oxford University Press, 1996.

Hopkins, I. W. J. "Nineteenth-Century Maps of Palestine: Dual-Purpose Historical Evidence." *Imago Mundi* 22 (1968): 30-36.

Horsfield, George. *Official Guide to Jerash with Plan*. Amman: Government of Transjordan Department of Antiquities, 1930.

Hourani, Albert. *Arabic Thought in the Liberal Age, 1798-1939*. Cambridge: Cambridge University Press, 1983.

———. "Ottoman Reform and the Politics of the Notables." In *The Modern Middle East*, edited by Albert Hourani, Philip S. Khoury, and Mary Wilson, 83-109. London: I. B. Tauris, 1993.

Hoyland, Robert G. *Arabia and the Arabs: From the Bronze Age to the Coming of Islam*. London: Routledge, 2001.

Hurvitz, Nimrod. "Muhibb al-Din al-Khatib's Semitic Wave Theory and Pan-Arabism." *Middle Eastern Studies* 29, no. 1 (1993): 118-34.

Ibrahim, Moawiyya. *Dirasat fi Athar Filastin* (Studies in the Archaeology of Palestine). Amman: Dar al-Baraka, 2010.

Jacobson, Abigail. *From Empire to Empire: Jerusalem between Ottoman and British Rule*. Syracuse: Syracuse University Press, 2011.

Jacobson, David. "Introduction to the Palestine Exploration Fund Explorations at Jerusalem, 1867-1870." In *Survey of Western Palestine including a Survey of Eastern Palestine, 1881: Essays to Accompany the Archive Editions Facsimile*, 1-31. London: Archive Editions in association with the Palestine Exploration Fund, 1999.

Jacobson, David, and Felicity Cobbing. "'A Record of Discovery and Adventure':

Claude Reignier Conder's Contributions to the Exploration of Palestine." *Near Eastern Archaeology* 68, no. 4 (2005): 166-79.

Jankowski, James, and Israel Gershoni, eds. *Rethinking Nationalism in the Arab Middle East*. New York: Columbia University Press, 1997.

Johns, C. N. *Pilgrim's Castle ('Atlit), David's Tower (Jerusalem) and Qal'at Ar-Rabad ('Ajloun): Three Middle Eastern Castles from the Time of the Crusades*, edited by Denys Pringle. Aldershot: Ashgate Variorum, 1997.

Kaicker, Abhishek. "Visions of Modernity in Revisions of the Past: Altaf Hussain Hali and the 'Legacy of the Greeks.'" In *Classics and Imperialism in the British Empire*, edited by Mark Bradley, 231-48. Oxford: Oxford University Press, 2010.

Karp, Jonathan, and Adam Sutcliffe. "Introduction: A Brief History of Philosemitism." In *Philosemitism in History*, edited by Jonathan Karp and Adam Sutcliffe, 1-26. Cambridge: Cambridge University Press, 2011.

————, eds. *Philosemitism in History*. Cambridge: Cambridge University Press, 2011.

Karpat, Kemal. *The Politicization of Islam: Reconstructing Identity, State, Faith and Community in the Late Ottoman State*. Oxford: Oxford University Press, 2001.

Katz, Kimberly. *Jordanian Jerusalem: Holy Places and National Spaces*. Gainesville: University Press of Florida, 2005.

————. "Jordanian Jerusalem: Postage Stamps and Identity Construction." *Jerusalem Quarterly* no. 5 (1999): 14-26.

Katzenstein, H. J. "Philistines." In *The Anchor Bible Dictionary*, edited by David Noel Freedman, 326-28. New York: Bantam Doubleday Dell, 1992.

Kaufman, Asher. *Reviving Phoenicia: In Search of Identity in Lebanon*. New York: I. B. Tauris, 2004.

Kayalı, Hasan. *Arabs and Young Turks: Ottomanism, Arabism, and Islamism in the Ottoman Empire*. Berkeley: University of California Press, 1997.

Kersel, Morag. "License to Sell: The Legal Trade of Antiquities in Israel." PhD diss., Lucy Cavendish College, Cambridge University, 2006.

————. "When Communities Collide: Competing Claims for Archaeological Objects in the Marketplace." *Archaeologies: Journal of the World Archaeological Congress* 7, no. 3 (2011): 518-537.

Khalidi, Rashid. *Palestinian Identity: The Construction of Modern National Consciousness*. New York: Columbia University Press, 1997.

Khalidi, Rashid, Lisa Anderson, Muhammad Muslih, and Reeva Simon, eds. *The Origins of Arab Nationalism*. New York: Columbia University Press, 1991.

Khouri, Rami. *The Desert Castles: A Brief Guide to the Antiquities*. Amman: al-Kutba, 1988.

Khoury, Philip S. *Urban Notables and Arab Nationalism: The Politics of Damascus, 1860–1920*. Cambridge: Cambridge University Press, 1983.

King, Philip J. *American Archaeology in the Mideast: A History of the American Schools of Oriental Research*. Philadelphia: American Schools of Oriental Research, 1983.

Klein, Rev. F. A. "The Original Discovery of the Moabite Stone." *Palestine Exploration Quarterly* (March–June 1870): 281-83.

Kletter, Raz. *Just Past? The Making of Israeli Archaeology*. London: Equinox, 2006.

Koçak, Alev. *The Ottoman Empire and Archaeological Excavations: Ottoman Policy from 1840–1906, Foreign Archaeologists, and the Formation of the Ottoman Museum*. Istanbul: Isis Press, 2011.

Kuklick, Bruce. *Puritans in Babylon*. Princeton: Princeton University Press, 1996.
al-Kurd, 'Abbas. *Tarikh al-'Arab wa al-Muslimin* (The History of the Arabs and the Muslims). Amman: Ministry of Education, 1970.
al-Kurd, 'Abbas, Radi 'Abd al-Hawi, and 'Abd al-Rahman Jaber. *al-Hadarat al-Qadima fi al-Sharq wa al-Gharb* (The Ancient Civilizations in the East and West). Amman: Ministry of Education, 1968.
al-Kurd, 'Abbas, Mahmud Rushdan, Yusuf Jum'a, 'Abd al-Hassan Jaber, and Husni 'Aish. *al-Mujtam'a al-'Arabi al-Urduni* (The Jordanian Arab Society). Amman: Ministry of Education, 1967.
Layne, Linda L. *Home and Homeland: The Dialogics of Tribal and National Identities in Jordan*. Princeton: Princeton University Press, 1994.
Ledger, R. T. *Philatelic History of Jordan, 1922–1953*. Amman, 1953.
Leval, Gerard. "Ancient Inscription Refers to Birth of Israelite Monarchy." *Biblical Archaeology Review* 38, no. 3 (2012).
Lewis, Bernard. *The Arabs in History*. London: Hutchinson University Library, 1966.
———. "Ibn Khaldun in Turkey." In *Studies in Islamic History and Civilization*, edited by M. Sharon, 527–30. Jerusalem: Cana, 1986.
Lewis, Norman N. *Nomads and Settlers in Syria and Jordan, 1800–1980*. Cambridge Middle East Library. Cambridge: Cambridge University Press, 1987.
Luke, Harry Charles, and Edward Keith-Roach, eds. *The Handbook of Palestine and Trans-Jordan*. London: MacMillan, 1934.
Lynch, William Francis. *Narrative of the United States' Expedition to the River Jordan and the Dead Sea*. Philadelphia: Lea and Blanchard, 1849.
MacKenzie, Duncan. "Dibon: The City of King Mesha and of the Moabite Stone." *Palestine Exploration Quarterly* (April 1913): 57–79.
al-Madi, Munib, and Suleyman Musa. *Tarikh al-Urdun fi al-Qarn al-'Ashreen, 1900–1959* (The History of Jordan in the Twentieth Century, 1900–1959). Amman: Maktabat al-Muhtasab, 1959. Reprint, 1988.
Maffi, Irene. "New Museographic Trends in Jordan: The Strengthening of the Nation." In *Jordan in Transition*, edited by George Joffe, 208–24. New York: Palgrave, 2002.
———. *Pratiques du Patrimoine et Politiques de la Mémoire en Jordanie: Entre Histoire Dynastique et Récits Communautaires*. Lausanne: l'Université de Lausanne, 2003.
Mahadin, Salam. "An Economy of Legitimating Discourses: The Invention of the Bedouin and Petra and National Signifiers in Jordan." *Critical Arts* 21, no. 1 (2007): 86–105.
———. "Tourism and Power Relations in Jordan: Contested Discourses and Semiotic Shifts." In *Tourism in the Middle East: Continuity, Change and Transformation*, edited by Rami Farouk Daher, 308–25. Clevedon, Buffalo, Toronto: Channel View Publications, 2007.
Makdisi, Saree. *Romantic Imperialism: Universal Empire and the Culture of Modernity*. Cambridge: Cambridge University Press, 1998.
Makdisi, Ussama. "After 1860: Debating Religion, Reform, and Nationalism in the Ottoman Empire." *International Journal of Middle East Studies* 34, no. 4 (2002): 601–17.
———. *Artillery of Heaven: American Missionaries and the Failed Conversion of the Middle East*. Ithaca: Cornell University Press, 2008.
———. *The Culture of Sectarianism: Community, History and Violence in Nineteenth-*

Century Ottoman Lebanon. Berkeley, Los Angeles: University of California Press, 2000.

———. "Ottoman Orientalism." *American Historical Review* 107, no. 3 (2002): 768–96.

Manners, Ian R. "The Development of Irrigation Agriculture in the Hashemite Kingdom of Jordan, with Particular Reference to the Jordan Valley." PhD diss., Oxford University, 1969.

Marchand, Suzanne L. *Down from Olympus: Archaeology and Philhellenism in Germany, 1750–1970.* Princeton: Princeton University Press, 1996.

Markoe, Glenn. *Phoenicians.* London: British Museum Press, 2000.

Marrus, Michael R. *The Unwanted: European Refugees from the First World War through the Cold War.* Philadelphia: Temple University Press, 2002.

Massad, Joseph A. *Colonial Effects: The Making of National Identity in Jordan.* New York: Columbia University Press, 2001.

Mazar, Amihai. *Archaeology of the Land of the Bible, 10,000–586 B.C.E.* New York: Doubleday, 1990.

Mazar, Binyamin, ed. *Journal of the Israel Exploration Society.* Nelson Glueck Memorial Volume. Jerusalem: Israel Exploration Society, 1975.

Mazza, Roberto. *Jerusalem from the Ottomans to the British.* London: I. B. Tauris, 2009.

McQuitty, Alison. "George Horsfield." In *The Oxford Encyclopedia of Archaeology in the Near East,* edited by E. Meyers, 90. New York: Oxford University Press, 1997.

Mendenhall, George. "Amorites." In *The Anchor Bible Dictionary,* edited by David Noel Freedman, 199–202. New York: Bantam Doubleday Dell, 1992.

Merrill, Selah. *East of the Jordan: A Record of Travel and Observation in the Countries of Moab Gilead and Bashan during the Years 1875–1877.* New York: Charles Scribner's Sons, 1881. Reprint, Darf, 1986.

Meyers, Eric M. "American Schools of Oriental Research." In *The Oxford Encyclopedia of the Ancient Near East,* edited by E. Meyers, 94–98. Oxford: Oxford University Press, 1997.

Mitchell, Timothy. *Colonising Egypt.* Cambridge: Cambridge University Press, 1988.

Moore, James R. *The Post-Darwinian Controversies: A Study of the Protestant Struggle to Come to Terms with Darwin in Great Britain and America, 1870–1900.* Cambridge: Cambridge University Press, 1979.

Moscrop, John James. *Measuring Jerusalem: The Palestine Exploration Fund and British Interests in the Holy Land.* London: Leicester University Press, 2000.

Munif, Abd al-Rahman. *Story of a City: A Childhood in Amman,* translated by Samira Kawar. London: Quartet Books, 1996.

Naʿaman, Nadav. "Amarna Letters." In *The Anchor Bible Dictionary,* edited by David Noel Freedman, 174–81. New York: Bantam Doubleday Dell, 1992.

Najam, Raʾif Yusuf. *al-Hafriyyat al-Athariyya fi al-Quds* (Archaeological Excavations in Jerusalem). Amman: Dar al-Furqan, 2009.

Nasser, Riad M. *Palestinian Identity in Jordan and Israel: The Necessary "Other" in the Making of a Nation.* New York, Oxon: Routledge, 2005.

Ochsenwald, William. "Opposition to Political Centralization in South Jordan and the Hijaz, 1900–1914." In *Religion, Economy, and State in Ottoman-Arab History,* edited by William Ochsenwald, 183–92. Istanbul: Isis Press, 1998.

Owen, Roger. "British and French Military Intelligence in Syria and Palestine, 1914–

1918: Myths and Reality." *British Journal of Middle Eastern Studies* 38, no. 1 (2011): 1–6.

Özdogan, Mehmet. "Ideology and Archaeology in Turkey." In *Archaeology under Fire: Nationalism, Politics and Heritage in the Eastern Mediterranean and Middle East*, edited by Lynn Meskell, 111–23. London: Routledge, 1998.

Palestine and Transjordan, edited by Naval Intelligence Division. London: Kegan Paul, 2006.

Palmer, E. H. "The Desert of the Tíh and the Country of Moab." *Palestine Exploration Quarterly* (1870): 3–80.

Parmenter, Barbara McKean. *Giving Voice to Stones: Place and Identity in Palestinian Literature*. Austin: University of Texas Press, 1994.

Peake, F. G. *A History of Jordan and Its Tribes*. Coral Gables: University of Miami Press, 1958.

Peckham, Brian. "Phoenicians." In *The Anchor Bible Dictionary*, edited by David Noel Freedman, 349–57. New York: Bantam Doubleday Dell, 1992.

Provence, Michael. *The Great Syrian Revolt and the Rise of Arab Nationalism*. Austin: University of Texas Press, 2005.

———. "Ottoman Modernity, Colonialism, and Insurgency in the Interwar Arab East." *International Journal of Middle East Studies* 43, no. 2 (2011): 205–25.

Radwan, Abdullah, and Sadik I. Odeh. *Arar: The Poet and Lover of Jordan*. Amman: Greater Amman Municipality, 1999.

Redford, Donald. "Mernptah." In *The Anchor Bible Dictionary*, edited by David Noel Freedman, 700–701. New York: Bantam Doubleday Dell, 1992.

Reed, Stephen A. "Jebus." In *The Anchor Bible Dictionary*, vol. 3, edited by David Noel Freedman, 652–53. New York: Bantam Doubleday Dell, 1992.

Reid, Donald Malcolm. "Egyptian History through Stamps." *Muslim World* 62, no. 3 (1972): 209–29.

———. "The Symbolism of Postage Stamps: A Source for the Historian." *Journal of Contemporary History* 19, no. 2 (1984): 223–49.

———. "The Syrian Christians and Early Socialism in the Arab World." *International Journal of Middle East Studies* 5, no. 2 (1974): 177–93.

———. "Syrian Christians, the Rags-to-Riches Story, and Free Enterprise." *International Journal of Middle East Studies* 1, no. 4 (1970): 358–67.

———. *Whose Pharaohs? Archaeology, Museums, and Egyptian National Identity from Napoleon to World War I*. Berkeley: University of California Press, 2002.

Reimer, Michael J. "Becoming Urban: Town Administrations in Transjordan." *International Journal of Middle East Studies* 37 (2005): 189–211.

———. "Control of Urban Waqfs in al-Salt, Transjordan." In *Held in Trust: Uses of Waqf in the Muslim World*, edited by Pascale Ghazaleh, 103–20. Cairo: American University in Cairo, 2011.

Reisz, Emma. "Classics, Race, and Edwardian Anxieties about Empire." In *Classics and Imperialism in the British Empire*, edited by Mark Bradley, 210–28. Oxford: Oxford University Press, 2010.

Retsö, Jan. *The Arabs in Antiquity: Their History from the Assyrians to the Umayyads*. London: Routledge, 2003.

Robinson, Edward. *Biblical Researches in Palestine, Mount Sinai and Arabia Petraea. A Journal of Travels in the Year 1838, by E. Robinson and E. Smith. Undertaken in*

Reference to Biblical Geography. Drawn up from the Original Diaries with Historical Illus. by Edward Robinson. 3 vols. Boston: Crocker and Brewster, 1841.

Rogan, Eugene. "Aşiret Mektebi: Abdulhamid II's School for Tribes (1892–1907)." *International Journal of Middle East Studies* 28, no. 1 (1996): 83–107.

———. "Bringing the State Back: The Limits of Ottoman Rule in Transjordan, 1840–1910." In *Village, Steppe and State: The Social Origins of Modern Jordan,* edited by Eugene Rogan and Tariq Tell, 32–57. London: British Academic Press, 1994.

———. *Frontiers of the State in the Late Ottoman Empire: Transjordan, 1850–1921.* Cambridge: Cambridge University Press, 1999.

———. "Instant Communication: The Impact of the Telegraph in Ottoman Syria." In *The Syrian Land: Processes of Integration and Fragmentation, Bilad al-Sham from the Eighteenth to the Twentieth Century,* edited by Thomas Philipp and Birgit Schaebler, 113–28. Stuttgart: Franz Steiner Verlag, 1998.

———. "The Making of a Capital: Amman, 1918–1928." In *Amman: Ville et Société, the City and Its Society,* edited by Jean Hannoyer and Seteny Shami, 89–107. Beirut: Centre d'Études et de Recherches sur le Moyen-Orient Contemporain, 1996.

———. "The Physical Islamization of Amman." *Muslim World* 76 (1986).

Rogan, Eugene, and Tariq Tell, eds. *Village, Steppe and State: The Social Origins of Modern Jordan.* London: I. B. Tauris, 1995.

Rogers, Stephanie Stidham. *Inventing the Holy Land.* Lanham: Lexington Books, 2011.

Rook, Robert. *The 150th Anniversary of the United States' Expedition to Explore the Dead Sea and the River Jordan.* Amman: American Center of Oriental Research, 1998.

Royle, Trevor. *Glubb Pasha: The Life and Times of Sir John Bagot Glubb, Commander of the Arab Legion.* London: Abacus, 1992.

Sa'id al-Dura, 'Abbas al-Kurd, Sadiq 'Awda, Muhammad 'Ali al-Shami, and Khalil Zeki al-Dajani. *Tarikh al-Hadara al-'Arabiyya al-Islamiyya* (The History of Islamic Arab Civilization). Amman: Ministry of Education, 1965.

Salibi, Kamal. *The Bible Came from Arabia.* London: Jonathan Cape, 1985.

———. *Khafiya al-Tura wa Asrar Sha'ab Isra'il* (Secrets of the Torah and the People of Israel). London: Dar al-Saqi, 1988.

Sanders, James A., ed. *Near Eastern Archaeology in the Twentieth Century: Essays in Honor of Nelson Glueck.* Garden City: Doubleday, 1970.

Satia, Priya. *Spies in Arabia: The Great War and the Cultural Foundations of Britain's Covert Empire in the Middle East.* Oxford: Oxford University Press, 2008.

Sauer, J., and L. A. Willis. "History of the Field: Archaeology in Jordan." In *Oxford Encyclopedia of the Ancient Near East,* edited by E. Meyers, 51–56. Oxford: Oxford University Press, 1997.

Sauer, James A. "Syro-Palestinian Archaeology, History and Biblical Studies." *Biblical Archaeologist* 45, no. 4 (1982): 201–9.

———. "Transjordan in the Bronze and Iron Ages: A Critique of Glueck's Synthesis." *Bulletin of the American Schools of Oriental Research (BASOR)* 263 (1986): 1–26.

al-Sawah, Firas. *al-Hadath al-Turati wa al-Sharq al-Adna al-Qadim* (The Phenomenon of the Torah and the Ancient Near East). Damascus: Dar 'Ala' al-Din, 1999.

Schamm, Sandra. "Disinheriting Heritage: Explorations in the Contentious History of Archaeology in the Middle East." In *Archaeology and the Postcolonial Critique,* edited by Matthew Liebmann and Uzma Z. Rizvi, 165–75. Lanham: AltaMira Press, 2008.

Seale, Patrick. "Jordan Calms Fears for Scrolls." *Observer*, 4 December 1966.

Shalabi, Suhaila S., and Shadia H. al-ʿIdwan. "al-Masuhat wa al-Tanqibat al-Athariyya fi Filastin wa al-Waʿi li Abʿadiha mundhu Muntasaf al-Qarn al-Tasiʿa ʿAshar hata al-Harb al-ʿAlamiyya al-Ula" (Archaeological Surveys and Excavations in Palestine and the Awareness of Their Dimensions from the Middle of the Nineteenth Century until the First World War). *al-Majala al-Urduniyya li-l-Tarikh wa al-Athar* (Jordanian Journal for History and Archaeology) 5, no. 4 (2011): 19–61.

Shanks, Hershel. *Jerusalem's Temple Mount from Solomon to the Golden Dome.* New York: Continuum, 2007.

Shaw, Wendy K. *Possessors and Possessed: Museums, Archaeology and the Visualization of History in the Late Ottoman Empire.* Berkeley, Los Angeles: University of California Press, 2003.

Sheppard, Kathleen L. "Flinders Petrie and Eugenics at UCL." *Bulletin of the History of Archaeology* 20, no. 1 (2010).

Shlaim, Avi. *Collusion across the Jordan: King Abdullah, the Zionist Movement, and the Partition of Palestine.* New York: Columbia University Press, 1988.

Shryock, Andrew. *Nationalism and the Genealogical Imagination: Oral History and Textual Authority in Tribal Jordan.* Berkeley: University of California Press, 1997.

Silberman, Neil Asher. "Desolation and Restoration: The Impact of a Biblical Concept on Near Eastern Archaeology." *Biblical Archaeologist* 54, no. 2 (1991): 76–87.

———. *Digging for God and Country: Exploration, Archeology, and the Secret Struggle for the Holy Land, 1799–1917.* New York: Alfred A. Knopf, 1982.

———. *The Hidden Scrolls: Christianity, Judaism, and the War for the Dead Sea Scrolls.* New York: G. P. Putnam's Sons, 1994.

Somel, Selçuk Akşin. *The Modernization of Public Education in the Ottoman Empire, 1839–1908.* Leiden: Brill, 2001.

Souan, K. C. R. *Philatelic History of Jordan, Diamond Jubilee, 1920–1980.* Kuwait: Author.

———. *Philatelic History of Jordan, Stampexo Jubilee, 1920–1995.* Kuwait: Author.

Stanley Gibbons Stamp Catalogue, Part 19, Middle East. 6th ed. London: Stanley Gibbons, 2005.

Stephan, Stephan Hanna. "Animals in Palestinian Superstition." *Journal of the Palestine Oriental Society* 9 (1929).

———. "Modern Palestinian Parallels to the Song of Songs." *Journal of the Palestine Oriental Society* 2 (1922).

———. "Palestinian Animal Stories and Fables." *Journal of the Palestine Oriental Society* 3 (1923).

———. "Studies in Palestinian Customs and Folklore." *Journal of the Palestine Oriental Society* 8 (1928).

Stocking, George W. *Victorian Anthropology.* New York: Free Press, 1987.

Storrs, R. H. A. *Orientations.* 2nd ed. London: Ivor Nicholson and Watson, 1945.

Stransky, Thomas. "Origins of Western Christian Missions in Jerusalem and the Holy Land." In *Jerusalem in the Mind of the Western World, 1800–1948*, edited by Yehoshua Ben-Arieh and Moshe Davis, 137–54. Westport: Praeger Press, 1997.

Strauss, Johann. "The Disintegration of Ottoman Rule in the Syrian Territories as Viewed by German Observers." In *The Syrian Land: Processes of Integration and Fragmentation, Bilad al-Sham from the Eighteenth to the Twentieth Century*, edited by Thomas Philipp and Birgit Schaebler, 307–29. Stuttgart: Franz Steiner Verlag, 1998.

al-Tabari, Abu Jʿafar Muhammad bin Jarir bin Yazid. *Tarikh al-Rusul wa al-Muluk* (The History of the Prophets and Kings). Vol. 2. Albany: State University of New York Press.

Tamari, Salim. "Factionalism and Class Formation in Recent Palestinian History." In *Studies in the Economic and Social History of Palestine in the Nineteenth and Twentieth Centuries*, edited by Roger Owen, 177–202. Carbondale: Southern Illinois University Press, 1982.

———. *Mountain against the Sea: Essays on Palestinian Culture and Society*. Berkeley: University of California Press, 2009.

———. *Year of the Locust: A Soldier's Diary and the Erasure of Palestine's Ottoman Past*. Berkeley: University of California Press, 2011.

Tawalbeh, Mahmud, and Hassan Riyan. *Mudhakkirat fi Tarikh al-ʿArab al-Hadith* (Remarks on the Modern History of the Arabs). Amman: Ministry of Education, 1979.

Taylor, Richard Loring. *Mustafa's Journey: Verse of ʿArar, Poet of Jordan*. Irbid: Yarmouk University, 1988.

Thiel, Winfried. "Omri." In *The Anchor Bible Dictionary*, edited by D. N. Freedman, 17–20. New York: Doubleday, 1992.

Tidrick, Kathryn. *Empire and the English Character*. London: I. B. Tauris, 1990.

———. *Heart Beguiling Araby*. London: I. B. Tauris, 1990.

Trigger, Bruce G. *A History of Archaeological Thought*. Cambridge: Cambridge University Press, 1989.

Tristram, H. B. *The Land of Israel, a Journal of Travels in Palestine*. London: Society for Promoting Christian Knowledge, 1882. Reprint, Gorgias Press, 2002.

Urice, Stephen. "The Qasr Kharana Project, 1979." *Annual of the Department of Antiquities of Jordan* 25 (1981).

ʿUthman, ʾAdnan Lutfi. *al-Watan al-ʿArabi* (The Arab Nation). Amman: Ministry of Education, 1965, 1967.

Varisco, Daniel Martin. "Metaphors and Sacred History: The Genealogy of Muhammad and the Arab 'Tribe.'" *Anthropological Quarterly* 68, no. 3 (1995): 139–56.

———. *Reading Orientalism: Said and the Unsaid*. Seattle: University of Washington Press, 2007.

Vollat, François. "Elamites." In *The Anchor Bible Dictionary*, edited by David Noel Freedman, 423–29. New York: Bantam Doubleday Dell, 1992.

Warren, Charles. "The Moabite Stone: Captain Warren's First Account of the Inscription from Moab." *Palestine Exploration Quarterly* (January–March 1870): 169–82.

Wasserstein, Bernard. *The British in Palestine: The Mandatory Government and the Arab-Jewish Conflict, 1917–1929*. 2nd ed. Oxford: Basil Blackwell, 1991.

Watzinger, Carl. *Theodor Wiegand*. Munich, 1944.

Wensinck, A. J. "al-Khidr." In *Encyclopedia of Islam*, edited by P. Bearman, Th. Bianquis, C. E. Bosworth, E. Van Donzel, and W. P. Heinrichs. 2nd ed. Brill Online, 2012.

Wheeler, Brannon. *Moses in the Quran and Islamic Exegesis*. London: Routledge, 2002.

Whitelam, Keith W. *The Invention of Ancient Israel: The Silencing of Palestinian History*. London: Routledge, 1996.

Wilson, Mary C. *King Abdullah, Britain and the Making of Jordan*. Cambridge: Cambridge University Press, 1987.

Zahran, Ibrahim Ahmad, and Ibrahim Muhammad al-Faʿuri, eds. *al-Nutq al-Sami li Jalalat al-Malik al-Husayn bin Talal al-Muʿatham: Hawal Shuʾun al-Urdun al-Ijtimaʿiyya* (The Royal Speech of His Majesty King Hussein Bin Talal the Great: Regarding the Social Conditions of Jordan). Amman: Unlisted, 2000.

Zeine, Zeine N. *The Struggle for Arab Independence: Western Diplomacy and the Rise and Fall of Faisal's Kingdom in Syria*. Beirut: Khayat's, 1960.

Zuwiyya, Z. David. *Islamic Legends concerning Alexander the Great: Taken from Two Medieval Arabic Manuscripts in Madrid*. Binghamton: Global Publications, 2001.

Index

Aaron (Moses brother). *See* Harun (Aaron)

Abbasids, 240n72

'Abd al-Malik (Umayyad caliph), 131–132

Abdülhamid II (sultan in Ottoman empire), 4, 49, 53, 54–55, 61, 62, 63, 141; as caliph, 59–60; and CUP, 222n44; role of Islam, 86–87

Abdullah I (king of Jordan), 1, 17, 91, 124, 126, 127, 128, 129–131, 144, 151, 204, 243n110; assassination of, 151–152, 242n98; as deputy in Mecca, 130; efforts to make Jordan a core space, 131–144; as Emir, 8–9, 110, 125, 126, 142, 147, 148, 149, 160, 168, 204, 239n60; showdown with Philby, 107, 108; on stamps and currency, 140, 141, 145, 240n65, 242n98

Abdullah II (king of Jordan), 1, 199, 201, 202, 251n15

Abraham/Ibrahim, 42, 70, 72–73, 74, 79, 88, 98, 111, 127, 132, 153, 177; becoming the patriarch, 6; Beni Israel as first Children of Abraham, 7, 52; God of Abraham, 26, 74; languages spoken by, 75–76, 78; origin of, 175, 177, 226n103; recognition of in Islam, 72, 185. *See also* Ishaq (Isaac); Ishmael (Isma'il)

Abrahamic antiquities, 11, 18, 43, 51, 98

Abrahamic faiths, 4, 12, 60, 61, 181, 198, 199; Abrahamic history of Jerusalem, 153; Abrahamic scriptures, 123, 127, 132, 208; Abrahamic traditions, 77, 98, 116, 154, 155, 178; Children of Ibrahim (Abraham), 7, 52, 70, 72; conflation of Abrahamic and Semitic identity, 158; and the Hashemites, 9–10. *See also* Christianity; Islam and Islamism; Judaism

Abu el-Haj, Nadia, 13, 84, 171

Abu Jaber House, 203–204, 252n24

Abu Mahjoob (cartoon character), 3

Abu 'Ubayda ibn al-Jarrah, 208

Acre, 159

ADAJ. *See Annual of the Department of Antiquities of Jordan*

'Adnan, progenitor of northern Arabs, 72, 118, 175

'Adnaniyeen Arabs, 175

Afghani, Jamal al-Din al-, 82–83

Ahab (king of ancient Israel), 171

ahl al-kitab (People of the Book), 60, 131. *See also* Christianity; Judaism

Ain Ghazal statues, 201

Ajloun (district in Jordan), 91, 131, 143, 148, 192. *See also* Jabal Ajloun

Ajloun Castle, 90, 109, 140, 143, 168, 188, 192

Akkadians, 79, 179

Albright, William Foxwell, 47, 111–112

Alexander Romance and Islam, 224n77
Alexander the Great, 71, 224n75, 231n65
Alexandria (Egypt), 71, 76, 224n75
Allenby, Edmund, 91
Allenby Bridge, 140, 143, 187, 241n82
Alon, Yoav, 13
al-Amarna, Tell, 78
Amarna Letters, 78, 226n107
American Palestine Exploration Society (APES), 37, 40, 41, 42, 45
American Point IV Program, 182
American Schools of Oriental Research (ASOR), 45, 47, 111, 112
American University of Beirut, 66, 216n74, 248n76. *See also* Syrian Protestant College
Amman (city), 2, 126, 209; as "Arab Culture Capital," 3; during British Mandate, 107, 108–109; Greater Amman Municipality, 203; Hashemites governing from, 10, 17, 125, 148, 153, 157, 158–159, 166, 186, 239n60; hotel bombings in 2005, 3; "liberalization" since 1990, 204; tourism in, 90, 142, 184, 186–187, 191, 192–193. *See also specific landmarks*
Amman Citadel, 110, 163, 164, 187, 193, 204
Amman Message, 199, 251n15
Ammon, ancient kingdom of, 38, 39, 113–114, 117, 178, 205
Ammonites, 8, 39, 110, 115, 117, 128, 201, 248n78
Amorites, 78–79, 120, 179, 205
Amos (prophet), 181
'Amra (castle/qasr), 142, 168
Anbar School in Damascus, 147
Ancient Times (al-'Usur al-Qadima) (Breasted), 120, 122, 175–176
Anderson, Benedict, 133
Anderson, Betty, 13, 149, 166
Anglo-Jordanian Treaty of 25 May 1946, 109, 144, 145–146, 151, 157, 244n13
Annual of the Department of Antiquities of Jordan (ADAJ), 163–164, 170
"Anonymous Five" (archaeologist), 206

"Anonymous Four" (archaeologist), 205, 206
anti-Catholicism, 26
anti-imperialism, 122, 157, 163
antiquities, 65, 222n48; Abrahamic antiquities, 11, 18, 43, 51, 98; contested ownership of antiquities in British Mandates, 92–124; defined as before AD 1700 (thereby excluding Ottoman heritage), 106, 109, 205; Egyptian antiquities, 9, 24, 31, 45, 46, 65, 74–75, 76, 82, 105, 135, 173, 185; Hashemite Transjordan in mandatory space, 125–152; Hashemite use of for nation-state narrative in Jordan, 153–194; Helleno-Byzantine antiquities, 53, 55, 57, 65, 99–100; Jordan's handling of after loss of West Bank and Jerusalem, 195–210; and modernity, 3, 15, 48, 87, 158, 175, 193, 200, 201, 203, 208; search for in the Holy Land before First World War, 20–48; in Southeastern Bilad al-Sham under Ottoman Empire, 49–87, 220n21
Antiquities Ordinance of 1920, 94, 106, 109
anti-Semitism, 43, 213n17, 217n95
anti-Zionism, 122
Antonius, George, 124
APES. *See* American Palestine Exploration Society
Aqaba (city), 90, 116, 185, 203, 204; imaginary grand tour of, 187, 188, 189, 191, 193; ownership of, 144–145, 242n94; on stamps and currency, 144, 145, 241n87, 241n91
al-Aqsa Mosque, 95, 131, 151–152, 160, 161, 185, 189, 192, 245n21
Araba, Wadi, 46
Arab Awakening, The (Antonius), 124
Arab Bureau, 20
Arabian Peninsula, 4, 63–64, 155; peoples of, 73, 119–121, 173, 176, 178, 179, 205, 248n76
Arabic language, 62, 66, 69, 70, 77–78, 82, 164, 165, 170, 206

Arabism, 7, 81, 142, 147, 169, 185, 194, 199; pan-Arabism, 10, 128, 158, 193. See also *qawmiyya*

Arab League resolution in 1946, 159–160

Arab Legion, 125, 158, 159, 244n12

Arab nationalism. See nationalism; *qawmiyya*; *watan*

Arabness/Arab-izing, 4, 56, 58, 59, 65, 69, 83, 87, 141, 158, 166, 178, 182; of all ancient peoples, 124, 127, 171, 178, 198; of all ancient Semitic people, 178, 199; progenitors of Arab peoples, 72, 118, 148; and self-determination, 118–124. See also identity

al-ʿArab project, Wadi, 145

Arab Revolt (1916), 9, 63, 195, 200

Arabs, ancient, 17, 43, 44, 81, 118–119, 128, 133, 154, 155–156, 166, 171, 179, 247n61

Arab Socialism, 10

Araʾir, excavation at, 150

Arameans, 31, 179, 180

ʿArar (Mustafa Wahbi al-Tal), 17, 137, 146–150, 151, 152, 243n105

Archaeological Museum on Amman Citadel, 163

archaeology: archaeological explorations of the Holy Land before First World War, 20–48; in British Mandates, 8, 88–124; competitive archaeology in the Holy Land, 1–19; and nationalism, 10, 18–19, 65, 209; reconciling history and archaeology through education, 164–172; role of in Ottoman Empire, 6–7, 49–87; scientific affirmation of understood origins, 68–73; use of to further self-determination, 118–124

al-ʿArif, ʿArif, 122

Ariha. See Jericho

Arslan, Emir Amin Mujid, 70–71, 223n72, 224n75, 225n86

Artemis, Temple of, 139, 140

Ascalon, 168

Ashbee, Charles Robert, 94, 99, 229n28

ASOR. See American Schools of Oriental Research

al-Assad, Hafiz, 196

Assur (Iraq, Mesopotamia), 105

Assyria, 25, 31, 74, 78, 79; language of, 25, 76, 80

Assyrians, 79, 176, 179, 181

Assyriology, 213n17

Austria and archaeology, 101, 103

Awqaf, Ministry of (Religious Endowments), 97

awqaf (religious endowments), 61, 168

Ayalon, Ami, 67, 68, 223n67

Aya Sofya (St. Sofia), 99, 100, 103

Azraq (castle/*qasr*), 164, 168

Azraq Oasis, 197

Baʿal (Canaanite god), 181

Baalbek, ruins of, 1, 71, 138

Bab al-ʿAmud. See Damascus Gate

Bab edh-Dhra, excavation at, 164

Babylon, 25, 39, 74, 76, 78

Babylonian Exile, 39, 181, 182

Babylonian Exploration Fund (BEF), 45

Babylonians, 179, 181

Baghdad, 60, 240n72

Baghdad Pact, 159

Baʿir (castle/*qasr*), 168

al-Bakhit, ʿAdnan, 206

Balfour Declaration, 98

Balkans: Ottomans loss of territories in, 4, 21, 54, 58; war in (1911–1913), 49, 84

Balqa (district), 4, 91, 131, 148, 239n60

Balqa Mountains, 188, 192

Banu Israʾil, 247n71. See also Beni Israel

al-Barghouthi, ʿUmar Salih, 121

Bartoccini, Renato, 110

Barton, George, 120

Bayt Lahm. See Bethlehem

Bdul (inhabitants of Petra), 134, 135, 150

bedouins, 28n35, 58–59, 88–89, 122, 134–135, 137, 140, 156, 167, 196, 236n13, 239n60; Jordan embracing idea of, 16, 195–196, 197, 205; as the "real" Arabs, 44, 56, 156, 181; similarities to peoples of the Bible, 17,

42, 120, 123, 235n138; symbolism of, 115, 117, 197. *See also* nomadism

Beer Sheva. *See* Bir al-Saba'a (Beer Sheva)

BEF. *See* Babylonian Exploration Fund

Beisan, historical value of, 189

Beit Mirsim, Tell, 112

Bell, Gertrude, 20

Beni Hassan tombs, paintings in, 173, 175

Beni Israel, 7, 52, 72, 78, 80, 128, 135, 247n71; and the Exodus, 72, 74, 79, 123; as first Children of Abraham, 7, 52; hailing from Arab tribes, 81. *See also* Hebrews; Israelites, ancient

Bennett, Crystal, 169

Ben-Yehuda, Nachman, 13

Bernhardsson, Magnus, 13, 47, 102–103, 105–106

Bethany Baptism site (al-Maghtas), 199–200

Bethlehem (Bayt Lahm), 88, 100, 161, 163, 183, 189, 190, 191, 192, 245n21

Bezalel School of Arts and Crafts, 123

Bible, Hebrew, 11, 35, 122; ancient peoples of, 6, 8, 15, 23, 38, 78, 120, 139, 226n102, 248nn76–78; and archaeology, 31, 55, 74, 76–77, 84, 111, 117, 127, 139; British interest in, 15, 23, 32; Christian religions differing on focus (Old vs. New Testament), 26–27; connecting State of Israel to ancient Israelites, 116; deconstruction of, 213n17; defining lands of, 38, 39; historicity of, 25, 26, 28, 31, 36, 46, 79–80, 111–112, 117, 171, 234n126; place of the "others," 8, 38, 117

Biblical Citations: Genesis 10, 72, 226n102; Genesis 20, 76; Genesis 25, 90; Leviticus 18, 248n78; 2 Kings 18, 31; 2 Chronicles 24, 31

Biblical Researches in Palestine, Mount Sinai and Arabia Petraea (Robinson and Smith), 28, 29

Bilad al-Sham (Greater Syria), 6, 73, 179–180, 225n88; archaeology in,

5, 7, 37, 78; British in, 91, 124, 131; Canaanites in, 78, 177, 179; centralization project in, 62, 85; French interest in, 37, 91; in late Ottoman Empire, 5–6, 7, 16, 49–87; Muslim conquest, 168; Nabateans in, 37, 91; possible burial site of Alexander the Great, 71; rebellions in, 180; southeastern Bilad al-Sham, 4–5, 7, 16, 49–87, 147; Umayyad period, 200. *See also* Transjordan; Transjordan Mandate

bin al-Husayn, Abdullah. *See* Abdullah I

Bir al-Saba'a (Beer Sheva), 175, 190, 247n64

Bliss, Frederick Jones, 45, 46, 54, 81–82, 84

"borrowed colonialism," 56

Brand, Laurie, 13, 203

Breasted, James Henry, 120–122, 175–176

Britain, 9; and air transport in Jordan, 144, 241n86; Anglo-Jordanian Treaty of 25 May 1946, 109, 144–146, 151, 157, 244n13; and archaeology, 21–22, 24, 26–28, 35, 45, 46, 101–107, 216n67; Colonial Office (CO), 104, 124, 242n96; and Egypt, 74, 105, 126, 130, 145, 183, 244n14; Foreign Office (FO), 104; in India, 30, 35, 39, 91, 105–106, 214n43; and Jordan after the Mandate, 125, 126, 128, 130, 141, 157, 158, 159, 163, 243n110, 244n13; mapping of Holy Land, 5–6, 8, 21, 22, 23, 34–35, 37–42, 45, 56, 112, 217n87; mediating the Hadda Agreement of 1925, 142; Royal Engineers, 29, 32–33, 34–35, 37–38, 41; War Office, 5–6, 33, 37, 38, 39–40, 41, 42, 45, 46, 47, 95; and wars with Russia, 30; withdrawal from Palestine in 1948, 195

British Academy, 103

British Mandates (1921–1946), 8, 10, 22, 88–124; and antiquities, 100–107, 109, 133–144; archaeology and self-determinism, 118–124; British interventions in cultural heritage, 92–100, 103, 105; Iraq Mandate, 14, 103, 125; Levantine Mandates, 103; protecting Hashemite kingdom of the Hijaz, 144–145; and Zionist aspirations, 98. *See also* Palestine Mandate; Transjordan Mandate

British Museum, 102, 103, 106, 216n67

British School for Archaeology in Jerusalem (BSAJ), 89, 106, 108, 110, 163, 245n27

Bronze Age, 38, 78, 80, 114, 117, 180, 201, 205

Brown, Jonathan M., 113

BSAJ. *See* British School for Archaeology in Jerusalem

Burckhardt, Johann, 40, 42, 120, 136

al-Bustani, Butrus, 68

Byblos, excavation in, 24

Byzantine. *See* Helleno-Byzantine antiquities

Byzantine churches, 99, 100, 103, 185. *See also* Greek Orthodox Church

Caesarea (Qaysariyya), 168, 190

Canaan, Amarna Letters as source for studying, 78; ancient kingdom of, 37, 38, 39, 78, 80, 173, 180, 205, 226n102; Canaanite cities, 37, 78, 90; Israelite conquest of, 114, 177, 181. *See also* Bilad al-Sham

Canaan, Tawfiq, 109, 121–122, 123, 124, 134–135, 137, 146, 150

Canaanites, 121–122, 173, 175–177, 179; Arab Canaanites, 121, 177, 178; Ba'al (Canaanite god), 181; Canaanite language, 80; paintings of in Beni Hassan tombs, 173, 175; and the Phoenicians, 173, 176–177, 226n102; as Semitic peoples, 78, 120, 121

Capitulations in the Ottoman Empire, 24, 50

castles. *See* "Desert Castles" sites; *qasr*

Catholic Church, 30, 86, 110, 212n6, 221n27; focusing on New Testament spaces, 24, 26–27, 28

Cave of the Seven Sleepers, 199

Chaldeans, 76, 79, 176, 179, 226n103

Chautauqua Institution's Palestine Park, 47

Children of Ibrahim (Abraham). *See* Christianity; Islam and Islamism; Judaism

Christianity, 4, 39, 52, 60, 73, 83, 90, 119, 121, 177, 185, 198, 201, 221n27, 248n85; archaeology related to, 11–12, 18, 90, 97, 150, 160, 162, 199–200, 201, 205; Christian hired to create Jordan's first stamps, 140–141; Christian tourism/pilgrimages, 18, 24, 190, 192, 199, 200; and civil war in Lebanon, 247n61; and education in the Middle East, 59, 67, 165, 182, 185, 199; "Judeo-Christian" concept, 11, 12, 23, 48, 128; "Lead Codices," 207; *al-nasari*, 190; in the Ottoman empire, 7, 59, 66, 70, 83, 86–87; Syrian Christians editing journals, 66, 225n88. *See also* Catholic Church; Greek Orthodox Church; Protestant Church

Chronicles, 31, 226n102

Church, Frederic, 43

Churchill, Winston, 14, 91, 108, 149

Church of England, 33

Church of the Holy Sepulchre, 98, 161, 189

Church of the Nativity, 161, 163, 185, 189, 192, 245n21

cisjordan, 39, 91, 116

classicist historicism, 22

Clermont-Ganneau, Charles, 33–34, 39

Cleveland, William, 124

Cold War, 10, 13, 80, 152, 154, 157, 172, 183

Colla, Elliott, 13

Committee of the Society for the Protection of Ancient Buildings, 99

Committee of Union and Progress. *See* CUP

Companions of the Prophet (Sahaba), 197; mosque and shrine of Abu 'Ubayda ibn al-Jarrah, 208

Conder, Claude R., 34, 37–38, 41–42, 216n69, 217n87
Cook's Traveller's Handbook to Palestine, Syria and Iraq, 90
Council of Ministers (Jordan), 145, 195
Cox, Henry, 110
Creation, as beginning of Islamic history, 73
Crete, 228n1; Philistines originally from, 176, 180, 247n67
Crimean War, 30, 214n43
Crusades, 23–24, 39, 40, 89, 127, 185, 186. Crusader-era castles, 90, 108, 109, 140, 142–143, 148, 168, 192, 193, 204, 241n80
cultural heritage, 11, 38, 53, 56, 58, 64–65, 110, 160; British interventions in, 92–100, 103, 105; and globalization, 203; and imperialism, 49–50, 54, 55, 57, 65, 71; Jordanian/ Transjordanian, 129, 160, 182, 188, 193, 197, 203, 206, 207–210; and nationalism, 209; Palestinian, 160, 207; and tourism, 229n28
CUP (Committee of Union and Progress in the Ottoman Empire), 63, 64, 84, 130, 222n44
currency in Jordan, 1, 129, 133–134, 138, 139–144, 145–146, 168, 240n65, 241n91, 242nn96–98; small bills having widest circulation, 238n49; use of Palestine pound, 242n95
Curzon, George, 52, 99, 101
Cyprus, 80, 94, 105–106

al-Dabbagh, Mustafa Murad, 172–173, 175–177, 178, 181, 247nn67–71
Daher, Rami, 204
Dajani, ʿAwni, 164, 169, 245n28, 249n94
Damascus, 62, 91, 97, 125, 130–131, 143, 147, 240n72, 244n15
Damascus Gate (Bab al-ʿAmud), 93, 192
Darwaza, Muhammad, 122
Darwin, Charles and Darwinists, 21, 22, 26, 42, 66

David (Dawud) (king of Israel), 39, 110, 177, 181, 199, 207, 226n102, 234n126
Davis, John, 43, 217n97
Davis, Rochelle, 224n73
Dawn, C. Ernest, 119
Dawud, Abu, 150–151, 152
al-Dayr monastery (in Petra), 140, 160, 189
Dead Sea, 41, 184, 185, 189, 199, 245n21, 248n78; Dead Sea Panorama (environmental museum), 204; first westerner to complete voyage of, 29
Dead Sea Scrolls, 163, 164, 168, 206–207, 245n21; Copper Scroll, 195, 206
Decapolis, Jerash of the, 138
Decapolis, Pella of the, 164
Deities and Dolphins (Glueck), 113
"de-Palestinianization" of government of Jordan, 196–197
Department of Antiquities. *See under name of country*
Deringil, Selim, 56
"Desert Castle" sites, 40, 55, 90, 101, 105, 141–142, 163, 168, 185, 197, 219n10, 240nn71–72. See also *qasr*
Dhiban, Tell, 150
Dhiban (Dibon), 31, 35, 36, 46, 129, 146, 150–151, 164
Dhu al-Qarnayn. *See* Alexander the Great
Di-Capua, Yoav, 67
Diodorus Siculus, 75, 154
Documentary Hypothesis of Wellhausen, 26
Dome of the Rock (Qubbat al-Sakhra/ Masjid al-Sakhra), 113, 131–132, 185, 189, 192; categorized as a Muslim site, 97–98; restoring tile façade of, 95–99, 100–101, 104, 105, 109, 245n21; on stamps and currency, 159–162, 245n21
Doughty, Charles, 42, 120

East Bank core, 183, 188
East Jerusalem under control of Jordan (1950–1967), 158–163, 166

Ebla, excavation at, 37, 79
edicts of 1839 and 1856, 60
Edom, ancient kingdom of, 38, 39, 43, 113–114, 117, 125, 178, 188, 205, 234n126
Edomites, 8, 39, 43, 113, 114, 115, 117, 128, 135, 155, 226n102, 248n78
education in Jordan, 164–172; training of Jordanians to work in antiquities, 169–170; youth summer camps, 247n53, 250n115. *See also* textbooks in Jordan
EEF. *See* Egypt Expeditionary Force; Egypt Exploration Fund
Egypt, 3, 5–6, 13, 14, 138, 154, 166, 172, 179, 180, 189, 242n100; antiquities of, 9, 24, 31, 45, 46, 65, 74–76, 82, 105, 135, 173, 185; Arab interest in, 74, 225n88; and Britain, 105, 126, 130, 145, 244n14; language of, 76; Napoleon's invasion of, 21–23; under Nasser, 13, 156–157, 159, 180–181, 244n14; national commemoration in, 166–167; Ottoman Egypt, 66, 74; revolution of 1952, 10; and tourism, 90, 102; trouble in during the 1880s, 45; union with Syria (1958–1961), 159; war in 1948 against Israel, 157, 244n14
Egypt, ancient, 71; defeat of the Philistines, 226n102; ethnicity of, 79–80, 81, 127, 173, 179, 180; and the Exodus of the Beni Israel, 72, 74, 76, 79, 123; Hyksos in, 173, 175; under Roman rule at time of Christ, 76–77; written documents from, 36, 76, 78, 170
Egypt Expeditionary Force (EEF), 95, 97
Egypt Exploration Fund (EEF), 45
Egyptian Museum of Antiquities, 79, 210
Eilat (city), 116
Eisenhower Doctrine, 159, 183
Elamites, 79, 226n103
Elgin, Thomas Bruce, Lord, 54
Emir Abdullah. *See* Abdullah I

emirülhac (hajj caravan), 129
Enlightenment, 24–25
Esau (Biblical figure), 43, 248n78
Eteocypriots, 94
ethnicity, 79, 83, 112, 158, 172–182; Arab ethnicity, 69, 119, 121, 171, 172, 175, 177; Cypriot ethnicity, 94; multi-ethnicity, 7, 50, 60, 71, 94; race and identity, 39, 73, 78, 81, 83, 120, 225n98; Turkish ethnicity, 56. *See also* Arabness/Arab-izing; identity; Turkishness
Europe, 22, 25–26, 55, 56, 65; and archaeology, 7, 35, 41, 45, 54, 57, 65, 71, 96, 105, 123, 208, 220n21; clarifying ownership of Middle Eastern antiquities, 100–107; colonialism of, 60, 61, 69, 71–72; creating national boundaries in Middle East after World War I, 14, 38, 122, 216n72; interest in cultural heritage of Holy Lands, 39, 40, 42, 44, 50, 58, 70, 79, 85, 139; museums in, 53, 67, 71; and Ottoman Empire, 21–22, 49–50, 52, 55–56, 123. *See also specific countries*
Evans, Arthur, 88, 228n1
Exodus, 43, 72, 73–77, 113, 114, 123, 135, 181, 185; dating of, 114, 233n112
Ezion-Geber (biblical city), 90, 116

fada'il al-urdun, 186–193, 250n115
Farajat, Suleiman, 136
Faynan, Wadi, 207, 234n126
Faysal I (king in Syria and later in Iraq), 91, 125–126, 130–131, 147, 160
fedayeen sympathizers, 196
Filastin (newspaper), 223n67
firman (decree), 33, 42, 103
First National Parliament of Jordan, 144
First Temple (in Jerusalem), 39, 181
First World War, 46, 47–48, 49, 118, 143, 157; aftermath in the Middle East, 16, 20–21, 22, 32, 38, 109, 119, 158; Middle East before the War, 4, 16, 22, 67, 105, 141; Ottoman Empire's entry into, 64; Paris Peace

Conference, 20; Versailles Treaty, 103, 105
Fischbach, Michael, 13, 133
Foreign Ministry (Israel), 195
France, 6, 14, 21, 22, 23–24, 30, 104, 125, 130, 163, 214n43; and archaeology, 24, 35, 41, 45, 101, 103, 216n67; and Lebanon, 24, 38, 212n8; planning a Holy Land survey, 32, 34, 37; receiving Mesha Stela, 31, 32, 34, 36–37
Franco-Prussian war, 34
Frederick William (crown prince of Prussia), 33
Free Officers (Egypt), 152, 157, 243n110
Friends of Archaeology Society, 209

Gadara, 199
Garstang, John, 89, 90, 106–107, 108, 109
Gaza, 173
General History of Semitic Languages (Renan), 82
Genesis, Book of, 79, 114; 10, 72, 226n102; 20, 76; 25, 90
Gerasa. *See* Jerash
German Archaeological Institute, 219n10
German Oriental Society, 216n65
Germany, 6, 47, 212n11; and archaeology, 24, 27–28, 41, 45, 96, 101, 103, 105, 212n11; and Dome of the Rock, 96, 101; interest in cultural heritage of Holy Lands, 25–26, 28, 40, 111–112; and Mesha Stela, 33–34, 35, 208; and Ottoman Empire, 21, 54–55, 103; and Qasr al-Mshatta, 55, 101, 105, 141, 219n10; rise of anti-Semitism, 213n17; use of philological science, 25–26, 28, 72, 73, 120
Gershoni, Israel, 166–167, 179
Gezer, excavation at, 78
Ghassan (fictional character) and an imaginary grand tour of Jordan, 186–190
Ghassanids, 155, 185

al-Ghazawiyya (tribe), 167
Ghor al-Safi, 204
Gilead, ancient kingdom of, 38, 42, 125
Glubb, John Bagot (Pasha), 158, 159, 163
Glueck, Nelson, 8, 16–17, 92–93, 110–118, 120, 121, 123, 134, 169, 178, 234n126
Gomorrah (biblical city), 114
Goode, James, 13
Goshen (Jasan), 76, 79
Great Arab Revolt, 130, 144, 236n13
Greater Amman Municipality, 203
Greater Syria. *See* Bilad al-Sham
Great War. *See* First World War
Greece, 22, 24, 54, 55, 94, 155, 167, 178, 179, 180; Greek Phoenecians, 226n102, 247n61. *See also* Hellenism; Helleno-Byzantine antiquities
Greek Orthodox Church, 23, 24, 28, 86, 108, 161–162, 212n6, 221n27
Grove, George, 29, 35, 36

Hadda Agreement (1925), 142
Hagia Sophia. *See* Aya Sofya (St. Sofia)
Hague Convention of 1954, 206
Hajjaj, Emad, 3
Hallabat (castle/*qasr*), 168
Ham (Noah's son), 78
Hamdi, Osman, 54, 55–58, 64, 84, 141
Hamida, Bani/Banu (tribe), 33, 167
Hammurabi, 81
Handbook of Palestine and Transjordan, The (Luke and Keith-Roach), 88–89, 98
Hanssen, Jens, 105
hapiru, 80, 226n106, 248n85
al-Haram al-Sharif (Noble Sanctuary), 95, 98, 189, 192; burial site for Husayn bin ʿAli, 131, 132, 151, 160, 189; illicit dig within the Jerusalem *haram*, 83, 84, 85. *See also* al-Aqsa Mosque; Dome of the Rock
haramayn. *See* Mecca; Medina
Haram of Ibrahim, 189, 192, 245n21
Harding, Gerald Lankester, 113, 137, 141, 150, 163, 233n108

Harun (Aaron) (Biblical figure), 135, 181, 199

al-Hasa, Wadi, 113, 142, 242n99

Hasan (fictional character) and an imaginary grand tour of Jordan, 186–190

Hashemite dynasty, 9, 13, 63, 149, 208; development of the Jordanian Kingdom, 125–152; and education, 164–172; and Greater Syria, 155, 156; HKJ ("Hashemite Kingdom of Jordan"), 160; need for legitimacy, 9–10; opposition to Communism, 157; and struggle against colonialism, 10; tracing lineage back to the Prophet, 9, 63, 132, 154, 173, 175; trying to create Hashemite historicity in Holy Land, 18; use of antiquities for national and pan-national purposes, 153–194; wanting larger hereditary possession of Jerusalem, 17; working with the Zionists, 157, 158. See also Abdullah I; Abdullah II; Faysal I; Hashim; Hussein; Talal

Hashim (progenitor of the Hashemites), 118, 126–127, 132, 173

Hassan, Banu (tribe), 167

Hebrew language, 31, 76, 79–81; relationship of Hebrew and Semitic languages, 80, 83, 226n106, 227n115

Hebrews, 113, 128, 175–176, 177, 180; as Semitic peoples, 46, 79–80, 119, 120–121, 126, 179–180, 181, 199, 248n76; similarity of *hapiru* and Hebrew, 226n106; use of terms Jews and Hebrews interchangeably, 181, 247n71. See also Bible, Hebrew; Israelites, ancient

Hebrew Union College, 112, 116

Hebron (Khalil) (city), 159, 189, 190–192, 245n21

Hellenism, 4, 56, 58, 59, 65, 87

Helleno-Byzantine antiquities, 53, 55, 57, 65, 99–100

Herodotus, 73, 75, 225n86

Heshbon (Hesban), 90, 164

el-Hesi, Tell, 45, 112

Hezekiah (king of ancient Judah), 31, 80

Hijaz, 5, 74, 85, 126, 131, 136, 138, 142, 144, 168, 185; birthplace of Islam, 4; end of Hijazi kingdom, 130; expelling the Hashemite family from, 10, 125, 131, 151, 204; as a focus in the late Ottoman empire, 16, 51, 58, 59–60, 62–64, 85, 129; "Hijazi Ma'an," 4; Medina separated from, 63. See also Holy Land

Hijaz Railway, 1, 55, 62, 89, 141, 144, 188, 216n65, 241n87

al-Hilal (publication), 68

Hill, Gray, 45, 142

Himyarites, 155

al-Hindawi, Dhuqan, 175–176, 177, 186

Hisham (Umayyad caliph), 192

Historical Passageway, 200, 205, 206

historicism, 22, 67, 70

historicity, 6, 21, 23, 39, 46, 91, 154; in archaeology, 10, 83, 170, 210; of the Bible, 25, 26, 28, 31, 36, 46, 79–80, 111–112, 117, 171, 234n126; Israel's historicity, 18, 126, 158, 171, 172, 177, 207, 208; Jordanian and Hashemite historicity, 18, 158, 171–172, 193–194, 208; of peoples of the Holy Land, 5, 7, 8, 21, 69, 93, 158

Hittites, 76, 78, 79, 180, 225n98, 226n102, 248n85

Hogarth, David, 20–21, 47, 88, 96, 97

Holy Land, 15, 21–22, 23, 39, 133–144; creating a Hashemite core out of peripheral space, 9, 17, 131–133, 153–154, 156, 178, 183, 184, 193–194, 196, 197; defining the core and periphery, 20–48; East Bank core, 165, 166, 183; historicity of peoples of, 5, 7, 8, 21, 69, 93, 158; Palestine as core space, 6, 21, 37, 45, 51, 88, 92, 111, 124, 127, 128, 151, 172–173; Palestine as periphery space, 152, 153, 157, 193, 196; PEF assigning roles of "chosen" and "others," 38; Pope Paul VI's visit to, 161–162; River Jordan used to define, 6, 28, 37, 39, 40, 42, 90–91, 93; Transjordan Mandate

as periphery space, 88–124; trying to create Hashemite historicity in Holy Land, 18, 193–194. *See also* Hijaz
"Holy Places" stamp series, 245n21
Holy Sepulchre, 185, 192, 245n21
Homer, 73, 225n86
Horsfield, Agnes, 137
Horsfield, George, 89, 108, 109, 110, 134, 137, 233n108
HUC. *See* Hebrew Union College
Humayma and the Abbasid family, 240n72
Hurrians. *See* Hittites
hurriyya (freedom), 61
al-Husayn, Abdullah bin. *See* Abdullah I
Husayn bin ʿAli (Sharif Husayn of Mecca and king of the Hijaz), 63–64, 91–92, 126, 130, 160, 204, 222n44; Husayn-McMahon debacle, 91–92, 204; site of burial, 131, 132, 151, 160, 189
Husn (town), 148
Hussein (king of Jordan), 10, 18, 151, 152, 159, 183, 196, 243n110; on archaeological and heritage sites, 169, 197–198, 202; on education, 165–166; on stamps and currency, 160, 161, 162
al-Husseini, Kamil Effendi, 96
al-Husseini Mosque, 108
Huwaytat tribe, 156, 167
Hyksos, 79, 175

IAA. *See* Israel Antiquities Authority
Ibn ʿAmar, plains of, 191
Ibn Battuta, 75
Ibn Jubayr, Hani ibn ʿAbd Allah ibn Muhammad, 75
Ibn Khaldun, 69, 73, 79, 121, 123
Ibn Saʿud, 108, 125, 129, 130, 142, 144–145, 204
Ibrahimi Haram, 189, 192, 245n21
Ibrahimi Mosque, 192
identity, 85, 94, 133, 147, 176; Arab identity, 81, 84, 86, 87, 119, 120, 177, 199, 225n98; Hashemite co-

opting Palestinian identity, 158–163, 186, 187, 193–194, 196; Hashemite national identity, 131, 132, 139, 153–194; Jewish identity, 177, 182; Jordanian efforts to create new identity after loss of Jerusalem and West Bank, 196–210; Muslim identity, 199, 251n15; race and identity, 39, 73, 78, 81, 83, 120, 225n98; understanding archaeology to achieve sense of, 70, 73, 85, 129, 136, 209, 210. *See also* cultural heritage; ethnicity; Semitics
IDF. *See* Israel Defense Forces
imaginary grand tours of Jordan, 186–193, 250n115
Imperial Museum (Ottoman Empire), 53, 54, 55, 56, 65
al-ʿImran, 175
India, British in, 30, 35, 39, 91, 105–106, 214n43
Iraq, 3, 5, 105, 125, 127, 131, 138, 142, 166, 172, 176, 179, 189, 200, 225n86; and the Abbasids, 240n72; Abraham coming from, 175, 177, 226n103; archaeology and anthropology in, 9, 13, 74, 103, 189; British in, 14, 91, 103, 125, 131; Hashemites in, 91, 125–126, 131, 159, 166, 181; Iraq war, 12; Nabateans in, 154, 155, 156
Iraq al-Amir, 90
Irbid (city), 90, 147, 148, 189, 244n15
Iron Age (1200–550 BCE), 38–39, 94, 114, 115–116, 201, 205, 233n112, 234n126
irrigation projects, 145, 242n99, 242n100
Isaiah (prophet), 181
Ishaq (Isaac), son of Abraham in Jewish tradition, 42, 72, 98, 111, 132, 189
Ishmael (Ismaʿil), son of Abraham in Muslim tradition, 90, 98, 132, 175, 177; as progenitor of northern Arabs, 118
Islam and Islamism, 4, 55, 56, 58, 59, 62, 65, 86, 90, 118–119, 135, 167, 168, 179, 185; Alexander Romance,

224n77; the Amman Message,
251n15; and Arabness, 87, 119; Creation as beginning of Islamic history,
73; feelings upon viewing mummy
of Ramses II, 210; and the Hashemites, 9, 10, 11, 18, 170, 188, 198, 200,
251n15; importance of Jerusalem, 60,
84, 97, 98, 185, 192, 200–201; importance of Petra, 135, 136, 155, 201;
Islamic arts, 55, 59, 62, 94; Islamicate traditions, 7, 12, 50, 64, 66, 69,
70, 71, 72, 84, 123, 169, 196, 199,
200, 240n72; Islamic military district, 216n72; Islamic period heritage and archaeology, 12, 18, 40, 55,
65–66, 71, 73, 84, 95, 119, 127, 142,
165, 196–210, 224n73; Islamic sciences, 70, 82; Islamization, 18, 60,
196–210; isnad, 71, 224n73; and the
Ottoman Empire, 59, 61, 62, 66,
86–87, 136; synthesizing Muslim
and Jewish history, 119–120. See also
Muhammad, the Prophet; Qur'an
Isma'il (Ishmael). See Ishmael (Ismail)
isnad (reliability of sources in Islamic
tradition), 71, 224n73
Israel, ancient kingdom of, 31, 167, 178,
226n107, 234n126; conquests of, 31,
114, 176, 177, 181; defining lands of
during Iron Age, 38; uniting with
Judah, 39
Israel, state of, 8, 10, 18, 38, 116, 159,
177, 182; creation of modern state,
22; Department of Antiquities, 195;
and Palestine, 18, 159, 171; war in
1948 against Egypt, 157, 244n14
Israel Antiquities Authority (IAA), 207
Israel Defense Forces (IDF), 159
Israelites, ancient, 6, 23, 25, 158,
226n102; attempt to Judaize (ancient Israelites equaling modern
Israeli Jews), 177, 182; Babylonian
Exile, 39, 181, 182; and bedouins, 42,
123; British interest in, 15, 23, 32;
as a chosen people, 26, 38; defining
space for in Surveys by PEF, 37–38;
Protestants feeling connected to, 28,

40; twelve tribes, 181. See also Beni
Israel; Exodus; Hebrews; Semites
Israel Museum, 207
"Isra'iliyeen," 247n71
'Issa. See Jesus
Issac. See Ishaq (Isaac)
Istanbul, 23, 33, 42, 60, 129, 130; Aya
Sofya restoration, 99–100, 103; as
imperial center of the Ottomans, 58
Italy, 104, 110

Jabal Ajloun, 4–5, 143. See also Ajloun
Jabal al-Ashrafiyya (mosque), 193
Jabal al-Qal'a. See Amman Citadel
JAC. See Joint Archaeological
Committee
Jacob (Y'aqub) (Biblical figure), 42, 76,
79, 111, 189
Jankowski, James, 166–167, 179
Japanese International Cooperation
Agency (JICA), 143, 203, 204
Jasan (Goshen), 76, 79
Jebusites, 79, 226n102, 248n76
Jeddah (city), 62
Jenin (city), 191, 193
Jerash (city), 1, 90, 108, 110, 128, 134–
139; archaeological sites, 9, 40, 109,
128, 137–138, 139, 150, 168, 170, 184,
185–186, 197; Jerash Festival, 197; on
stamps and currency, 1, 128–129, 138,
139, 141, 145, 156, 160, 162; tourism
in, 137, 138, 139, 184, 188–189, 191,
192, 197, 238n46
Jeremiah (prophet), 181
Jericho (city), 164, 168, 185, 189, 191,
230n55, 238n46; tourism in, 90, 192
Jerusalem, 3, 4, 30, 31, 131–132, 145,
183, 195; Abrahamic history of,
153; under British Mandate, 89, 91,
93–100; coin issued honoring cityscape, 162–163; as the cradle of
Islam, 185; destruction of by Titus,
248n83; and Hashemite dynasty, 10,
11, 14, 17, 18, 39, 153, 157, 169, 194,
195; illicit dig within the Jerusalem
haram, 83–84, 85; Jordan controlling
West Bank and Jerusalem (1950–

1967), 10, 14, 17, 144, 151, 158–163, 166, 168, 183, 184; Jordan's loss of West Bank and Jerusalem, 18, 159, 160, 169, 195; Kingdom of (during Crusades), 39; known as al-Quds, 189, 190, 191, 192; in the late Ottoman empire, 58, 59, 60–61, 63, 64, 85; original inhabitants of, 226n102; and religio-national identity building, 16, 83; role of Jews in and rise of anti-Semitism, 217n95; tourism in, 187, 232n88. *See also specific sites*
Jerusalem Water Relief Fund, 29
Jesus, 185, 192, 199, 200, 207, 249n86
Jethro (Biblical figure), 199
Jews. *See* Judaism
JICA. *See* Japanese International Cooperation Agency
Jidda (city), 130
jinns, 150–151
Jiza (castle/*qasr*), 90
Job (Biblical figure), 199
John the Baptist, 90, 199, 200
Joint Archaeological Committee (JAC), 103, 104, 105, 106
Joktan (son of Shem). *See* Qahtan (Joktan)
Jordan, 8, 9, 13–14, 48, 153, 160, 163–164, 182, 196; ancient kingdoms in, 39, 178; Anglo-Jordanian Treaty of 25 May 1946, 109, 144, 145–146, 151, 157, 244n13; archaeology and antiquities, 10, 11–15, 18, 110–118, 125–152, 153–194, 195–210, 231n77, 234n126; civil war in (1970–1971), 196; control of West Bank and Jerusalem (1950–1967), 10, 14, 17, 144, 151, 158–163, 166, 183, 184; creating concept that Jordan was the Holy Land, 193–194; currency and stamps in, 1, 129, 133–134, 138, 139–144, 145–146, 159–160, 161, 162, 168, 238n49, 239nn56–57, 239n60, 240n65, 241n87, 241n91, 242nn95–96, 242n98; Department of Antiquities, 137, 164, 197; development of museums and gardens in, 200–206;

education in, 164–172, 182–193, 245n33, 246n45, 250n115; finding modern identity in, 49–87, 196–210; under the Hashemites, 125–152; international reputation of tolerance and moderation, 200, 252n17; "Jordan First" publicity campaign, 2–3; "Jordanian Jordanian" compared to "Palestinian Jordanian," 15; loss of West Bank and Jerusalem, 18, 159, 160, 169, 195; Mesha the Moabite as a national symbol, 178; as part of Bilad al-Sham, 4, 49–87; as a peripheral area in the late Ottoman Empire, 85–87; role of nomadic peoples in, 114–115; transition of Transjordan into Hashemite Jordanian kingdom, 144–146; use of term Transjordan, 14–15; youth summer camps, 171, 247n53, 250n115. *See also* Ammon, ancient kingdom of; Edom, ancient kingdom of; Hashemite dynasty; Moab, ancient kingdom of; Ottoman Empire; tourism; Transjordan; Transjordan Mandate
Jordan Currency Board, 145, 242n96
"Jordan First" publicity campaign, 3, 206, 208
Jordanian Arab Army, 189
Jordanian Committee for the Dead Sea Scrolls, 206
Jordanians differentiated from Transjordanians, 14–15
Jordan Ministry of Education, 165, 166, 245n33
Jordan Ministry of Planning, 2
Jordan Museum, 195, 202–203, 204–206, 251n21
Jordan Tourism Authority, 184, 192, 199, 203, 249n94
Joseph (Biblical figure), 76, 79, 189
Joshua (Biblical figure), 199, 233n112
Joucka, Jamal, 200, 206
Journal of the Palestine Oriental Society (JPOS), 121–122
Judah, ancient kingdom of, 31, 38, 39,

43, 114, 115, 116, 167, 178, 181; conquests of, 117, 176, 181
Judaism, 4, 12, 60, 121, 178, 181, 189,
199; Holy Land rooted in, 111; Jewish history based on a pan-Semitic
narrative, 121; Jewish humor, 83;
Jews and Hebrews, use of terms,
247n71; Jews under Roman rule,
248n83; Jordan as cradle of, 185; Reform Judaism, 111, 112; synthesizing
Muslim and Jewish history, 119–120.
See also Bible, Hebrew; Hebrews
Judeans, 115
jund al-urdun, 216n72

Ka'aba in Mecca, 62, 113, 175
Katz, Kimberly, 13, 138, 165
Keith-Roach, Edward, 89
Kemosh (Moabite god), 31, 39
Kenyon, Frederick, 102–104, 105–106,
230n55
Kenyon, Kathleen, 169, 230n55
Kerak (district in Jordan), 4, 45, 86, 90,
91, 131, 168; imaginary grand tour
of, 187, 188, 189; Kerak Revolt of
1910, 84, 85, 87, 142–143; tourism
in, 90, 184
Kerak Castle, 108, 109, 140, 142–143,
193, 204, 241n80
al-Khabiri. See hapiru
Khalidi, Tarif, 124
Khalil. *See* Hebron (Khalil) (city)
Khammash, Ammar, 1
Kharana (castle/*qasr*), 141–142, 163
Khatib, Anwar, 195
al-Khatib, Muhibb al-Din, 121
Khazna Fara'un. *See* Pharaoh's Treasury
el-Khelifeh, Tell, 116
Khirbet al-Qeiyafa, 207
Khirbet al-Tannur, 113
al-Kindi, Abu Yusuf, 75
King Hussein Bridge, 241n82
King Hussein Gardens, 200–202, 204
2 Kings 18, 31
Kirkbride, Diana, 150
Kisch, F. H., 126
Kitchener, Horatio H., 34, 37–38, 130

Klein, Frederick Augustus, 33, 34, 45
Knossos, excavation of, 228n1
Kovach, George, 183–184, 249n94
Kuklick, Bruce, 26
Kutler, Laurence, 113

Lachish (biblical town), 112
La'iqa (Leah), 189
al-Lakhmi, 'Amr bin 'Adi, 73, 225n86
Land Department (Transjordan), 133
languages, 80–81, 83, 115, 123, 129,
177, 226n104, 241n80; of Abraham,
75–76, 78; Arabic language, 62,
66, 77–78, 82, 164, 165, 170, 206;
Hebrew language, 31, 76, 79–81,
226n106; Semitic languages, 25, 28,
72, 73, 77–78, 80, 81, 83, 226n106,
227n115
Lapp, Paul, 169
Latin Christians. *See* Catholic Church
Lawrence, T. E., 20, 46, 90, 97, 111, 116
Lawrence of Arabia (film), 197
Layard, Austen Henry, 40–41
Layne, Linda, 13
"Lead Codices," 207
League of Nations, 88, 103
Leah (La'iqa), 189
Lebanon, 1, 4, 9, 71, 75, 105, 130,
247n61; French in, 14, 24, 38, 212n8
Levant (Levantine), 97, 103, 173
Leviticus 18, 248n78
Liatneh (inhabitants of Petra), 135, 150
Libya, Italian invasion of, 49, 84
Lisbon Collection, 105
Lot (Biblical figure), 199, 248n78
Lot's Cave, 204, 248n78
Louvre, 31, 34
Luke, Harry Charles, 89
Lynch, William Francis, 29, 41

Ma'an (district), 1, 68, 90, 109, 131, 137,
244n15; divided into Syrian Ma'an
and Hijazi Ma'an, 4; imaginary
grand tour of, 188, 189, 193; museum
in, 203, 204
Macalister, R. A. S., 78, 82
MacKenzie, Duncan, 46

Madaba (town), 31, 90, 141, 160, 188, 189, 191, 193, 199, 225n93
Mada'in Saleh (city), 136, 153
Maffi, Irene, 203, 204
Mafraq, 189
al-Maghtas (Bethany Baptism site), 199–200
al-maghul (barbarian tribes), 78, 79, 226n102
Makarius, Shahin, 66
Makdisi, Ussama, 56, 57, 225n98
al-Mamlaka al-Urduniyya al-Hashimiyya ('Anabtawi, et al.), 191
mapping of Palestine. *See* Survey of Eastern Palestine; Survey of Western Palestine
Masih/Messiah. *See* Jesus
Masjid al-Sakhra (The Mosque of the Rock). *See* Dome of the Rock
Massad, Joseph, 13, 14, 44
McMahon, Henry, 91, 92, 204
Mecca, 62, 125, 130, 132; hajj caravan, 129; Ka'aba in, 62, 113, 175; sharif and emir of Mecca, 63–64, 91–92, 126, 129, 160, 204. *See also* Husayn bin 'Ali
Medina, 62, 63, 125
Megiddo, excavation at, 98, 216n65
Meir, Jacob, 126
Merneptah (pharaoh in Egypt), 31, 76, 78, 79
Merneptah Stela, 78, 226n107
Merrill, Selah, 216n65
Mesha (king of Moab), 31, 32, 36, 39, 150, 171, 178
Mesha Stela (Moabite Stone), 31–32, 33–37, 38, 80, 129, 171, 201, 208
Middle East, 12, 21, 23–27, 32, 44, 48, 50, 120, 215n62; archaeological considerations in, 3, 7, 11–12, 15, 16, 18, 20, 22, 28, 35, 36, 46, 47, 70, 74, 102–103, 105–106, 170, 240n71; artificial borders after First World War, 3, 10, 14, 15, 16, 17, 18, 21, 23, 38, 40, 48, 90–91, 122, 132–133, 145, 148–149, 216n72; and First World War, 4, 16, 20–21, 22, 32, 38, 46,

47–48, 49, 64, 67, 103, 105, 109, 118, 119, 141, 143, 158; Roman empire in, 40, 170, 179, 180, 191, 192, 248n83
Milkom (Ammonite god), 39
millet (confessional community in Ottoman Empire), 60, 100, 132, 221n31
Minaeans, 155
Ministry of Education (Ottoman Empire), 54
Ministry of Interior (Ottoman Empire), 61
Minoan civilization, 228n1
Minya (town), 173
al-Miqdadi, Darwish, 122
Mlayh (town), 39, 76, 225n93
Moab, ancient kingdom of, 31, 35–36, 38, 39, 42, 113–114, 117, 125, 178, 188, 205
Moabites, 8, 39, 113, 114, 115, 117, 128, 142, 201, 248n78; defeating Israelites, 31, 171; language of, 80, 115, 241n80. *See also* Mesha; Mesha Stela
modernity, 6, 12, 15, 24, 48, 71, 88, 175, 200; analysis of by *al-Muqtataf*, 68, 69, 70, 75; and archaeology/antiquities, 3, 15, 48, 87, 158, 175, 193, 200, 201, 203, 208; imperial modernity, 21, 22; in Jordan/Transjordan, 3, 87, 115, 134, 152, 158, 188, 189, 193, 196–197, 201, 203, 208; national modernity, 6, 44, 56; Ottoman modernity, 4, 58
monotheism, 27, 39, 44, 52, 116, 179, 181
Morrison, Walter, 29
Moscrop, John, 29, 32
Moses (Musa), 72, 75, 76, 79, 80, 135, 181, 185, 224n77
Mosque of 'Umar in Bethlehem, 100, 192
Mosul (city), 40
Mount Lebanon, 24, 37
Mount Nebo, 90, 109, 199
Mount Sinai, 113. *See also* Sinai
al-Mshatta (castle/*qasr*), 141–142, 168, 219n10; façade of, 55, 90, 101, 105
Muhammad, the Prophet, 60, 63, 120,

136, 167, 197, 240n72; Hashemite descent from, 9, 18, 63, 125, 126–127, 131, 173; lineage of, 72–73, 118, 127, 132, 154, 173, 175; mosque and shrine of the Prophet's Companion, 197, 208; Night Journey (*al-Isra*ʿ), 98, 132, 185

Mujib, Wadi, 142

Mukawir (site where John the Baptist was beheaded), 90, 199

Munif, Abd al-Rahman, 110

al-Muqaddima (Prolegomena) (Ibn Khaldun), 69, 123

al-Muqtataf (journal), 6, 7, 16, 36, 51–52, 66–75, 119–120, 123, 139, 168, 169, 170, 199, 210, 225n98, 226n107; end of publicaton of, 152; identifying Semites, 73–83; letters from readers, 75–77

Musa. *See* Moses (Musa)

Muʾta (village), 86, 188

Muʾta, battle of, 168

Nabateans, 8, 9, 90, 113, 114, 121–122, 205; and Petra, 40, 43, 90, 136, 139, 154–156, 200–201; seen as "Arabs," 136, 154, 155, 156, 185

Nabil (fictional character) and an imaginary grand tour of Jordan, 186–190

Nablus (city), 33, 176, 189, 190, 192

Nablus Mountains, 191

nahda ("renaissance" or "awakening"), 66, 69, 71, 118–119, 122–123

Nahr al-Shariʿa. *See* River Jordan

Napoleon Bonaparte, 21–22, 23

al-Naqab. *See* Negev Desert

narrative map of Jordan, 186–193

al-Nasira (Nazareth), 189, 190

al-Nasser, Gamal abd, 10, 13, 163, 172; death of, 196; and Hashemites in Jordan, 17, 156–157, 159, 168, 180–181

Nasserism, 10

National Geographic (TV special), 207

nationalism, 17, 82, 83, 94, 122, 123–124, 130; Arab nationalism, 12, 18, 166, 195; and archaeology, 10, 18–19,

65, 209; in Hashemite Jordan, 153–194. See also Arabism; Arabness/Arab-izing; identity; pan-Arab/pan-Arabism; *qawmiyya*; *watan* (nation)

Nationality Law of 1869, 60

National Parliament of Jordan, 144

nation-state historicism, 22

Nativity Church. *See* Church of the Nativity

Nazareth (al-Nasira), 189, 190

Near East. *See* Middle East

Negev Desert (al-Naqab), 46, 113, 140, 239n60

Neo-Babylonians, 117

Neolithic Period (ca. 8500–4500 BCE), 18, 201

New Testament: Catholic interest in, 24, 26–27; Protestant non-interest in, 28

NGOs in Jordan, 203

Nimr, Faris, 66

Nimrud, excavation of, 40

Noah (Biblical figure), 72, 78, 118, 170, 199

Noble Sanctuary. *See* al-Haram al-Sharif

nomadism, 5, 15, 31, 69, 81, 114–115, 121, 123, 125, 146, 154, 167; ʿ*arab* as word for nomadic pastoralism, 79, 120; nomadic origins of Semitic peoples, 79, 224n81. *See also* bedouins

Notes on Studies in the Topography and Folklore of Petra (Canaan), 109, 134

Nuʿuman (fictional character) and an imaginary grand tour of Jordan, 186–190

Nymphaeum, 139

Occupied Enemy Territory Administration (OETA) (Britain), 91

Ochsenwald, William, 62

Office of Strategic Services (OSS) (U.S.), 116

"Oh Neighborhood of the Ban Tree" (poem by ʿArar), 148, 243n105

Old Testament. *See* Bible, Hebrew

Omar al-Khattab Mosque, 245n21

Omri (king of Israel), 31, 171, 178, 190
Order in Council of 1924, 229n18
Ordnance Survey, 32–33, 36
Organic Law of Transjordan (1928), 133
Orientalism, 20, 21, 33, 43, 56, 82, 120, 123, 135, 136, 169, 225n98
Ormsby-Gore, William, 97, 99, 229n44
Orthodox Christians. *See* Greek Orthodox Church
OSS. *See* Office of Strategic Services
"other." *See* "self" and "other," concept of
Other Side of the Jordan, The (Glueck), 114, 115–116
Ottoman Empire, 4, 9, 13–16, 33, 188; and antiquities, 53–58, 64–66, 100–107, 109, 220n21; Arab Revolt (1916), 9, 20, 63, 91, 130, 143, 144, 195, 200; and archaeology, 6–7, 49–87; British laws leaving Ottoman heritage without protection, 106, 109, 205; Capitulations, 24, 50; diversity in, 7, 52, 83; education in, 54, 59, 67–68, 86; Great Arab Revolt, 130, 144, 236n13; Holy Lands (cores and periphery in), 58–64; illicit dig in Jerusalem, 83–84, 85; Islamic identity of, 60, 61, 62; Kerak Revolt of 1910, 87, 142–143; laws and edicts, 54, 60, 103, 104–105, 106, 109; literacy in, 67–68; modernizing of after mid-19th century, 4, 21, 41, 49, 58–59, 60, 64, 143, 221n31; museums in, 53–54, 65, 67; treatment of Arabs, 118, 167; wars with Russia, 4, 58; Young Turk Revolution (1908), 49, 61, 63, 84, 129
Ottomanism, 4, 56, 58, 59, 60, 62, 65, 87
"Ottoman Orientalism," 56
Oultrejordain, 39, 216n72
Oval Forum, 140, 162

Palestine, 8, 14, 21, 49–87, 135, 138, 144, 195, 207, 209, 225n88, 245n95; Arab loss of in 1967, 195–196; and archaeology, 3, 5–6, 11–12, 18, 46–47, 48, 84–85, 94, 106, 107, 112, 126, 127, 163–164, 207–210; biblical Palestine, 15, 177, 226n102, 247n76, 248n76; and Britain, 6, 9, 10, 23, 29, 34, 48, 143, 145, 195; as core space in Holy Land, 6, 21, 37, 45, 51, 88, 92, 111, 124, 127, 128, 151, 172–173; Department of Antiquities, 89, 106, 108, 110, 137, 138; and Hashemites, 10, 126, 131; importance to Abrahamic faiths, 4, 6, 24, 28, 208; Jews in, 17, 121, 125, 126; Occupied Palestine, 14; and the Ottoman Empire, 4, 50–51, 52, 56, 61, 74, 84, 138; "Palestinian Jordanian" compared to "Jordanian Jordanian," 15, 209; Palestinian movement, 159; Palestinian refugees, 183, 196; seen as periphery space, 152, 153, 157, 193, 196; and State of Israel, 18, 159, 171; war in 1948 against Israel, 151, 157; as West Bank claimed by Jordan, 151–152, 158–194, 196; "wounded Palestine," 186; Zionist movement in, 83, 84, 127, 234n126. *See also* Palestine Mandate; Survey of Eastern Palestine; Survey of Western Palestine
"Palestine Aid" stamp series, 159–160
Palestine Antiquities Ordinance, 106
Palestine Archaeological Museum (PAM), 110, 122, 195
Palestine Exploration Fund (PEF), 27, 29–30, 45, 47, 130; assigning roles of "chosen" and "others" to peoples in the Holy Land, 38; and the Mesha Stela, 31–32, 33; work on mapping and surveying projects, 32–33, 35–36, 45; work with the War Office, 5–6, 33, 37, 38, 39–40, 41, 42, 45, 46, 47. *See also* Survey of Eastern Palestine; Survey of Western Palestine; Wilderness of Zin Survey
Palestine Exploration Quarterly (journal), 36, 82
Palestine Mandate, 4, 8, 9, 14, 16–17, 22, 38, 88–124, 126, 131, 140, 143, 145, 195, 229n18, 242n95; British interventions in cultural heritage and

antiquities, 92–107; high commissioner of Palestine, 88, 89
Palestine Oriental Society, 109, 126
Palestine Park (in western New York State), 47
Palestinian Authority, 206, 207
Palestinian Liberation Organization (PLO), 159
Palmer, E. H., 35, 36, 41
Palmyra, ruins in, 1, 138
PAM. *See* Palestine Archaeological Museum
pan-Arab/pan-Arabism, 10, 93, 128, 130, 158, 193; Hashemite use of antiquities for national and pan-national purposes, 153–194. See also *qawmiyya*
pan-Babylonianism, 25
pan-Islamism, 55
pan-Semitism, 178
Parliament Building (Jordan), 144
Parr, Peter, 163, 169, 245n27
Parthenon Marbles, 54
"Patriarchal Period," 117
patriotism, 27, 30, 32, 47, 49, 59
Paul VI (pope), visit to Holy Land, 161–162
PEF. *See* Palestine Exploration Fund
Pella of the Decapolis, excavation at, 164
People of the Book. See *ahl al-kitab*
PEQ. See *Palestine Exploration Quarterly* (journal)
Pergamon Museum, 141
Persia, 24, 55, 127, 167, 180, 181, 225n86
Petra, 40, 90, 150, 205, 209; antiquities in, 9, 43, 127, 128–129, 135, 137, 153, 155, 164, 168, 184, 185–186, 197; imaginary grand tour of, 188, 189, 191, 193; and the Nabateans, 40, 43, 90, 136, 139, 154–156, 200–201; role of in developing nation-state of Jordan, 128, 134–139, 153–156; on stamps and currency, 1, 134, 138, 139, 140, 141, 145, 156, 160, 162; tourism in, 109, 127, 136–137, 138, 139, 140,

184, 197, 232n88, 237n35, 238n46. *See also specific sites*
Petrie, Flinders, 31, 36, 43, 45, 81, 112, 123, 215n62
Pharaoh's Treasury (Khazna Fara ʿun), 139, 140, 189, 193
Philby, Harry St. John Bridger, 20, 108, 109, 110, 232n88
Philistia, ancient kingdom of, 39
Philistines, 38, 79, 121; originating in Crete, 176, 180, 247n67; struggles with ancient Israelites, 177, 181, 226n102
philo-Semitism, 43
Phoenicians, 34, 79, 173, 176–177, 179, 180, 226n102, 247n61; Phoenician language, 80
Picot, François Georges-, 204
PLO. *See* Palestinian Liberation Organization
Plumer, Herbert, 107, 109
Portugal, seizure of Lisbon Collection, 105
Pro-Jerusalem Society, 93–94, 109, 229n18
Protestant Church, 22–23, 24, 25–26, 86, 111; affinity with the Old Testament, 26–28, 91; interest in the Middle East, 24, 40, 46–47, 212n11; interest in the "real" Arab bedouin, 44; sharing characteristics of Reform Judaism, 112
Protestant Reformation, 6, 24, 26

Qahtan (Joktan), progenitor of southern Arabs, 72, 73, 118, 127, 148
Qalʿat al Rabad. *See* Ajloun Castle
Qalqilya (city), 190
qasr, 101, 105, 141–142, 163, 168, 192, 240n71. *See also* "Desert Castle" sites; *names of specific locations*
al-Qastal (castle/*qasr*), 90
qawm (people), 156
qawmiyya, 10, 151, 152, 156, 158, 196, 208. *See also* pan-Arab/pan-Arabism
Qaws (Edomite god), 39
Qays, 73

Qaysariyya (Caesarea), 168, 190
Qibya (village), 159
Qubbat al-Sakhra. *See* Dome of the
Rock
al-Quds, 189, 190, 191, 192. *See also*
Jerusalem
Qumran, excavation at, 164, 245n21
Qur'an, 62, 72, 79, 129, 132, 176; 3:67,
175; 10:90–92, 80; 17:1, 132; 7:73–
78, 136; *kuttab* (Qur'anic recitation)
schools, 67
Quraysh tribe, 118, 154, 167
Qusayr 'Amra (antiquity site), 142

Rabad (castle/*qasr*). *See* Ajloun Castle
race and identity. *See* ethnicity; identity
Raghadan Palace, 1, 3
Ramallah (city), 192
Ramses II (pharaoh of Egypt), 78,
79–80; feelings upon viewing
mummy of, 210
Ras al-Ain. *See* Jordan Museum
Rebecca (Rifqa) (Biblical figure), 189
Reformation. *See* Protestant
Reformation
Reform Judaism, 111, 112
Reid, Donald, 13
Renan, Ernest, 82
Richmond, Ernest, 20, 95–97, 99, 101,
109
Ridwan (celestial being), 148
Rifqa (Rebecca) (Biblical figure), 189
River Jordan, 31, 35, 44, 91, 171, 187,
192, 196; archaeological sites west of
river, 28, 36, 46, 90–91; as basis for
defining areas for mapping, 5, 23, 24,
34–35, 36, 37, 39, 40, 41, 45; Jordan
River Valley, 40, 90, 164, 188; lands
east of the river, 6, 36, 40, 41, 45,
92–93, 113, 114, 117, 139, 187; stamp
issued featuring, 140, 143; unification
of "East and West Banks" of Jordan
River in 1952, 160; used to define
core and periphery Holy Land, 6, 28,
37, 39, 40, 42, 90–91, 93. See also
cisjordan; *transjordan*
River Zarqa, 189, 231n80

Robinson, Edward, 28–29, 41, 43, 111
Rockefeller, John D., 110, 195
Rockefeller Museum, 110, 122, 195
Rogan, Eugene, 13, 142–143
Roman Empire in Middle East, 40, 170,
179, 180, 191, 192, 248n83
Roman Theatre, 2, 108, 110, 140, 164,
170, 186, 193
Rothschild, Edmund de, 84
Royal Automobile Museum, 200, 204
Royal Engineers (Britain), 29, 32–33,
34–35, 37–38, 41
Rum, Wadi, 197, 241n87
Rusayfa (city), 189
Russia, 6, 21, 24, 30, 86, 130, 212n6;
and the Ottoman Empire, 4, 58, 137,
214n43

Sabeans, 155
Sahaba. *See* Companions of the Prophet
Saida (ancient Sidon), 56, 105, 231n65.
See also Sidon
St. Sofia (Aya Sofya), 99–100
St. Sofia (Aya Sofya), restoration of, 103
Sakhr, Bani/Banu (tribe), 33, 167
Salah al-Din (first sultan of Egypt and
Syria), 142, 143, 167, 192
Salibi, Kamal, 248n76
Salih (God's messenger), 135–136
Salt (city), 90, 148, 189, 203–204,
239n60, 252n24; education in,
67–68, 86; first capital of Transjor-
dan, 140
Samaria, 176, 181
Samaritans, temple of, 189
Samuel, 226n102
Samuel, Herbert, 88–89, 98, 106, 107
sancak, 61, 63
San Remo Conference, 91
Sara (Sarah) (wife of Abraham), 76, 189
Sarruf, Yaqub, 66
Sauer, James, 117
Saul (king of Israel), 181, 199
Sayce, A. H., 120
Schick, Conrad, 45
Schliemann, Heinrich, 54, 224n75
School of Archaeology in Jerusalem. *See*

British School for Archaeology in Jerusalem scouting camps in Jordan, 191, 250n115

Sebastiyya (Sebastia), 168, 176, 189–190, 191–192

Second Temple (on site of Solomon's Temple), 98, 182

Seetzen, Ulrich, 40

"self" and "other," concept of, 38, 71–72, 98–99; idolators as "others," 128; Orientalized "other," 56

self-determination, 83, 88, 118–124, 152, 156, 195

Selim III (sultan in Ottoman Empire), 54

Semitic languages, 25, 28, 72, 73, 77–81, 82, 226n106, 227n115; relationship of Hebrew and Semitic languages, 80, 83, 226n106, 227n115

Semitics, 7, 16, 72, 74, 81–83, 154; antiquity of Semites, 52; antiquity of the "Arab homeland" and achievements of Arab Semites, 178–179; and Arabism, 81; Arab-izing all ancient peoples, 124, 127, 171, 178, 182, 199; Arabs and Hebrews sharing Semitic origins, 79–80, 120–121, 126, 180, 199; ethnicity and the ancient connections between Jews and Arabs, 172–182; Exodus and the Semites, 73–77; *hapiru* way of life, 226n106; original inhabitants of Jerusalem not Semitic, 226n102; pan-Semitic historical consciousness, 120, 121, 178; Ramses II and Menepteh as Semitic, 79–80; relationship of Semite and Aryan, 124; Semites as the first monotheists, 179; Semitic humor, 82–83; Semitic origins, 69, 70, 72, 73, 87, 119–121, 128, 179, 248n76; Semitic scriptural narrative, 127; Shem as progenitor for Semites, 118. *See also specific peoples*

Semitic Wave Theory, 79, 121, 123, 176, 248n76

Sèvres, Treaty of, 91

sha'ab (people), 148, 152

shari'a, 87

Shaw, Wendy K., 53, 54, 56, 57, 65

Shawbak (castle/*qasr*), 168

Shawbak (town), 68, 138, 188, 193, 238n44

Shechem (Canaanite city), 164

Shem (son of Noah), 72, 118, 127

Shi'i, 198, 251n15

al-Shita, Wadi, 148, 149

Shlaim, Avi, 13

Shrine of the Nativity. *See* Church of the Nativity

Shrines and Tombs of the Prophets and Companions, 197, 198, 200

Shryock, Andrew, 13, 15, 224n73

Sidon (city), 24, 71, 80, 224n75. *See also* Saida (ancient Sidon)

Silberman, Neil Asher, 42

Silwan (Siloam), 31, 80, 84

Sinai, 30, 32, 35, 45, 113, 156, 159, 181

Sirhan, Wadi, 142

Smith, Eli, 28, 29, 41

Social Darwinism, 21, 66

Sodom (biblical city), 114, 248n78

Solomon (Suleyman) (king of Israel), 78, 116, 177, 181, 199, 207, 234n126

Solomon's Temple (First Temple), 39, 98, 132, 181

"Sons of Qahtan," 118

stamps in Jordan, 129, 133–134, 138, 139–144, 145, 168, 239n57, 239n60; first air mail stamp, 160; first stamp series for Mandatory Transjordan, 139, 140–144, 239n56, 240n65; "unity stamp" issued in 1952, 160; use of to co-opt Palestinian identity, 159–160

Storrs, Ronald, 20, 93–95, 99, 104, 130, 229n18

Sudan, trouble in during the 1880s, 45

Suez Canal, 5, 30, 159, 163, 183

Suez Canal Company, 30

suicide bombings of 3 hotels, 3, 252n17

Sukkar, Y'aqub, 140–141, 145, 240n65

Suleyman. *See* Solomon (Suleyman)

Sumeria, 74

Sumero-Akkadian texts, 79

Sunni, 198, 251n15
Supreme Muslim Council, 99
Surat Yunus (Jonah), 80
Survey of Eastern Palestine: by APES, 37–38, 40, 41, 216n65; Glueck's survey, 113; by PEF, 5, 23, 42, 45, 56, 217n87
Survey of Western Palestine (1871–1878): by the British, 5–6, 8, 21, 22, 23, 34–35, 37–38, 39–41, 42, 45, 56, 112, 217n87
Sykes, Mark, 97
Sykes-Picot debacle, 91, 204
Syria, 125, 130–131, 147, 151, 154, 229n44, 240n72; archaeology and antiquities, 1, 9, 78–79, 90, 138, 240n72; invasion of northern Jordan, 196; Jordan as "southern Syria," 14; separating Lebanon governance from, 212n8; "Syrian Ma'an," 4; union of Egypt and Syria (1958–1961), 159. *See also* Bilad al-Sham
Syria, ancient, 74, 76, 80–81, 155
Syrian Protestant College, 40, 45, 66, 216n74. *See also* American University of Beirut
Syrians, ancient, 36, 49, 83, 175, 179, 247n67
Syrio-Aramaic culture, 121–122

al-Tabari, Abu Ja'far Muhammad bin Jarir bin Yazid, 73, 136
Tafila (town), 68, 188, 189, 193
al-Tahtawi, Rifa'a Raf'i, 69
al-Tal, Mustafa Wahbi. *See* 'Arar (Mustafa Wahbi al-Tal)
al-Tal, Wasfi (prime minister), 147
Talal (fictional character) and an imaginary grand tour of Jordan, 186–190
Talal (king of Jordan), 140, 242n98, 243n110
Tamari, Salim, 121, 124, 225n88
Tanzimat (restructuring, 1839–1876), 4, 49, 60, 143
Tarikh Filastin (The History of Palestine) (Barghouthi and Tutah), 121

Tel Aviv (city), 190
Teleilat al-Ghassul, 109
tell, definition of, 215n62. *See also names of specific tells*
Temple of Artemis, 139, 140
Tenth Century Debate, 234n126
textbooks in Jordan, 164–172, 245n33, 246n45; an imaginary grand tour, 186–193, 250n115; sense of "Jordanian-ness," 185–193; teaching ethnicity, 172–182; and tourism, 182–185
Thamud, ancient civilization of, 135
Thomas Cook and Sons, 29, 46, 90
Thompson, William, 27, 30, 32
Tíh, Desert of the, surveying of, 35
Timnah, copper mines of, 116
Touqan, Ja'afar, 204
tourism, 2, 10–11, 18, 28–29, 229n28, 250n115; Christian tourism, 18, 24, 190, 192, 199, 200; in the Holy Land, 46, 89–90, 94, 98, 184, 191–192, 193, 195, 232n88, 241n87; Islamic tourism, 129, 185, 192, 198, 199; in Jordan, 109, 136–138, 140, 143, 157, 158, 160–161, 182–193, 195–210, 237n34, 238n46, 249n94, 250n4
Tourism Plan of Action for Jordan, 183–184
Tourism Sector Development Project, 203
Toynbee, Arnold J., 100
Transjordan, 4, 16, 24, 39, 48, 58, 86, 150–151, 196, 201, 221n27, 234n126, 241n86; Arabness in, 87; 'Arar's poetry reflecting, 146–150, 152; and archaeology, 16–17, 89, 90, 107, 108–109, 110–118, 125–152, 163, 168, 208, 231n77, 234n126; currency and stamps in, 140, 145–146, 239nn56–57, 239n60, 240n65, 241n86, 242n95; Department of Antiquities, 106, 108, 109, 110, 113, 137, 138, 141, 163, 168; education in, 59, 67–68, 86; as an Emirate, 125, 126, 142,

147, 148, 149, 160, 168, 204, 239n60;
Hashemite attempts to develop
Transjordan into a nation-state, 110,
129–146, 151–154; as land of non-
Jews, 8, 15; legal and bureaucratic
classification of spaces that became,
58–64; in Ottoman Empire, 4, 59,
64, 74, 87, 129–131, 188; as periphery rather than core, 15, 17, 39, 44,
124, 126, 127, 131–133, 146; seen as
home to bedouins, 17, 44; survey of,
110–118; Transjordan Land Department, 133

transjordan, 39, 48

"Transjordania" as part of Syria, 101,
229n44

Transjordanian Frontier Force, 244n12

Transjordanians differentiated from Jordanians, 14–15

Transjordan Mandate, 8–9, 16, 39,
88–124; British defense of Aqaba in
1925, 144–145; British interventions
in cultural heritage and antiquities,
92–93, 100–107, 109; independence
of, 151; introduction of air transport by British, 241n86; irrigation
projects in, 145, 242n99; promise of
eventual independence in 1923, 108

Treasury in Petra. *See* Pharaoh's
Treasury

Tribal School (Aşiret Mektebi), 115

Tristram, H. B., 29, 41, 45

Troy, excavations of, 54, 224n75

turath (heritage), 3, 13, 14, 17, 93

Turjman, Ihsan, 68, 236n13

Turkey, 3, 57, 81, 103, 104, 167; archaeology and antiquities, 9, 78, 79,
99, 100, 101, 102–103, 104; feelings
about in Jordan, 130, 167; and the
Hittites, 78, 225n98; War of Independence (1919–1923), 49. *See also*
Ottoman Empire

Turkish language, 129

Turkishness (Turkish identity), 4, 56,
58, 59, 65, 81, 87, 225n98; "Muslim
Turks," 129

Tutah, Khalil, 121

Tuthmoses III (pharaoh of Egypt), 80,
180, 248n85

Tyre, excavation at, 24

Tyrwhitt Drake, Charles, 35, 36,
216n69

UAR. *See* United Arab Republic

Ugarit (Canaanite city), 37

'Umar, Mosque of (Bethlehem), 100

Umayyad caliphs, 131, 192, 200, 240n72

Umayyad desert castles, 141, 142,
240n72

umma (nation), 66, 76, 82–83, 84, 132,
165, 167

Umm al-Jimal (city), 90

understood origins, 68–73

United Arab Republic (UAR), 159

United Monarchy, 207. *See also* David
(Dawud); Solomon (Suleyman)

United Nations, 162; Amman as "Arab
Culture Capital," 3; UNESCO
World Heritage site, 136, 142, 197,
200

United Nations Relief and Works
Agency (UNRWA), 166

United States, 6, 12, 13, 41, 103; aid to
Jordan, 182–183, 184, 197, 247n53,
250n115; American modernity, 15;
and archaeology, 22, 27–28, 39, 41,
45, 46, 65, 103, 104, 106, 110–118,
124, 139, 142; bringing Holy Land
to Americans at Chautauqua, 47;
impact of American Protestantism,
22, 25–26, 27–28, 91, 217n97; and
Middle Eastern scholarship, 24, 26,
28; not recognizing Jordan's independence until 1949, 183. *See also*
American Palestine Exploration
Society

United States Agency for International
Development (USAID), 182–183,
184, 197

"unity stamp," 160

Universal Postal Union (UPU), 140, 144,
239n57, 241n85

University of Chicago Oriental Institute, 120
University of Liverpool, 89, 106
UNRWA. *See* United Nations Relief and Works Agency
Ur, as home of Hebrews, 177, 226n103
"al-urdun awalan." *See* "Jordan First" publicity campaign
USAID. *See* United States Agency for International Development
al-ʿUsur al-Qadima (Ancient Times) (Breasted), 120, 122, 175–176
ʿUthman, ʿAdnan Lutfi, 155, 178–182, 248n85

Varisco, Daniel, 118
Versailles Treaty, 103, 105
vilayet (province in Ottoman Empire), 61, 62, 63

Wadi Musa (village), 136–137, 188, 189, 193
wadis, 46, 113, 142, 145, 197, 207, 234n126, 241n87, 242n99
War Office (Britain), 5–6, 33, 37, 38, 39–40, 41, 42, 45, 46, 47, 95
Warren, Charles, 32, 33–34, 36, 41, 82, 215n52
watan (nation), 3, 13, 14, 66, 124, 126–127, 139, 145, 157, 185, 186, 191; imagining and historicizing the Tranjordanian *watan*, 146–151; and the narrative of antiquity, 131–132, 133–144, 185–193; *wataniyya* (nation-state, nationalism), 10, 119–120, 127, 128, 132, 147–148, 151–152, 156, 190, 196, 208. *See also* nationalism
"We are all Jordan," 3
Wellhausen, Julius, 25, 26, 42, 121
West Amman. *See* King Hussein Gardens

West Bank, 163–164, 165, 191; during 1948 war, 158; under control of Jordan (1950–1967), 10, 14, 17, 144, 151, 158–163, 166, 183, 184; Jordan's loss of West Bank, 18, 159, 160, 169, 195; Palestinians living in occupied West Bank, 196; unification of "East and West Banks" of Jordan River in 1952, 160
Western Wall, 98
Wilderness of Zin Survey, 46, 116
Wilhelm II (kaiser of Germany), 55, 141, 240n69
Wilson, Charles, 29, 30, 32, 34, 36
Wilson, Mary, 13
Woolley, Leonard, 20, 43, 46, 116
World War I. *See* First World War
Wust al-Balad, 108

Yadin, Yigael, 110–111, 114
Yaffa (Jaffa), 190
Yahweh (god of the Israelites), 31, 39, 181
Yahya. *See* John the Baptist
Yaman, 72, 73
Yʿaqub. *See* Jacob (Yʿaqub)
Yarmouk River, 244n15
Yellin, David, 126
Yishuv, 126, 151
Young Ottomans, 49, 59
Young Turk Revolution (1908), 49, 61, 63, 84, 129
Yusuf (Joseph), 76, 79, 189

Zarqa (city), 189
Zaydan, Jurji, 68, 81, 169
Zionism and Zionist movement, 6, 10, 61, 83–84, 93, 116, 119, 121, 123–124, 126, 152, 166, 177–178, 191, 199, 234n126; and Hashemites, 157, 158; Zionist imperialism, 167
Zionist Commission, 97, 98